9/96

# MOTHERGUILT

ALSO BY DIANE EYER, PH.D.:

*Mother-Infant Bonding: A Scientific Fiction*

# MOTHERGUILT

*How Our Culture Blames Mothers
for What's Wrong
with Society*

Diane Eyer, *Ph.D.*

TIMES BOOKS

RANDOM HOUSE

*Grateful acknowledgment is made to the following for permission to reprint previously published material:*

*Cambridge University Press*: Excerpts, including condensation and paraphrasing, from *Adolescent Mothers in Later Life* by Frank F. Furstenberg, Jr., J. Brooks-Gunn, and S. Philip Morgan (1987). Reprinted with the permission of Cambridge University Press.

*Harvard University Press*: Excerpts, including paraphrased text and quotations, from pages 16–17, 34, 47–48, 53–54, 56, 84, and 91 from *Divided Families* by Frank Furstenberg, Jr., and Andrew Cherlin (Harvard University Press: 1991). Copyright © 1991 by the President and Fellows of Harvard College. Reprinted by permission of Harvard University Press.

*The Progressive*: Excerpts, including close paraphrasing, from an article by Linda Baker from the June 1994 issue of *The Progressive*. Reprinted by permission from *The Progressive*, 409 East Main Street, Madison, WI 53703

*Kyle D. Pruett*: Excerpts, including close paraphrasing, from *The Nurturing Father* by Kyle D. Pruett (Warner Books, 1987). Copyright © 1987 by Kyle D. Pruett. Reprinted by permission of the author.

*Teachers College Press*: Excerpts and close paraphrasing, from *Raised in East Urban: Child Care Changes in a Working Class Community* by Caroline Zinsser (New York: Teachers College Press, © 1991 by Caroline Zinsser. All rights reserved.), pp. 138–143. Excerpts and close paraphrasing from *Good Day/Bad Day: The Child's Experience of Child Care* by Lyda Beardsley (New York: Teachers College Press, © 1990 by Teachers College, Columbia University. All rights reserved), pp. 7–22.

Library of Congress Cataloging-in-Publication Data

Eyer, Diane
Motherguilt : how our culture blames mothers for what's wrong with society
/ Diane Eyer. — 1st ed.
p.    cm.
Includes bibliographical references (p.    ) and index.
ISBN 0-8129-2416-9
1. Working mothers—United States—Psychology.   2. Motherhood—
United States—Psychological aspects.   3. Attachment behavior.
4. Child care—United States.   I. Title.
HQ759.48.E94   1995
306.874`3—dc20                                         95-7692

# *Acknowledgments*

I have enjoyed writing this book, and I have many many people to thank for making the challenge of this undertaking both pleasurable and rewarding. Most enjoyable has been the sharing of this project with my husband, Jack Byer, a professor of theater and communications and a great seeker of knowledge. His enthusiasm has sustained me through the inevitable moments of doubt (mostly "Will I ever manage to complete this endeavor?!" and "Have I really got this right?!"); his research acumen has provided me with the equivalent of a whole team of sophisticated research assistants. But most of all, I have enjoyed working through many of the ideas in the book, in valuable coffee-laden discussions, so often sitting in, or looking out over, our peaceful Japanese garden.

Much of the reward in this undertaking has come from discussions with parents, especially mothers who have been wonderfully open, honest, and often funny about their experiences in the realm of motherhood and motherguilt. I would especially like to thank: Cissi and Bill Clement, Mary and Jack King, Donna Liotta, Lori and Brian Cooper, Lynne and Bill Headley, Joy Sill-Hopkins, Kate and Gerry Moran, Margaret Salinger Pinto, Jean Wallace, Suzannah Lachs, Serrill Headley, Valerie McLaren, Susan Clarke, and the newest mother, my agent Beth Vesel.

Several colleagues have read chapters of the book and provided me with helpful feedback, including Jackie Litt, Jean-Jacques Steichen, and Mary Beth Apple. Gladys Topkis, my former editor at Yale University Press, continues to be an inspiration. Elizabeth Eyer, my mother, has been a great clipper of relevant news items, and I also thank her and my father, Charles Eyer, for their interest and support. I have also been helped by the excellent staff at the University of Pennsylvania Libraries and Bucks County Community College libraries, with special thanks to Warren Troust. These libraries, of course, are the repositories of information that constitutes the considered efforts of many fine minds—both within and outside the academic world—information that I feel privileged to reflect upon and turn around in the light. While I am critical of some of the bias and shortsightedness of many social science researchers, I also have a great deal of respect for the complex technology of research design and analysis that they have mastered and which they employ in the interests of discovery.

Finally, I am most grateful for my agent Beth Vesel, whose integrity, insight, and sensitivity have contributed greatly to this effort. My editor at Times Books, Betsy Rapoport, has the gift of seeing both the whole picture—and its required structure—and the importance of every detail. Her judgment is impeccable, and I am truly fortunate to have her guidance.

# Contents

# Introduction

It was a sunny April morning in 1993, and I was happy to be walking toward my departure gate in the Cleveland airport. I had survived another television interview and was still trying to find an adequate perspective on the surprising tidal wave of public attention that had followed the publication of my book, *Mother-Infant Bonding: A Scientific Fiction.* My gaze settled rather absentmindedly on some travelers heading toward me, and for just a moment in my imagination they acquired the long-necked, rather sweet-faced countenances of those grumbling humpbacked creatures that transport the paraphernalia of entire tribes across deserts. The young man and woman were piled high with bundles of baby equipment—the baby traveling on her mother's hip, almost lost amidst the diaper bag, infant seat, and pastel-colored stuffed animals and rumpled storybooks. Suddenly the caravan lugged its way right up to me. The mother told me, "I can't thank you enough. I saw you on TV this morning and you changed my life. I was sick after my baby was born and I didn't get a chance to bond with her. I wrote her a three-page letter for when she grows up, apologizing for not giving her that experience. But I've felt so guilty. I can never get that time back. Now I see it's all right. I didn't deprive her!" I was still shocked by such statements, even though by then, I had heard hundreds of them.

I had written my first book primarily for my undergraduate college students who, I felt, needed to know more about how science is influenced by the prejudices, ineptitudes, and professional agendas of scientists. I also wanted them to see how easily bits of data, especially in psychology can become politicized and turn into fads. Bonding research was a good example. It is based on the fact that mother goats will reject their infants if you separate them for just a few minutes after birth. In the same way, according to the bonding theory, human mothers will reject their children if you interrupt their natural instincts by separating them after birth. Based on research with mothers claiming to support this notion, American hospitals instituted mandatory bonding rituals after birth, varying in strictness and detail. While the research evidence for such maternal instincts was soon discredited, the idea lived on.[1] My book was an exploration of how such flimsy research became such a powerful force. (See chapter 3 for further discussion.)

I had expected my book might relieve parents of guilt and regret as so many of them were inevitably unable to have such a "bonding" experience because of exhausting births, C-sections, adoption, and so forth. But I was completely unprepared for the deluge of publicity that ensued. I received requests for articles and interviews from major newspapers, magazines, talk radio and TV shows, even from lawyers wanting me to be an "expert witness" in legal cases involving "bonding." This enthusiasm was not primarily because I had shown how very subjective and political scientific research can be. Rather, it was because I seemed to be touching on some deeply held beliefs regarding maternal instinct and the ideology of motherhood. Indeed, "bonding" had apparently lived on as a powerful idea because it was identified with these myths. In the 1980s, pediatricians and psychologists had begun to use the pseudoscientific concept to set out revised rules of mothering to encourage mothers to stay with their children full-time, which obviously necessitated curbing women's enthusiasm for work outside the home. Mothers told me they were being advised to stay home from work for the entire first year of their child's life in order for proper bonding to be attained. I was astounded. There was absolutely no research that I knew of to prove the existence of a special "bonding" period during this time or to show that women's employment interfered with mother-child relationships.

The new and improved claims for bonding were made possible by an old psychological cousin, born in the 1950s, called "attachment." Technically speaking, bonding refers to a *maternal* instinct that requires postpartum mother-infant proximity; attachment refers to an instinct in the *child* that requires early childhood proximity to mothers. Attachment research began with the work of British psychiatrist John Bowlby, who claimed that mothers who work during the first three years of their children's lives have doomed them to "maternal deprivation." In the 1980s "bonding" and "attachment" apparently came to be used interchangeably to discourage women from working outside the home.

However, more than half of mothers with young children worked outside the home by the mid-1980s, and they had to scramble to find decent care for their children. Rather than studying the parameters of good supplementary care for children in order to help parents with this new challenge, however, psychologists and pediatricians tended to cling to the familiar attachment idea in which they had vested their professional reputations, predicting dire consequences for those who transgressed their precepts by working. Dr. T. Berry Brazelton, the era's premier child-raising expert, insisted mothers who did not stay home for the first year of their infants' lives risked turning them into "terrorists"! If Brazelton did not convince mothers who (guiltily) continued to work, he did persuade the officially appointed judges of women. No doubt fearing a generation of terrorists, American judges have begun denying custody to mothers because of their outside employment (see chapter 1).

I am not a mother. Therefore, I had a great deal of trouble understanding why the working mothers I encountered were feeling so guilty. It seemed to me they had done nothing wrong. Yet they were hearing not only from child-raising experts but also from other mothers and coworkers, that they had gone back to work too soon, or were working too much, or were going to lose some fixed quantity of attachment energy to competing caregivers. They were also hearing from their employers that they could not be taken seriously if they devoted time to their children. Husbands worried for them about their plight. I was frankly perplexed by it.

I thought perhaps if I wrote an article disentangling the research on attachment from mythology about motherhood, I could free these working mothers from the unnecessary worry and regret about bonding/attachment that was apparently quite a burden to them. As I began to talk to them, however, the plot thickened. It was not simply the strictures of attachment theory that were constraining them.

Mothers, it seemed, were coming once again to be seen as the root of all evil—the original Eve of our Puritan past. Psychological theories simply provided the underpinnings for a scapegoating game conducted by politicians and pundits: If mothers were working, they were damaging bonding/attachment.

That is, unless they were poor and on welfare, in which case they were damaging their children if they were *not* working! If mothers were single, not only were they damaging their children by working (or not working), but also by depriving them of a resident father.

In fact, single mothers caused the 1992 Los Angeles riots, as well as drug addiction, violence, poverty, teenage pregnancy, and probably tooth decay, according to Vice President Dan Quayle, and a horde of like-minded public officials. If mothers were divorced, they were damaging every aspect of their children's psyche. If they remained in a bad marriage, they were blamed for not rescuing their children from a hostile environment. Even the middle-class married (i.e., "good") mothers who stayed at home full-time with their children were not to be exonorated. One third of their kind could not form a secure attachment with their children, according to the legions of researchers quantifying attachment *ad infinitum*. In addition, these stay-at-home mothers were depriving their children of strong role models for female independence and accomplishment, which apparently exist only outside the home.

Motherhood was beginning to look as strange to me as a caravan of camels lumbering through an airport. Mothers, I began to realize, are encumbered with the burdens of a society unwilling to carry its own weight. I saw the need to analyze the myriad ways that mothers in America are blamed by experts and public officials alike for a wide range of problems that are really a collective matter. After reviewing the research evidence, I concluded that these allegations of maternal guilt are without foundation. Moreover, it became clear to me that far from failing their children and society, mothers are carrying a disproportionate share of responsibility for children. Instead of facing the need for family-friendly business practices and public support of families by providing substantial tax cuts, paid parental leave, and regulated subsidized day care, a national blame game substitutes for a constructive family policy in this country. Its purpose is to deflect attention from the need for a redistribution of resources that will be more fair to children, one quarter of whom live in poverty and the majority of whom receive child care that is deleterious to their growth. The truth is that mothers need to redirect all these fingers of blame at a society that is too cheap to care for its children, and business that is too sexist to recognize the importance of women's work.

This book demonstrates that the indictment of mothers in the kangaroo courts conducted by social scientists, child-care experts, and public officials is not sustained by the evidence. The crimes committed against our children are committed by our entire society, and these are devastating. The solution, once the bullying of mothers has been stopped, requires the spending of collective money and the genuine involvement of men as equal partners with women and as co-stewards of American family life. Moreover, such a stewardship requires an acceptance of the fact that there are many legitimate family forms.

In Chapter 1, "Motherblame," I describe the din of mother bullying which has been midwifed by the baby gurus T. Berry Brazelton, Penelope Leach, and Benjamin Spock, among others. Their psychobabble about attachment and bonding has facilitated a backlash against working mothers in the courts and in the workplace. Mothers are being blamed by child psychologists and pediatricians, whose professional advice she seeks; by the double-speak of women's magazines; by other parents who see her falling short of the ideals of mothering; by politicians who use her as a scapegoat; by social reformers who want to restore the 1950s family; and even by judges who increasingly deny her custody in court cases. The bullying of mothers may be the necessary tactic to draw attention away from the fact that their free domestic labor and cheap commercial labor currently subsidize American business. The workplace, designed for the male breadwinner, thwarts mothers at every turn with unequal pay, glass ceilings, maternal walls, inflexible hours, and outright hostility to family obligations. The blaming of mothers is not about the welfare of children; it is about restricting women's labor in the guise of defending motherhood.

It is no wonder mothers feel guilty for just about anything that ails even their adult children. Mothers have been taught by generations of ideal-manufacturers to blame themselves for the son or daughter who is unemployed, unhappily married, divorced, substance abusing, or even just cranky. Chapter 2, "Framing Motherhood," explores the origins of the basic ideals of motherhood that are now being used to manipulate mothers. These amount to a virtual frame-up. The images and ideals of motherhood have constantly shifted with the Zeitgeist. In Colonial times, it was fatherhood that received all the acclaim. It was fathers who comforted children in the night and saw to their instruction. Mothers, because of their allegedly sinful natures, were subordinate to their husbands and relegated to what were considered custodial tasks regarding the care of infants and young children. In fact, nurses and even slaves were thought to be as suitable for breastfeeding other peoples' infants.

Motherhood, as most people think of it, was really fashioned in the 1830s as a response to the labor dilemma posed by the Industrial Revolution, which threatened to draw work out of the home and into the factory. Women should stay home, it was decided, and become "hearth angels," exemplars of moral virtue to inspire the children who were mere "clay" in their hands. (Imagine how easily mothers could be cast as sinners if they failed to live up to the angel standard.) As mothers were given a greater role in rearing their children, they attempted to create their own high standards by making motherhood into a profession. And so they enlisted the assistance of scientists and found themselves increasingly reliant on professional—male—experts to tell them how best to raise their children. The advice mothers received throughout the twentieth century, however, was a virtual roller-coaster ride of inflated and conflicting dicta.

When feminists challenged the hearth angel mythology in the 1960s, women were increasingly working outside the home. The need for child care was so great that Congress eventually passed a comprehensive child care bill. However, it was vetoed in 1971 by President Nixon—not because of budget constraints—but because, according to Nixon, it threatened "family values." The ideology remained in place. The expert advice that kept middle-class mothers at home while sending poor mothers to low-wage jobs required an extraordinary ideological balancing act that proffered standards no mother could adequately meet. One of the most virulent of such standards was the invention of attachment.

In chapter 3, "Crimes of Attachment," I examine the maternal-deprivation idea out of which attachment/bonding theory emerged.

The fundamental discovery—that infants are very social creatures and require consistent, loving relationships—was virtually lost because researchers were so steeped in hearth angel ideology. Upon discovering the emotional deprivation of infants kept in institutions designed by doctors and psychologists, the scientific community termed their suffering "maternal deprivation" even though the infants had been deprived of any consistent caregivers and even of play and stimulation. There ensued all kinds of studies, from war orphans to abused monkeys, in which the suffering of the young was deemed the inevitable consequence of the loss of their mothers' love. Such love, researchers concluded, could be provided only through exclusive (stay-at-home) maternal care. Of course, the factors that contribute to infant mental health and to building a foundation for trusting interpersonal relationships depend on far more than the continual or exclusive presence of mothers. The research on mother-child attachment burgeoned, however, perhaps because it was so simplistic and so consistent with convenient myths of motherhood. The content of the research is virtually useless in guiding parents or paid caregivers in meeting the emotional needs of infants and young children, however, because of its ideological distortions.

In chapter 4, "Deviant Motherhood," I examine the evidence that mothers who deviate from the imaginary norm of the stay-at-home married mother are chiefly responsible for damage to children. Are working mothers, single mothers, poor mothers, teen mothers, welfare mothers, and divorced mothers bad for children? Psychologists have a propensity to look at mothers as the sole cause of their children's problems rather than seeing children as part of a complex, interdependent system in which they, with their very different god-given personalities, interact with parents (including fathers who make occasional cameo appearances in the research), siblings, peers, teachers, and other adult caregivers. Sociologists tend to see divorced and unmarried mothers as a social problem and therefore search only for deficits in their childrens' lives. There is no sound evidence that the mothering of any one of these categories of mothers is damaging to their children. The research on these different types of mothers is once again caught up in the maternal-sculptress notion. More than that, however, it is predicated on the assumption that the two-parent married family is best and all other forms are deviant. The evidence, however, does not support the exclusive superiority of the two-parent married family. To give the reader some insight into some of these mothers' typical experiences, I provide some composite portraits based on both national statistics and actual case studies.

In chapter 5, "Fatherguilt?," it becomes clear that mothers and children need a little help from the men, 40 percent of whom do not live with their children. But the caring men are unlikely to be motivated by guilt, as are their female counterparts. There are no studies lamenting damage to attachment caused by fathers' employment, and there is certainly no guilt culture for men. Public officials do not blame riots, juvenile delinquency, drug addiction, and the decline of the family on single fathers. In fact, there are no psychological prescriptions for the competent father. Bad fathers are simply the ones who don't pay child support. Granted, there are the "New Fathers," middle-class young men who are interested in nurturing their infants and children and who may be secretly creating a daddy track at work by choosing family over promotions. But even this hopeful trend is embedded in debates about what is masculine rather than what is good for children. Unfortunately, the New Father, who believes in equality with his wife, is already under attack from advocates for the "New Traditionalist" father, whose hearth angel wife stays home while he, though a little more nurturing of his children than the old-fashioned breadwinner, is still the boss and is not genetically programmed to change diapers.

In chapter 6, "The Real Crime: American Child Care," I analyze the shameful state of American child care. Scientists have been so busy pursuing the bogus distinction between day care and mothercare that they have failed to pay attention to the real damage being done to children by the unregulated, unsubsidized patchwork of care. The handful of recent studies that has examined this care find the vast majority of it harmful to children—regardless of their socioeconomic status. Parents are ignorant of the quality of care their children are receiving because psychologists have not sufficiently studied these situations and can provide only fragmentary information. Parents deserve care that is regulated, as they have no way of gaining access to some of the information necessary to making an adequate evaluation. With several composite case studies, I illustrate some of the typical experiences of day care centers, family day care, nannies, and the vicissitudes of selecting care. I conclude that without a regulated subsidized system, serious damage to families will continue.

In chapter 7, "Reformed: Care in Other Countries," I discuss some of the alternative models of early care found in other countries that have moved away from the ideal of exclusive mothering. Sweden, of course, provides by far the most nurturing environment for families, with a full year of paid parental leave at 80 percent of salary and a system of subsidized day care that provides all families with stable caregivers and beautiful child-centered facilities. The Israeli kibbutz, where children are actually raised collectively, provides the antithesis of our exclusive mothercare notion, yet children raised nonmaternally turn out to be perfectly psychologically healthy. A more likely model for America (which currently seems to view government programs as akin to occupation by enemy forces) is the French system, in which day care, attended by 90 percent of preschoolers, is a public/private enterprise, and is regulated, subsidized, and viewed as highly advantageous for all children. And finally, there is the Japanese model, where sole responsibility for young children belongs to mothers, who now view preschool as absolutely essential to their children's educational success. Because this trend is new and there is a shortage of Japanese preschools, mothers who work receive priority. Consequently, many Japanese mothers take part-time jobs to secure a preschool education for their children; some even claim to work when they do not.

In chapter 8, "The Way It Ought to Be," I conclude that the key to ending the litany of motherblame from parenting experts, public officials, and even mothers themselves, is to recognize that mothers are not the primary cause of the problems afflicting American children.

Mothers are being asked to do too much. They must therefore outsource some of their operations to employers, who also have vested interests in the new generation, and demand the provision of family infrastructure from their government and business community. First off, however, mothers must insist that social scientists and parenting experts undergo retraining to become more aware of their own biases. Parents who seek guidance from experts have a right to the fruits of a more sensible and complex family psychology. Instead of fabricating endless versions of the exclusive mothering mythology or searching only for deficits in all families that don't conform to the married, two-

parent middle-class family, researchers must put aside their prejudices and develop more useful directions for their investigations. The
fact is, there are many legitimate and healthy family forms and they
are here to stay. Parents deserve accurate information about their
strengths and pitfalls. Moreover, one of the best ways of preventing
weak and contentious families, after economic supports are provided,
is the extensive education of our schoolchildren for family life.

After setting her guardians straight, the New Mother must call on
men to be New Fathers, asking them to put aside concerns about
which aspects of parenting are sufficiently masculine and to fully em-
brace the responsibility for nurturing and providing for their children
in concert with mothers. Together, mothers and fathers must insist on
a genuinely family-friendly workplace and the kind of family supports
provided by every other Western nation, including paid family leave
and a first-rate subsidized, regulated child-care system.

Because single mothers and many two-parent impoverished families spend a quarter of their income on child care and the cost of child
care prohibits welfare mothers from being able to afford to work, universal subsidized child care could virtually eliminate child poverty
with the benefits going directly to the children. And finally, of course,
parents and all concerned with the well-being of families must become activists at both the local and national level.

If we, as a society, are to live well—as our tremendous wealth
promises—we must come to distinguish more fairly between personal
responsibility and collective guilt. Once we recognize how the blame
game operates, we have a real chance of behaving like a whole village
that truly cares for all its children.

# MOTHERGUILT

# Motherblame

Open up your newspaper, flip through a parenting magazine, or tune into the nightly news, and you'll discover that the American mother has become the prime target in a national blame game. Society's ills—welfare, child poverty, latchkey kids, and even riots, indeed the changing family, with its abundance of overworked dual earners, divorces, and single motherhood—are all being assigned to her authorship. Employed or not employed, rich or poor, educated or uneducated, today's mother is given the lion's share of blame for problems she couldn't possibly have fomented alone.

Her blamers come from every quarter. They are child psychologists and pediatricians whose professional advice she seeks; they are women's magazines that always have a bland take on the problems she is confronting; they are other parents, who see her falling short of their ideals of mothering; they are politicians who use her as a scapegoat; they are social reformers, who want to restore the 1950s family; they are even judges who increasingly deny her custody in divorce cases. How and when did mothers become such a viable target? Why are they held to an impossible standard (the term "supermom" is a dead giveaway) of the "Good Mother"? And why do mothers believe the rhetoric?

## THE BABY GURUS

One of the most exasperating sources of maternal guilt is that it's peddled by the very authorities who are supposed to be a mother's most friendly advisers: the baby gurus. Mothers usually acquire their sacred texts—T. Berry Brazelton, Penelope Leach, Benjamin Spock, and their fellow clergy—before they even give birth. In any case, they are bound to meet up with these high priests on TV or read echoes of their advice in the glossy magazines and commercial pamphlets that help while away the hours at the obstetrician's and pediatrician's offices. These authorities love babies and know a lot about them and are great advocates for better child care, national family subsidies, and a reformed workplace. But while they care deeply about children, they perpetuate a constricting stereotype of mothers as little more than architects of the perfect child, not people with their own legitimate needs and diverse talents. If today's mothers are feeling guilty, it's a good bet it's because the Holy Triumvirate has told them in so many words that they *are* guilty.

When it comes to working outside the home, the baby gurus stand grandly in their pulpits, which bear the signature of Freud, and pontificate about the sinfulness of mothers who work. Conceding to reality, they all claim to accept the "need" and "right" of mothers to work. But fundamentally, they believe "othercare" is inferior to mothercare and pass along this message—tacitly or explicitly—to new mothers primed to accept it as gospel.

British psychologist Penelope Leach is one of the world's most widely read child care experts, with her own TV show and worldwide public appearances to promote the word. In a 1993 parent and educator conference, Leach admonished working mothers, "You've spent so long getting where you are—how does a baby fit in when you can't afford to give up one income? If you continue to work, however, you give up raising your child."[1] (As far as I know, the women in her audience continued to sit respectfully in their seats, hands perhaps folded neatly in their laps to restrain them from bobbing up into unmotherlike gestures. Why no one rioted right then and there is the mystery this book attempts to unravel.) In her most recent book *Children First,* she criticizes all forms of nonmaternal care during the first eighteen months of a child's life because, she proclaims, it is inherently inferior to the care provided by the one-and-only "special adult"—mother.[2] Leach even trots out the old Freudian notion that "for a woman, having a baby is a culmination of adult sexuality" and her role as mother is therefore her biological destiny and should come before all else. She touts breast-feeding as a fundamental and necessary part of the attachment process and incompatible with working. In *Your Baby and Child,* she even chastises women for feeling trapped when they stay home. "Some women hate [the first six months of infancy] . . . Instead of taking pleasure in being so much enjoyed and needed, they feel shut in and consumed by the baby's dependence . . . Understanding your own importance is both the prevention and the cure . . . Like it or not, you are the family now."[3] Poor Dad.

American neonatologist T. Berry Brazelton, with some dozen baby books, magazine columns, commercial videos, and a TV show to spread his gospel, has tried to accept the legitimacy of mothers working, but his own long-standing bias is constantly overtaking his rhetoric of tolerance. In *Infants and Mothers,* he continues to hope that women's enthusiasm for work will recede, and they will come to understand how crucial a job mothering is: "My bias is that a woman's most important role is being at home to mother her small children . . . [women should see] mothering as a goal that is as important as anything they can achieve in their professional life."[4] (Here's where the power question, which we'll hear more about in a minute, tiptoes in, because you soon get the impression his "bias" does not concern mothers who work as office functionaries or schoolteachers. Let the litigator, legislator, or theoretical physicist like her work, though, and you can be sure she has little chance of a pediatric dispensation.) Not surprisingly, Brazelton depicts mothers' work as a trial. In *Working and Caring,* the mothers he profiles do not enjoy their work—it is simply a burden that makes them frantic, guilty, and faced with inferior child care.[5] According to Dr. Brazelton, women's guilt about working is legitimate, and he further compounds the load of guilt with some of his psychoanalytic prowess—he claims your children are going to experience your guilt as anxiety so your working and then your anxiety over it puts them "at risk."[6] What the term "at risk" actually means here is anybody's guess. At one time, it belonged to epidemiology and predicted your likelihood of contracting a disease. In the last decade, however, it has become a scientific-sounding bogeyman trotted out by experts implying the risky ones will become everything from drug addicts to psychopathic murderers.

If you think I'm exaggerating, you might want to rent the video of journalist Bill Moyers's interview with Brazelton in his *World of Ideas* TV series. Moyers and Brazelton discuss whether women should stay home from work to rear their infants during the "bonding period," which Brazelton describes as lasting a year. "Does the first year really make a difference?" asks Moyers. "It does," replies Brazelton. "The child gets a sense of being important . . . if he doesn't have that through infancy, it's hard to put it in later . . . and these kids that never get it . . . will become difficult in school, they'll never succeed in school, they'll make everybody angry; they'll become delinquents later and eventually they'll become terrorists." Moyers asks, "And you think that goes back . . . to this bonding period?" "Yes."[7] (Imagine! The control of terrorism in our world is in the hands of mothers at bonding time. Surely the gurus should be working to see that all mothers receive lavish subsidies and room service during that critical period of the incipient criminal's life.)*

Dr. Spock, in his best-selling book *Baby and Child Care,* studiously substitutes the terms "men and women" or "parents," for "women" and "mothers" in his more recent sermons, and advocates gender equality in all matters. But such politically correct thinking often breaks down with the weight of its own rigidity, masking the lack of a genuine change of heart. For instance, he claims in the 1985 edition that "parents" who stay home with their children and find this makes them irritable should not think this is necessarily because they want a career; it also goes back to their own childhoods and they really should consult a therapist about it. In the 1992 edition, Spock omits the prescription for therapy and allows that "parents" may "need a career for fulfillment."[8] (Now, if we hear that a "parent" may need to stay home with *his* baby for fulfillment, we might just be able to credit Spock's professed egalitarianism.) In his 1994 finger-wagging lecture, *A Better World for Our Children,* Spock admonishes it's better for one "parent" (guess who) to stay home for the first two or three years of a child's life, although he recognizes the need for "parents" to work.[9]

---

*I'm not suggesting children can't be severely damaged at this tender age. But the equation between mothers at home and terrorism doesn't compute. As far as I can tell, the IRA and the PLO (the original terrorist organizations in Ireland and Palestine, respectively) took hold in countries where a greater proportion of mothers stayed home with their young children than in most places.

So you would think that at least mothers who do stay home would escape the guru-induced "guilts."* But stay-at-home mothers also get a healthy sense of their own sin, because the domestic world the baby gurus describe is so romanticized. The experts' image of the Good Mother is more like a religious icon than a flesh-and-blood woman. Most baby books describe this mother as if she really spends her entire day doing nothing but beaming at a cooing baby and playing developmentally appropriate games to stimulate intelligence and self-confidence. The virtuous mother is allowed the occasional outburst of anger, of course, which the gurus help her manage, but never chronic frustration with the isolation and tedium that often attends child rearing. Poor mothers who stay home at the behest of Uncle Sam because they must do so to receive public assistance are entirely invisible to the good doctors, as are poor mothers who work. Mothers' employment, of course, is described as a "career" "choice," a problem that interferes with women's parenting. Staying home remains a middle-class ideal sponsored by the gurus. It would therefore be sheer heresy to suggest mothers might, in some cases, overwhelm their children with developmentally appropriate attention when their energy and expectations (prescribed by the experts) are focused solely on their children.† And, of course, it is unimaginable to these experts that the best mothers might actually be women who have the option of a reasonable mix of working and caring.

## MOTHERS' MAGAZINES: THE GUILT MONGERS

The parenting and women's magazines are as bad as the gurus (whom

*Like the rest of our society, I use the term "working mother" to apply to mothers who work for wages. I use the term "work" as if it were the same as paid work. However, I believe that mothering is an aspect of domestic labor which is productive. But like so much of what women, alone, do, domestic labor deserves to be in some special category that is not the same as salaried work, yet not the same as nonwork because it is so entwined with personal and private relationships.

†There are, of course, advice books that are beginning to break free of the gurus' mother-unfriendly moralizing. One mother-and-daughter team has produced several very popular books for new parents that recognize a more diverse mother population (albeit strictly middle class). But because the authors are conveying pediatric knowledge, they still get tangled up in the stay-at-home-mother strictures of bonding and attachment while affirming that mothers' desire to work is legitimate: i.e., the ongoing double message—it's okay to work/your children will suffer. For example, see: Arelene Eisenberg, Heidi Murkoff, and Sandee Hathaway. What to Expect the First Year (New York: Workman Publishing, 1989), pp. 587–590.

they often feature) because they purport to have concern for mothers' predicament while communicating a fundamentally conservative message that will do nothing to further the serious plight of mothers and children in our society. In spite of all the psychological advice, the majority of mothers have entered the paid workforce, and the magazines claim to help them manage this transition.[10] In fact, 52 percent of mothers of infants and 60 percent of mothers with children under six are in the workforce as are 76 percent of women with school-age children.[11] (Imagine the hordes of terrorists we can expect to meet up with a few years from now.) Apparently mothers are not enjoying it, though—in fact, they can barely manage it according to the virtual chorus of "I-told-you-sos." The supermom of the 1980s who managed to stagger into the '90s is now being told that she just can't "have it all" and presumably she should feel guilty for continuing to try. She has failed at her task of gracefully balancing career and family through time management techniques and stress reduction classes. In the best end-of-century advice literature, from *Parents* magazine to *Redbook,* unhappy working mothers are told they must now learn to manage their guilt about not being supermom, since they are just going to have to live with it.

Most of these recipes for self-torture insist that you are the greatest instigator of your own guilt. Even those other women who ask you how you feel about having gone back to work "so soon" after having your baby or ask what prevented you from breast-feeding your baby cannot be blamed for your unease. You wanted to be just like June Cleaver, you also wanted to find fulfillment from your job, and *you* drove your*self* crazy with worry about the psychological impact of day care.[12] To help mothers conquer these maternal failings, some advisers have identified the "top ten guilt trips" which mothers inflict on themselves and they provide "tips" on how to cope with them. For example, how do you feel less guilty about not being able to stay home with a sick child or missing work if you do? The answer is so easy. Bring work home. If you can't do that, just weigh the guilt and choose between child and work—whichever makes you feel less guilty.[13] (The exhortation to run for Congress and legislate generous family support or organize the parental labor force has yet to be incorporated into any working mother's "guilt makeover.") Mothers should "ask yourself if the cause of your guilt is within your control. If the answer is no, your guilty feelings are self-defeating. Let them go . . . If your guilt is triggered by a lack of time with your kids, set a timer for twenty minutes and play—giving them your full attention. When the buzzer goes off, return to other responsibilities."[14]

Of course, the maternal advisers offering this self-imploding balm are the very people who continue to throw women's perfectly good consciences into a frenzy by suggesting working mothers' difficulties are the product of their own inadequacies. (If only they would use those twenty-minute timers!) Women are being asked to choose between family and work or to shortchange both, not to mention themselves. Moreover, the nonmaternal care available to their children is genuinely inadequate. Working mothers do not have real choices. The only way for a woman to actually resolve the "work/family conflict," which is said to be *her* problem, is to demand a more flexible workplace and genuine family support from the entire society to whom the children ultimately belong.

## THE DAY CARE HYSTERIA

But at a time when the Supermom icon was gaining currency and women were thinking seriously about demanding a national child care policy, day care became a magnet for all the confusing fears about whether mothers' employment might damage their children. In 1984 child sexual abuse was suddenly "discovered" in preschools, and the nation has yet to recover from that nightmare.[15] Millions of miles of print, megawatts of electronic images, and scores of real-life witchhunts in which innocent people actually served prison time were spawned by the day care fear-mongering. The hysteria was tailor-made to drive working mothers up the wall—what more horrifying sign could there be that consigning their children to day care was tantamount to handing them over to the devil?

In the more than half-dozen most sensational cases, almost all defendants have now either been acquitted for insufficient evidence or released from prison on appeal because higher courts have declared that the evidence was obtained by improper methods.[16] It appears that therapists and health officials, in their zeal to coax sensitive admissions out of children, actually *created* many of the children's accusations by their aggressive questioning.

The most notorious case involved the McMartin preschool, a small one-story building in Manhattan Beach, California, and resulted in a trial lasting six years at a cost of $16 million.[17] In the hundreds of news media stories about the case, only a handful were skeptical about the guilt of the defendants before the verdicts were rendered. Extensive investigations by the FBI, the U.S. Customs Service, and Interpol, and the parents' offer of a reward of $25,000, yielded no physical evidence of the crimes. Many charges were dropped, and formal indictments obtained only against Raymond and Peggy McMartin Buckey, who were found not guilty on all but thirteen of sixty-five counts, and on those thirteen the jury was deadlocked. In the relatively brief retrial, the jury could not agree on a verdict and a mistrial was declared.

In 1995 the conviction for child sexual abuse of New Jersey preschool teacher Margaret Kelly Michaels, who served five years in jail, was overturned on appeal when an appellate division ruled that her trial had been full of egregious prosecutorial abuses, including questioning of the children that planted suggestions, tainting their testimony. Michaels is now suing state and local agencies for $10 million. Similarly, in 1995, a judge ordered a new trial in Massachusetts for Violet Amirault and her daughter, Cheryl Amirault LeFave. And in North Carolina an appeals court in 1995 ordered retrials for two more day care workers, Robert Kelly, Jr., owner of the Little Rascals Day Care center in Edenton, and Dawn Wilson, a cook at the center.

While the mid-1980s witch-hunts were fueled by a zealotry about the horrendous problems of child abuse and sexual abuse, they occurred at the site of day care because of our perception that day care is a fundamentally less appropriate environment for children than being at home with their mothers. This strong belief about the superiority of stay-at-home mothering has even inspired recent advertising campaigns to persuade mothers to stay home.

## THE "NEW TRADITIONALIST" PLOY

During the late 1980s, middle-class mothers kept on working and liking it. (Poor mothers, of course, have always worked.) The media spin on this phenomenon, though, was that mothers weren't really enjoying themselves and the most trendy mothers were repenting of their sinful work. The message was that mothers *could* just say no to work, since they were feeling so guilty. In fact, it was widely proposed that they could easily make up for lack of income from outside employment and enjoy the bonus of being there for their kids if only they would give up some of the material comfort that is really a sign of their self-centered and shallow values anyway. In the late 1980s, *Good Housekeeping* actually waged a campaign consisting of full-page ads in America's leading newspapers, insisting there was a growing phenomenon they called the "new traditionalist" woman who stays home with her children. While evidence of the new traditionalist trend is hard to discover, a round of stories in the national media and copycat ad campaigns by other publications and manufacturers of clothing and household goods, spread the nostalgic rumor.[18] At the moment there is little demographic evidence of this phantom.[19] In fact, even the small number of upper middle-class mothers who are "stopping out" of the workforce to care for their children at home say they would return to work if better day care were available. Conceding to reality, *Good Housekeeping* finally dropped the campaign in 1995.

## THE ATTACHMENT CANON

Few women fell for the new traditionalist trick. (Most could not afford to.) So the big guns of psychology were trotted out again to curb women's enthusiasm for the workplace. They are old guns, actually, in the shape of attachment theory; this theory, first developed in the 1950s, as I'll discuss in chapter 3, rests on the bedrock assumption that only mothers can provide the caring, nurturing relationship their children need to survive. Magazines in the late '80s and early '90s reported on the growing arsenal of attachment research that was pouring forth from the psychology departments of universities, where it had become something of a fad. The latest findings include the inevitable failures of mothers to do it right (only two thirds of mothers have "securely attached" babies) and cautions about the effects of nonmaternal care (it "risks" inferior attachment). The baby gurus, of course, stepped up their doublespeak about working mothers: Women are biologically designed for exclusive stay-at-home mothering, but let's not neglect their "understandable" (say this with a little pat on a mother's head) need for self(ish)-fulfillment in work, despite

that "risk" to children posed single-handedly by mothers' working.[20]
A popular book enshrining the attachment canon was even published, and promotions for the treatise warned: "The bond you form
with your mother will influence your own children, their children and
generations to come."[21] (Gee, if it's that critical, why don't you have
to pass it in high school? Shouldn't it be on the SAT exams?) In this
same vein, recent issues of *Mothering* magazine continue to trot
out all the old warnings about early separation from the mother
interrupting the natural "psychobiological mother-child unit" and
deficiencies in maternal-child attachment causing "partial psychopaths."[22] (No mention of who might be turning *mothers* into partial psychopaths with all the nutty advice.)

But in spite of all the warnings from the attachment quarter, mothers, like the Energizer Bunny, just keep on marching into the labor
force, working two and three jobs sometimes, and bumping up
against those glass ceilings with perpetual determination.* They continue to feel torn and guilty, however, because it's impossible to give
both their jobs and their children the time they deserve.[23] But if mothers have pretty much failed to heed their advisers, they are now coming in for some advice they will not be able to refuse: The legal system
is now attempting to be the enforcer of the baby gurus' standard of
the Good Mother.

## THE WORKING MOTHER CUSTODY BACKLASH

By the mid-1990s, it is clear the baby gurus' teachings have fueled
something far more sinister than simply the inevitable tarnishing of
the impossible Good Mother image or fear of the day care bogeyman.
Women are finding that they can actually lose their children because
they work.* The highly publicized situation of Marcia Clark, the Los
Angeles prosecuter in the O.J. Simpson murder trial, indicates one
ominous direction of the working mother debate.[24] In 1995 Clark's estranged husband, Gordon Clark, asked a judge to give him primary

---

*In 1970 about 44 percent of mothers with preschoolers were employed during the year; in 1992, 67
percent were employed. Howard Hayghe and Suzanne Bianchi, "Married Mothers' Work Patterns: The
Job-Family Compromise," Monthly Labor Review, June 1994, pp. 24–31.

custody of the couple's sons because she was rarely home to care for the boys during the trial. This custody dispute became public after Clark told Judge Lance Ito that she could not stay for a proposed evening session of the trial because of her child care needs and defense lawyer Johnnie Cochran accused her of attempting to delay testimony of an important defense witness. Mr. Clark's bid for custody apparently came after Ms. Clark requested increased child support payments based on her need for increased child care due to the demands of the trial.

In another highly publicized case, Sharon Prost, a counsel to Senator Orrin Hatch, was ordered to relinquish custody of her two sons to her former husband. The judge portrayed Ms. Prost as a driven workaholic, while her husband was portrayed as a doting father who put the children first. The husband, however, even while unemployed for a substantial period, maintained his children in full-time day care. In another recent child custody battle, a nineteen-year-old honor student and mother, Jennifer Ireland, lost custody of her daughter when she enrolled as a freshman at the University of Michigan, where she was on a scholarship. Her three-year-old daughter was to be given into the custody of her father, Steven Smith, because Ireland would have placed her daughter in day care while she attended classes. Smith had rarely visited his daughter, had never been married to Ireland, and had to be forced by the court to pay child support when Ireland decided to attend college. Yet Smith, a part-time maintenance worker at a local park, lived with his parents and intended to have his mother, a full-time homemaker, look after the girl while he was at work. Judge Raymond Cashen indicated that day care was the deciding factor against the mother, expressing skepticism about the long-term impact of "strangers" on a child's emotional well-being. (Fifteen months later the decision was reversed by the state court of appeals.)[25] Men and women are being held to such a different standard of conduct in the divorce courts that some women are now being advised by their attorneys to refrain from taking more demanding jobs or even seeking further education for fear they will be accused of devoting too much of themselves to their work and will lose custody of their chil-

---

*In chapter 4 I will analyze social science research on the effects of maternal employment on children.

dren. While mothers are increasingly being denied custody of their children because of their work, fathers are rarely, if ever, held to the same standard.[26]

The mother who does not read the newspapers or listen to electronic newscasts can still be intimidated by this backlash through such TV docudramas as "Because Mommy Works," which aired on NBC in November 1994.[27] Based on a true story, a divorced nurse who works full-time loses custody of her seven-year-old son. Her husband, a journalist who left the West Coast for the East Coast and rarely ever saw the son for two years, successfully sues for custody upon returning to the neighborhood. Although he continues to work full-time (and more), his new wife stays home, and so he is awarded custody of the boy.

Clearly, underlying all the motherguilt is a realistic maternal fear of being pilloried for not adhering to the standards of psychologically correct mothering as defined by the baby gurus.

## ILLEGITIMATE MOTHERS

In addition to the impossible strictures of the psychologizers who blame mothers for their work/family conflict, mothers are feeling guilty because they are the target of a gathering assault by politicians and pundits. If you were worried about the effects of your working on your children, you'll wonder if you're not in for capital punishment if you accept public funds designated for mothers or experience divorce, fail to marry, remarry, or even neglect to make a lot of money. The mere mention of mothers receiving welfare payments seems to turn most Americans into sputtering, blue-faced jabberwockies. But behind all the venom currently directed at "welfare mothers" is an agenda that posits all renegade mothers as the cause of our social problems.

Republican Speaker of the House Newt Gingrich delights in using mothers as examples of the moral corruption of the entire society, which he claims to know how to cure. Just before the 1994 election, Gingrich spoke of the widely publicized case in which two children had been drowned by their divorced mother, Susan Smith. "I think the mother killing her two children in South Carolina vividly reminds every American how sick society is getting . . . the only way you can get change is to vote Republican." In November 1995, speaking to Republican governors in New Hampshire, Gingrich spoke of the killing of Debra Evans, a mother who was receiving welfare. Her assailants slashed open her abdomen and removed her unborn child, and also killed her ten-year-old daughter and eight-year-old son. The leader of the House of Representatives said: "Let's talk about what welfare has created. Let's talk about the moral decay of the world the left is defending . . . What's wrong is a welfare system which subsidizes people doing nothing . . ."[28]

Gingrich's "Personal Responsibility Act" is designed to punish poor, unmarried mothers for their presumed irresponsibility in producing "illegitimate" children. (As it happens, only 30 percent of mothers require AFDC because they are unmarried and have a child, 45 percent because they are divorced or separated).[29] The illegitimate label originates in the English Common Law that conferred upon such children the term "filius nullius"—child of no one. Unmarried mothers (at the moment, primarily just the poor ones) are perceived as a kind of social plague by our congressional exemplars of virtue because they are manless and only men are apparently able to confer legitimacy upon children. In fact, the Heritage Foundation, which seems to have replaced Harvard as the prime supplier of nonelected Washington advisers, warns us: "The primary goal of conservative reform [is]: To wipe out the scourge of illegitimacy in the United States."[30] According to social psychologist Charles Murray, another linchpin of conservative thinking whose ice-cube-hearted and racist ideas about welfare reform and the inferiority of the poor have now been fully embraced by the Republican if not Democratic mainstream: "Illegitimacy is the single most important social problem of our time—more important than crime, drugs, poverty, illiteracy, or homelessness because it drives everything else."[31] According to *Washington Post* commentator Richard Cohen, "illegitimacy" is now even a "national security issue."[32]

## LEGITIMATE FATHERS

Anyone listening carefully to the attack on single mothers would think that all those loose females and their little bastards causing our horrendous social ills were produced by parthogenesis. The alert observer, however, might just as legitimately insist that the plethora of women and children breaking up the family and wallowing in poverty are the fruits of male weakness, callousness, selfishness, and sexual vanity. After all, almost half of all mothers receiving welfare are on the rolls because of divorce or separation—i.e., the failure of judges to order, or husbands to pay, adequate child support.* While the standard of living of divorced mothers and children declines by a third after divorce, that of fathers increases 15 percent. Child support as currently calculated covers less than half the cost of rearing a child— in fact, it usually does not even cover the average cost of day care.[33] Moreover, close to half the families on welfare were started while the mother was still a teenager[34] and two thirds of those girls were either raped or sexually abused, nearly always by fathers, stepfathers, or other male relatives or guardians (60 percent also suffered severe physical violence from males and females alike).[35] Our elected reformers are so clueless about women's lives, though, that they actually want to deprive teenage mothers of welfare in hopes that these same families will continue to care for them or they will get married (or perhaps disappear into thin air). While our leaders seek out "deadbeat dads" for their outstanding child support dollars, they ignore the fact that 30 percent of fathers of babies born to girls under sixteen are men in their twenties or older.[36]

If we haven't yet spelled "f-a-t-h-e-r-b-l-a-m-e," how about the connection between the high rates of male violence against women and the poverty and fatherlessness many children face?† More than a

---

*Methods of calculating child support are based on the costs of raising a child in a two-parent family where women's caregiving is not paid. Therefore, when divorced women become employed and pay for the work they once did for free, they receive no comparable award. The average child support award is $2,995 a year in 1995—less than the average cost of day care! Vanessa Gallman, "GOP Welfare Plan Ignores Fathers," Philadelphia Inquirer, January 20, 1995, p. A1. In part, because of this inequality, 39 percent of divorced women and children live in poverty; 20 percent receive some type of welfare income. Demie Kurz, For Richer, For Poorer: Mothers Confront Divorce (New York: Routledge, 1995), p. 3.

†In a randomly selected sample of 129 divorced mothers, sociologist Demie Kurz found that 50 percent of her subjects had experienced violence by their ex-husbands, 37 percent had experienced frequent or severe violence; only 30 percent had never experienced violence. (Demie Kurz, For Richer, For Poorer: Mothers Confront Divorce, pp. 52–3. (Several other studies that corroborate this finding include: J. Wallerstein and J. Kelly, Surviving the Breakup: How Children and Parents Cope with Divorce [New York: Basic Books, 1995]; and Ellis and Wight, "Post-separation Woman Abuse: The Contribution of Lawyers," Victimology 13 [1987]. Studies indicate that 50 to 90 percent of battered women try

third of divorced women are likely to have experienced serious violence at the hands of their husbands. Are our moral reformers suggesting cutting off unemployment insurance or inventing a social stigma for batterers? Are they lamenting the irresponsibility of macho men who use women and have no use for children? Are they suggesting vasectomies for these irresponsible dads? Are they considering reviving statutory rape laws?

## SINGLE MOTHERS

Millions of those irresponsible mothers, on the other hand, seem to be the ones who get up every morning and cook breakfast, get the bastards dressed, sing the Barney song to them, and even hock their few remaining valuables to get the kids high-top sneakers when they reach puberty while their fathers have no idea where or how or who their children are. These men are going to make children "legitimate?"

If single mothers are truly a scourge, we are in trouble. In America, 27 percent of all children are born to unmarried mothers.[37] Nowhere are single mothers being congratulated for becoming independent enough to avoid bad marriages or for taking on the responsibility of caring for their children with little or no support. Instead, their lack of a legal husband is designated a social problem regardless of the reason for not being married. Dan Quayle (vice president at the time), of course, kicked off the '90s by blaming the Los Angeles riots on single mothers. Quayle stated his case in Los Angeles in the wake of riots sparked by a jury decision to exonerate L.A. policemen of the brutal videotaped beating of Rodney King, a black man. Quayle argued the riots were "directly related to the breakdown of the family." He drew a connection between poor, unmarried black mothers and Murphy Brown, an affluent white television character, who, he said, mocked the importance of fathers by bearing a child and "calling it just another lifestyle choice."[38]

The outcry against single motherhood began to spread with a 1993

---

*to escape abusive situations but their efforts are hampered by the economic deprivation that so often goes with domestic violence. Even women whose mates are not poor, may be financially isolated. (See Martha Davis and Susan Krahan, "Beaten, Then Robbed," Letters to the Editor, New York Times, January 13, 1995, p. A31.)*

*Atlantic Monthly* cover story, "Dan Quayle Was Right" by Barbara Dafoe Whitehead, a member of the Institute for American Values, a research group in New York City that studies families and children. The author boasts that the accumulating body of social science evidence* supports Quayle's assertion that single mothers are a virtual cornucopia of social problems.[39] Whitehead, along with the now resounding chorus of conservatives, paints a devastating portrait of divorced and never-married mothers (widows are okay apparently), whose poverty, social isolation, and even remarriage are so damaging to their children that they drop out of school, become parents too early in life, and remain dissatisfied with their lives. The proposed remedy for this alleged plague is to restrict divorce laws, provide tax breaks and cash incentives for married couples, stigmatize out-of-wedlock births, and force couples into therapy before they may be allowed to divorce. Some conservatives have even proposed a constitutional amendment forbidding divorce to couples with children under eighteen.[40]

By 1995, as part of the growing chorus of single-mother blamers, David Blankenhorn, president of the Institute for American Values, even posits single motherhood is the cause of "our nation's tragic decline."[41] In the same vein, an Institute colleague of Blankenhorn, Rutgers University sociologist David Popenoe claims delinquency, teenage suicide, child abuse, and other social problems are "demonstrably worse" in single-mother families.[42]

It appears our leaders view single motherhood as a kind of crabgrass that inexplicably appeared on the lawn of family life and now needs a dose of legislative weedkiller to make us a happy land again. Its roots—impoverished, quarrelsome, exploitive, unloving, battering, substance-abusing marriages—are never discussed. All will be well when the cleared single-mother patches are replaced with co-parent turf, regardless of men's paternal character, employability, abusiveness, criminality, or otherwise general suitability for being marital partners or dads.

The nation's most powerful leaders now declare they want to confine motherhood to marriage, and they may believe they have started the stampede back to marriage by gutting funding for welfare and

---

*An analysis of this social science evidence is the subject of chapter 4.

mandating welfare-to-work policies without providing the accompanying funds to train the immoral workforce, create the jobs to employ them, or provide supplementary care for the 67 percent of welfare recipients who are children. But just in case poor mothers and children can't be starved into marrying, the Speaker of the House advocates a "return to Victorian morality" wherein the concept of shame will be reactivated. Gingrich, while calling mothers immoral, is leading a truly immoral crusade to cut programs that maintain minimum health and nutrition standards for some children and provide preschool education for children in poor families (while at the same time proposing tax cuts and other benefits for those who are very well off). But Gingrich's longings for morality concern only women's shame and children's stigma caused by that missing wedding ring.[43] Hopefully, Mr. Gingrich will be remembered in history along with Marie Antoinette—who lost her head to the French Revolution after suggesting the starving peasants eat cake—for his suggestion that welfare families (who are known to clip coupons so they can buy a cheaper can of Spaghetti-O's) should each be given $1,000 toward the purchase of a laptop computer. Shame.[44]

## THE BIG, BAD ("BLACK") WELFARE MOTHER

While it is racism itself that has negotiated a place for African Americans at the bottom of the socioeconomic ladder, those of us who have benefited from their exclusion have the pleasure of believing our society is a just place if we also believe they are deserving of their poverty. Therefore, the black "welfare queen" has been added to the pantheon of racist stereotypes that serve to dehumanize entire groups of people as the portion of impoverished mothers burgeons. That black women and children are disproportionately represented in the welfare roles is no surprise. Unfortunately, what may surprise many is that the majority of recipients are *not* black.[45]

The contemptuous allegations of public figures about the immorality of welfare mothers (who are most often imagined to be black) abounds now that the Congress has legitimized the trashing of these women and their children by its righteous abandonment of them. The governor of Mississippi, Kirk Fordice (in whose state the average cash benefit for a mother with two children is $120 a month), for instance, proclaims that mothers on welfare became pregnant precisely so that they could collect the $24 a month in extra benefits offered by the state for an additional child. "We can't keep subsidizing the production of additional illegitimate children," he admonished.[46] In the same vein, several states applying the "family cap"[47] have cut benefits to women who bear another child while receiving AFDC even though the average welfare mother has her statistical 1.8 children (the same as the rest of us) and half have only one child, and even though there is no correlation between higher welfare payments and higher birthrates.* This legislation feeds the requisite stereotype of the promiscuous welfare mother as unthinking baby factory.

One of the most dangerous proposals, in its implications for the freedom of all women, is to force women receiving welfare to have Norplant contraceptive rods implanted under their skin as a condition of receiving benefits, even though rates of childbearing automatically decline while women are receiving public assistance.[48]

Politicians have been using the war on welfare as a galvanizing force to propel their political careers by capitalizing on the dissatisfaction of the growing population of hardworking families that keeps losing financial ground as the bottom falls out of the middle class and jobs are outsourced to the "third world." An early winner with this tactic, Wisconsin governor Tommy Thompson's "Two years and you're out/Work-Not-Welfare" slogans helped to provide the GOP with a viable organizing principle in the post-communist world where voters might otherwise have found enemies in government waste and corporate callousness.[49] Those promiscuous, lazy, TV-watching, imagine-them-to-be-black-and-overweight from eating so many tax dollars (nonvoting) ghetto females provided the perfect scapegoat.[50]

---

*In 1994, Rutgers University researchers conducted a rigorous study comparing families receiving AFDC to a comparable group who were not receiving assistance and found the birth rates were identical. Teresa Amott, "Reforming Welfare," Bucknell World 40 (September 1995), p. 40. There is no correlation between higher benefits and higher birthrates. Benefit levels in the states with the five highest birthrates to single teenage mothers—Mississippi, Louisiana, South Carolina, Arkansas, and Alabama—rank among the seven lowest welfare benefits in the nation. (Kevin Ryan and Jill Chaifety, Letters to the Editor, "Cutting Welfare Won't Reduce Teenage Births," New York Times, April 21, 1995, p. A21.) Correcting for inflation, the average AFDC benefit has fallen 50 percent over the past 25 years, while out-of-wedlock births have risen dramatically. Moreover, two thirds of all out-of-wedlock births are to women who are not poor. (Teresa Amott, "Reforming Welfare," p. 40.) Also see: June Axinn and Amy Hirsch, "Welfare and the Reform of Women," Families in Society, November 1993, p. 569.

Governor Thompson has even instituted a "Bridefare" program to bribe teenage parents to marry by offering them a hike in benefits so the government won't have to help them with food stamps or AFDC.[51] (Imagine the gratefulness of the girls and their legitimized babies when they get to marry their seducers and abusers, and then experience soon after, the likely divorce.)* Such sound-bite solutions have yet to produce actual changes, but they did seem to get votes.[52]

While working mothers and single mothers continue to be admonished for giving too much time to their careers and not enough to their children, mothers who receive welfare and stay home are being held in such contempt for *not* working that reformers would put their children in orphanages (to save the taxpayer money?)† if those mothers cannot find sufficient work to support their children—Brazeltonian blandishments about attachment notwithstanding.

There's just one thing I don't understand in all this moral zeal to reform mothers: Who is going to be responsible around the clock, around the week, the month, the year, for all that feeding, clothing, comforting, cooking, washing, changing, translating, diagnosing of fevers, rashes, runny noses, earaches, stomachaches, eye infections; constantly watching to prevent injury from the stove, electrical outlets, harmful household substances, injury from running out of the yard, the parking lot, the store, the park, and into a dangerous street, falling out of the grocery cart, pulling down boxes from shelves, pulling tables and chairs on top of themselves; constantly telling the kids what to do—"Brush your teeth," "Tie your shoes" (or tying their shoes for them), "Wash your hands," "Eat your XYZ"; stopping fights, drying tears, helping with homework, shopping for clothes that are constantly being outgrown, dealing with a barrage of requests for expensive toys, deciding on the use of TV, finding baby-sitters, getting them to play groups, preschools, and other activities while managing to make three meals a day with food you've tried to get the best prices on while reading the labels to screen out the ingredients most

---

*Divorce rates for teenage parents are much higher than for parents who married in adulthood; the divorce rates for their second marriages are also higher. Amy Butler, "The Changing Economic Consequences of Teenage Childbearing," Social Service Review, March 1992, pp. 1–31.

†According to the Child Welfare League of America, the cost would be about $36,500 per child per year; foster care is about $4,800, and a child's share of welfare and food stamps is $2,644. Editorial, "Orphanages Are No Solution," New York Times, December 12, 1994, p. A18.

recently promoted to the harmful substances list, and always trying to be patient and understanding even while they are screaming and crying? I just thought I'd mention it. These are the duties of the slatternly slackers.

How can we explain the irrational fuss over these women and children, whose welfare costs about 1 percent of the federal budget—hardly a big-ticket item?[53] Mothers receiving AFDC are to be forced out of the home to do anything else but this lazy good-for-nothing life according to our leaders—"even leaf-raking, if that's all they are capable of," says Mickey Kaus, senior editor of *The New Republic* and author of a book about welfare reform written without a single interview with a welfare mom.[54] While long-term welfare recipients constitute a small drain on the federal coffers, the brouhaha over their not working for wages and their alleged inferiority as human beings is reminiscent of the anti-communist fervor of the 1950s.

## THE CULTURE OF POVERTY = SINGLE MOTHERHOOD

One of the most insidious ways of blaming mothers for the nation's social and economic ills is the notion of a "culture of poverty" that presumably gets passed on from generation to generation. This notion conveniently suggests that the poor are really very different from us, less good, less moral, and therefore deserving of their poverty.\* While the term was first applied primarily to men, it has more recently been leveled at women to suggest they are responsible not only for their own poverty but that of their children and men, as well. This concept has evolved into the convenient notion that to break the "cycle of poverty" transmitted from generation to generation by single mothers accepting welfare, public assistance must be withdrawn so the poor

---

*This culture of poverty epithet is based on a distortion of anthropologist Oscar Lewis's studies of Latin American poverty. See Oscar Lewis, "The Culture of Poverty," in On Understanding Poverty: Perspectives from the Social Sciences, ed. Daniel Patrick Moynihan (New York: Basic Books, 1968), pp. 187–200. He found that poor people eventually adapt to their marginal position and do not seem to be psychologically geared up to take advantage of new opportunities. However, on further study (this latter hopeful finding is completely ignored by policy makers), he discovered that people were more resilient than he had at first thought, and when presented with genuine opportunities, he found they quickly adapted and grasped them.*

will be forced out of their habit of laziness and into the work ethic. A common quip to be heard in late-1995 Mississippi captures the concept: "The only job training that welfare recipients need is a good alarm clock."[55]

Or, as Mickey Kaus put it, welfare is "the enabling force that indulges ghetto residents' propensity for living in squalor." He compares black mothers' "attachment to poverty" with junkies' addiction to drugs.[56] (The income support of husbands, apparently, would not be addicting.) The pronouncements of MIT social psychologist Charles Murray and antifeminist author George Gilder also center around the conviction that a culture of single-mother households with "illegitimate" children transmitted intergenerationally from mother to child is at the root of the poverty problem. Poverty is here the product of a shared character defect—an unwillingness to refrain from sexual activity outside the institution of marriage. Poverty is the price these women pay for their transgressions. In fact, another chorister, commentator Michael Novak, tells us poor families have insufficiently developed "moral skills": Single mothers' immorality is evidenced by their high illegitimacy rates, willingness to avoid marriage, and reliance on welfare "rather than work." Novak portrays the woman-headed family as the epitome of all that's wrong with society, referring to such arrangements as "moral hazards."[57]

Recently, Charles Murray's attack on these mothers has broadened and deepened the argument. He claims that women who give birth out of wedlock "generally have low intelligence."[58] According to his recent best-seller *The Bell Curve,* African Americans, who are over-represented in the welfare population, are inherently less intelligent than white people, and therefore special programs to help them would waste taxpayers' money. (Well, isn't that a relief.) Murray's racist book is old-fashioned Social Darwinism/Eugenics encrusted with an illogical high-tech barrage of statistics.* Poor people are inherently unfit and should be allowed, even encouraged, to die out. (Get those Norplants ready.) Of course, if we are going to try corre-

---

*Their book (Charles Murray and Richard Herrnstein, The Bell Curve: Intelligence and Class Structure in American Life (New York: Free Press, 1994) links race, inherited intelligence, and success in life. The premise that IQ is a measure of intelligence is, of course, notoriously false. But even assuming IQ is a useful measure of some aspects of thinking, the authors simply ignore pertinent studies in their own field of social psychology, such as those of Robert Rosenthal, which vividly illustrate the profound

lating IQ with power and success, then won't it soon be found that all those people who make 71 cents for every dollar made by their male counterpart, have inferior brains too?

In addition to welfare mothers' inferior brains, what really sets off Murray and his followers, though, is that these women are getting along without husbands. Never mind that if women are widowed and collect Social Security, they are not perpetuating a culture of dependency. Never mind that if they receive unemployment insurance (a traditionally male entitlement) they are also not at risk for moral corruption. Whether a mother should stay home apparently depends on who pays. But even if she gets off AFDC and works for wages, she will not be exonerated by the mommy police unless she also marries (in which case she can become a lazy addict again and stop all that selfish work).

## A CULTURE OF INCOMPETENCE?

Should the embattled mother manage to break free of the shackles of guilt now weighing her down, she could just as easily imagine there is a "culture of incompetence" caused by the "pathology" and "immorality" of the powerful. She might even begin to see the rich and governing as guilty of so badly mismanaging the society they control (would it be impolite to mention their gambling with other people's money to the tune of a $500 billion savings and loan debacle that the rest of us taxpayers subsidized?) that a significant portion of their own workforce is hungry, homeless, and hopeless. Would it be too inconsiderate to mention that one in twelve American children already suffers from hunger and over a million children each year suffer abuse

---

effects of environment. Children randomly assigned to a group that was then presented to teachers as having high IQs gained 15 points in IQ tests in a year (exactly the number of IQ points Murray claims distinguishes the inferior black race). But more important, the authors seem to be utterly ignorant of evolutionary biology. Genetically based intelligence cannot be linked to race. Superficial adaptations like skin color and those features that serve to make up this construct we call race can evolve very quickly in a matter of several thousand years. Changes in brain structure and capacity, however, take far longer—on the order of hundreds of thousands of years. Innate differences in intelligence among the races have simply not had enough time to evolve. For a sample of the dozens of demolishing critiques of the book, see: Jim Holt, "Anti-social Science?" New York Times, October 19, 1994, p. 22; Myron Hoefer, "Behind the Curve," New York Times, December 26, 1994, p. 39; Russell Jacoby and Naomi Glauberman, eds., The Bell Curve Debate, New York: Times Books, 1995.

directly related to their poverty?[59] Could it not as easily be construed as immoral that the prospect of personal gain causes the owners of industry to pollute their own country or market lethal tobacco to their own youngsters or outsource their work to third world countries where they can get away with paying people 40 cents an hour and polluting someone else's land with no financial penalties? And is it too much to suggest that the increasingly tawdry style of political campaigns, the ever more frequent revelations of our legislators' corruption and disregard for the laws they themselves make is pathological? Would it be unfair to cite the loss of will to deal with poverty, sexism, and racism and the failure to exercise strong, constructive means to end the abandonment of the nation's children to poverty (while so many new billionaires are hatching) as irresponsibility incarnate? Oh well. Everybody knows it's really mothers who are the irresponsible and powerful ones.

## THE INCREDIBLE POWER OF MOTHERS

Mothers should actually be very proud. Apparently the critical structures of second millennium civilization are maintained by them alone, since they alone are guilty of causing our demise. Only 27 percent of American mothers of young children stay home with their offspring while their husbands work to support them.[60] If the experts are right, that means three out of four mothers should feel guilty for not staying home while their husbands (they'll each have to have one) work. Not only that—something swift and sure should be done! Perhaps we should guarantee every woman who is married with children that her husband will be paid a minimum annual salary of $75,000 if she stays home. Surely then, everyone would marry. And we would apparently be able to call off the drug war, end violent crime, raise children's test scores, experience universal love, maybe even abolish cigarette addiction, and all be very moral again. Even with the government subsidizing that wage, we would still save billions in law enforcement, psychotherapy, cancer treatment, drug rehabilitation, remedial education, orphanages, and laptop rebates. We could even convert the prisons (which are a lot nicer than most schools) into schools.[61] We could turn in our guns and knives and have a colossal meltdown, recycling the congealed metal into John Deere tractors (the swords-into-plowshares approach); our smarter children could probably even figure out a way to grow something besides tobacco in Virginia. Alcohol and Valium, I imagine, would be necessities, as they were in the '50s and '60s, especially for the stay-at-home mothers. So with all this power—why do mothers feel so powerless to control their lives? Because they are, indeed, too busy working, working, working to "balance work and family."

## MOTHERS *WORK*

Mothers and family support advocates should not ever apologize for asking business and government to "subsidize" the family. It is women who are now subsidizing the economy.[62] The few studies that now recognize the importance of women's unpaid labor are beginning to tell a surprising story. Women's unpaid work—child care, cooking, cleaning, gardening, and chauffeuring—is worth about $27,000 per woman a year in the paid labor market.[63] Moreover, women's mothering labor is absolutely vital to productivity. It is "human capital" that actually determines a nation's economic performance. As long as women are willing to take on the burden of maintaining the household for free, the household members can survive with lower wages, which therefore raises business profits. The tremendous pressure that mothers are experiencing is the result of exploitation.[64]

Mothers are doing two jobs and being paid at a consistently lower rate for only one job because the definition of productive work in our society is sexist. Women's productive and reproductive labor is not counted as part of the productivity of nations. And since these things are not accounted for in gross domestic capital formation, they are not figured into the accounting systems that determine all public policy. In other words, much of women's work is invisible to the officials who budget our collective money.

Given the standard production framework of conventional economics, it is impossible to prove, for instance, that child care facilities are needed, because "nonproducers"—housewives and mothers, who, according to economists at the Labor Department, the House and Senate Banking committees, the World Bank, and so forth, are "inactive" and "unoccupied"—i.e., not noted in the official economic

ledger, cannot, therefore, be shown to be in need. This economic system inhibits our ability to see what is in our own interests—what we
do and do not wish to pay for.

When women's work is computed into the national accounts, the
difference is sometimes staggering. In America, women's "unproductive" child care labor, alone, would be worth about $240 billion
per year. Were such a figure computed into the national budget, the
resistance to public support of families would seem clearly self-
defeating.*

While mothers have increased both their paid and domestic labor,
their male partners have done little to ease their burden. In fact, the
presence of a husband adds five hours of housework a week to a
woman's domestic load. Working mothers perform 75 percent of domestic work in addition to their wage work including 70 percent of
the child care.[65] By adding more and more unpaid labor to their day,
they enable employers to reduce wages and benefits without seriously
damaging the workforce, although the increasing hunger and homelessness indicate we have exceeded the limits of amelioration that
even women's free labor can provide.

A revealing study of household division of labor by sociologist
Arlie Hoschchild, shows that women work a second unpaid shift at
home, in addition to the first shift they work in the paid labor force.
Hochschild estimates that over a year, women work an extra month
of twenty-four-hour days more than their partners. (Three months of
eight-hour days!)[66] While women in the study revealed over and over
again that they accept this inequality in order to keep the peace, they
tend to suffer chronic exhaustion, low sex drive, and frequent illness
as a result. Husbands' unwillingness to share the burden eventually
proved to be a major cause of divorce.[67]

In addition to the double shift, women's paid labor is also ex-
ploitative. Officially, women make 71 cents for every dollar made by
men for equal work.[68] Mothers start work with two main economic
detriments—unequal pay for the same work, and, related to this,

---

*What economists figure into the official ledger book is highly value laden. The first national income
accounts were evolved in order to justify paying for wars, and so only cash-generating activities were
listed as productive. This cash-only system is now very useful to the international banking community,
which needs to know the cash-generating capacity of debtor countries—not their productive capacity,
so the system is perpetuated. Marilyn Waring, If Women Counted (New York: Harper Collins, 1988).

work ghettoization, which keeps them in low-paying jobs. Women are 98 percent of secretaries; 98 percent of nursery school and kindergarten teachers; 97 percent of child care workers; 93 percent of registered nurses; 93 percent of dieticians; 91 percent of bank tellers; 89 percent of information clerks (includes receptionists, ticket and reservation agents, and hotel clerks) and so forth. And in each of these categories except RN, the males make more than the women!*[69]

One of the most powerful factors preventing mothers from protesting their pervasive disadvantage has been the spectre of the ignominious poor mother. When the poorest mothers in the land are seen as vampires, sucking the lifeblood of a struggling society, when they are portrayed as authors of a culture of poverty or immoral breeders of kids for profit, the fear of poverty is enough to keep any nonpoor mommy's mouth shut and even inspire her to salute her employer every day (if not her husband) for fear of becoming one of "them."

The feminization of poverty which has taken place in the last two decades, as mothers have taken on more and more responsibility, deeply affects all mothers. In fact, one in three mothers now experiences official poverty for at least some portion of her child-rearing years as even dual earner working couples increasingly sink below the poverty line.[70] Eighty-two percent of people in poor families are mothers and children and they are poorer than anybody in this society could possibly deserve to be.†[71] One in four mothers with children under three live in poverty, as do almost half of single mothers.[72] Two thirds of them are just a divorce away from the official poverty line.[73]

Half of all single mothers have accepted welfare at some point. About half of those mothers receiving welfare use it to bridge some process of digging out following a major crisis—divorce, a job loss, or

---

*Moreover, a recent study by the National Academy of Sciences found that each time the number of women in a given occupation went up by one percentage point, salaries in that field went down by $42 per year. Ellen Bravo, national director of 9 to 5. Naomi Barko, "Equal Pay in Your Pocketbook," Working Mother, November, 1993, p. 42.

†If the government used the same formula today for measuring the cost of necessities that was used to calculate its own original poverty line in the 1960s, it would discover that a family of four now needs at least 50 percent more than its official standard. Using these criteria, the poverty line for a family of three in 1995 would have been $18,163 instead of the official $12,112. European countries define the poverty line as being one half the median income, which, in the United States, in 1995, was $50,025 for a married-couple family. (Edward Wolff, "How the Pie Is Sliced: America's Growing Concentration of Wealth," The American Prospect, summer 1995, pp. 58–65.)

perhaps the death of a spouse, and they are self-sufficient again in two or three years.*[74] However, quiet as it's kept, the vast majority of mothers receiving welfare work outside the home (albeit intermittently, at low wages, and often paid under the table). In fact, the majority of recipients, trying over and over to find and keep jobs, ultimately leave welfare through work.[75] For most recipients, in fact, welfare is the mother's version of unemployment compensation.[76]

## THE MATERNAL WALL

In addition to the "glass ceiling" that makes it look like the sky is the limit for women's advancement—until they bash their heads against the glass when they actually try to ascend to the top—there is also a "maternal wall" that keeps mothers from having access to work they have already been hired to perform, and even keeps them out of the workplace altogether. A new study of 900 graduates of Harvard's business, law, and medical schools, shows that even the most elite working mothers face discrimination. These women often face punishment on the job for daring to get pregnant, taking a few weeks of maternity leave, and shortening their workweek. For example, one woman's clients were reassigned to others only because she announced she was having a baby; another was told by a male mentor, "Take my advice. Don't take your whole maternity leave. Not if you want to keep your job." Several women had their babies on Friday and returned to work on Monday for fear their standing at work would be jeopardized. An obstetrician said she was asked to be assistant chief of her hospital department, but the offer was withdrawn when she announced she was pregnant. While male doctors could miss weekend hospital rounds to catch a big football game without anyone raising an eyebrow, she had to hide the time she took to attend her son's birthday party.[77] More than half the women said missing work because of a sick child was detrimental to their career.

*In 1995 a breakdown of families currently on welfare indicates that 28 percent have received assistance for two years or less; 24 percent: two to five years; 19 percent: five to nine years; and 28 percent more than nine years. Sixty-three percent of those remaining beyond five years had less than a high school diploma; 32 percent had a high school diploma; 20 percent had some post–high school education. Source: study by La Donna Pavitti, The Urban Institute. Celia Dugger, "Iowa Plan Tries to Cut Off the Cash," New York Times, April 7, 1995, p. 1.

Mothers are also faced with a workplace that is prejudiced against them and sees the family responsibility of workers as a threat to profit. In spite of all the talk about a family-friendly workplace, study after study suggests there is more talk than action.[78] The few legal structures designed to accommodate working parents benefit them very little. The Family Medical Leave Act (FMLA), signed into law in 1993, was designed to guarantee all working parents an unpaid three-month parental leave for the birth, adoption, or serious illness of a child, as well as a job when they returned. However, 95 percent of businesses are exempt from the FMLA because they hire fewer than fifty employees. Moreover, most parents cannot afford to be without a paycheck for three months. In any case, businesses are apparently resisting even these meager benefits.[79]

The other legal protection for working mothers is the Pregnancy and Discrimination Act of 1978, which makes it illegal to fire or refuse to hire a woman just because she is pregnant, and it entitles her to paid "disability" for the birth of her baby. Discrimination against pregnant women and new mothers is not only pervasive, it is increasing as part of widespread layoffs—in part because prejudice against pregnant women is deep-seated.[80] Between 1990 and 1994, pregnancy discrimination complaints filed with the Federal Equal Employment Opportunity Commission rose 48 percent from women who were either unjustly fired, denied leave, or otherwise punished for giving birth.[81]

Because it is now prohibited by law, maternity discrimination is always disguised and is difficult to litigate. According to a 1991 survey by the Families and Work Institute, even if they are not fired, many working mothers say they contend with underlying tensions at the office. Only 16 percent said their supervisor was supportive when they needed to take care of family matters, and only 7 percent said their coworkers were supportive. More than half felt they had to choose between advancing their careers and devoting attention to their families. One woman in her mid-thirties, a bond salesperson for a Wall Street investment firm, put off having children until she felt she'd earned the respect of her mostly male colleagues. When she returned from her three-month maternity leave, she found her desk had been moved to a far end of the office and her accounts given to others, who then sabotaged her. She worked twice as hard and won back the traders and coworkers and landed new accounts. Her desk has neve. been moved back. She does not keep a photo of her child on it.[82]

## UN-FAMILY-FRIENDLY

The workplace, of course, is currently designed for the male bread-winner who has a wife at home, and it is still hostile to parents' time predicaments. Even public schools maintain hours that do not accommodate working parents. In a recent California court case, a mother of five couldn't drop her children off at school before 8:00 A.M. which often meant she was *five minutes* late to work. In response, her employer, the California Department of Motor Vehicles, docked her pay. She challenged the pay cut, and a state administrative judge ruled that "inadequate child care and inadequate public transportation" had caused her tardiness. Nonetheless, the state personnel board overruled the judge and cut her pay.[83]

Many corporations are now advertising that they are "family-friendly." In a study conducted by New Ways to Work, the authors found that 50 percent of the large companies they studied claimed to offer flextime. Because flexibility appears at the top of the list of what parents say they want, this sounded promising. However, they found that top-level supervisors and managers were far more likely to be offered a flexible work schedule than administrative staff. When you consider that 80 percent of all clerical workers and 98 percent of all secretaries are women, even the "family-friendly" company starts to look less friendly to mothers. Most top-level business managers are men between the ages of fifty and sixty, and many still equate women having babies with a lack of commitment to work. The net effect of a workplace designed for breadwinning men is that women are penalized for having children.[84]

## THE NEED FOR SCAPEGOATS

How can we explain the growing assault on mothers who won't play Harriet Nelson? Mothers are obviously doing more of the work of mothering and breadwinning than at any time in history. How can they even have time to cause the current rates of American poverty, divorce, teen pregnancy, violence, and incarceration that are higher than any of our industrialized counterparts?

Two related and unhappy social changes contribute to all this scapegoating. The American family has changed dramatically in the last two decades, and men have increasingly been estranged from it. Between 1960 and 1982, the rate of divorce tripled and the amount of time American men spent with their children declined by 40 percent.[85] In 1955, 60 percent of American households consisted of a working father, a mother at home, and two or more children. By 1986, such households constituted only 4 percent of U. S. households.[86] Men lost much of their status as breadwinners—in fact, many even lost their jobs.[87] Between 1973 and 1993 men's wages decreased by 14 percent and by the mid-1980s working mothers' incomes accounted for two thirds of the two-parent-family income.[88] Married women who work full-time now earn 40 percent of the family income. One out of every three makes more than her husband.[89] Not only that— men have lost contact with their children through divorce and women's growing propensity to bear children without marrying or cohabiting. Nostalgia for Ozzie and Harriet is certainly enhanced by men's loss of economic power and control over their children (and wives).

The other great change inspiring motherblaming is the tremendous economic losses experienced by the majority of Americans. America has the most unequal distribution of income of any industrialized nation in the world, with 15 percent of the population falling below the official poverty line.[90] In the 1980s much of the middle class fell into poverty, the working poor became very poor, and the nonworking poor required the invention of a new term: "hyperpoor." There was an unprecedented redistribution of America's wealth during which "trickle-down" economics actually worked in reverse. In the first half of the 1980s, for instance, the poorest fifth of the population lost $6 billion while the richest 5 percent experienced a 60 percent growth rate.[91] The distribution of income in America during the previous hundred years looked pretty much like a normal bell-shaped curve. The majority of people, about 60 percent, clustered around the middle, another 20 percent were poor, and 20 percent were upper class. (Of course the top 5 percent at the rich end of the curve actually owned half the nation's wealth.) But in the 1980s, for the first time in a hundred years, the curve flattened out and tilted, leaving fewer people in the middle and a lot more filling up the poor end.[92] The growing loss of well-paying jobs and decrease in economic security has many looking for a visible culprit. In mothers, they believe they have found it.

## FAMILY VALUES

The outcry over our lost "family values" and the mothers who no longer fit the Good Mother corset is misplaced. The values of love, respect, nurture, sharing, comfort, sacrifice, and cooperation are no more lacking in families than in other institutions. Although humane behavior may be declining in our society, the family alone will not be able to rehabilitate us. The current lament over our lost family values is really about the loss of values that were once given to mothers alone to guard. As keepers of the hearth and homemakers of the family's "haven in a heartless world," women have long been the designated guardians of these ideals.

However, in the 1990s, the word "family" means a range of relationships, including gay couples, cohabitees, househusbands at home, single male and single female parents, two or three generations of women and their children living together, grandparents acting as parents, adults officially fostering children not born to them, and of course the vast preponderance of mothers who now have a salaried relationship with the workplace. Women are going to continue to bear and rear children in all types of families, and they are going to continue to work outside the home. Family life has changed dramatically in the past two decades, and the clock will not turn back, no matter how much women are persuaded they are guilty for failing to put it all together again properly.

Family relations have been steadily changing throughout history and will continue to do so. Moreover, the status of women is changing all over the planet—a revolution probably more significant than any in recorded human history. So now is the time for all of us, men and women, parents and nonparents, rich and poor, to become more like mothers and assume a caring stewardship of the land and its people.

If we are to develop more appropriate expectations for mothers and fathers and enhance our changing family relationships rather than cripple them as we do now, we must understand how the story of the "Good Mother" has been concocted and how fathers have been reduced to dollar signs in the process. From its inception in the Industrial Revolution of the 1840s to its devaluation in the feminist revolution of the 1970s, an ideology of motherhood has "framed" mothers by creating rigid, unrealistic ideals and then faulting mothers for not adhering to them. It is this ideology that has led us down the dead-end road of motherblaming.

# Framing Motherhood: The Brief History of an Icon

We all have ideals. These are important. They inspire us to behave well. They also define certain ready-made roles that help to organize our society. But if we want to understand how the motherblamers are getting away with their outrageous scapegoating; why mothers accept such a vast burden of guilt; how mothers and children have fallen into such shameful poverty and disrespect at the end of the twentieth century—we ought to become aware of the strange life history of the "Good Mother" icon in America. The framing and reframing of her portrait has helped to organize labor and to compensate for collective sin. It has also been, again and again, the means of restricting women's world and prohibiting them from engaging equally in the public world of men.[1] As you will discover, the Good Mother needs to be relegated to the museum so that we can come up with a new parental icon that respects *all* guardians of children.

## THE FIRST "GOOD MOTHERS" WERE FATHERS

It is no accident that when we talk about our country's history, we refer to our "founding fathers." In Colonial times, it was fatherhood that carried all the importance that we attribute to motherhood today. When infants and children awoke in the night, it was their fathers they turned to for comforting. Fathers rocked their infants, walked them when they cried, and cuddled them when they traveled. Fathers played with their children, taught them their three R's, and schooled them in religion.[2] Women were considered devious, sexually voracious, emotionally inconstant, and physically and intellectually inferior. Their sinfulness made it necessary for husbands to rule over them and their children.[3] Maternal bonding was simply not an issue, mothers' care of infants was considered custodial. Breasts were usually provided by mothers, but those of servants or slaves were often substituted. Routine care of infants was provided by adults and children of both sexes. When children began to be able to reason around the age of seven, they were dressed as little adults and mothers then trained girls in cooking, canning, textile making, and other household skills while fathers provided vocational training for their sons who became farmers and craftsmen. Many children left their homes as early as ten years old to work and train in other households, where they provided domestic service or learned a trade.[4]

In cases of the death of a parent or divorce, few children ended up with their mother. It was thought their best interests would be served by sending them to the family member, however distant, with the most potential to give them a financial future. Mothers, in this arrangement, were least likely to retain their own children.[5] This is not to suggest that mothers and children did not love each other or have a close relationship, but rather that motherhood, as we know it, simply was not recognized. Children were economic assets claimed by their fathers. Interestingly, as their economic value declined, so too, did the importance of fatherhood.

In Colonial America, a significant portion of the population were Native Americans and African Americans, and these communities fostered a different ideal of motherhood. Among Native Americans, for example, women were generally responsible for nurturing. However, these societies tended to be communal and egalitarian. Women were spiritual and tribal leaders, property was often passed along matrilineal paths, and the emphasis was on identification with the group, not standing out from it. Moreover, there was considerable tolerance for those who did not follow traditional sex roles. Mothering, in this context, was not an isolated experience in which one mother was charged with the exclusive care of her own biological children, but a shared and powerful enterprise.[6]

American slave mothers were generally bought and sold with their "increase" so that children under ten remained with their mothers. Mothers were sent back to the fields a month or two after delivery, and infants were then looked after by older siblings and enfeebled older men and women.[7] Illegitimacy was not condemned, and relationships between mother and child superseded those between husband and wife.[8] These practices, of course, served to increase the population of slaves belonging to the planter. Slave fathers, it must be noted, were even more disenfranchised, as their owners viewed them as irrelevant to preserving the "increase." Roughly 20 percent of slave marriages were broken up by sale, and often a father's only way to preserve the connection with his children was to give them his name.[9]

## VICTORIAN MOTHERHOOD

In the 1830s, as the country expanded westward, roads and bridges needed building, cities burgeoned, and men and women began to inhabit separate spheres, a highly idealized and exalted concept of motherhood came into prominence. Male membership in the church declined, leaving the role of domestic religious instruction to the female congregation they left behind.[10] The newly ordained mothers were not exactly left in charge of the children, however. They followed the orders of their clergymen and were assisted in the home by domestic servants. (By the latter part of the century, even working-class white families often had African-American maids.)[11]

The exaltation of motherhood was facilitated by a new religious conception of the infant. In Colonial America, the Puritans had considered infants to be born "full of the devil." Young children therefore needed the strict discipline taught by a male clergy and executed by the male parent who was to periodically beat the devil out of them. The new Victorian view of infants, occasioned by the growth of Romanticism and the religious cult of the baby Jesus, was that babies were born pure and innocent. They now needed the clergy to protect them from a corrupting world and a kind and virtuous mother to set an example of piety and obedience.[12]

## THE NEW EDUCATIONAL PHILOSOPHY

Eighteenth-century European philosophy also fueled the new ideal of motherhood.[13] French philosopher Jean-Jacques Rousseau and Swiss educator Johann Pestalozzi emphasized the special needs of small children who, they claimed, were more successfully governed by persuasion than coercion, and by rewards than punishment. In his novel *Emile*, Rousseau described the ideal education of a boy. Like all children, he is born good and proceeds through natural stages of development that simply need to be managed by mothers who, of course, consult regularly with their (male) physician. Women are nature's creatures and have an instinct to please men and bind children to their fathers. "Her strength is in her charms . . . She is the bond that connects the children with their father . . . What tenderness and care must she not exert to preserve unity in the family!"[14]

Inspired by this educational philosophy, infant schools were introduced in the 1820s to assist poor children whose mothers worked. It was thought the schools would be better at nurturing these children than their mothers, who were encouraged to continue working. (The idealized attributions made to the female sex are somehow never applied to poor women.) Once middle-class mothers heard of the educational benefits of these schools, they insisted on having them too. As middle-class women began to take advantage of these schools, however, a prominent New England physician claimed that early intellectual activity diverted energy necessary for the physical development of the female brain and would result in teenage or adult insanity. His views were publicized extensively and contributed to a national movement against early childhood education.[15] This movement, however, had less to do with any evidence regarding the harm done by infant schools than the growing need to secure a new division of labor. Such schools would free middle-class mothers to compete with men in the new wage-paying workforce.

## THE CULT OF TRUE WOMANHOOD

The most important force in creating the new maternal ideal was the economic upheaval created by the Industrial Revolution. By the 1840s the growth of commerce and industry had seriously begun to change the way the family was organized.[16] The traditional productive skills of women—textile making, garment making, and food processing—were transferred to the factory system along with the men who left the home for industry. What then, was to keep women from entering the world of industry and leaving the home behind? There were proposals for communal dining halls, child care services, and housekeeping services so that women, too, could join the wage labor force. However, the factory system was brutal, and it was feared that these commercial services would turn out to be extensions of the hated factory system. Moreover, to take women from the household would be to take away the only thing that cushioned men from psychic destruction in the rough world of the marketplace.[17] Women, it was decided, would stay home, where their domestic labor would underwrite the factory system.

As women were not to be paid for their work at home, it was important that there be a compelling rationale for their being there. The apparent solution was a new ideology: polar-opposite ideals of masculinity and femininity in which *men* were now the sinners (albeit licensed ones able to pursue material values frowned upon by the puritan church).[18] Women were persuaded that their femininity was contingent upon their being "the angel of the hearth" who exemplifies the Christian virtues for her children. Women were suddenly discovered to be altruistic, tender, and intuitive; men were now rational, competitive, and self-interested. Men would be breadwinners, working for wages to build the bridges and railroads and produce goods in the factories; women would stay home and teach the Christian virtues to the children. The growing conflict between the Puritan values of thrift, asceticism, and piety, on the one hand, and the material values of getting and spending, on the other, was relieved by this arrangement.

Historians refer to this new role for women as the "Cult of True Womanhood," for domestic motherhood became a sacred ideal fashioned by an absolute flood of propaganda. The women's magazines, gift annuals, and religious literature of the 1830s insisted women would be "another better Eve, working in cooperation with the Redeemer, bringing the world back from its revolt and sin." *The Young Ladies Class Book* was sure that "the domestic fireside is the guardian of society against the excesses of human passions." *The Lady at Home* expressed its convictions in its title and concluded that "even if we cannot reform the world in a moment, we can begin the work by reforming ourselves and our households . . ."[19] Sacred scripture was used to confirm these views. "St. Paul knew what was best for women when he advised them to be domestic," said a Mrs. Sanford in another magazine.

The American mother was now placed under the sternest pressure. She was to be constantly at the center of the child's life and take the most minute interest in all his activities.[20] Poor women were not invited to be hearth angels as their cheap labor was needed to make the hierarchical system work. Bad examples of the unholy poor lent special status to the sacred middle-class hearth angel. Many advice books warned mothers against relying on servants, since they, with their own "bad habits" could reduce or eliminate entirely the mother's indispensable control over the child's development.[21] Middle-class and wealthy women came increasingly to minister to these poor women and children, in part out of genuine concern, but also because in Victorian America, it was the only respectable public role for them.[22] The double standard regarding poor and middle-class motherhood set in motion feelings of suspicion and resentment between privileged and poor women that continue to obscure the common predicament they share today.

The shift to the hearth angel/breadwinner ideals contributed to a decline in fathers' involvement with their children. With industrialization, fathers had less control over their own future and had few skills to pass on to their offspring as farming declined and crafts died out. Men in the growing middle class often commuted to downtown offices from the streetcar suburbs that began developing even before the Civil War and saw less and less of their children.[23] With the early nurturing function transferred to mothers and the occupational tie severed, what fathers now had to offer their children was money. Their personal involvement seemed more and more superfluous. And as fathers became more and more caught up in the world of commerce, their lives came into greater and greater conflict with Christian values. Rather than reforming and becoming more altruistic, however, it was left to women and children to stand for piety.

## THE CHILD AS REDEEMER

As America became more industrial and commercial, the conflict between the traditional Calvinist ideals of asceticism and piety, and the commercial values of individualism and worldly pleasure, continued to grow. The increasingly secular nurture experts, however, managed to create yet another rationale for resolving the conflict by proposing that the character of children was especially flexible: "Its character is as yet of wax," they opined. If children were properly guided, their self-centeredness and conscience would not be in conflict.[24] Key words in the nurture literature such as "impress," "mold," "form," and "shape," indicated the importance of the new role for woman as a maternal sculptress in managing this conflict.[25] In fact, child-nurture expertise in the latter half of the nineteenth century became an obsession perhaps as a means to avoid the actual clash of values. Increasingly, the child was viewed as the principal means by which the society would progress—the infinitely malleable child would now be the redeemer.[26]

By the turn of the century, Darwin's popularizers had managed to link evolution with progress and Christian morality. The laws that science was discovering would turn out to be the expression of God's will. Therefore science could provide moral guidelines. Darwin's theory proposed a constantly evolving race, led to its destiny by selective adaptation to the environment. His discovery prompted some to study evolution as it is expressed in individuals, especially in the early years of growth, to uncover ways in which the adaptation process might be enhanced. Thus, the field of child development was born. By learning how individual infants evolved, or developed, child raising could be scientifically tailored to the course of evolution. *The Century of the Child,* a best-selling book published in 1909, claimed that if women would focus all their energy on children, they could bring forth "the completed man—the Superman."[27] Now the infant was seen as a kind of evolving protoplasm by which the society adapted and progressed.* This "sacrilization" of children helped spur the abolition of child labor and made it less acceptable to value children for their economic contributions to the family.[28]

---

*The religious motive had become so deeply entwined with the scientific that, as one American woman told an international conference on "scientific motherhood" in 1908: ". . . The goal is nothing less than the redemption of the world through the better education of those who are able to shape it or make it. The keeper of the gates of tomorrow is the little child upon the mother's arms . . . and that child's hands a woman holds." (Barbara Ehrenreich and Deirdre English, For Her Own Good: 150 Years of the Experts' Advice to Women [New York: Doubleday, 1978] p. 190.)

## BIOLOGICAL MOTHERHOOD

Meanwhile, science also found motherhood to be biologically based and proclaimed it women's evolutionary duty to obey the newly discovered laws of nature. In the latter half of the nineteenth century, increasing numbers of women began to strain against the Victorian role of virtuous exemplar in the home. They became leaders in the movements for humanitarian reform, improved educational opportunities, and (more covertly) birth control. Not coincidentally, it was at this time that medical theories about women's restricting biology rose in opposition to this threat to the social order.[29] Women, it was claimed, were biologically destined to be mothers, and women who gave their energies to anything else were more prone to illness and more likely to produce defective offspring. Not surprisingly, medicine discovered that education was causing American women to deteriorate by using energy that was needed for reproduction. In 1873 Dr. Edward Clarke of Harvard published a review of the medical theories of female nature, concluding that higher education would cause women's uteruses to atrophy. The book went through seventeen editions in just a few years.[30]

Curiously, the mothering energy of poor women, who were presumably also biologically female, did not require them to remain sedately at home. In fact, they were encouraged to work outside the home, creating an abundance of young children who either wandered the streets or were locked in small apartments because their mothers had to work and had no one to care for them.[31] Philanthropists who offered support to these women and children simply facilitated their working. They provided nursery care centers, which often included job training and placement for the mothers.[32] Settlement house workers tried to create a comprehensive program for the children, providing education, medical care, and mental hygiene (teaching good habits), but the need was far greater than the sporadic help.[33]

## PROFESSIONAL MOTHERHOOD

Science provided a new and appealing set of reasons for middle-class mothers to stay home. At the turn of the century science could make the hearth angel into a professional. As science became a source of moral precepts, the scientist became its priest. Asked what creed best suited Americans, one social commentator wrote in 1890: "The answer is, that which he knows to be true—and that, in one word is *Science*. The majority of American people are already *practically secularists . . .* Our people are unconsciously welcoming the incoming sway of Science and Man . . ."[34] At the turn of the century, progressive Americans campaigned for scientific medicine, scientific social work, and even scientific child rearing. In all areas of endeavor, making something scientific became synonymous with reform. As the professions began to develop along with the authority of science, motherhood was recast to resemble a profession and mothers formed associations to study the pronouncements of the emerging scientific experts.

## DOMESTIC SCIENCE: HEARTH ANGEL BECOMES HOUSEWIFE

By the turn of the century, much of the productive domestic function that had once given dignity and purpose to womanhood had disappeared. Of course, before the Industrial Revolution there had never been any question about what women should be doing in the home. Colonial and early-nineteenth-century women were making bread, butter, cloth, clothing, soap, candles, medicines, and other things essential to their families' survival. The pressures of home production left very little time for the tasks that we would recognize today as housework. However, while much of the home manufacturing function was usurped by industrialization, 95 percent of married women continued to remain in the home through the end of the nineteenth century, even as the birth rate declined from 7 births per woman to around 3.5 in 1900.[35] The home was becoming a major issue—especially regarding woman's proper role. Some feminists, such as Charlotte Perkins Gilman, urged women to move into the world of industry, science, and public affairs. Clergymen, popular magazines, and politicians, however, harped on the sanctity of the home and the need for women to remain there. *The Ladies' Home Journal* suggested that what women needed more than anything "is some task that would tie her down."[36] The 1909 White House Conference on the

Care of Dependent Children declared that "home life" is the highest and finest product of civilization. Even most feminists at the time insisted that the reason women deserved the vote was because they were homemakers. The new ideal carved out for women was the scientific version of the hearth angel—the housewife.

Enter Ellen Swallow Richards, a chemist by training, who founded the new "science" of "home economics."[37] Richards had had a genuine scientific education, complete with laboratory training. She represented the necessary link to the transcendent world of science. Richards graduated from the new college for women, Vassar, and then battled for acceptance to MIT (which, like most universities, was a strictly male enterprise) to study chemistry. She was finally allowed to study, but permitted only a bachelor's degree. She was essentially barred from the male world of chemistry, however. So Richards turned her formidable energies toward the creation of a new science in which she would be on an equal footing with men.

Richards and her domestic scientists hoped to forge a direct pipeline between the scientific laboratory and the average home, and they seized any science, any discipline that could conceivably be used to upgrade a familiar task. Richards believed that biochemistry could eventually transform cooking into a precise laboratory exercise, economics could revolutionize budgeting and shopping, and bacteriology could sanctify cleaning. In fact, germ theory, which had become known to the public in the 1890s, had set off a wave of public anxiety about contagion. Any public place or object was suspect, as were the lower classes. Housecleaning was thus transformed from a matter of dilettantish dusting to a sanitary crusade against "dangerous enemies within." In light of germ theory, cleaning became a moral responsibility. The woman whose child died of a preventable disease, they warned, would, in the coming "sanitary millennium" be seen as a murderer! The domestic scientists claimed the major household germ carrier was dust, although there was (and is) little evidence to establish dust as a source of infection. (To this day, there is no scientific research on the actual effects of various kinds of household cleaning.)[38] Manufacturers of soap and cleansing agents, of course, picked up on the theme with ads that played directly to maternal fears and guilt.

But domestic science's major innovation was the discovery of efficiency through management. In 1912, *The Ladies' Home Journal* promoted the managerial revolution in the home, advising women that ironing boards should be at the proper height, appliances should be chosen with care, and schedules should be made for daily and weekly chores.[39] For the homemaker, household scientific management turned out to mean new work—the new managerial tasks of analyzing one's chores in detail, planning, recordkeeping, and so forth. *The Journal* advised, for instance, that, first, each task had to be studied and timed. Only then could precise weekly and daily schedules be devised. And everything in the household had to be accounted for in a master file, including the location and condition of each item of clothing possessed by the family. The scientific housekeeper now saw herself not only as a microbe hunter but as a manager, operating on principles of industrial efficiency. Enthusiasm for this new calling was so great that women were told that with the time they had saved, they should study home economics! Indeed, domestic science also became a way of justifying higher education for women, and home economics departments were established in universities.

The architects of domestic science were, of course, repelled by the cloying nineteenth-century romanticism of the hearth angel. To them the home was not a haven from society—it was a factory for the production of citizens. Beyond the managing and cleansing of the home, the real center of life for women was to become the child—that miraculous key to the management of human evolution. Indeed, while child rearing was to become women's vocation, they would not actually be allowed to manage it themselves. In their study of the tyranny of male expertise over women's lives, *For Her Own Good: 150 Years of the Experts' Advice to Women,* Barbara Ehrenreich and Deirdre English conclude that once the child became so important at the turn of the century, it was "as if the masculinist imagination takes a glance over its shoulder and discovers it has left something important behind in 'woman's sphere'—the child . . . It follows that if children must be left with their mothers, they must not be left *alone* with them. A new figure will enter the family tableau—a man equipped to manage both children and mothers and to direct the interaction—the scientific expert in child rearing."[40]

## THE CHILD-REARING EXPERT

The experts did not come uninvited, however. At the turn of the century, a mothers' movement was under way, and in 1887 became a formal organization: the National Congress of Mothers. Mothers were eager to obtain information from scientific experts in child rearing and convened national conferences to educate themselves. A more scientific approach to child rearing promised to elevate the status of women (which also helped the case for female suffrage). The function of mothering, of course, had changed. In the Colonial and even Victorian family, the mother-child relationship had been shaped by the round of daily tasks—it was always, in part, an apprenticeship relationship. Child rearing meant teaching children the skills and discipline required to keep the home industries running. But with the separation of home and work, the standards for "success" in child rearing were less clear. As children were increasingly to be prepared for life outside the family, paradoxically, they were to be reared by women whose experience was to be limited to the home. Male psychologists would provide the view from outside.[41]

According to Ehrenreich and English, the great achievement of early psychology was to transform biology into a kind of generalized philosophy that would provide these goals. Granville Stanley Hall was America's first developmental psychologist and a prime mover in creating psychology as an academic discipline. A former theology student and lecturer on education, Hall had studied with the great German experimental psychologist Wilhelm Wundt in Leipzig. Returning to the U.S. to take a position at Johns Hopkins University, Hall proceeded to organize one of the first psychology laboratories in America. The science laboratory, of course, was the ultimate symbol of the power and authority of science and so other psychologists, with Hall's encouragement, were quick to acquire them, even though few (including Hall) had much idea what to do with them.[42] Hall's real focus was to organize the field of child study and as president of Clark University, he began to train the new psychologists.

Hall, whose name was now linked with the holy laboratory, was a popular lecturer who awed his audiences with glimpses into mysterious Germanic investigations and simultaneously reassured them with his exalted theories on childhood. His lectures at the National Congress of Mothers meetings promised a glorious union of science and motherhood. But, of course, the laws of this particular science had yet to be uncovered so mothers were enlisted to assist Hall with developing a complete description of childhood from birth through adolescence. He urged mothers to keep a "life book" for each child, recording "all incidents, traits of character, etc., with frequent photographs, parental anxieties, plans, hopes, etc."[43] Hall was full of theories about children and liberally gave mothers advice, which they avidly consumed. He believed that the development of children recreates the evolution of the animal world—children are at first like invertebrates, then monkeys, and eventually savages. Child rearing is a matter of keeping all these atavistic tendencies in check. So Hall dispensed such scientific bits of advice such as "children need lots of exercise," presumably to keep the little animals from going completely wild.[44] As Hall's influence subsided and more psychologists began to populate the landscape, mothers' careers as data gatherers soon disappeared and thenceforth only scientists could gather data and formulate rules.

## THE EXPERT ADVICE

While early-twentieth-century child-rearing experts drew their prestige from science, the content of their advice came more from the factory than the laboratory. Mothering in the teens and twenties would be like modern industry—highly technical, mechanized, and measured by the clock. Women would require advanced education to master it. The goal of child rearing was to produce the industrial man—disciplined, efficient, precise. The key to producing such a man was regularity, and this meant that spontaneity would have to be subdued in the cradle. Parents were not to play with their infants, indeed they were not even to pick them up between scheduled feedings. To do so was to risk creating moral laxity. Modern psychology soon found specific methods for instilling workers with obedience, punctuality, and good citizenship while they were in the cradle.

The industrial approach to child rearing achieved scientific footing in the late teens with the development of "behaviorism." According to experimental psychologist John B. Watson, the ideal child was " . . . one who finally enters manhood so bulwarked with the stable work and emotional habits that no adversity can quite overwhelm him."[45] Like the industrial efficiency experts, Watson broke behavior down into components. Struck by the conditioning experiments of Pavlov in Russia, Watson found that he could condition infants by causing them to associate behaviors and expectations with conditions chosen by the psychologists. For example, Watson showed infants a series of white furry things that they liked and then paired the presentation of those things with a loud sound that scared them. They quickly came to fear the white furry things. So Watson set out a catechism of behaviorist rules for mothers. Mothers who picked up their infants every time they cried, he claimed, would be forever conditioning them to cry. Mothers were then told by the new experts to let their babies "cry it out" and to care for them only according to schedule. According to Watson, mothers torment their children with their display of love. "She picks the infant up, kisses and hugs it, rocks it, pets it and calls it 'mother's little lamb,' until the child is unhappy and miserable whenever away from actual physical contact with the mother."[46] Watson made grandiose claims that he could, using similar behaviorist techniques, make a child into any kind of adult—from thief to statesman. Indeed he asked himself whether children would not be happier brought up in institutions than at home with their mothers. Women who insisted on rearing their own offspring were admonished to teach their infants discipline to prepare them for a world where machines marked the time, kept trains on schedule, and cranked out a cornucopia of factory goods. Scientific, properly scheduled bottle feeding, of course, was the logical choice of the professional mother.[47]

## POOR CHILDREN ARE REDEFINED AS PATHOLOGICAL

In the 1920s a whole army of child-rearing experts was being launched by the Laura Spelman Rockefeller Memorial Foundation. The foundation's goal was to promote "scientific" solutions to social problems, and psychology was to be one of its tools. According to a report sponsored by the fund, mothers and educators were far too ignorant of scientific child-rearing techniques and experts were needed. They would be trained and sent out to standardize child rearing and make it a more "rational" process. Between 1923 and 1929 the foundation spent over $7 million to fund institutes and research stations at universities across the country. The new professionals were not mothers themselves, of course. But thanks to the mothers' movement, there was a maternal congregation looking to the new corps of priests for advice.[48]

The poor, of course, were also modernized. New psychological advisers developed a therapeutic ethic that equated good families with personal growth through mental hygiene, and the poor were now considered "pathological." This view was inspired by the new Rockefeller Child Guidance centers, which treated juvenile delinquents psychologically instead of merely incarcerating them. Even nursery care for young children of the poor shifted from trying to affect the child's health and socioeconomic situation to preventing juvenile delinquency through child psychology.[49] Poor mothers in this scheme, were, by definition, responsible for creating juvenile delinquency.

## THE MIDDLE-CLASS CHILD IS TO BE INDULGED

As the century progressed, a fundamental cultural inversion took place as households became consumers of mass-produced goods that they had once produced at home. In the 1930s private fulfillment became more of an end in itself and indulgence became the code of the nursery. The experts who had been concerned with discipline and self-control now "discovered" that self-indulgence was healthy for the individual personality. The infant who had been seen as full of dangerous impulses that needed to be reigned in was now viewed as natural and able to regulate his own impulses. Developmental aspects of behavior received attention, and temper tantrums or thumb sucking or lying or bad manners were seen as passing phases in a child's life that could best be treated by ignoring them.

Dr. Arnold Gesell, a pediatrician and researcher, studied children's stages of development (in the laboratory) and established timetables for such maturational milestones as the age at which a baby crawls, walks, talks, and so forth. Gesell's work was interpreted to mean that whatever problems mothers might be concerned about, need not be great cause for concern—the child was "just going through a stage." The ideal mother of scientific permissiveness applied her understanding of the vicissitudes of child development with inexhaustible patience and always through indirection. Gesell and his colleagues suggested techniques of "household engineering" through which the well-organized mother could simply eliminate conflict.[50] To create in her children the congenial, self-pleasing personality who sought happiness in private life had become the new child-rearing goal for the middle-class mother.

## FATHERS' REACTION

The emphasis on the importance of full-time "professional" mothering seemed to contribute to the decline in the importance of fathers. Men's role of financial provider was becoming increasingly divorced from family life as the industrial system began to mass produce that which had been made at home on farms and by craftsmen. Fathers who had worked at home and had a skill or trade to pass on to their sons, lost even that function as work became more complex, and formal mass education replaced education at home.

So, in the early 1900s, social scientists, home educators, counselors, and newspaper columnists began to promote a kind of "new fatherhood," urging fathers to be more involved in family life. Many middle-class fathers took that advice. They led Girl Scout troops, held "democratic family meetings," and wrote letters to advice columnists, worried about their children's hygiene, study habits, and personalities. While fathers became somewhat more involved in their children's lives, the shift posed no challenge to the gender division of labor that relegated women to doing the lion's share of housework and child care. Men's home involvement was important, but it was a "gift" men made to women and children, not part of a restructured conception of masculinity and parenthood.[51]

By 1910, less than one third of American men were economically autonomous whereas before the Civil War 90 percent of men were independent farmers or self-employed businessmen or artisans. At the same time, the northward migration of newly freed slaves and the dramatic immigration of swarthy Southern Europeans signaled new competitors for white, middle-class men's power in the public domain. What's more, women were demanding equality not only in the ballot box or the classroom, but also in the workplace and the bedroom as social feminists argued for the right to birth control and "sex rights." Suddenly men felt themselves to be on the defensive and launched a critique of turn-of-the-century culture that blamed their decline, in part, on the dominance of women. Soon, coeducation was feared because it was thought women would sap the virility of male students. Strict separation of "boy culture" was to be maintained to ensure that boys would grow up to be real men. The founding of Boy Scouts of America in 1910 was necessary because, according to its founder, Ernest Thompson Seton, women were turning "robust, manly, self-reliant boyhood into a lot of flat-chested cigarette smokers with shaky nerves and doubtful vitality."[52]

## MORE WORKING MOTHERS

While the family experts were busy redrawing the rules of the stay-at-home mother role and trying to boost fathers' egos, mothers were increasingly leaving the home to enter the wage labor force. In 1900, less than 10 percent of married women worked for wages. By the 1930s the figure was 15 percent.[53] During the Great Depression, women's work was thought to be taking jobs away from male breadwinners, so there was a temporary hiatus in the growing migration of women into the workplace. The New Deal rescued some of the poorest mothers and children at this time, with the 1935 Aid to Dependent Children Act.[54] This plan was not designed to make hearth angels out of poor mothers. Its purpose in providing women with subsidies instead of jobs and child care was to reduce competition with male workers. Typical of this attitude, one proposal declared: "There are approximately 10,000,000 people out of work in the United States today, there are also 10,000,000 or more women, married and single who are jobholders. Simply fire the women who shouldn't be working anyway and hire the men. Presto! No unemployment. No relief rolls. No depression."[55] Laws were indeed passed prohibiting the employment of women in certain sectors if their husbands could support them.

By the end of the 1930s, the country was rapidly advancing toward full employment as it prepared for World War II.[56] Growing numbers of working women had no one to care for their children while they worked, and the country was soon faced with scandals regarding the plight of these children. In some cities, bands of children roamed the streets while their mothers worked, and it was not uncommon to find children locked in parked cars near a factory.[57] Because of these scandals, the 1942 Lanham Act was passed, which allowed child care centers to be considered public works in war-impacted areas. It provided brief and meager assistance of questionable value, however.[58] The few facilities were shabby, overcrowded, expensive, and often lacked outdoor play space. In Auburn, Maine, in 1945, sixteen babies and preschoolers burned to death in a fire at one of these nurseries for children of women war workers. The ideal of the stay-at-home mother, however, was preserved.[59]

## THE FEMININE MYSTIQUE

The mid-twentieth-century version of True Womanhood (what Betty Friedan was to call "the feminine mystique")[60] derived its central authority from the strictures of psychoanalysis, that described a moral order in which neurosis was seen as equivalent to the wages of sin. According to Freud, the adult personality is shaped by the resolution of a fundamental conflict occurring in childhood when girls realize their biology is inferior to that of males. They must learn to accept that their female nature can be realized only in motherhood. Otherwise they will be neurotic: competitive, frigid, and maybe even homosexual. According to Freud, little girls, at about the age of three, as genital drives become important, discover that they do not have a penis. Automatically they think they are castrated and inferior. The female first blames her mother "who sent her into the world so insufficiently equipped."[61] She then expects her father to prove magnanimous and give her a penis. Later, disappointed in this hope, she learns to content herself with the aspiration of bearing a baby, but even then she might still succumb to this penis envy if she doesn't find complete fulfillment in motherhood.[62]

Some female psychoanalysts claimed the reverse was really true—that males started off with "womb envy," but that idea never caught on. A woman who chose a career, of course, was clearly suffering from penis envy and was a candidate for the couch. This theory is the mother of all twentieth-century fairy tales about the Good Mother. Freud was trying to describe how we develop our sex roles. In fact, the truth is greater than his fiction—women often do envy the (owner of the) penis.

Increasingly, motherhood was a mysterious matter only psychologists could sufficiently understand. Freud's theory indicated that serious flaws in adult character were due to traumatic childhood events tied to critical psychosexual periods in early development. Therefore, if a mother, through inept child rearing in infancy, tipped the delicate balance between the demands of the child's pleasurable instincts and her own imparting of the reality demands of civilized society, she could create a child whose character was stunted or fixated at the oral level. The result would be, not so much a character that was immoral or ungodly, as one that was "neurotic" or maladapted.

This powerful and pathologized concept of motherhood emerged at a time of major cultural ferment brought about by World War II and dramatic changes in the economy that once again threatened to alter cherished cultural values. While the majority of women were supposed to be suited only for the home and hearth, their labor was needed in the early 1940s for the war industry. Initially, persuading women to take such jobs required a delicate ideological balancing act and a newly idealized woman worker was invented.[63] She was young, white, and middle class, even though she was often represented in work sectors where poor and minority women actually predominated. Advertisers artfully conveyed the message that the employment of women would not disrupt the family.[64] Women were portrayed as pioneers, helping to load their husbands' rifles to fight off the Indians. They were depicted in advertisements, dressed in work clothes, spinning stories about their important day at work for the war effort, surrounded by their admiring children and caregiving grandparents.* By emphasizing that women's primary duty was to guard the home by holding down men's jobs until they returned, advertisers avoided showing war work as leading to new roles for women. The campaign was successful. Between 1940 and 1945, women increasingly took over jobs that were well paid and that only men were thought to be

---

*A Maxwell House coffee ad, for instance, published in the Saturday Evening Post in 1944, portrayed an attractive young middle-class woman war worker resting after a hard day's work at the factory, still wearing her coveralls and identification badge; her lunch bucket is prominently displayed on the dining room table. She is flanked by an older couple, probably her parents, and a little girl, her daughter, hugs her closely while she sips the coffee that her mother has just poured. All three are eagerly listen-

capable of handling. Women did the work successfully, undermining the mythology that only men could handle the really tough jobs of industry and giving women a sense of power and satisfaction.

## AFTER THE WAR, WORKING MOTHERS ARE BAD MOTHERS

Working women during the war years were still made to feel guilty, however. Social scientists and child-rearing experts criticized women who were said to be neglecting their children by working. Most mothers managed to keep their children at home with relatives or friends while on the job but, inevitably, many were left unsupervised. Who was blamed for the trouble that befell these children? Wartime conferences on the family were filled with complaints—not about the paucity of day care centers but about the fact that some mothers were actually using them.[65] When congressional hearings in 1943 took up the issue of juvenile delinquency, working mothers received a disproportionate blame.[66] There was to be little help for them, though.

During the war, only the heroic woman could both work and manage the home. When the war was over, only the villainous woman would try to do both. There were strong political pressures to save money and reduce unemployment by pushing women back into the home. As manufacturers began to convert to production of consumer goods, advertisers intensified the attack on working mothers. In one persuasive ad in the *Saturday Evening Post* in 1945, a factory worker has to plead before a judge for her teenage son, who is labeled a "Victory Vandal," and a hysterical girl is carted away to a foster home because her mother has to work.[67] Such propaganda was apparently necessary. A 1944 Women's Bureau study showed that 80 percent of

---

*ing to her working-day tales and clearly full of respect for what she is doing. (The proportion of women in the labor force jumped from 25 percent to 36 percent between 1940 and 1945 with the help of this campaign.) (Honey, Creating Rosie the Riveter, pp. 118–119.) Readers of one of the most prestigious social science publications, The Annals, learned that mothers who resorted to day care "forget that there are many children who have a dangerous feeling of insecurity when they are away from their mothers from dawn to dark . . ." In this tug of war between children and jobs, the children are losing. (E. Boll, "The Child," Annals of the Academy of Political and Social Sciences 229 [September 1943].)*

the women who worked throughout the war wanted to continue in their jobs.[68] However, from September 1945 to November 1946, 2.5 million women left work and an additional million were laid off, especially in the higher-paying manufacturing jobs, where dramatic gains for women had been made during the war. The hearth angel had finally tasted the wages of the labor market—the fear was that she would not return to her pedestal. Indeed she had been quietly, steadily leaving it since the 1920s, a fact that did not come to public awareness until the 1970s.[69]

## THE ROMANCE OF OZZIE AND HARRIET

After the war, cultural and economic realities turned motherhood into a powerful, almost sacred institution, and domesticity became a safe harbor in worldly turmoil, appealing to both men and women alike. Women and children came to stand for those cherished qualities that had been snuffed out by carnage and danger: innocence, gentleness, idealism, continuity, and safety. The deprivation of the war years made a close family life attractive. The fear of a recession, even another depression, gripped the nation as conversion of the war industry to a consumer industry caused inevitable unemployment and labor unrest.[70] Consequently, in the 1950s, 60 percent of female undergraduates dropped out of college to marry, and they extolled marriage and motherhood with Freudian arguments. The family was romanticized in movies, TV, and popular magazines. A middle class affluence made possible by the soon booming postwar economy reinforced the romance with newly built private suburban homes and a host of new consumer items. Ozzie and Harriet were born. The term "day care" disappeared altogether and in its place the occasional baby-sitter appeared in discussions of motherhood.[71] Psychologists contributed to the domestic trend, warning again of the detrimental effects of "brainwork" on women's biology. According to one typical adviser, Margaret Ribble, the prospective mother should avoid "mental activity during pregnancy, lest she produce a nervous infant . . . the more educated the woman is, the greater the chance there is of sexual disorder . . . The greater the disordered sexuality in a given group of women, the fewer children do they have."[72]

## THE FEMININE MYSTIQUE INTENSIFIES

A flood of propaganda once again emerged to sell the mother-at-home ideal to women whom the labor market was continuing to try to dislodge. Typical of the new advice literature was *Modern Woman, The Lost Sex,* published in 1947 by Dr. Marynia Farnham, a psychiatrist. It was used as a textbook in college courses on "marriage and the family," "life adjustment," and other innovative courses.[73] The book advised women that they should consider themselves only a temporary reserve labor pool, available to fill in the gaps when the men decided it was necessary. The book also claimed that the problems of modern society—including the war and the Depression—could be traced to the fact that women had left the home. (Sound familiar?) Women had given up their femininity to compete in a futile battle with men, causing their children to become delinquents or neurotics and their husbands to become alcoholics or sexually impotent.[74] This textbook advised that woman should be domestic and self-subordinating.*

## PATHOLOGICAL MOTHERHOOD

The discovery of the theories of maternal deprivation and attachment (see chapter 3) coincided with the need to persuade women to give their higher-paying jobs to the men returning home from the war and to preserve a family life that might provide a haven from the more harsh and uncertain public world of war, communism, and commerce. Reports of stunted children deprived of their (working) mothers filled the scientific literature and filtered into the mainstream, standing as cautionary tales for mothers of children living in normal family situations. Popular books on child rearing began to feature

---

*"[Woman should] devote all her efforts to improving it [the home] in every way. When she is not tending to the children, she should be an amateur interior decorator, chef, mender, home nurse, retail buyer, and member of the local parent-teacher association. She should be ever ready, upon the homecoming of her husband, to be a spirited companion, tricked out like a debutante for a cocktail party. In order to be a good companion, she should give some time to reading a few current books and the newspapers. It would not do at all for her not to know what the conversation was about at dinner. It would be especially humiliating to her husband if she were unable to contribute to the conversation about some public matter in the company of friends . . ." (pp. 1, 8–9).

ominous references to orphaned animals and institutionalized children.[75] They showed a tragic picture of the maternally deprived child—sunken eyes, wan cheeks, limbs thin and flaccid, prey to every passing infection—all presumably for lack of "constant attention day and night, seven days a week and 365 in the year."[76] Women were told their sensitivity to their infant's every need was critical for healthy personality development. Infants should be picked up every time they cried. Failing to do so would make them emotionally maladjusted. Women could now "infect" a generation of children with the germs of mental illness unless, of course, the modern clergy of psychologists and social scientists saved them.

The prevalent view of disturbed children was that mothers caused all their problems, from autism to delinquency. Rene Spitz identified the "psychotoxic diseases of infancy" in which "the mother's personality acts as the disease-provoking agent." Such maternal attitudes as "primary anxious overpermissiveness," he said, produces the three-month colic, "hostility in the guise of manifest anxiety" was responsible for infantile eczema, and so on.* Mothers who devoted themselves according to the experts' advice, however, were still in danger of harming their children. In 1946, Dr. Edward Strecker, a psychiatrist, found that the almost 3 million men who were rejected for military service because of psychiatric disorders and who "lacked the ability to face life, live with others, think for themselves and stand on their own two feet," were all suffering from "momism"—the mother who makes a child's home life such a haven that he doesn't ever want to leave it and manage on his own.†

Troubled children were now seen as "overprotected." Psychiatrist David Levy wrote an influential book in this vein entitled *Maternal Overprotection*. He used case studies from a child guidance clinic to

---

*"[O]scillation between pampering and hostility," was responsible for rocking in infants; "cyclical mood swings of the mother," for fecal play and coprophagia; "maternal hostility consciously compensated," for hyperthymia in the child (Rene Spitz, The First Year of Life: A Psychoanalytic Study of Normal and Deviant Development of Object Relations [New York: International Universities Press, 1965], p. 206.)

†According to Dr. Strecker, ". . . mom is sweet, doting, self-sacrificing . . . She supervises the curl of their hair, the selection of their friends and companions, their sports and their social attitudes and opinions. By and large she does all their thinking for them . . . It is the perfect home . . . Failing to find a comparable peaceful haven in the outside world, it is quite likely that one or more of the brood will remain in or return to the happy home, forever more enwombed." (Edward Strecker, Their Mother's Sons [Philadelphia and New York: 1946], pp. 52–59.)

illustrate various types of overprotection; the children involved had been referred to the clinic for such problems as poor schoolwork, withdrawal from group activities, chronic bedwetting, quarreling, and disobedience. According to Levy, what determined whether a woman would lean more toward overprotection or rejection was probably the amount of "maternal-type hormones" she possessed. Curiously, Levy proclaimed that a woman could even be both rejecting and overprotecting at the same time—an expression of her "unconscious hostilities."[77] (One can only imagine the required admixture of hormones!)

As the economy began to stabilize, the old "masculine" characteristics of aggressiveness and strength were threatened by the necessity of corporate conformity and docility.[78] As a counterforce, medicine and the social sciences forged a conception of femininity so intense and so at odds with women's actual experience that it was bound to come undone. All women were to derive total fulfillment from complete devotion to their husbands and children. Should women have any doubts, psychologists, bolstered by Freudian theory, admonished them one and all that to want anything other than motherhood was a sign of maladjustment requiring the aid of a psychotherapist.*

## INCREASING DEPENDENCE ON THE EXPERTS

In the flowering of this new era of motherguilt, women had become dependent on these expert authorities as never before because they were increasingly isolated. For the first time in American life, women spent their days at home alone in the newly affordable private housing. Women were also isolated from the traditions of the past—the wisdom of mothers and grandmothers had been replaced by the esoteric knowledge of experts. The advice book of one expert, published

---

*A typical female advisee wrote to Child Study, a parent-oriented periodical whose advisory board included Benjamin Spock, Rene Spitz, and David Levy: "I am a professional woman with a son five years old . . . though I keep planning to quit [work] so far I haven't . . . I'm not at all sure it would be wise for me to give up my work and try to be just a mother". The response: ". . . you may want to get some professional help in finding out what has caused you to lose confidence in your capacities. It may be that you're more the domestic type than you think and that under the right circumstances your powers as wife and mother could be liberated in the service of your child . . ." (Ehrenreich and English, For Her Own Good, p. 224.)

in 1946, sold almost as many copies as the Bible—enough, in fact, for every household with a child to have a copy.[79] Pediatrician Benjamin Spock, in his *Common Sense Book of Baby and Child Care,* sounded reassuring and old-fashioned, telling mothers to just use their "common sense" at the same time, of course, telling them what to do every single step of the way.[80] Spock announced a shift from the tyranny of scheduled technicalities in child rearing to a theory of managing the unconscious. He was a Freudian (he had even been psychoanalyzed) and was especially concerned that mothers not re-create the "authoritarian personality"—i.e., the personality of a Nazi—by frustrating their children or being too strict. Spock advised permissiveness and avoidance of conflict with children. The mother's goal was to create in her child a congenial, well-adjusted personality. (Fathers continued to be in the background, providing support for their wives by being good breadwinners and distant role models for their children.) The infant should now be indulged, a prescription that was in keeping with the intensified emphasis on consumerism that altered the function of the family to one of indulgence. The Harriet Nelsons of the 1950s, however, apparently indulged everyone in their families except themselves.

By the early 1960s, the growing discontent among these Freudian mothers was surfacing. In September 1960 *Redbook* ran an article called "Why Young Mothers Sometimes Feel Trapped." Readers had been invited to send written responses to the article, drawn from their own experience. The editors expected to receive a few hundred manuscripts at most. They received fifty thousand.[81] In the words of Betty Friedan, "The problem that has no name burst like a boil through the image of the happy American housewife."[82] With day after day of infant colic, malfunctioning refrigerators, chicken pox, and grape juice spills, women were wondering whether there shouldn't be something more to their lives. But the experts had told them they were experiencing (feminine) fulfillment and so they endured. Sort of. Doctors and magazines began to identify a malady they called "housewife's syndrome." Women were waking up one morning and deciding to stay in bed, permanently. They were suffering from uncontrollable weeping, exhaustion, insomnia, headaches, and drastic weight changes. So doctors began prescribing amphetamines and tranquilizers. Women also prescribed alcohol for themselves. Magazine analysts speculated on whether the problem was overeducation, over-work, or maybe just incompetent appliance repairmen.[83]

Fortunately for these women, there were better remedies for their problems than the prescriptions of doctors and the glib analyses of the news media. By the early 1960s, the life of the full-time housewife had become financially untenable for growing numbers of families. The mid-century ideal of a fully equipped house and kids turned out to be so expensive that full-time mothers were quietly, steadily creep-ing into the labor market to support them. The number of employed women with children under six rose from 12 percent in 1950, to 16 percent in 1960, to 30 percent in 1970.[84] Full-time motherhood was losing its financial and psychological underpinnings.

## FEMINISM REJECTS FEMININITY

In 1963 Betty Friedan interviewed these troubled middle-class house-wives and concluded in her landmark book *The Feminine Mystique* that the problem they were having was femininity itself.[85] It was, she declared, a myth concocted by medical authorities and social scien-tists. Friedan was succeeded by a host of feminist theorists who con-tinued the critique. Sex roles were not rooted in biology, as Freudians insisted, but were simply socially constructed. Kate Millett cited the work of Margaret Mead, who noted that in some cultures it was con-sidered masculine to be passive and feminine to be aggressive and even to dislike child rearing. She also cited the studies of John Money, who treated people for sexual anomalies they were either born with or acquired through injury. Money, in deciding to which sex these people should be medically reconciled, found that the most important factor predicting their later adjustment was how they had been so-cialized, not whether they ultimately had the female XX or male XY chromosomes.[86]

Friedan's book had struck a chord and sparked the feminist move-ment of the 1970s, which was facilitated by other movements for so-cial change such as the antiwar movement and the civil rights movement. Married women gathered in groups to raise their con-sciousness regarding the ways their lives had been unfairly restricted by the ideology of sex roles and discovered that "the personal is po-litical." Being single became a fashion, and the vocation of motherhood fell out of favor with the new feminists, not to mention a generation of seekers of personal fulfillment.

Motherhood in the 1970s was not radically transformed by the feminist movement—it was simply dismissed as having been a source of women's oppression. In addition, the women's movement failed to recognize that the domestic pedestal had never even been offered to poor and minority women, and to them the constrictions of sex role seemed secondary to economic deprivation, which was often the product of discrimination.[87] Black and Hispanic women had always worked outside the home. The source of their oppression was as much about racism, which kept them in the lowest-paying jobs, as it was about sexism. Moreover, their husbands were often barred from the higher-paying jobs open to white men, and they sometimes had to live away from their families to find work. Native American women were sequestered on reservations, where they had been taught to abandon their traditions. The prime source of their oppression was the loss of their culture and terrible poverty.[88]

The feminist movement did recognize the need for day care, however, and launched a campaign to provide it. The 1968 National Organization for Women (NOW) Bill of Rights demanded the establishment of child care facilities on "the same basis as parks, libraries, and public schools, adequate to the needs of children from the preschool years through adolescence . . ." Feminists, educators, child advocates, and congressmen succeeded in enacting a national child-care policy available not just to the poor, but to all children. These efforts resulted in the passage of the Comprehensive Child Development Act. It authorized medical, nutritional, and educational services for children from infancy to fourteen years of age. The services would be provided free to the poor, and those above the poverty line would pay on a sliding scale. President Nixon vetoed the bill in December 1971, not because of budgetary constraints, but because the program would facilitate women's work outside the home. Nixon said it would, "commit the vast moral authority of the national government to the side of communal approaches to child-rearing over and against the family-centered approach."[89]

While the struggle for day care continued, middle-class women were so busy carving out new roles for themselves in the public arena and cobbling together their own nonmaternal care assistance, that any reconceptualization of motherhood was put on a back burner (insofar as it was even considered). Consequently, its parameters were still left to the experts to define and they continued to do so as they had throughout the century, taking bits of data and theory and fashioning it into advice that shifted with the cultural climate and the economy. That advice, however, continued to be predicated on the hearth angel ideal.

## THE MATERNAL SCULPTRESS REFASHIONED

Medical and psychological experts in the early 1970s managed to reestablish the idea of a biological basis for motherhood—albeit in a form that wouldn't be laughed off by wise feminists and mothers who now worked full-time. The 1972 "discovery" of maternal-infant bonding (later debunked, as I'll describe in chapter 3) showed that maternal instincts were so powerful they could affect children's IQ and even cause child abuse if they were interfered with. This bonding could only occur if mothers were allowed to hold their infants right after birth. Why would enlightened, liberated women accept an idea that claimed their behavior toward their newborns was as unthinking and mechanical as that of barnyard goats, whose postpartum bonding was the basis for this idea?

One of the most powerful reform movements of the 1970s was the natural childbirth movement. In America, unlike most modern nations, childbirth is managed almost entirely by doctors in hospitals. Doctors tend to use drugs, surgery, and technology in a manner that treats childbirth like an illness or injury, and hospitals tend to restrict and regiment their patients in order to manage them. Before the reform movement of the 1970s, women giving birth in hospitals were isolated from their families, routinely prepped for surgery, and were managed by doctors who made all the decisions.[90] The new bonding research seemed to promise women less isolation and more control. Fathers and other family and friends who had been relegated to waiting rooms in the past, could—should—be with birthing women for bonding. Hospitals, which were in danger of losing their obstetric business to the midwives and alternative birth centers, made bonding part of their official policy—complete with special homey rooms to simulate a home birth. As part of the romanticism of everything natural, breast-feeding underwent a revival and was intertwined with bonding philosophy. Reformers in the natural childbirth movement, many of them feminists, embraced the bonding notion because it appeared to give women more power in their own birth and allowed them to continue to use the hospital, which seemed safer than home or even the alternative birth center. For working mothers, bonding provided an added psychological bonus: If they went back to work right away, at least they could feel they had gotten their infant off to the right start. Bonding was a bad bargain for women, though. This seemingly liberating idea of postpartum bonding ultimately served to reconfirm the idea that women were in some very specific way, the natural, the best, the only ones really fit to care for their own young children. Not incidentally, it also became another way for mothers to blame themselves or be blamed if they failed to bond adequately with their children for whatever pesky reason—cesarian section, illness, employment, fatigue.

## MOTHERS AS COGNITIVE STIMULATORS

While the biological basis for motherhood was propped up once again, another scientific discovery was also used to make a case for the importance of mothers to their young children. In the late 1960s psychologists began to figure out how to study the infant mind. Intelligence was an issue that greatly concerned adults at this time, in part because the achievements of Communist countries (like the launch of the first space satellite *Sputnik* in 1957) sparked a great fear that the Russians were proving to be smarter than the Americans. Studies began to show that the world of infants was not just the "blooming buzzing confusion" psychologists had thought it to be—infants were "intelligent."[91] Studies with rats further contributed to how this data would be interpreted. One researcher found that rats kept in cages with "enriched environments"—i.e., more tunnels and toys—developed bigger brains than rats kept in the usual cages. (Of course rats with the biggest brains are those that inhabit natural environments.)[92] This increased brain capacity of laboratory rats was even passed on to subsequent generations of rats. According to these studies, stimulation could permanently increase basic intelligence, so needless to say mothers were prevailed upon to stimulate their infants' intelligence and of course they could only do that if they stayed at home and devoted themselves entirely to their young children.

The 1970s saw the dawn of a technological revolution that threw many adults into "future shock" as they began to worry about the capacity of their own minds to process the rapidly changing culture and technology.[93] This worry was then projected onto children—it was their intelligence that needed to be honed. Mothers would do the honing by every possible means according to instructions as technical as those given mothers in the 1920s. Harvard psychologist Burton White, through popular books, columns, and even television, prescribed the new cognitive technology. "The limits for our capacity for future achievement may be irrevocably fixed during the first thirty-six months of our lives," White proclaimed. In White's instruction book, these critical three years are broken down into seven phases in which week-by-week developments are described, complete with flowcharts![94] Such advice fostered a sense of urgency, even desperation among middle-class parents, especially women who were rapidly leaving the home to work. Between 1970 and 1984, the percentage of mothers in the labor force with children under age six rose from 30 percent to 52 percent.[95]

## THE ABANDONMENT OF MOTHERS

While the mothering experts were going on about the critical power of very early education and maternal nurture, the maternal sculptresses and their children were being abandoned. The 1970s had been a time of extraordinary change. The feminist movement, the widespread emphasis on pursuing individual desires, the rebellion against established authority—all contributed to a massive breakup of the nuclear family. The divorce rate rose to 50 percent of all marriages and stayed there. The amount of time American men spent with their children declined by 40 percent.[96] Between 1970 and 1985 the number of families headed by women with one or more children increased to one fifth of all households.[97] By the end of the decade, one in four babies was born to an unmarried woman. The most profound effect of the dissolution of the American family was the impoverishment of women and children who were left on their own with little assistance from fathers or anyone else, for that matter.

Most women were invested in their mothering role and were not well equipped for the breadwinner part that was thrust upon them. They were stuck in the pink-collar ghetto and they were poor. But whether women were at the bottom of the pink-collar ghetto or had pushed their way into the male-dominated jobs, they were consistently paid less. Whatever their work, women discovered the glass ceiling of discrimination, which prevented them from advancing to the highest-paying jobs, and the maternal wall, which prevented them from both working and caring for their families.

While single mothers were not permitted to enter the economy on equal terms with men, they were expected to be both provider and nurturer for their children. In over 90 percent of divorces, children remained with their mothers and yet only about 60 percent of these women were awarded any child support; moreover, the payment of these awards was erratic and covered less than a quarter of the cost of rearing a child.[98] The experts had told men their importance to their children was as a (breadwinning) role model and occasional play buddy. Men were under little social pressure to maintain their involvement with their offspring. Therefore women and children were increasingly alone and impoverished. By 1989, 59 percent of poor families were headed by single mothers.[99]

## THE ARRIVAL OF SUPERMOM

With the devastation of the old hearth angel and her plunge into poverty, a strange new maternal ideal emerged in the 1980s—a model more unreal and impossible than any since the overprotecting/rejecting Freudian mother of the 1950s. Her very name suggested there was going to be no realistic remedy for the problems that plagued working mothers. Women were doing more work and getting less help than at just about any time in our history. In place of fair wages, family leave and child care support, the "supermom" of the '80s would have to learn to be a superhero. She was discovered by the media, running around in her three-piece suit, fending off stress and burnout with time management techniques and exercise classes. She was the subject of endless magazine articles that claimed her difficulties were simply the product of the role strain she had brought on herself.[100] The supermom of the 1980s was the new Good Mother who endured her plight by suffering "stress" without becoming indignant or pointing the finger at a workplace designed for the days of the male breadwinner or at a husband who retained the privileges of breadwinning while bringing home an increasingly smaller loaf. In the popular portrayals of supermom, she never wore a pink collar, so she certainly never complained about the poverty so many of her kind were coping with.

## CASHING IN ON MOTHERS' ANXIETY

Supermom was a yuppie maternal ideal who represented the prospect of status and power so many were losing. If she succeeded with her child and her job, she would rescue her family by handing the mantle of middle-class privilege to her offspring at a time when the middle class was on the verge of sliding down the socioeconomic ladder. She was portrayed as a kind of air traffic controller trying to coordinate all the complicated schedules of the various family members and her own high-powered work. Of course, she never considered going on strike for better working conditions (the real air traffic controllers had lost everything by such tactics).

Her greatest hurdle, however, was her preschooler, whose emotional development she was warping by being at work. Fortunately, she could compensate in this matter, too, at considerable cost to herself. She could buy help to stimulate his IQ so he could compete successfully with his peers for that secure spot in the economic sun. Sensing a new market, all kinds of commercial services sprang up to help the working mother with her crucial task. Nursery schools renamed themselves early childhood development centers and offered programs based on the findings of the cognitive psychologists. These schools often had long waiting lists and even entry tests for aspiring toddlers. The educational toy industry boomed; the physical fitness industry reached out with "Gymboree" classes for little tykes; and the clothing industry marketed expensive designer kiddie clothes to parents who were trying to do their very best for their 1.8 children. One popular organization even gave workshops to parents so they could teach their infants to read and do basic math. The intelligent infant had become the "superbaby." Parents were flashing reading cards at their three-month-olds, spending $4,000 a semester on developmental day care and even reading to their fetuses, who were all presumably very intelligent and in need of intellectual stimulation.[101] At the same time, most of the little geniuses' mothers had left home. By 1988, only one in four families were the Ozzie-and-Harriet sort (down from 44 percent in 1975).[102]

Mothers were frantically trying to make up for their time in the workforce—time, they were told, when their mothering was crucial to their infant's future. Dr. T. Berry Brazelton became the decade's Dr. Spock, delivering the same old message that working mothers were really threatening their children's emotional development by weakening attachment.[103] Should the new supermom wish to give up her professional strivings and stay home to relieve her stress (as she was increasingly persuaded to do) the spectre of the evil poor mother would keep her on her treadmill. Supermom had every reason to fear: fully half her kind would lose her husband and his income in divorce. If she didn't want to risk the ignominy of poverty, she must equip herself with viable job skills. And poor women were air traffic controllers with a fleet of broken-down planes and outmoded radar equipment— they had very few resources with which to do their job. Poverty grew like a plague, with hunger and homelessness not seen since the Depression.

## FAMILY VALUES

By the turn of the decade, a new social invention, like some ethereal genie uncorked from a bottle, filled the public stage and promised to grant the wishes of a troubled society: "family values" would now be the redeemer of a nation on the verge of crumbling. The conservative right equated family values with the traditional image of the nuclear family in which the mother stays at home. The family restorationists did not agree on a program for reducing the number of single-mother families, although they used the language of moral failure and cultural decline to account for the changing shape of the family. Many proposed to revive the stigma that used to surround divorce and single motherhood. They proposed making it harder to divorce, by restricting legal channels for divorce. They proposed restricting welfare benefits for unmarried mothers and eliminating benefits entirely for mothers who have children while receiving welfare.

But the family values Good Mother is about as likely to gird up the

changing family as a whalebone corset is likely to enhance the working mother's power suit—it's simply a useless fantasy for the wrong
times.

In fact the relationship of changing times to the Good Mother fantasy is what this chapter is really about. The Good Mother changes
form with the Zeitgeist and is an ideal that is always grossly overstated, not so much for the sake of the children, but rather for the re-
striction of mothers who must be kept in "their place." Therefore,
mothers are hardly guilty of hurting their children if they do not conform to these hyped-up images of the Good Mother. Yet it may not
be enough to describe how these ideals have been socially constructed, because mothers are now faced with a greater arsenal of scientific studies directed at them than ever before. Even the mother
who knows this history may find it difficult to argue with contemporary study after study that says her very biology has programmed her
to care exclusively for her young children. A whole cadre of Ph.D.'s
in psychology have been hard at work once again, proving this verity
through research on attachment. How can the innocent mother defend herself against such august expertise? Let me provide the argument for her.

3

# Crimes
# of Attachment

## THE INDICTMENT

One of the reasons mothers take their expert advisers so seriously is
that the advisers draw upon science. And we all assume that science
is a rational operation that yields facts we can rely upon. But scientists
are human beings and they, too, have been steeped in visions of the
Good Mother. The questions scientists ask and the way they interpret
the results of their studies are bound to be influenced by their unexamined assumptions about what makes a Good Mother. One of the
most popular ideas in psychology is the notion of attachment, "discovered" (one might even say "invented") in the 1950s, which claimed
mothers are biologically programmed to care for their children. And
not coincidentally, this idea acts as the bedrock foundation for our
contemporary standards of the Good Mother.

Attachment is said to be instinctual behavior that programs a child
to stay close to its caregiver as a means of survival; bonding, a poor
cousin of attachment, is described as a *maternal* instinct, also designed to ensure survival, that requires mothers to lovingly hold their
babies right after birth and stay close to them in the ensuing months.
Maternal bonding and attachment have become the *sine qua non* in
child psychology as predictors of children's emotional development
and yet these concepts are so elastic they are often used interchangeably. Moreover, as we are about to discover, the "science" on which
these notions are based is about as reliable as those old wives' tales the
experts love to warn us about.

Before we wade into this "science," it must be emphasized that the general concept of attachment is an important one. It is this: Infants are very social creatures; they can distinguish people from one another, and they need to have loving, consistent relationships if they are to thrive. Infants and young children *require* loving, consistent caregivers. But the distance between this fact and the increasingly distorted doctrines of attachment (and bonding) is interplanetary. Attachment doctrine is so convoluted that virtually every mother is guilty of attachment "crimes," if the experts are to be believed.

## CAUTIONARY TALES

One of the most consistent warnings from the psychopediatric pulpit has been that mothers who work outside the home "risk" damaging their children's emotional development. But as mothers continue to disobey the experts in greater and greater numbers by heading into the workplace (and I guess the experts are disobeying themselves as they deliver one in four American babies by cesarian section, which certainly inhibits congenial postpartum bonding), the attachment rhetoric is beginning to sound rather shrill. Recent newspaper headlines, for example, read, "Scientists say the fundamental glue between mothers and infants is something like a heroin fix. Mother and child really can get hooked on one another." These scientists claim, "We think we have a handle on the biochemical underpinnings of mother-infant bonding," because their studies with monkeys show that endorphins (opiatelike substances produced by the body) are released in a monkey mother and her infant when they are reunited after a separation. These researchers then make the astounding claim that motherlove is so powerful a biochemical event that problems with this "fix" could result in later drug abuse for the child.[1]

In addition to such periodic preposterous "scientific discovery" headlines, attachment theory often comes to mothers through cautionary tales posing as entertainment. In the fall of 1992, CBS aired a docudrama, produced by a child psychologist, about children without a conscience. These murderous children who attacked their loving families were said to be suffering from "attachment disorder." One troubled boy burned down the hotel in which the family was staying, presumably because his mother returned to work too soon. A woman psychiatrist in the drama told concerned parents that this murderous behavior could be caused by failure of postpartum bonding. The day after the program aired, calls poured in to the pediatric ward of one city hospital (and possibly hospitals across the country) from concerned mothers who felt they had not been able to bond properly with their babies and might be guilty of having caused such severe damage. Some of the real-life subjects on whom the docudrama was based had already made the rounds of *Donahue, Oprah, Geraldo,* and dozens of other talk shows.[2] These disturbed children had usually been adopted by loving parents who eventually came to fear for their lives. The adopted children tortured and killed pets, abused and molested their siblings, and threatened to kill their adoptive families. Oddly, the children were superficially charming and friendly (their way of controlling people), but they were unable to feel any genuine connection with people and were bubbling underneath with a murderous rage. They all had one thing in common: they had been severely abused and neglected before the age of two and could not therefore consciously remember the source of their rage and mistrust. In their need to be invulnerable, these children could not let themselves be loved nor could they love in return. They were "unattached."[3]

By now the reader will not be surprised that much of the blame for these atrocities is leveled at working mothers. In the foreword to one of the first books about these children, it is, oddly, working mothers, not abusing home-staying mothers or fathers, aunts or uncles, not the takers of drugs nor the abandoners of children, but working mothers—who are told they will feel grief and guilt when they read this book, and they are admonished to pay closer attention to what is happening to their children. Sadly, the foreword is by U.S. Representative from Colorado Pat Schroeder, one of America's foremost advocates for working parents. Congresswoman Schroeder does not suggest that women should stay home from work, but she does see these children as women's responsibility and women's work as an endangerment to their children.[4] If the foreword of the book doesn't provide the maternal reader with that familiar defendant's quiver, the authors' assertions certainly will. They claim that children are so vulnerable to "attachment disorder" that any factor that damages or distorts attachment puts them "at risk" for a serious disturbance. These risk factors include day care, working mothers, divorce, adoption, foster care, and teenage pregnancy.

"At risk," "attachment," "bonding": It's a wonder mothers don't break out in a rash every time they hear these psychobabble terms. And they hear them constantly from the professional child-rearing advisers on whom parents have come to rely. The vocabulary of the late-twentieth-century mother is unavoidably replete with the commandments of bonding and attachment: Thou shalt worry that anyone but yourself who takes care of your children will shame you and damage them. Thou shalt see your husband, baby-sitter, neighbor, day care provider, aunt, and grandmother as a threat to your standing as a Good Mother. Thou shalt regret involvement in any activity that you enjoy more than being with your children. Most of all, thou shalt feel guilty about working outside the home. It is doubtful either mother or her ministers have a clear idea of where this maternal virtue of fostering attachment leaves off and sin begins. The high priests of child-rearing advice claim to be deriving their standards of nurture from the sacred text of science, a source not easily understood by the mere layperson. Indeed the text is full of esoteric language and a mystifying use of numbers; it is also full of human foibles, especially pride and prejudice. The scientific text from which the clergy pontificates consists of hundreds of studies a year regarding something called "bonding" or "attachment" and, as we will see, these terms are used to describe everything from the wellsprings of religion to the machinations of business management. In reality they accurately define very, very little.

## THE BREAST-FEEDING POLICE

I guess this is a good place for a little aside about breast-feeding because it is certainly a codefendant among crimes of attachment. Even though there is no research that links breast-feeding to attachment, the experts all advocate breast-feeding as a means of promoting bonding and attachment. Breast-feeding is another highly idealized aspect of mothering that in our society has irrationally gone from one extreme to another. Currently, it is strongly associated with socioeconomic status. About 70 percent of college-educated mothers

breast-feed compared to 32 percent of those with a grade-school education. In the 1950s and 1960s, when attachment theory was at its
most virulent, the psychopediatric community promoted bottle-
feeding. In fact, from the 1930s to the early 1970s, only about 25 percent of mothers breast-fed at birth and only about 10 percent
continued beyond the early weeks. Although the psychopediatric
community now claims breast is best, the health advantages do not
seem dramatic. Entire generations have been raised safely on formula.
Yes, certain immunities are transmitted through breast-milk and it is
easier for many babies to digest. But studies that find a correlation between bottle-feeding and inferior infant health may really be finding
the effects of poverty because poor women, whose health and nutrition is more likely to be inferior, also tend not to breast-feed.[5] I'm certainly not disagreeing with the assertion that "breast is best" for the
majority of women and babies. But I do believe that breast-feeding
has become one more overstated imperative that holds women to an
impossible standard and contributes to their guilt. While it can be a
very gratifying experience for a mother, it can also be exhausting, burdensome, and quite painful; moreover, many women must take med-
ication for their own health, making breast-feeding inadvisable. For
middle-class women, breast-feeding is becoming another pseudo-
index of good mothering; for poor women, it may become an imperative for different reasons—bottle-feeding costs money, and
government programs that underwrite the cost are now promoting
breast-feeding because it is cheaper.[6]

## FROM THE PULPIT

Parents consume more child-rearing advice than even pizza or Big
Macs. The number of child care books rolling off the assembly line
has flooded a seemingly insatiable market in the past few decades.
(My own local small-town Encore bookstore boasts 783 titles in "Child
Care.") As I indicated in chapter 1, parents rely on the baby gurus and
the surrounding expert advice industry more now than at any time in
our history, in part because since they have so few children to practice on, they feel they have to "get it right" the first time; in part because the circumstances of family life have changed so dramatically

that even their own parents' advice is based on a very different experience; and of course in part because science is always making discoveries that only the experts can explain.

I've alluded to the prominence of the baby gurus; the spread of their gospels is breathtaking. Dr. Benjamin Spock, whose first book was published in 1945, is the author of seventeen books and is one of the century's best-selling authors. His *Baby and Child Care* is in its sixth edition and has sold over 40 million copies. Spock has also been a parenting columnist for a number of magazines including *Redbook, Ladies' Home Journal,* and *Parenting.*[7] Dr. T. Berry Brazelton has written thirteen books and many columns in newspapers and magazines, including *Redbook.* His first book, *Infants and Mothers,* has sold more than a million copies and has been translated into eighteen languages. Since 1984 he has starred in his own daily Lifetime cable TV program, *What Every Baby Knows,* reaching millions of viewers.[8] British child psychologist Penelope Leach is the author of four books on parenting as well as many articles for parenting magazines. Her *Baby and Child,* first published in 1977, has sold 2.5 million copies in the United States alone.[9] She also hosts her own question-and-answer show, also broadcast on Lifetime: *Your Baby and Child with Penelope Leach.* The more parent-friendly mother-and-daughters team of Arlene Eisenberg, Heidi Murkoff, and Sandee Hathaway, authors of the *What to Expect* books, first published in 1984, are also doing a booming business, with 4 million copies currently in print, of *What to Expect When You're Expecting.*[10] There are now a half dozen TV programs on child rearing on Lifetime, which markets primarily to women, including: *American Baby, Healthy Kids,* and *Growing Up Together.* All deliver advice either direct from the experts or via young attractive TV host mothers, in three-minute sound-bite segments.

Parents obviously count on the advisers a great deal. But the content of this advice is not always helpful to mothers, especially when it concerns the issue of attachment.

In T. Berry Brazelton's 1991 book *On Becoming a Family: The Growth of Attachment: Before and After Birth,* a mother asks the doctor: "Do you believe in mothers going back to work after they have their babies?" . . . "I am sure that the first few months are critical," the doctor replies. "At least six months and even a year might be the ideal time span [before mothers can return to work]."[11] In Penelope

Leach's 1994 advice book, the author admonishes: "Most day care advocates gloss over babies' need to be breast-fed and to establish the primary attachments on which later development depends." Leach adds that women should not only breast-feed, they should carry their babies on their body at all times to allow for "more natural" feeding and sleeping cycles, and, of course, better attachment.[12] Dr. Spock, in the 1992 edition of his book, chimes in, telling "parents" that mothers have better relationships with their babies if they had contact "soon after birth" for the "attachment and bonding" process.[13]

Brazelton, Leach, and Spock claim their advice is based on the research of Rene Spitz, John Bowlby, Mary Ainsworth, John Kennell, and Marshall Klaus, whose science, we will discover, sometimes borders on fiction. Brazelton explains everything that happens in family relationships involving a new baby as "stages of attachment," the "cementing of bonding," and the vagaries of "detachment," all of which are said to occur in critical phases that have been identified by these experts. This delicate process requires mothers to stay home from work for the first three months at a minimum, but preferably the first year. Dads can work around the clock, apparently, because they have no maternal instincts. In fact, Leach insists that dads are in the way when mothers are attaching to their infants, which mothers do hormonally, through breast-feeding. Since dads don't have breasts or maternal hormones, their job is to stand back and support their wives.*[14]

By now the reader must wonder if these experts really know what they are talking about. Where did this idea come from? What research, exactly, is it based on? The story of attachment began six decades ago with the discovery of infant suffering in institutions that was promptly and inappropriately termed "maternal deprivation."

## MATERNAL DEPRIVATION

In the 1930s a new pediatric problem was identified: "hospitalism." It occurred when infants actually became physically ill because of poor

---

*Why Dr. Leach and her colleagues have failed to investigate the parallels with animals here, as they did with maternal bonding, is, of course, curious. Many normal male domesticated goats, for instance, with normal testes and proven ability to inseminate females, spontaneously grow udders and secrete milk. (Jared Diamond, "Father's Milk," Discover, February 1995, pp. 83–87.)

hospital conditions: lack of sanitation, inadequate nutrition, and so forth. A decade later, researchers discovered that infants could also contract a kind of "emotional hospitalism" produced by the practices of hospitals, nurseries, and orphanages. In the hospital wards and nurseries, a philosophy prevailed in which the pain of a parent's frequent coming and going was considered worse than one long separation; so parents were discouraged from frequent visiting. In fact, some institutional policies even discouraged staff from becoming involved with infants lest the inevitable separations cause emotional distress. Moreover, in orphanages, social scientists claimed that abandoned infants were likely to come from inferior genetic stock and therefore adoption should be forestalled for a couple years until one could see what kind of character the child developed.[15] In addition to these misguided theories, institutionalized children suffered from understaffing and other inadequacies of the institutions run by pediatricians, psychologists, social workers, and other scientific authorities.

When it was realized that infants did not generally do well in these institutions, however, the cause of their impairment was termed "maternal deprivation." The studies of psychoanalysts Rene Spitz and Katherine Wolf provided some of the most dramatic findings.[16] They studied infants in an orphanage and a nursery attached to a penal institution where juvenile delinquent mothers could visit with their infants. They found that the nursery infants fared better, while the infants in the orphanage were literally dying of what they called "anaclitic depression." The pattern of depression took a regular developmental course. At about six months the orphaned infants began to cry all the time, and at nine months they completely withdrew from humans. Spitz filmed the infants, and their faces are absolutely haunting. In the orphanage, a third of the infants died of greater susceptibility to disease brought on by their depression, according to Spitz. The babies were adequately fed and clothed, and the researchers concluded that they had died from "maternal deprivation"—lack of motherlove.

There are just a few things Spitz and his colleagues forgot to mention to the worried mother who would try to avoid causing maternal deprivation herself: The infants lay in their beds all day long with nothing to do, had as many as fifty different caretakers in their first eighteen months, and died of a measles epidemic. Mothers, quite frankly, had nothing to do with it. But Spitz and Wolf were essentially right in their analysis of the severe emotional depression that babies experience for want of loving attention, stimulation, and consistent care. However, the interpretation of this data was that mothers *alone* must be the primary and constant source of such care for their babies.[17]

## JOHN BOWLBY

Spitz and Wolf's studies helped to reform institutions. They were also taken up by the British psychiatrist John Bowlby. With social worker John Robertson, Bowlby documented the negative reaction of children when they are separated from their mother for a stay in the hospital or a residential nursery. Their work helped to reform institutional care by encouraging parental visits and more consistent emotional attention from staff. In 1950 Bowlby was asked by the World Health Organization to study the plight of children who had been orphaned by the war. Bowlby found that they were often emotionally disturbed, developmentally delayed, and unhappy. In his 1951 report, *Maternal Care and Mental Health,* the reader can by now anticipate what Bowlby concluded: These children—who had experienced the devastation of war, the loss of both parents, and often the loss of their childhood homes—were really just suffering from "maternal deprivation."[18]

Bowlby went beyond the data on institutionalized children and claimed such deprivation could take place in the seemingly normal home if mothers did not thoroughly enjoy every moment of mothering. He asserted that a warm, intimate, and continuing relationship with a mother is an essential precondition for the mental health of children. A disturbed emotional bond between mother and child was said to cause irreparable damage, not only to the child, but to society as a whole: "Deprived children, whether in their own homes or out of them, are a source of social infection as real and serious as are carriers of diphtheria and typhoid."[19] (Here we certainly are witness to one prime source of our current river of motherblame.)

In an attempt to curb the "infection" at its source, Bowlby proposed the adoption of a large number of policies: more attention for individual children in institutions and hospitals; the encouragement of foster parenting instead of using orphanages; more caution in placing children outside their homes except in the case of unmarried mothers. According to Bowlby, unmarried mothers were often psychologically disturbed and their children would be better off if adopted by a "normal family."[20] Bowlby advised mothers of young children not to work outside the home. The report, which became a best-seller in England, claimed that in terms of risk to the child, "full-time employment of a mother" is on a par with the "death of a parent, imprisonment of a parent, war, famine" and so forth. (Could the fact that Bowlby considered his own parents to have been very cold and distant and the fact that he was cared for by nannies have any bearing on this rather extreme romance of doting motherhood?)

## HARLOW'S MONKEYS

Bowlby continued to look for data to bolster his theory regarding the power of motherlove. He found the work of Harry Harlow, a psychologist at the University of Wisconsin, who experimented with monkeys. Harlow had decided to isolate infant monkeys in his colony in order to keep them from contracting infection. Accidentally, he learned that this complete social isolation caused the monkeys to develop bizarre behavior—they would rock back and forth, bite themselves, attack monkeys bigger than themselves, and if they managed to mate and produce offspring, they often abused the offspring. Of course the reader knows the refrain by heart now. Bowlby and Harlow concluded the little monkeys were suffering from "maternal deprivation."[21]

Harlow then launched a series of studies of "motherlove." He conducted experiments in which he set inanimate dummy "mothers" in the monkeys' cages. The dummies were equipped with crude plastic faces and either a terrycloth towel or a baby bottle filled with milk. Harlow scared the babies in a variety of ways and noted that the terrified infants sought out the terrycloth dummy even though it did not give milk. How did Harlow interpret his sadistic games? He had, of course, made a scientific discovery: Motherlove is not based on oral gratification, as Freudian theory suggested, but rather on an attachment to a comforting mother.

There was, of course, no objective observer present at these doings to mention that one could as easily conclude from the "data" that mothers could leave an inanimate terrycloth dummy in their place whenever they wish to go off somewhere! Moreover, not wanting to drink milk when you're frightened to death might be a sensible way of avoiding an upset stomach, not an illustration of the true well-springs of motherlove. In any case, Harlow's infant monkeys grew up in solitary confinement, deprived of all animal contact—not just their mothers. The one lesson Harlow's experiments did illustrate is the profound need infants have for tactile comfort and sociable care. Harlow's studies, however, were reduced to yet another cautionary tale to suggest what babies would be like if their mothers did not love them every moment of the day, which, of course, they could not do if they went to work.

## GOSLINGS AND IMPRINTING

Bowlby also found other animal studies to bolster his maternal deprivation theory. (By now his theory was being criticized by some psychologists as lacking sufficient scientific evidence.) He found the studies of Konrad Lorenz, an Austrian ethologist, to be very useful. Ethologists study the behaviors of animals in their natural habitat in order to learn more about the social mechanisms that help them to survive in the Darwinian process of adaptation. How, for example, do monkeys communicate with each other and decide who will be their leader? Which monkey is in charge of pointing out the approach of a hungry lion, for instance, and how does he or she communicate the information?

Lorenz was studying the social behavior of birds when he noted that there is a critical time in the life of a baby bird when it is ripe for "imprinting." About the second day of a graylag gosling's life, for instance, it will learn to follow its mother or anyone who has some very specific characteristics that make it resemble the mother. (Nature would not have the baby bird follow a creature resembling the predatory fox, for instance.) Lorenz found that the goslings would not imprint on any creature before or after the second day. Further, if they attached to him, they could not later be persuaded to follow their own mother. (In later research, Lorenz found that goslings *could* form other attachments and that the critical period was more flexible than he had first thought.)[22]

Bowlby claimed that human infants are equipped with a similar survival mechanism. He pointed out that infants also have ways of fostering attachment by promoting proximity to a caretaker, such as cooing, gazing, gurgling, crying, and later creeping, crawling, and walking. The critical period during which nature has equipped human infants to form their survival-based attachment is the first three years of life, according to Bowlby. He claimed they could attach only to their mother, or, if she were unavailable, then a mother substitute.[23] According to Bowlby, human attachment figures serve two interrelated functions for young infants. They provide children with a secure base for exploration of the environment, thereby facilitating the growth of their intelligence. And they afford children a haven of safety when they encounter threats, thus permitting them to regulate their level of stress. This early experience profoundly influences later life.

It should be noted that there are some aspects of caring relationships that are not considered attachment behaviors. Strictly speaking, Bowlby and colleagues decided that play is not attachment, the constant police work of parenting, however caring, is not attachment, and teaching is not attachment, although of course, all these behaviors are inspired by affection. Attachment, according to the orthodoxy, is formed essentially by responding to the infant's needs in a sensitive and appropriate manner. Through this primary attachment relationship, a child develops a model of human relationships that suggests her own needs are legitimate and are likely to be met with appropriate care. Upon this framework she builds other healthy relationships. The infant develops trust that she can rely on the care and comfort of her caregiver and therefore becomes an emotionally secure person.

## AINSWORTH: THE SECURE AND THE INSECURE

Bowlby's claims about attachment were aided by a disciple who came to dominate attachment research in America. Mary Ainsworth had been a protégée of Bowlby in England. In the late 1950s, she followed her husband to Uganda where she studied infants and mothers and described three main types of attachment that she claimed were the results of three types of mothering. One type was good or "secure" attachment, which she found in about two thirds of mothers and infants studied, and the other two were bad or "insecure." Good mothers were presumably more sensitive to their infant's every need. In America, Ainsworth studied a small number of mothers and infants (twenty-three pairs) and found that in a laboratory setting, although not at home, there was a pattern similar to the one in Uganda, of two thirds, secure, and one third insecure attachments.

Ainsworth made her assessments according to the results of a Strange Situation Test she designed, which has since been widely used to assess attachment. In this test the degree to which an infant uses his mother as a secure base from which to explore and play, and the degree to which he seeks comfort in the mother when distressed, determines the quality of attachment. Babies and mothers are observed in a laboratory in several episodes over twenty minutes: First the mother and baby are together and the baby plays alone; then a stranger joins them; then the mother leaves unobtrusively, returns a few minutes later, and settles the baby; she and the stranger leave—this time saying good-bye; then the mother returns. It is assumed that the strange place and person will upset the baby, who will seek security in the mother. If the baby seeks comfort in the mother when she returns, he is securely attached. If he avoids her or is ambivalent about the reunion, then he is insecurely attached.[24]

Of the twenty-three mother-infant pairs Ainsworth studied, she found about 20 percent of the infants were "anxiously attached or avoidant." These children conspicuously avoided their caretaker during the reunion episodes, did not cling when held, and tended to treat the stranger the same as, or even more positively than the mother. According to Ainsworth, this type of attachment was the product of an angry and rejecting mother. About 65 percent of her subjects were securely attached. These babies tended to seek proximity and contact with their mother, particularly during reunion episodes. They preferred their mothers to the stranger. These mothers were said to be more affectionate, more effective in soothing their infants, less intrusive, and better able to assess the infant's needs and to engage in more physical contact. The remaining infants were "ambivalently attached or resistant" and tended to resist interaction and contact with their mother although they also sought contact and proximity. Ainsworth deemed this the product of the insensitive and inept but not rejecting mother.

## THE DAY CARE WARNINGS

Fueled by the findings of Bowlby, Ainsworth, and others, the women's and parents' magazines began to provide an endless supply of articles equating attachment with motherlove and motherlove with staying out of the workforce. By the 1960s, even brief separations from mothers were considered toxic. For example, *Parents* magazine described a mother who was separated from her boy and girl for a few months because she was very ill. No further mention is made of the girl, but the boy calls his mother a "Bad Mommy" when she returns. For this terrible slur, the mother contemplates whether to send him to his room or even to spank him "for calling someone 'bad.' " Although he was taken care of by "a very fine couple who adored him," referred to thereafter as Mrs. Williams, and his own father, he became "a scrawny skeleton of a little boy" due to the mother's absence. The reader is advised of the very elaborate preparations she must make if she has to leave her child, however briefly, to take care of a sick relative for instance, or give birth to another baby, or, at the bottom of the author's list, take a job to help support the family.[25]

By the end of the 1960s a great many women had defied the experts' advice and separated daily from their young children to work outside the home. Between 1960 and 1984, married women with children under six nearly tripled their labor force participation. There was, however, no mention in the psychological literature of any surge in children suffering from the disorders of attachment.[26] Did the researchers consider this real-life experiment a disproof of their theory? Certainly not. They simply expanded the concept of attachment. Children who experienced day care, could, after all, remain attached, but probably their attachment would be inferior to the home-reared children. However, psychologists found no increase in clinical problems among children who attended day care, so they simply reduced the official period of time mothers were required by their theories to stay home to ensure attachment, thus preserving the concept. Now, even though there was absolutely no research to establish this, the first year of life became the new bonding/attachment critical period when mothers were presumably creating "risk" by working outside the home.

If working mothers read the women's magazines or listened to their pediatricians, they could only feel a constant sense of guilt about the deprivation they were causing their children by being on the job. Psychologists mounted study after study searching for the negative effects of day care on children who were increasingly leaving their mother's side to join other children in the homes of friends and relatives and the growing number of professionally run day care centers. (It was not until the late 1970s that any major studies—accidentally, while looking for damage—found positive effects of day care for the middle class.)[27]

By now you won't be surprised to hear that while psychologists continued to lament the damage (middle-class) working mothers were doing to their children's IQ and attachment, they were enthusiastically promoting day care for poor children. Poor children were to be provided with a preschool experience so positive it would propel them out of poverty. The Head Start program, launched in 1965, taught cognitive and social skills to children and instructed their mothers on how to tutor them. The assumption was that these mothers, by virtue of their poverty, were incompetent to teach their own children unaided. Ironically, one cannot help but notice that since the average salary of a Head Start teacher was below the poverty level, the teachers themselves should likewise have been ruled incompetent![28]

## MOTHER-INFANT BONDING

In the early 1970s a new twist in the attachment idea sprang to life with the emergence of "maternal-infant bonding" research. Two pediatricians, John Kennell and Marshall Klaus, had been concerned about the difficult problems of parents whose babies were kept in the new neonatal intensive care units. Parents were not allowed to enter these units because they might interfere with the complicated technology and spread infection to the precarious infants. Later these same infants often returned to the hospital, suffering from failure to thrive, neglect, and even abuse. Doctors and nurses who had used heroic measures to save these babies were at a loss to explain why so many of their parents did not seem to care about them as much as *they* did.

Klaus had been reading about research with goats that showed that right after birth, if the baby goat was taken from its mother for as little as five minutes and then given back to her, the mother would butt it away and refuse to feed it. Klaus thought a similar instinctual process was at work in human mothers: He hypothesized that the extended mother-infant *separation* of the intensive care unit could be causing the problems of these babies, including abuse and failure to thrive. Klaus and Kennell therefore conducted a study to see if there was a similar period in human mothers. They observed twenty-eight low-income mothers of healthy babies, half of whom got to hold their infants for sixteen extra hours during their hospital stay.[29]

By now, you can guess how they assessed their subjects and what they concluded. They said the extra contact group showed "better mothering," because on the average, more of the mothers in this group didn't leave home without their infant in the first month after birth—or if they did go out, they felt guilty about it. In fact, mothers who don't feel guilty score zero in these assessments of Good Mothering. (Could we want better evidence that motherguilt is sheer gold bullion with these guys?!) Also, more of the "extra contact" mothers stayed close to their infant in a pediatric exam, and fewer of them thought their baby should be left to cry rather than be picked up.

Armed with this evidence of superior mothering in fourteen women, they claimed to have found a universal instinctual phenomenon in all women. Right after birth, they claimed, women are sensitive to "bonding" with their infant and therefore hospitals should do everything to promote this phenomenon. If you think this has to be foolish hubris, you'll be sobered to learn that their study was published in *The New England Journal of Medicine* in 1972. Moreover, as mentioned earlier, it helped usher in a reform of hospital childbirth. Parents were given entry into the neonatal intensive care units to help care for their babies, and whole families were allowed to participate in the birth process based on this science.[30]

Dozens of subsequent bonding studies based on the Kennell and Klaus model were conducted, attempting to predict not only better mothering but also child abuse and failure to thrive. Nurses even produced bonding checklists in order to police the bonding process in the hospital. Although nurses consistently confused bonding and attachment, they trained each other to teach bonding to new mothers. In the ensuing research on bonding, its definition varied from study to study, as did the measures of "better mothering," which included everything from how long a mother breast-fed to whether or how soon she returned to work. Some of the subjects of these studies were middle class, many were poor; no studies showed that abuse or failure to thrive resulted from faulty postpartum maternal bonding, although in obstetric wards maternal bonding was taught and assessed as if it were a direct cause of abuse and neglect. Some studies claimed to find better mothering in the bonded group; others found no differences. Kennell and Klaus followed their twenty-eight subjects for five years, and even though they lost track of a third of them, they continued to make claims for better child development (essentially more complex speech) in the bonded group. The one study that attempted to replicate the original Kennell and Klaus study found no differences between the two groups.[31]

The research on bonding is probably the most poorly conceived research in the entire maternal-deprivation canon. Neither Kennell and Klaus nor the other investigators of bonding attempted to assess any biological phenomena that would establish their findings as something instinctual or universal. Moreover, in the original study, out of some seventy-five mothering factors that Kennell and Klaus assessed for the twenty-eight women, they found only a handful in which the bonded group did "better" than the regular group, and the few mentioned above should give some indication of their usefulness as measures of nurturing. Surely a good mother could go out and have a good time without feeling guilty, although having a trusted caregiver might be an important factor in her decision; a mother who never went out might be too impoverished or without social supports or might be depressed—she might not feel she had a choice and might therefore even feel resentful toward her baby, thus experiencing a decline in her "bonding" capital. Staying close to the baby in the pediatric exam could mean anything—feeling friendly toward the doctor, being anxious, and so on. Finally, of course, the problems of the intensive care unit babies are special. These babies are often sick and difficult babies to care for, are more likely to come from environments where there is drug and alcohol abuse, are more likely to be born into poverty, where social supports for parenting are scarce, and are as likely to be abused or neglected by men as by women. Of course, many people take great pleasure in greeting their newborn right after birth. Just as many, however, do not—because they are tired, it's their tenth baby, they are depressed or anxious, or they just haven't gotten to know this little creature yet; or maybe their child is adopted and they are not even present at the birth. These experiences in no way predict how well the baby will be loved and cared for nor what kind of relationships she will have in the future.

In the early 1980s the bonding research met with an avalanche of criticism. Some critics admitted they had held their criticism in check because they approved of the hospital reforms ushered in by bonding. However, as bonding turned into a rigid and restricting doctrine, and as a body of research emerged that was clearly a morass of badly designed studies full of conflicting definitions and conclusions, the demolishing criticism poured forth and after the mid-1980s the bonding research died out.[32]

Although bonding research was largely discredited by the scientific community, it seemed to develop a life of its own as its definition expanded. The term now seems to cover the growth of an emotional connection between mothers and fathers with their fetus; grandparents and friends with fetuses and babies, stepparents with children, and so on. Today bonding is virtually interchangeable with attachment.[33] Moreover, the gospel continues to be spread by the baby gurus.

## THE BABY GURUS PROMOTE BONDING

Dr. Spock, for instance, insists the stakes are too high to just let women bond with their babies in their own natural way. (Never mind that "instinctual" is supposed to mean you're on automatic.) The scientifically established rules of bonding dictate that mothers must hold their babies postpartum no matter what. If they are separated right after birth, their relationship is damaged—possibly resulting in the infant's failure to thrive, and even child neglect and abuse. According to Spock, "some say" it's good for fathers to bond, too. Spock explains that women's postpartum behavior toward their infants "suggests an instinct."[34] The reader is then provided with some examples that presumably illustrate the power of women's maternal drive, but of course, serve once again as bizarre cautionary tales: If pregnant rats are prevented from licking themselves, they won't exhibit normal mothering behaviors. If a chimpanzee has a very short labor, it will be frightened by the baby and climb to the top of its cage. Infant monkeys deprived of their mothers become socially bizarre and self-destructive.

Spock truly believes that human mothers—who read, write, and speak in thousands of complex languages, perform microsurgery and psychotherapy, compose symphonies and make movies—are fundamentally like these animals. In case the thinking mother should feel just a little wave of skepticism coming on as she contemplates her likeness to rats and monkeys, Spock alludes to the science of his colleagues Kennell and Klaus. (He fails to mention the goats—perhaps he didn't want to push his luck.) Spock explains: "In their experiment, mothers who didn't get to hold their babies after birth developed the idea that when your baby cries, you let him cry it out rather than pick him up; the ones who did 'bond' believed you pick up your baby right away when he cries."[35] If by now women still have any lingering doubts about their maternal-bonding proclivities after all this scientific evidence, Spock is determined to subdue them with one final admonition: "the high rate of violent crimes in our society may be related, in part, to the infrequency of close contact between babies and mothers." Perhaps sensing he might have gone a bit too far, Spock intones the ritual disclaimer of his priesthood: ". . . we know the majority of American children who have experienced [faulty bonding] turn out to be bright and warmhearted. So don't rush—this minute—to pick up and hug and joggle your baby to try to make up for lost opportunities."

Bonding is so complicated, according to Brazelton, that the pediatrician's guidance is crucial and should start before the baby is even born. Brazelton explains bonding from a different point of view—that of the natural childbirth advocate who throws in a bonus for the woman who gives birth without drugs or surgery (which Brazelton and the natural childbirth movement recognize as bad for babies): her child will have a higher IQ. According to Brazelton, postpartum bonding is really a reward for the mother who gives birth naturally *"all* by herself . . ." and when mothers can "hold, inspect and put their infants to the breast on the delivery table . . . there tends to be better mother-infant bonding and significantly better developmental performance in the infants." Moreover, the participation of fathers helps to "cement" the family.

Again, having perhaps gone a bit far in representing claims for bonding (with or without breasts), Brazelton asks, "What of parents who cannot pull off such a delivery? Will they miss an opportunity to give their babies a higher IQ? Will they miss out on bonding to their babies and endanger the baby's ultimate psychological development? (I will deal with these issues in detail in a future article.)" Alas, the future article is still in the future and the guilt induced by the insinuation that bonding à la natural childbirth is a critical necessity was apparently intentional: Brazelton claims women need guilt to goad them to do right by their children: "Guilt is an important motivator"; "Women should allow themselves to feel anxious and guilty about leaving their children—those feelings will press them to find the best substitute care."[36] (Why do I think that if these men ever had to give birth, childbirth would be the occasion of months of spa-side pampering and the perfect designer painkilling drugs would have been fully developed and marketed to obstetricians?)

## THE ATTACHMENT BONANZA

In the 1980s attachment research was positively booming as its definition kept on expanding. By 1985 the term "attachment behavior," according to the *Thesaurus of Psychological Index Terms,* officially replaced and consolidated a dozen different categories of research into its simplistic mechanistic maw: "Anaclitic depression, dependency, emotional development, intimacy, love, object relations, parent-child relations, postpartum depression, separation anxiety, separation individuation, stranger reactions, and bonding," all became understandable as relatives of attachment.[37] In the twenty years between 1974 and 1994, some 3,535 attachment studies were published and the annual rate of publication grew from 35 in 1975 to 280 in 1993.[38] What these studies actually amount to in terms of useful information is frankly dubious, since they all begin with the unvarnished assumption that mothers are the prime architects of their children's lives, rather than one of many influences on the lives of children who come into this world as unique as individual snowflakes.

"Parents," of course, had only to pick up *Parents* magazine to find the fruits of the boom translated into succinct verities for the conscientious mother. There were, as always, attachment accomplishments that reflected good mothering and bad mothering. What must have been baffling for the working supermom who was trying to do it all and remain the Good Mother, is that even if she stayed home, according to attachment studies, she still had a one-in-three chance of fostering a bad attachment.[39]

That same mother must have positively developed vertigo when she began to read, toward the end of the 1980s, that day care could actually be *good* for her child. *Parents* magazine advised that while it is best for a mother to stay home, especially for the first year of a child's life, "studies have shown that a well-run day care experience" produces children who are less shy, more socially adept, and more cooperative with adults.[40] The attachment experts had finally actually studied their own precepts and found them to be false.

## THE NEW "RISK": INFANT DAY CARE

As quality day care turned out not to be so harmful after all, advisers in the late 1980s tended to restrict their warnings to mothers who work during the child's infancy. Now a new cautionary tale emerged, alleging harm done to *infants* in day care. In 1986 developmental psychologist Jay Belsky claimed his research showed that infants under twelve months and even under twenty-four months who experience more than twenty hours per week of day care are "at risk" for insecure attachment to their mothers and greater aggressiveness and noncompliance in early childhood.[41] While this study has now been criticized by many other researchers, Belsky was making the rounds of talk shows before the study was even published and occasioned a burst of newspaper and magazine articles with his contention that nonmaternal infant care was psychologically unsafe.[42] Among the problems with Belsky's study was his contention that the infants who experienced day care showed significantly more "insecure-avoidant" (i.e., "bad") attachment than infants kept at home with their mothers. But, in fact, there was a normal percentage of attachment types among the infants who attended day care.[43] However, because Belsky compared them to a group that had a higher than average percent of "securely" attached children, the discrepancy between the secure and the insecure in the two groups looked bigger. Moreover, some critics of Belsky contended that "insecure-avoidant" attachment could simply be evidence of independence and familiarity with encountering strangers. (See chapter 6 for Belsky's most recent study.)

Headline-grabbing studies such as Belsky's, the continual preaching from the baby gurus, and the chorus from parenting and women's magazines are proof of how firmly entrenched attachment theory has become. But how trustworthy is all this research? The alert reader who has taken note of the ready expansion and contradictions of the bonding and attachment period—now thought to be located somewhere between birth and the child's first three years of life—will be wondering how to draw any solid conclusions from such changeable evidence.

## MAKING SENSE OF ATTACHMENT RESEARCH

While the bonding research was so poorly conducted that it has been referred to as "pseudoscience,"[44] the problems of this paradigm are not dissimilar to more general problems in psychological research, which is, pardon the term, in its infancy. Research on bonding and attachment is a patchwork of varied and nonmatching studies. The realities of doing social science research greatly limit the number of factors that can be accounted for in any one study and also limit the likelihood that researchers will study the same consistent phenomena. Thus, in researching attachment, for example, one study may assess thirty middle-class married mothers and their fifteen-month-old infants in a day care center. Another study with the same research design may look at twenty-five single mothers of diverse socioeconomic backgrounds and their eighteen-month-old infants; and another may look at twenty divorced, impoverished mothers and their two-year-olds. (It is quite possible that the mother's marital and socioeconomic status will affect her relationship with her child, due to variations in her resources, anxiety level, availability to her child, and so forth.) Therefore, none of these studies could really corroborate the others, since some important variables have altered them. Moreover, the outcome of any social science study is rarely clear. A responsible researcher drawing conclusions should take care to limit them to a very specific group of people who are just like the ones they have studied. Human relationships are highly complex, changing over time and in different situations. To determine that regular proximity to a caregiver causes social, emotional, and cognitive characteristics in a child that are part of a constantly interacting web of factors is difficult. No study incorporates all the important interacting factors, so each one provides, at best, a fragment of the picture.

## RESEARCH PRINCIPLES

Should the layperson attempt to decode attachment research by reading the actual studies for themselves, an overview of research principles may be useful. One of the most highly esteemed forms of research in the social sciences and medicine, for example, is the experiment designed to determine whether one phenomenon actually causes another. This is presumably the kind of study Kennell and Klaus conducted. To find a cause-and-effect relationship between bonding and postpartum separation, for example, one would most logically begin with two groups of mothers who were exactly the same except for the bonding experience. In the *experimental* group, one factor or "variable" would be changed: in this case, the factor that we hypothesize will cause the "effect" (bad mothering), i.e., the mother's separation from her infant. The *control* group would have had their babies with them after birth, the experimental group would have experienced prolonged separation. If we found that the experimental group turned out to be, on the average, worse mothers, then we would have some evidence to suggest that the separation contributed to bad mothering, since that was the only difference between the two groups. You can already foresee the problems with this conclusion. If you're dealing with a small group of mothers, let's say fourteen, the presence of just one woman who just happened to be a bad mother for whatever reason, will drag down the score of whichever group she is in. In other words, it's difficult to draw broad conclusions based on a small number of study subjects.

This brings us to the next matter—there are so many variables that could account for differences in mothering that it is nearly impossible to account for them all and to distinguish their effect from the effect of separation. One way to soften the comparative significance of those "confounding" variables is to have a bigger sample. If you have one thousand mothers in each group, and the experimental group has more "bad" mothers, it is more likely that the separation from new-

borns caused the inferior mothering because all the confounding variables in each group are more likely to average each other out. In fact,
researchers can conduct a statistical test that tells you, based on your
sample size and the number of variables you are assessing, what the
probability is of something other that your experimental factor causing the effect. They might say the results are "significant at the .05
level" meaning that there are only five chances in a hundred that the
inferior mothering happened by chance instead of as an effect of the
separation. Another difficulty in such research is the interpretation of
results. Who decides who's a "bad" mother, anyway? And who decides whether a child's qualities are learned or innate? We're on shifting sands here.

Of course there are many nonexperimental forms of research in
psychology, too, and they are used to find correlations rather than to
establish cause and effect. Surveys and interviews, for example, are
common kinds of studies that are especially useful for counting people's opinions or determining specific, quantifiable data, such as
whether they are employed, use a day care center, and so forth. Another kind of study is the observational study, in which people are observed perhaps at home or in a day care center. Usually these studies
focus on specific behaviors—for example, children's aggression in a
day care center. Counting the number of aggressive acts a child com-
mits, whether she initiates the aggression, how the caregivers respond
or intervene, would all be recorded, revealing profiles of the children
or certain dynamics of teacher-child interaction. Often several methods are combined. The Kennell and Klaus bonding study was an experiment, but it also used an interview and observation of a pediatric
visit.

Most research in the social sciences is very limited. It deals with just
a few variables pertaining to a small subgroup of people at a specific
point in time. Thus, any valid conclusions must be extremely limited.
When we begin to look at research on bonding and attachment,
things become complicated. When the independent variable is something as complex and changing as "day care" or "maternal care," any
claims for cause and effect must be seriously questioned. Moreover,
the bonding/attachment research is so powerfully linked to deeply
held values that the very questions asked reveal a ready-made bias.
Asking a mother if she left her month-old baby with a caregiver and

giving her a score of "0" if she went out without feeling guilty is one example. And the notable absence of fathers, of course, clearly distorts every bonding/attachment study, since fathers have very important relationships with their young children.[45] *Caveat emptor* must be the motto of any parent looking to this research for guidelines in child rearing.[46]

## IS INFANCY A CRITICAL PERIOD?

One of the reasons attachment theory has gained such currency is the assumption that infancy is a critical period: If the right things don't happen during that time, you can't make them happen later. It is assumed that a deprived infant will grow up to be a disturbed adult. Bowlby began, after all, as a psychoanalyst working with disturbed and delinquent children. The first research he conducted compared juvenile thieves to a normal group of children. Bowlby concluded that the thieves were more often separated from their mothers in early life, and those who had been separated were more likely to be "affectionless."[47] Of course, losing their mothers also meant the kids were more likely to have had unstable early caregiving. Moreover, like Bowlby's war orphans, these boys had all kinds of deficits in their lives—abandonment by their fathers, poverty, the influence of criminal peers and adults, and so forth. Bowlby concluded, however, the cause of their delinquency was maternal deprivation.

Does what happens in infancy predict later behavior? To explore this assertion, we must approach it from two angles.[48] One is the matter of how we develop from children to adults. There is little consistent evidence that what happens to us in early childhood predicts what we will be like in adolescence, our twenties, forties, sixties, or old age. When you think about yourself in those various life stages, you probably see that in some way there is a core of you that remains the same, and many things that change dramatically depending on your experiences and what you learn from them. A stressful experience in early childhood does not necessarily produce a weakened adult—it might even make for an adult who is strengthened by what she learned from the experience. People respond very differently to events in their lives. And when you think about that constant core, you may even find yourself thinking about something distinct from your experiences—something that you were born with—a personality, a temperament, a unique identity.

On the other hand, severe experiences in the early years can, of course, distort and limit further growth. The human brain is developing very rapidly in the first few years of life and an optimal environment certainly promotes optimal growth, establishing a foundation for the rest of life. A child who has been abused in infancy has trouble consciously remembering what happened, partly because her brain was not sufficiently developed at the time of the trauma. She had no way to reflect on the experience. A child who does not learn language in childhood may never be able to learn it in adulthood because the brain requires linguistic stimulation at a distinct period of maturation to develop the capacity to process language. But these examples are extreme and hopefully rare. Most children's experience is within a fairly wide normal range. Moreover, humans are abundantly resilient. Even people with serious brain anomalies often defy prediction regarding their later competencies. Not surprisingly, the attempt to predict later behavior from early attachment quality has so far failed because it is impossible to disentangle attachment from more general conditions. Some studies that followed infants into later childhood have found some consistency between early attachment and later child development, but it appears the consistency is the product of the child's innate characteristics combined with an emotional environment that doesn't change much from year to year. Early secure attachment itself does not even predict later attachment, let alone all the global characteristics said to be associated with attachment.[49]

If, in spite of the lack of confirmation to date, there is some relationship between attachment and a better childhood or adulthood, it's very hard to prove for several reasons. For one thing, it's difficult to follow the same subjects over a long time period. Funding for a study that goes on for seventy years is hard to find, as is the researcher who can wait for seventy years to publish her results, and the subject who remains interested and hasn't lived everywhere from Atlanta to Kalamazoo in the course of her lifetime. Even if such a luxury of time did exist, there is another big hurdle in this research. How do you measure good attachment in infancy? In adolescence? In adulthood? And how would you distinguish its influence from the myriad other factors such as intelligence, quality of schooling, social status, talent, income, and luck? Moreover, how do you define good relationships and the contribution of attachment to them? These are questions far more complex than attachment theory can accommodate. Yet battalions of researchers seem undaunted by these reservations in their enthusiasm to measure the relative health of relationships built on motherlove.

## MEASURING ATTACHMENT: A HOUSE OF CARDS

Ainsworth's Strange Situation Test (SST) became the yardstick by which a virtual army of researchers have measured and compared the quality of mothering in every conceivable situation from day care to life in the !Kung bush. Unfortunately, this yardstick has proven quite faulty in its calibrations. The test, so long considered a gold standard in attachment research, has now been used all over the world and the proportion of "secure" and "insecure" infants changes with each culture. In north Germany, for instance (but not south Germany), more than half the infants are classified as "insecure-avoidant." This suggests that factors other than mom's capabilities have a strong effect on children's behavior. It's also clear that babies who have experience with separation will respond very differently to this test. In Japan, for example, where infants have had very little experience with separation from their mother, and in the traditional Israeli kibbutz, where infants have had very little experience with strangers, they are markedly distressed by the SST and show high rates of "insecure attachment."[50] Moreover, children who attend day care are used to daily separations from their mothers and may therefore appear less emotionally upset by the SST. We cannot rightly conclude that the security of their relationship with their mothers is inferior—the babies may just be used to strangers. It could be that the Strange Situation Test is just measuring a child's reaction to stress. Moreover, some researchers believe the behavior Ainsworth calls "insecure-avoidant" is actually autonomy or independence. Perhaps the child on reunion with his mother doesn't need to be held by her. It is also possible that an "avoidant" infant could really just be a placid, friendly baby. Moreover, a "secure" baby could really be dependent and even spoiled. Also researchers have discovered that the behavior they observe in a laboratory may have little to do with children's behavior at home.

Furthermore, when family circumstances change, so too does behavior in the Strange Situation.

Another fundamental problem with the Strange Situation Test is that it doesn't take into account the infant's own characteristics. Some babies are good-natured and easygoing, others may be sick or cranky, shy or extroverted, stubborn or compliant, and all these factors are going to interact with caretakers who also have different personalities. A very expressive and active caretaker might overwhelm an infant with a low tolerance for stimulation; and few caretakers can do "well" with a very irritable baby. Clearly, children express their security in relationships in different ways. Some like to stay close but do not want to be held, some want a lot of cuddling, and some are happy when wandering away but like to have a lot of conversation and attention from their parents. The balance between exploring the world and maintaining safe contact is maintained in a rich and subtle variety of ways by different parent-child pairs. How much any individual child will request these different kinds of contact will also vary with how he or she is feeling (the degree to which she is tired or frustrated, for example) and with the developmental stage.

At this point, we need to do more than question the validity of attachment research. We need to ask ourselves, why we are pathologizing the mother-infant relationship. Virtually every attachment study rests on the assumption that mothers must supply the nurturing that fosters attachment, and the Strange Situation Test is designed to look for deficits in that relationship. The threat of early behavior producing psychopathology drives much of the concern about the strictures of attachment. However, there is little evidence that insecure behavior as measured in the Strange Situation reflects pathology. In fact, the test does not appear to register even severe pathologies. For example, autistic children, who are virtually unable to form or manifest loving relationships, do not differ from normal children in their Strange Situation behavior![51] What is reflected in the SST is simply a normal range of human behaviors.

Some researchers have moved beyond the SST to measure attachment. However, the same value judgments about mothers as the prime architects of children's behavior are still a problem with other tests, and clearly there are many, many factors beyond the quality of mother-child relationship that account for differences in children. In fact, some research shows infants and toddlers prefer their mothers as attachment figures only about 60 percent of the time and often continue to like several people at once. Infants clearly develop attachments with close friends and family as well as paid caregivers. In fact, there is also research that suggests that infants with a disturbed or very unhappy parent thrive with a close attachment to a paid caregiver.[52]

## MATERNAL INSTINCT AND GOOD MOTHERING

What scientific rationale do researchers have for focusing so narrowly on mothers when they study attachment? It all goes back to Darwin and the concept of instincts. When researchers think about attachment they think about goslings and imprinting and imagine they are observing a well-known law of nature. But let's look for a moment at this law. Baby animals can imprint on inanimate objects (Styrofoam objects, cloth-and-wire surrogates, bouncing balls, television sets, and so forth). These objects can hardly be considered appropriate to meet animals' needs, yet they attach to them. Even more dramatic is that both animal young and human infants remain attached to their abusers.[53] As scientists continue to study the behavior of animals, they reveal how very complex is this behavior we call an instinct.*

Psychologists automatically assume that attachment is good because it has helped us to survive. But this, too, could be debated. A behavior that was adaptive in one environment might not be so in a contemporary one. Birds that evolved to peck at food under bark also fly into houses where they peck wallpaper, lampshades, and other objects that do not give them food and may even lead to an untimely death. Babies develop fear of strangers at about nine months. This

---

*The phenomenon of maternal postpartum bonding, for instance, does not occur for all species, but it is most pronounced in ungulates—hooved animals. Yet slight variations in environment can dramatically alter even their behavior. The bonding of goats, which Klaus found so illuminating, occurs primarily in barnyard goats and is really a matter of "olfactory labeling." When the kid is separated from its mother for a few minutes, the mother smells the scent of another animal on her infant and concludes the kid belongs to that animal. In the close-herd situation of the barnyard, she rejects the offspring because she doesn't want to get into a custody battle with a fellow mother. On the other hand, some free-ranging ungulates will actively adopt a newborn not their own. This makes survival sense in a wild environment where a stray baby needs immediate care to survive and its biological mother could be miles away. (P. Klopfer, "Mother Love: What Turns It On? Studies of Maternal Arousal and Attachment in Ungulates May Have Implications for Man," American Scientist 59 [July/August, 1971]: pp. 404–407.)

may have been useful in our earlier environment, but it is now as likely to hinder desirable social interactions as to facilitate development. Earlier in our evolution, it is likely that families remained in close proximity throughout an individual's life, rather than spreading over the planet as they are increasingly doing. Close and long-lasting family bonds were probably essential for survival then, but now different conditions prevail. For these reasons, any suggestion that a particular type of relationship is to be preferred over another because it is "natural" is suspect.[54]

One more problem with the instinct notion is that humans have language and a highly complex culture. Areas of our behavior that are profoundly influenced by our biology are, from the first moments of life, shaped by this culture. We know, for example, that if you show the same film of the same infant to two groups of people, they will describe the baby in completely different ways depending on whether you have told them the film is of a boy or girl baby. If they are told the baby is a girl, viewers assert her crying shows she is frightened. If they believe they are watching a boy, his crying is said to show he is angry. The biological fact of sex difference is immediately shaped by the stamp of culture.[55]

The ways that scientists interpret data about biological bases of behavior are not neutral. In fact, they are often interpreted in a way that rationalizes the status quo, indicating that the inferior status of certain groups is due to some inherent flaw rather than human injustice. For instance, at the turn of the century, led by sociologist Herbert Spencer, many people interpreted Darwin's theory of evolution to mean that poor people were poor because they were the least fit to survive. The new millionaires and robber barons, who had come under considerable criticism, were really the evolutionary cream that rose to the top. The poor simply hadn't adapted successfully to the environment, so we should stop trying to help them and just let them die out as nature intended.[56] A contemporary version of that self-serving nonsense is the assertion of Charles Murray and Richard Herrnstein that African Americans are less intelligent than white or Asian people due to genetic inferiority and that their low IQ leads to social pathology—poverty, welfare dependency, out-of-wedlock births, and crime.[57] (See chapter 1.) The Bell Curve contention has been heard throughout the history of social science, beginning with the nineteenth-century version of biological determinism—craniometry.

Using a variety of measures of skull size and shape, the races and sexes were ranked with the (surprise!) white man on the top and the women of each "race" always lower than the men of each race.[58]

In the 1970s, when the feminist movement was exposing the oppression of women in our society, sociobiology was used to rationalize inequality and injustice, especially regarding women. Sociobiology claims that humans have certain genetic tendencies, such as territoriality, male aggression, and female passivity, which are necessary because they are adaptive. One sociobiologist, for example, even claimed that rapists, while misguided, could easily be understood as just following a necessary law of nature in which men must dominate women if the species is to reproduce successfully. Rapists are just trying to get their genes into the gene pool.[59]

Once again, like craniometry, social Darwinism, and sociobiology, contemporary interpretations of biological bases of behavior provide the comfortable message that injustices and inequalities are natural and inevitable accomplices of human evolution, providing confirmation for those who find comfort in the status quo and its legitimation by science. The research on attachment serves a similar function. By interpreting it to mean that women are best suited to take care of their own children alone, it helps rationalize the lack of support for our impoverished mothers and children by suggesting that women's only necessary reward in caring for their children is satisfaction of their instinctual nature. Like the bonding notion that co-opted the natural childbirth movement, keeping birth in the hospitals, midwives out, and the obstetricians in charge of an increasingly surgical birth, attachment helps to co-opt the power of the working mother by seeming to make her of critical importance during the preschool period when institutions would otherwise have to change to accommodate her. The owners of businesses, the leaders of government, need only listen to the attachment theorists to hear the comforting notion that they don't have to support families, and that they don't have to pay for child care because biology dictates that instinct will do the work for free.

## BEYOND ATTACHMENT

Attachment is not an adequate framework for understanding the developmental significance of parent-child relationships. Security is just one dimension of such relationships. They also differ in mutual warmth and the mutual expression of affection; they differ in frequency of conflict; in shared involvement in daily activities; shared communication about feelings; shared humor; the ability to sustain a line of communication; and they also differ in the pattern of power and control—not just parental control but also control by children. Moreover, the qualities of parents as teachers, playmates, and caregivers are not separate from the apparent ability to give their child security, as orthodox attachment theory claims.

Attachment theory misses essential aspects of the strength and variety of parent-child relationships. Using attachment to define good mothering also misses the fact that parents relate to each of their children differently. Even orthodox attachment studies show that more than a third of siblings have a different attachment status from their brothers or sisters. The same parent can find one child congenial, another difficult; a parent can have a relationship with one child in which humor is the key theme and a relationship with another in which intellectual curiosity is the prime connection. Parents usually respond differently to their children based on gender as well, with girls getting more cuddling and boys more playful affection, for example. Parents and children also differ greatly on the dimension of control and discipline; and they differ in cognitive sophistication and verbal ability. All of these factors differ with the age of the child. Moreover, things that are going on at different times in the adult world—marital difficulties, satisfaction with work, financial problems, and so forth—can profoundly affect parent-child relationships at various times so that a relationship might feel good at one time, troubled at another. The concept of attachment is simply inadequate to capture the range of socioemotional influences that comprise the foundation of children's developing capacity for trusting relationships.

## THE VELCRO OF POP-PSYCH IDEAS

One of the appeals of attachment/bonding theory is the simplicity of the idea. It is a concept everyone can readily grasp—put two people together and you have a relationship. It seems like a kind of social Velcro. Everyone can visualize bonding and attachment. The notion that these processes are instant and automatic adds to their appeal; at least there is one area of life—the relationship of mothers and children—that is secure and predictable. The broadness and simplicity of the concept also make it a convenient and scientific-sounding framework for examining other kinds of relationships. In fact, the meaning has been stretched so far that attachment research has become like a one-size-fits-all garment: just about all relationship phenomena can be fit into it, but it successfully fits none of them.

Attachment is now used to assess every aspect of human relations, from the mother-infant dyad, to styles of coping with the Gulf War, adult's love of each other, people's love of their pets, people's patriotism, business management techniques, and people's choice of religion. See, for instance: "Attachment Styles, Coping Strategies, and Post-traumatic Psychological Distress: The Impact of the Gulf War in Israel";[60] "Attachment Styles and the 'Big Five' Personality Traits: Their Connections with Each Other and with Romantic Relationship Outcomes";[61] "Psychology, Human Violence, and the Search for Peace" (which explores the relationship of early attachment to patriotism);[62] "Attachment to Pets Among Eighth Graders";[63] "Attachment-Detachment and Non-Attachment" (which hypothesizes that the pursuit of Eastern spiritual practices by many Westerners is often driven by a disturbance in their attachments).[64]

If we allow that these articles may comprise the fringes of attachment research, a look at the more traditional attachment territory provides no comfort to the rational reader, the persecuted mother, or the parent who is buckling under the weight of college tuition that goes to pay for such research. The more mainstream attachment terrain involves research on animal instinct, mothering of children, mothering of fetuses, illnesses and mental illnesses caused by bad mothering, and child abuse caused by bad mothering. For example there is: "Mother-Daughter Bonds in Sheep";[65] "Maternal-Infant Bonding and Pediatric Asthma";[66] "Factor Analysis of the Maternal Fetal Attachment Scale";[67] "Parent-Child Interaction in the Etiology of Dependent and Self-Critical Depression";[68] "The Relationship Between Parental Attachment and Eating Disorders";[69] "Borderline Disorder and Attachment Pathology";[70] "Application of Attachment Theory to the Study of Sexual Abuse";[71] "Support Seeking and Support Giving Within

Couples in an Anxiety-Provoking Situation: The Role of Attachment Styles."[72] Well, actually, the distinction between fringe and mainstream is muddy.

Attachment, in fact, is often psychobabble pseudoscience clogging the research journals and draining your tax and tuition dollars. One of my favorite such specimens is: "Psychophysiology in Attachment Interviews: Converging Evidence for Deactivating Strategies" which finds that "individuals [adults] employing deactivating attachment strategies [avoiding the researcher's personal questions] experience conflict or inhibition [activity on an electroencephalograph] during the "Adult Attachment [quality of romantic relationships in college students] Interview."[73] Untroubled by the complexities or verities of such research, however, the psychopediatric priesthood continues to prescribe its homilies about bonding/attachment to mothers who invariably end up in mommy court defending themselves against the inevitable allegations of failing to abide by the Alice in Wonderland rules. Let me emphasize once again that the ministers are well meaning and often do have useful advice for parents. Wise parents, however, will treat their advice the same way they would follow the wisdom of Aunt Minnie or Grandma Ellen—they must correct for personalities. Advisers have their own character, quirks, perspectives, and biases.

Clinical psychologists, for instance, work with troubled children; developmental psychologists map age-related behaviors; pediatricians promote children's health: Each has a peculiar point of view or bias. Clinical child psychologists spend most of their time with children who are unable to concentrate, who constantly fight and break things, who hurt themselves—children who are seriously disturbed. These psychologists are trained to understand such emotional pathology. So their advice is often based on trying to prevent the serious distress they see so much of. When these psychologists give parenting advice about bonding/attachment, they have those very troubled children in mind. Yet such problems occur for only a small number of severely disturbed children who as often suffer from congenital problems as from problems caused by a troubled family system.

Developmental psychologists see children through a biological growth model in which the earliest period of life often directly determines later behavior. All children are generally seen to conform to age-related norms where one type of child is considered normal and all other types are considered deviations from the normal. Developmental psychologists put tremendous emphasis on infancy, sometimes imbuing very minute aspects of infant behavior with great importance because the critical-period concept is driving their concern.

Pediatricians are trained to care for the physical problems of children. Parents, however, ask them about all kinds of behavioral and emotional matters, as mind and body are hardly separate and the doctor is a respected authority. Pediatricians are often faced with problems that are far beyond their capacity to alter: children's behavior disorders, learning problems, dysfunctional family relationships, poverty, substance abuse, and mental illness. Therefore, they draw on the works of the child psychologists and dispense them as they would the prescriptions they have been trained to write. Unfortunately, there are very few psychological principles that work as well or as predictably as Tylenol or erythromycin.

Like the character of our aunts and grandmothers, then, these parental advisers have their own limiting and distorting tendencies that must be corrected for. There is one thing we can count on, however: they are most likely steeped in an ideology of motherhood that views women as the main source of their children's troubles.* The "discovery" of attachment, it must be emphasized, was not occasioned by any bad mothering. The phenomenon became apparent *only* when the practices of institutions, run by (mostly male) doctors and guided by psychologists, violated the fundamental relationship needs of children. The policies of hospitals, orphanages, and nurseries were based on bad psychological theories and fostered sheer neglect. Those institutionalized infants suffered dramatically from the deprivation of human love. Yet our psychologists and pediatricians continue to focus their search for the source of children's troubles in

---

*The maternal attachment theory as scientific "fact" can have many serious repercussions in our society. Consider the example of Baby Jessica, who for two and a half years was suspended between the would-be adoptive parents in Michigan who reared her and the parents in Iowa who gave birth to her and wanted her back. The Iowa parents eventually won custody of their birth daughter and experts predicted life-damaging attachment trauma for Jessica. But eight months later, the unhappy scenario had never materialized—she did not seem traumatized, did not cry, did not have trouble eating or sleeping. She did not regress. In fact, it appears she may have adjusted rather easily and is now Anna Jacqueline Schmidt. (Michele Ingrassia and Karen Springen, "She's Not Baby Jessica Anymore," Newsweek, March 21, 1994, pp. 60+.) Although we can't draw broad conclusions from this single famous case, it does suggest that we shouldn't make decisions regarding a child's welfare based solely on unproven theory.

the behavior of their mothers. By putting the spotlight on maternal attachment rather than the truly damaging effects of the grossly inadequate American child care patchwork, our psychopediatric priesthood has betrayed mothers and children.

## ATTACHMENT AND ADOPTION

The concept of attachment has become a tool for simplifying the moral dilemmas faced by social workers and the legal system. Decisions about adoption and foster care are a case in point. At its best, the broad concept of attachment is one of several key factors used in making decisions about a child's future. Attachment has become a priority factor only since the late 1970s and is responsible for a shift in policy that more often makes foster parents the preferred adoptive parents. Social workers now recognize that the continuity of a relationship is very important to infants and toddlers. Another related factor in decision making is the recognition that permanence is important, whether it is with the biological family, a relative, or long-term foster care. A third major factor to be considered in placing children is kinship, whether this refers to an ethnic or racial group or close biologically related people. For most children in need of placement, these factors are in conflict and must be weighed against each other.

For example, a nine-month-old child is taken from a neglecting, drug-addicted homeless mother.[74] She is a difficult child, given to hair-pulling temper tantrums and eating difficulties. She is placed in care with foster parents who are skilled with troubled children and do well with her. Six months after the child is taken from her mother, the maternal grandmother, who lives in another state, makes a bid for adoption. This bid languishes in the social service system for three months. In the meantime, the foster parents have made a request to formally adopt the child. The maternal grandmother obtains a lawyer and sues for custody. When the child is two years old the case goes to court. How does one make a just decision about custody? Wouldn't attachment theorists say the child is attached to the foster mother and will be severely traumatized if separated? And wouldn't they claim the grandmother is a bad mother because her daughter became a drug addict? If the grandmother adopts the child, there is always the possibility that the grandmother will return the child to her biological mother (to whom the child is bonded?). But what if the grandmother is forty-two years old, wealthy, and a community leader and her husband owns a toy company or is principal of a school? The foster parents are poor and uneducated. Such decisions are very complex and burdensome to those who must make them. There is a growing tendency in some regions of the country to see attachment as the paramount factor in placement. Using an attachment "test" loosely based on the Strange Situation Test, decisions are increasingly made that view the child as unable to adapt to a new relationship. While the presumed moral authority of science relieves these officials of the burden of uncertainty, such decisions may not be in the best interests of the child.

## CONCLUSION

In fact, it is the moral authority of science that is in question here. It is something we must no longer take for granted. Researchers must be held accountable to the women and children they investigate because they simply cannot afford the luxury of their prejudices. The distorted attachment model I've just described may seem like a weird fairy tale, but it is only one example of how the social and behavioral sciences provide a rich template on which to organize all the mother bashing. When the research spotlight attempts to illuminate the complex problems of modern family life, it should come as no surprise that mothers are singled out and found wanting. In fact, research on the family provides a stack of allegations that non-Nelsonian mothering is really deviant. And yet, embedded within all the indictments is clear evidence of mothers' innocence.

I fear, after all this evidence of distortion and prejudice, the maternal reader may still be filled with guilt and self-doubt. She may be ruminating, "Well, perhaps attachment is something of a myth, perhaps the researchers have been swayed by ideology, but still, doesn't my work outside the home damage my children in some way? And what about those of us who are single mothers, teenage mothers, divorced mothers, poor and welfare mothers? We've failed to give our children the Ozzie-and-Harriet dream. Aren't most of us really guilty of failing our children?" Like the evidence for attachment, the reader is about to discover that the evidence against the "deviant mother" is also a frame-up.

# Deviant Mothers

Those saviors of the family who devote themselves to the august endeavor of social science research seem to expect that mothers cause most of the problems of family life. They investigate "single-mother" families, "employed-mother" families, "adolescent-mother" families, "welfare-mother" families, and the mothers of divorced or "disrupted" families—searching methodically for the damage these mothers cause to their children by having deviated from the Ozzie-and-Harriet ideal. But even the hearth angel does not escape their accusations—she, apparently, is the cause of everything from cognitive deficits in her preschoolers to every imaginable sort of psychopathology. (So far, researchers have forgotten to accuse her of putting her children "at risk" for poverty, since when she divorces or fails to secure a husband she will almost certainly be poor unless she has a good earning record.)

In spite of the tendency to see most mothers as deviant, the family has changed—not just in America, but everywhere.[1] We would be far better served if the academic Sherlock Holmeses were searching for clues as to what makes these varied families function well. There are now a dozen "typical" family arrangements that are perfectly good for children: Mothers should not feel guilty if they are working, divorced, remarried, never married, cohabiting, lesbian, living with parents, are grandmothers acting as mothers, are foster mothers, are on welfare, or are even teens. All such mothers are legitimate and prevalent types of parent. Sixty-two percent of mothers of children under six work for wages.[2] Single mothers head close to 30 percent of families with one child under eighteen.[3] Within five years of divorcing, 60 percent of single parents are either cohabiting or remarried so 11 percent of children live with a stepparent.[4] At least 44 percent of single mothers have been "welfare mothers."[5] I could go on, but the point is—Harriet is really not around much anymore. Moralists claim these figures represent the corruption and disintegration of our society and that everything should be done to rehabilitate the Nelson model of family life. Could they be right? Let's see what the advice and research industry can tell us.

## A WORKING MOTHER'S EXPERIENCE

If we are talking about sheer numbers, working mothers are certainly the norm (about 76 percent) among these mother "types." Is there evidence that they are depriving their children by working? The advice industry, which presumably draws on research findings, suggests she is quite a problem. In the 1980s and '90s, the working mother is usually portrayed wearing a three-piece suit and toting an executive briefcase (even though she's most likely to be a secretary, clerk, teacher, or nurse—so maternal readers will automatically feel inadequate, since less than 7 percent are in the executive class). This supermom is always distraught, crumbling under the weight of a briefcase that drags one of her hands toward the ground as her baby wriggles out of the other hand and slides down her tightly skirted hip. Her fatigue and exasperation are attributed to her inability to gracefully balance work and family. Mothers who stay at home with their children, on the other hand, are counseled to take it easy in their attacks on this working mother in what the magazine industry has dubbed the "mommy wars"—mothers slinging the Bad Mother label at each other based on their employment status. These "wars," of course, are fueled by parenting and women's magazines, which are filled with double messages about working mothers and whether they should be classified as Good or Bad.

The psychological experts undergirding the 'zines are so reluctant to give up their old construction of the Good Mother (even though mothers are further than ever from wearing their ideological corset) that their psychobabble bunches up into doublespeak as they waver between a new paradigm demanded by the realities of mothers' lives and their stay-at-home bread and butter who was such a good listener. For example, in *McCall's,* a well-known psychologist and parenting expert, Ron Taffel, Ph.D., writes a column called "The Confident Parent" (who never seems to be a guy) subtitled "The Real Trouble with Working Mothers."[6] Taffel begins the piece with an anecdote about his own mother's return to work when he was ten years old— he resented it and wanted to make her feel guilty. He says that now, after talking to parents and kids for twenty years as a therapist, he has discovered five basic truths. The first is that women usually work for the "right" reasons—they need the money. They're not doing it, he says, for "a glitzy career." (Do consider becoming a nun or a street cleaner if you want the approval of this psychologist.) He concludes that there are, of course, mothers who "know themselves well and recognize that if they don't work, they'll drive themselves and their kids crazy." (They just can't restrain their sinful impulses.) To further baffle the working mother, Taffel then points out that kids don't always know what's best for them, so even if they seem distressed by mothers' working, this is not necessarily bad. (So if your kids *aren't* upset, you're damaging them?) Finally, we learn what is "the real trouble with working mothers." What's bad, he says, is that so many mothers don't have enough support from their husbands, and this causes them stress, and it is working mothers' subsequent stress from being overburdened that is what really hurts kids. (Working mothers *will* damage their kids—*of course!* It's not those stress-producing *fathers* who are at fault, though—do they read these columns?) And cleverly, it is *mothers' stress,* not their *job,* that is at fault. After all, who could argue with their "need and right" to hold a job—certainly not an adviser who doesn't want to offend the majority of his (working) constituency.

Should the scrambled brain of the maternal reader still be open to the search for affirming psychological verities, short circuits may be heard to sputter and snap when she glances at the series on "attachment parenting" in *Mothering.*[7] Psychologist Paul Klein quotes John Bowlby, in "one of the last interviews of his life," as saying that mothers should be responsible for their own children—they should be the principal caregiver. (This apparently leaves out dads, extended family, nannies, and day care.) Attachment is a biological survival mechanism that is universal, it forms the foundation for all social relationships and requires an empathically responsive mother. A baby, according to Klein, is "an indivisible part of a large psychobiological mother-child unit." The prematurely separated child caused by the "parent who repeatedly fails to respond to a particular self-object demand" may "begin to deny his relational needs and internalize mistrust and anger instead of affection and empathy." (Babbling is not the sole privilege of babies.) The author does not say whether mothers should work or not work (fathers are clearly only pinch hitters), but once again the threat of "partial psychopaths" is attributed to faulty *mother*-child attachment.

Should the working mother still be capable of reading anything more on the subject of her likely damage to her children, she may decide to skip the experts and see what other mothers have to say. *Child,* in a special issue entitled "To Work or Not to Work, How to Make Your Choice Work for Your Child," provides a survey of mothers who work and those who stay at home. They find, "It's not so much which path you take that makes a difference in how you feel about yourself, but the attitude you have about that path." If that doesn't clarify matters, in the same issue, they've thought to provide you with a look at how kids feel about their mothers working. The reader will discover that beneath a child's painful sense of loss (when her mother goes to work) is a primal fear of not surviving the separation. On the other hand, as kids grow, "they don't like mothers who hover over them."[8]

Will somebody *please* give me a straight answer! Perhaps a look at a typical real-life working mother will provide some perspective for gaining insight into the factors influencing the mental health of children and their working mothers.

## WENDY WORKHOLME

Wendy Workholme will serve as our working mother prototype.* Wendy works thirty hours a week as a computer and software trainer

---

*This composite portrait is based on Census Bureau information about average wages and job characteristics; a portrait of a working mother reported in* Child. *(Sara Nelson, "Four Women Share Their Strategies for Success,"* Child, *May 1994, pp. 84+; and miscellaneous interviews with working mothers.)*

at August College, making $14,227 a year. Her husband, Bob, is an operations analyst for Fairweather Insurance Company, a full-time job paying $29,421 annually. They have owned their own home, which cost $63,000, for two years. They have two children, a four-year-old girl, Amy, and a twenty-one-month-old girl, Anna. Wendy stayed home for the first six months after Amy was born, even though it meant losing her job at Maple County Hospital. She felt breast-feeding was very important and when she returned to work, she expressed her breast milk into bottles for Amy for the next six months. Then she found another job at the college and luckily, Anna was born in June, at the end of the academic year. The college could do without her until the fall, so she was able to stay home for three months and keep her job as well. Amy was first cared for by a neighbor, Mrs. Hart, whom she seemed to love. Mrs. Hart moved away when Amy was two, and she then went to Mrs. Apple, who also cared for her own son, Benjy, at home. The first few days, Amy cried at Mrs. Apple's and wanted to go home. But soon she seemed to enjoy going there and playing with Benjy, who was about her age.

At the college, Wendy shares an office with another part-timer, a woman who works for the registrar down the hall. They have separate desks but must share a phone and the computer. Wendy feels that she is not taken very seriously as a member of the staff, is not included in important meetings or in decision making, even though the work she does gives her an important perspective. However, she loves the problem-solving and teaching aspects of her work, and the sense of worth that comes from receiving a salary.

Wendy and Bob arise every weekday at 6:00 A.M. and usually get the children bathed and into bed around 8:30 or 9:00 P.M. They have two cars, one five years old, the other eight, and it seems every six weeks or so, one car has to be in the shop. So their transportation ends up taking one of them close to four hours a day. They take turns dropping off Amy at the Sprouts day care center. Wendy takes her Monday, Wednesday, and Friday, because on Tuesday and Thursday she has to stay home until the graduate student arrives to care for Anna. The student, who depends on a ride, can't get there until 8:30 or 9:00 A.M. On Mondays and Wednesdays, in addition to taking Amy to Sprouts, Wendy also takes Anna to the home of Mrs. Apple, who cares for Anna along with Benjy and her own new infant, Jessica. The trip takes between fifty minutes and an hour and twenty minutes, depending on traffic and social interactions. Bob doesn't usually leave work until 6:00 P.M. so Wendy is also the one who picks up Amy and Anna at day care, getting home about a half hour before Bob. On Fridays, Wendy takes Amy to Sprouts and Anna to her mother's house in the morning as she teaches an hour-long class at the college. (Wendy's mother also works but is free on Fridays.) She picks up Anna around noon and has lunch with her mother and then picks up Amy and returns home around 3:00 P.M.

Wendy and Bob spent $7,000 this year on child care. On Fridays, Wendy phones in a big supermarket shopping list, which is supposed to last the week, and has the fifteen bags of groceries delivered. While laundry gets done, it seldom makes its way into drawers and closets. Family members usually take what is needed from large plastic bags near the machines. On Tuesday nights they all go out for pizza where kids get to eat for free. One other night a week they usually eat at a family restaurant that runs kids' specials. Dinner seldom includes all the basic food groups, but no one seems to mind too much. Weekends fly by with Amy playing with friends in the neighborhood, Anna being cared for by Bob or Wendy, whichever one is not busy doing household chores or running errands or trying to catch up on a little office work; on Sunday, church and Sunday school take up most of the morning. The afternoon is finally spent relaxing a bit. Wendy's mother often comes over, and they have a nice Sunday dinner together. The Workholmes haven't had a vacation in five years.

If we can flash ahead into the future, we will see that after one month of the even more complicated fall schedule, Wendy quits her job, as she has been starting to get severe headaches from the tension. Now that Amy is in public school, there is an additional afternoon set of child care arrangements that Wendy is responsible for, taking Amy and several other children (they have a car pool) two days a week on the average, to an after-school day care center, Kidkare. Anna loves Mrs. Apple's house, but Wendy feels she should also be in a day care center because of the more stimulating educational program, so they compromise with three days at Sprouts and one with Mrs. Apple. Wendy finds that she is often in a cold sweat, trying to keep up with all the child care arrangements and give adequate attention to her own work. So Wendy decides to quit her job and devote herself entirely to her family. Both Amy and Anna seem to like their school and other-care situations, so Wendy lets Anna continue one day with Mrs. Apple and two half days at Sprouts. Amy comes home after school but seems to miss the other kids and activities at Kidkare, especially as many of her neighborhood friends are there. After two months, Wendy realizes they cannot afford to be without her salary, and she also realizes she needs to work with other adults because she likes the challenge and their company. She begins to develop a consultant business that allows her to set her own schedule, but she cannot always get as much work as she would like. Bob is offered a promotion that would entail a 25 percent raise but also longer work hours. He turns it down because he values family time but worries about his future and whether he will again receive such an opportunity or be taken less seriously at work.

## RESEARCH ON WORKING MOTHERS

The real-life problems of Wendy's family are not a prime concern of the research industry, which is stuck in its own self-aggrandizing Victorian time warp. No wonder the magazines are confusing—their readership is full of struggling Workholmes, yet their advisers are still in love with the hearth angel whom they can presume to manage with their perennial homilies. Notice they do not take on the analysis of corporate executives, workplace managers, elected public officials, and lawmakers, whose "psychology" contributes so much to the problems of children. And psychologists seldom concern themselves with damage caused to parents and children by the maddeningly inadequate child care patchwork, the family-unfriendly workplace, and the increasing poverty of so many families. Not surprisingly, economists, psychologists, sociologists, and other behavioral scientists have produced hundreds of studies attempting to evaluate the effects of mothers' work outside the home on their children; still, they cannot agree on the outcome of their investigation even though there is no consistent evidence of harm to children caused by their mothers' working. However, study after study still continues to divide children into those cared for exclusively by their (good) mothers and those reared outside the hearth angel's bosom.

Studies of "home-reared" versus "child-care-reared" children rest on the assumption that young children's separation from their mothers interrupts the attachment process and that "child-care-reared" children will be less secure. Some psychologists have even updated the term "maternal deprivation" to "maternal absence" in referring to working mothers.[9] Moreover, in these comparisons the "quality" of the child's attachment to her mother continues to be defined as *the* essential characteristic of emotional development in spite of the fact that no consistent pattern of attachment differences between home-reared and child-care-reared groups has emerged.[10] Some research claims to find increased aggression in some day care children, but others say the "aggression" is really just independent behavior. Also, some studies show that boys in day care have lower self-esteem and lower academic achievement, and that boys and girls in day care show less cooperative behaviors with adults.[11] However, it appears these effects are due primarily to some aspects of the child care curriculum rather than child care per se; and again, what is considered "uncooperative" may simply be greater independence.[12]

Most studies found that day care caused no clear evidence of harm to preschool age children and in fact offered benefits. For example, psychologist Alison Clarke-Stewart, using measures of attachment, language development, and intelligence tests, showed that high-quality child care could accelerate a child's social and intellectual development and therefore be superior to home care, although the differences between the two groups disappeared by the time the children were about the age of five.[13] Other studies that measured security, self-confidence, and overall emotional adjustment found that no differences exist between child-care-reared and home-reared children.[14] In the face of this good news, researchers in the early 1980s shifted their search for damage to infants and toddlers. Psychologist Sandra Scarr, for instance, went to Bermuda where many mothers work and infants and toddlers receive out-of-home care. She found the only children to suffer if their mothers worked were those in day care centers where the staff were poorly trained and poorly paid.[15]

Have all these studies demonstrating positive or neutral effects of day care on children stopped the war of research seeking to indict working mothers? Hardly. Although many investigators are beginning to see a more complex picture in which the quality of child care is evaluated and one where working mothers are more often seen as part of an interacting family system, the search for damage due to maternal employment continues.

Psychologists, of course, assume that employed mothers now spend less time with their children than in the Ozzie-and-Harriet days. But the few time-use studies that have investigated "mothertime" show that even these assumptions are faulty. In fact, the research suggests the real "victims" when Mommy works are mothers. One time-use expert, for example, recently found married women who work simply cut back in their own leisure and housework time, not the time they give to their children.[16] He also claims the differences in time mothers spend with each child has barely changed over the last fifty years. Another recent study shows that married working mothers spend as much time in direct care (bathing, dressing, and supervising) as stay-at-home mothers.[17] On the other hand, another study shows that the amount of time working mothers spend in "primary care"—i.e., direct interaction with their children—is somewhat less than what non-working mothers spend. Mothers who work full-time spend six hours a week in primary child care activities; mothers who work part-time spend nine or ten hours a week, and mothers who are not employed spend about thirteen.[18] While very small differences may exist, then, in the amount of attention children receive from their working and nonworking mothers, psychologists continue to search for negative effects of maternal employment, even though working mothers secure others (including fathers) to care for their children in their absence.[19]

But can we rely on a single one of these studies?

Researching the effects of mothers' work on children's well-being is like trying to find the effects of rain on the world economy—a vastly complex endeavor of highly questionable worth. Firstly, this phenomenon researchers call "maternal employment" is really many phenomena. Women sometimes find work that is personally fulfilling, secure, demanding an appropriate amount of time and energy, and well-paying; sometimes their employment is not secure, not well-paying, not personally fulfilling, and not requiring an appropriate amount of time. And these factors change over time for the same woman and are certainly going to affect children differently. So to seek causes of children's behavior in maternal employment, per se, is at best inadequate.

But let us suppose that some really alert researcher recognizes these distinct categories of maternal employment and compares ten or fifteen different types of employed mothers with at-home mothers. Then another question arises: Did these women differ in some consistent ways before they became variously employed and unemployed? And do mothers who elect to stay home also differ in a significant way? And do they differ significantly from one another? We do know that mothers who have more satisfying employment tend to be better educated, and better educated middle-class mothers are more likely to work than stay home (although this is changing as fewer women can afford to stay home). Better educated mothers (and fathers) tend to have higher-achieving children because they push for it and pay for it. So there were most likely differences in the groups of mothers that preceded and to some extent contributed to their employment experiences. These various types of mothers may also differ in their attitudes toward work and child rearing. So, for instance, if you somehow decided to pay all mothers to stay home, the groups of women would still behave differently toward their children and the children might therefore exhibit different characteristics.

Even if we accounted for all these factors, we would not be able to draw any conclusions about the effect of maternal employment on children, because it's hard to separate the effects of Mommy's job from other factors. First of all, mothers' employment has an impact on their attitudes and in turn, on the whole family environment. A mother who hates her work is bound to bring stress to the rest of her family. Employed mothers might have husbands who might be forced to become more involved in child care whether they want to or not; they might not have husbands; they might have people who share the domestic work and they might not; they might have mates who approve or disapprove of their working, and they might not have any mate at all. Women and men also have children who are born with different temperaments, different capacities for independent behavior, and different needs at different ages, and these children may have inherited and learned many of their own characteristics from both their differing parents. Children's temperament and inherited characteristics alone could account for many "effects of maternal employment" psychologists claim to find. (More recent studies sometimes do assess infant temperament, but they still lump together employed and not-employed mothers as monolithic and opposing categories.)

Also, families have different sources of stress—the emotional relationship between parents may be healthy or not healthy; parents may be warm and have appropriate expectations, or be cold and have inappropriate expectations; children may be exhibiting "insecurity" or getting low grades because of emotional tension in the family. Moreover, everything said about mothers' work could just as easily apply to fathers' work; fathers may be involved with their children or not involved; people may have reliable and affordable othercare or they may not; and people may be comfortably middle class, or struggling to stay middle class, or may be struggling to make ends meet. Children's behavior changes over time and varies with circumstances, yet few studies follow them throughout their childhood. So what can we say about the research on maternal employment? Not one study takes all these factors into account; very few ever look at several factors at once. Most of them use middle-class people as their subjects; some use teenagers; some use poor people (very rich people are never studied). Few studies have a representative sample of families, and "paternal employment" is never even mentioned.[20]

## SHOULD WE ABANDON RESEARCH ON WORKING MOTHERS?

One lone psychologist recently called for a halt to all this research on working mothers. Louise Silverstein proposes interrupting this research and following a new agenda that documents the negative consequences of not providing high-quality, affordable day care.[21] Sadly, her colleagues have self-righteously rejected this suggestion, claiming that they adhere to the highest principles of objective scientific investigation and that her proposal to abandon this area of research is a violation of scientific principles and is strictly "political."[22] A typical critic of Silverstein accused: "When strong personal, political views [Silverstein's, of course] . . . cloud scientific objectivity, psychologists risk weakening their credibility with those who most need to listen to what psychologists have to say."[23] One critic even saw Silverstein as a "divisive" "feminist" who should be censured: "Silverstein's argument . . . builds an axiom around some faulty propositions that motherhood is an idealized myth which must be deconstructed . . . I grant that Silverstein's proposed research agenda on the negative consequences of not providing high-quality day care should be examined, particularly in disadvantaged families. But that should not preclude or replace research on risk factors associated with nonmaternal care . . . [The] nurturing role of the mother has been determined through natural evolution for the purpose of species survival . . . Silverstein's emphasis on a feminist revision of the family system provides ammunition and further division of the already frail discipline of psychology into a battlefield in which the accumulated knowledge will be disgraced for the reason of not being feminist . . . The Board for Social and Ethical Responsibility in Psychology . . . should propose an urgent agenda to avoid hostile 'feminist language' in psychological research in the APA journals."[24] Few critics seemed able to deal with the assertion that their research is biased.

Interestingly, those eminently objective investigators in search of harm caused by maternal employment—whose science is above politics—have tended to ignore one of their own most common (albeit, accidental) findings: contented and independent mothers tend to have children who are thriving. The happiest children tend to be those of mothers who work and who love their work. The next happiest are likely to be children whose mothers stay home and love staying home.[25] The effect of maternal happiness on women's families, however, is never the subject of research.

Unfortunately, the alleged beneficiaries of all this investigation, children of employed mothers, are in fact, the victims of it. These countless studies searching for negative effects of maternal employment obscure the real child care needs of the modern family. Among the prime factors that promote good mental health for women and consequently their children, after all, is reliable, affordable child care. With so many mothers of young children in the labor force, you might think that psychologists would finally turn their attention to the real causes of inadequate caregiving, such as poorly paid caregivers, familial poverty, and lack of knowledge about child behavior, but they seem to be "fixated" on the wonders of biological motherhood.

## CHILDREN OF DIVORCED MOTHERS

If it is becoming clear that it is difficult if not impossible and certainly inappropriate to try to prove that mothers' employment harms children, perhaps we should turn to divorced mothers, another prime source of motherguilt and motherblame. Setting the stage for what is now the accepted wisdom on divorce, Barbara Dafoe Whitehead, in her article "Dan Quayle Was Right," claims that overall, children's well-being has declined because of the problems associated with our changing family structure. Whitehead asserts that children in families disrupted by divorce and out-of-wedlock birth or in stepparent families are more likely than children in "intact" families (i.e. two biological parents living with their children) to be poor, to drop out of school, to have trouble with the law, to bear children at an early age, to show maladjustment in relationships with their fathers, and to be impaired in love and work in adulthood. Even the high teen suicide rate, the increasing violence of juvenile crime, and the increased and more violent crime in American cities are all associated, she claims, with these "deviant" families. In fact, Whitehead asserts the biggest problem faced by American schools is the number of children who come from disrupted families!

Whitehead makes the allegation that the married two-parent family is being widely depicted as pathological (witness the "dysfunctional" family and the emphasis on describing family violence and substance abuse in two-parent families) and that this is an attempt to discredit that institution and therefore discredit a social norm. This discrediting, she says, can be understood as part of what Senator Daniel Patrick Moynihan has described as a larger effort to accommodate higher levels of social deviance. According to Moynihan, the amount of deviant behavior in American society has increased beyond levels the community can afford to recognize. One response has been to normalize what was once considered deviant behavior—such as out-of-wedlock birth.

Whitehead cites evidence by sociologist Sarah McLanahan and others, many of whom, including psychologist Judith Wallerstein, are associated with Whitehead at the Institute of American Values in New York. Whitehead claims the research clearly shows that non-intact families are inferior for children. She does not seem particularly concerned with what is best for mothers. She refers to the needs of mothers (and fathers) that cause them to divorce, remarry, or remain single as the consequence of individualism, a value that interferes with "communitarian" values and is at odds with the interests of children.

How the deviant mothers have managed to avoid causing acid rain and the budget deficit should certainly be the subject of an extensive study! Funding might be difficult to find, though, these days.

Probably second to working outside the home, mothers feel most guilty about divorce, especially since half of all marriages end in divorce and 90 percent of the time mothers become the custodial parent. Between the early 1960s and mid-1970s the divorce rate doubled, in part because of the increased employment of women which allowed them to survive independently.[27] It also soared because of a change in gender relations that made many marriages unacceptable to women;* and because of relaxed sexual mores that made finding a romantic partner a right of self-fulfillment. In broader perspective, the increase in divorce is a global phenomenon and part of an historical trend away from the obligations of kinship. Divorce has become such a commonplace occurrence that two out of five young children are likely to see their parents separate and be forced to encounter some or all of the consequences of family disruption: parental conflict, diminished contact with the noncustodial parent, residential change, and economic decline.[28]

As with studies of mothers' employment, researchers have assumed divorce is bad for children and have attempted to map the negative effects. Consequently, most studies compare children of divorce to children in married families and therefore find the children suffer from deficits in both academic achievement and emotional adjustment. But divorce is the result of a bad relationship or a good relationship that has gone bad. Therefore, the appropriate comparison group for children of divorce would be children in intact families in which the parents' relationship is troubled. This comparison is never made, however, and so all the claims about how children of divorce are faring (and the findings are far from clear or consistent) are, at best, in-

---

*The fact that 80 percent of divorced women, but only 50 percent of divorced men say they are happy that they divorced is some indication of the extent of the gender issue. (Demie Kurz, For Richer, For Poorer: Mothers Confront Divorce [New York: Routledge, 1995].)

appropriately named. Children of divorced parents are not so much the product of a divorce as of a bad relationship. If we outlawed divorce, these children would probably be no better off—and might be worse off as the marital relationship became even more contentious and dysfunctional. Children's lives can be enhanced by divorce as well as traumatized by it, and probably both scenarios are going to apply.

I have reached almost the same conclusions about the study of the effects of divorce on children that I made with the study of maternal employment's effects on children: Divorce, per se, has little predictable effect on children. However, there is one important caveat. In my ideal world, work would be so well integrated with family life that most mothers and fathers would have the opportunity to enjoy work and family equally. Mothers' employment would be a common and desirable fact of life. In my ideal world, adult relationships would be so mature and informed that when partners decided to have children, divorce would be very rare indeed. Divorced mothers would be a rare and undesirable fact of life.

## HELEN AND HERB HOLMESWORTH

To understand more about the complexities of the problem, let us take the example of prototypical Helen Holmesworth.* Helen was married to Herb for eight years. They had two children, Mickey and Sally. During this marriage, Helen and Herb had gotten along poorly much of the time. Helen complained that Herb was emotionally remote and constantly ridiculed her family. Herb, who hung out more and more with his male friends, complained that Helen was a nag. Both Helen and Herb came from stable families who encouraged them to work out their differences and so they did not contemplate divorce. Helen even went to a therapist for a while, but Herb refused to join her, although he did listen to her more carefully while she was seeing the therapist. The quarreling escalated again just before Helen's second pregnancy, and Mickey, their first child, who was now a toddler, was becoming increasingly difficult. Helen felt this was be-

*I am indebted to Frank Furstenberg and Andrew Cherlin (Divided Families: What Happens to Children When Parents Part [Cambridge, MA: Harvard University Press, 1991]), for this example from their book, which I have modified, primarily by condensing it.

cause the quarreling was taking a toll on him and she finally asked
Herb to join her in counseling or move out. Only when Herb moved
out, did the children officially learn of their parents' problems. During the eighteen-month separation before the divorce, Herb continued to make the house payments, and pay all the children's expenses.
He felt very guilty about the kids. Herb saw the children several times
a week, but their time together was often rather strained. He would
ask them what they had been doing in the intervening days, but they
could not easily remember. After the divorce was finalized, he continued to see them regularly for the next year or so. Three years after
the divorce, he saw his son only twice a month and his daughter even
less often.

At the time of their separation, Herb was assistant manager of a
fast-food franchise, earning $24,000 a year. Helen had recently re-
turned to work as a part-time secretary, making $8,000 a year. They
had moved into a $60,000 condominium only a year before the sepa-
ration. While Herb was deeply attached to his son, he assumed the
kids would stay with Helen. He kept the car but gave up his $10,000
equity in the condo and took only a few furnishings for his small
apartment. Helen was awarded $300 a month in child support, 15
percent of Herb's gross income. Helen was now fully responsible for
the mortgage. Her child care costs doubled. She also had counseling
costs for Mickey, who was having trouble at school; she was also badly
in need of a car to manage her complicated work and child care
schedule. A move to a smaller place would have saved about $100 a
month but would have taken her too far from her parents, whom she
relied on for child care. She asked Herb to increase his payments, but
he refused as he had little discretionary income and he had also begun
seeing Alice, who had two children whose own father paid no child
support. Helen, who soon found a higher-paying job, was supporting
herself and two children on an income of $17,600 ($14,000 salary plus
$3,600 in child support.) Herb was supporting himself, alone, on
$20,400. Helen fell behind in her bills and therefore sold the condo
and moved in with her parents while she took time to look for more
suitable housing. Finally, she found an apartment in a less desirable
section of town near her work but farther from her parents, and in a
different school district. A few weeks after she and the kids moved
into the apartment, Herb told her he would have to reduce the sup-

port payments because he was now living with Alice and her two children and was anticipating marriage. Herb's visits with Mickey and Sally were becoming less and less frequent as he shifted his attention to Alice and her children. All this made Helen feel desperate and abandoned, and now she even felt jealous of Alice. She was constantly fighting back a sense of rage. When the children came back from visits with Herb and Alice and Alice's two children, it was just impossible for her to hide her anger, which sometimes spilled over onto Mickey.

When Herb curtailed his contact with Mickey and Sally, that meant they also saw less of their paternal grandparents, with whom they had spent summer vacations at their lakeside home. Herb's parents encouraged him to bring the children along with his new family, but somehow those arrangements never worked out. Herb's new wife Alice wasn't crazy about sharing time with Mickey and Sally, since she wanted Herb's parents to get to know her own children. Besides, Sally was so demanding that the one time they had all gone together, she had nearly ruined the vacation.

Herb eventually backed down from his threat to reduce payments when he was notified by Helen's lawyer that he would face court action. He is, in fact, not making out badly. In the two years since the divorce, his salary had risen to $28,500, an increase of 20 percent, and his support payments had not increased at all. As Herb now lived with Alice, her earnings of $15,000 combined with his, gave them an income of $43,500. Helen, on the other hand, learned to make do with less; gradually, she became less depressed and started to find some time for her own needs.

After five years of sporadic dating Helen has become engaged to Lester, who shares custody of his two sons from his first marriage with his ex-wife. His parents, who have no granddaughter, have taken a special liking to Sally. This story goes on and on with the development of new relationships, and the growing and changing of personalities.

Divorce, then, is not a discrete event.[29] Rather, it is the demarcation of a transition, often from one bad situation to a different bad situation, which may eventually get better. For most children, divorce will mean acquiring a stepfamily and a whole new set of relationships to be negotiated. Children's continued adjustment will be greatly affected by the course of their mother's and father's love life. When we are concerned with the psychological fate of children, we must recognize that the divorce is a fracture in a fragile relationship, which, if it had continued, would have been bad for the children, not to mention the parents. The event of divorce precipitates a series of events and changed relationships that are quite varied. Among these changes, there is usually a terrible strain on mothers, far greater than that on fathers, primarily because of the unequal economic rearrangements.

## RESEARCH ON CHILDREN OF DIVORCE

What, then, can psychologists tell us about the well-being of children whose parents divorce? The answers, once again, are not terribly clear. Like most social science, the investigation of this problem is piecemeal and fragmented—studies vary in quality, in the types of families studied, the questions asked, and the answers considered useful. It is therefore difficult to compare one study with another, let alone find a dozen of quality that actually corroborate one another on more than a few points. A few findings do repeatedly stand out, however. The first is that interparental conflict, whether inside or outside of marriage, is very hard on children. It is also becoming apparent that change of residence after divorce, which also involves change of friends, schools, and activities, accounts for a considerable portion of the hardship that children experience and is related to post-divorce economic decline. The third factor—maybe this could become our theme song—is that happier mothers make for children who are more able to adjust and achieve.

Beyond these principles, however, the waters are muddy. Much research is based on the reports of parents and teachers who often expect to find differences in divorced children's behavior. Some researchers have been so convinced that they will find effects of divorce that they have failed to compare the children they studied to children who did not experience divorce. In fact, currently, one such study, conducted by Judith Wallerstein and Sandra Blakeslee, is being widely cited,* especially by those who want to restore the Ozzie and

---

*Judith Wallerstein and Sandra Blakeslee, Second Chances: Men, Women, and Children a Decade After Divorce (New York: Ticknor and Fields, 1989). For a typical use of this study, see: Barbara Dafoe Whitehead, "Dan Quayle Was Right," Atlantic Monthly 271, no. 4 (April 1993), pp. 47+.

Harriet family. (See chapter 1.) Wallerstein and Blakeslee paint a picture of a generation of children permanently scarred by divorce. They claim that almost half of the children in their study entered adulthood as worried, underachieving, self-deprecating, and sometimes angry young men and women—characteristics they attribute to the divorce. However, they studied sixty white, middle-class, recently divorced couples from San Francisco who had come to a clinic for counseling. They did not compare these children to a similar group of intact families. It is quite possible that the same characteristics can be found in almost half of white middle-class children of intact San Francisco families seeking psychological treatment in the 1980s.

The fact is, children appear to display a wide range of responses to divorce. Some children seem to do very well; others do poorly. Almost all children are distressed when their parents separate, and most continue to experience confusion, sadness, and anger for months and even years. On the other hand, some children experience a great sense of relief—especially in families where the noncustodial parent has been abusive and/or has suffered from drug and alcohol abuse. Children's responses vary a great deal though, depending on their age, sex, and other factors. In general, very young children, for instance, have trouble conceptualizing what has happened. They do not understand future time and tend to see themselves as the cause of the divorce since they cannot easily understand their parents' relationship. Older children can understand more about their parents' relationship but may also therefore be very angry at one parent or the other and experience divided loyalties. Many studies show there are more problems for boys than for girls, but this is quite possibly because girls are more likely to express their pain differently—boys often direct it outward at others, becoming unruly and disobedient; they fail at school, fight with other children. Girls tend to become depressed, withdrawn, anxious, or exceedingly controlled and well behaved. It is the behavior of the boys, however, that is reported more often by teachers and parents as troublesome and shows up as "effects" of divorce in the research.[30]

A central problem in the study of the effects of divorce on children is that families who divorce may be different from other families from the very beginning. For example, a couple who married very young or who married because the woman was pregnant have higher rates of divorce. There may also be, for some families, predisposing personality characteristics of parents that are then reflected in children's behavior. Low income or some personal trauma might also predispose people to divorce, and the psychology of children from these relationships might be significantly different from other divorced groups. The effects of divorce in a white middle-class family might have little in common with those in a very poor minority family because of differences in social supports stemming from both custom and money.

A small cadre of researchers is beginning to see divorce as a gradual disintegration of a fragile family system and to recognize the need to study families before divorce and into the adulthood of the children. Although Wallerstein's study failed to examine the influence of a large range of pre-divorce conditions, it did follow children long enough to suggest that some children who initially exhibit successful adaptation to divorce may encounter later problems adjusting to the developmental tasks of adulthood—achieving psychological and economic independence as well as being able to establish and maintain stable sexual partnerships.[31] One recent study, however, does examine pre-divorce characteristics and compares children of divorce with children from intact families. Sociologists Frank Furstenberg and Julien Teitler[32] found, consistent with many other studies, that children whose parents separated are less likely to complete high school or attend college, and are more likely to start their own families earlier. They are also more likely to be depressed, have sought psychological help, and to express discontent with their lives. However, Furstenberg suggests these differences may be due, in part, to "pre-divorce risk factors" having to do with socioeconomic class and education, the quality of marital relations, and parent and child characteristics. Families that eventually experience divorce may be different in a variety of ways from those that do not, long before marital disruption occurs. This analysis suggests that exposure to these conditions may compromise children's economic, social, and psychological well-being in later life whether or not a separation takes place. Thus it appears that divorce and its aftermath may not contribute as much to children's problems in later life as many have thought.

## FATHERS AND DIVORCE

Researchers looking for the damage produced by divorce assume that "losing" a parent is the source of the trouble.[33] (See chapter 5 for further discussion of fathers' absence.) It has been assumed that a family with both parents living in the same household as the child is a better environment for children's development than is a single-parent family. Mothers and fathers are each important resources for the child—each is a source of emotional support, practical assistance, information, guidance and supervision; they are also role models from which children learn social skills such as cooperation, negotiation, and compromise. Following divorce, many children experience a decrease in the quantity and quality of contact with the noncustodial parent. And because most custodial parents are in the labor force, they are constrained in the amount of time and energy they can devote to their children. A decline in parental support may increase the likelihood of children's problems, such as poor academic achievement, low self-esteem, and misbehavior. This combined with less parental supervision may increase the chances that children get into trouble through truancy, delinquent subcultures, or premature pregnancy.

Research does show that having two parents is not always the preferred situation. For example, some studies show that the more contact children have with their noncustodial fathers, the more problems they develop—presumably because of the increase in conflict between the parents and, also, the ongoing effects of abuse. On the other hand, when the conflict between parents is low (which apparently is rare), it appears that the more time kids spend with their fathers, the better they adjust. Mothers who don't live with their kids, however, tend to be more personally involved with their children, and their relationship seems to be more important to the children's adjustment than that of fathers.[34] In the future, fathers may become more involved in the daily caregiving of their children and therefore represent a greater emotional force in their children's lives than they generally do now, and the loss of their company may then prove more detrimental. Certainly a belief that the father's involvement is beneficial to children was an important reason why many states recently adopted joint custody statutes. However, to date, joint legal custody seems to be little different in practice from maternal sole custody in its effects on children. There is no difference in child support payments, or the amount of visitation or cooperation with their former wives; fathers don't even participate more in decisions about the children's lives. It would seem that many men just do not know how to relate to their children except through their wives. While few divorced families manage joint physical custody, studies of those who do indicate that these children fare no better than those whose mothers have sole custody. Researchers, once again, believe that the critical factor is not the custody arrangement, but the amount of conflict between the parents and how effectively the parent (or parents) function with their children.

Another finding discounting the importance of losing a parent is that having a live-in stepparent (usually stepfather), rather than making up for the absence of one parent, tends to increase problems for children, most likely because there is now another set of relationships to be negotiated. The presence of a stepfather may also result in a decline in the mother's emotional involvement with her children as the new mate takes a more prominent place in her affections.

Some studies compare children who have lost parents to divorce with children whose parents have died; once again, the similarities or differences are not clear. (Grief, while painful to the one who experiences it, may elude measurement.) The research on parental loss does little to establish the essential importance of the divorced father.

## RECOVERY FROM DIVORCE: MOTHER'S TASK

The emotional and economic burdens of divorce are carried primarily by mothers. Within two or three years, it appears that most single parents and their children recover substantially from the trauma of the crisis period. Almost all the advice books on divorce warn parents of the need to protect children from the emotional fallout that frequently occurs as the marital world collapses. They are urged to draw a boundary around the children, protecting them from the animosity between the former spouses. They must also protect their children from parental worries. Parents are warned not to take out their anger on the children. As women are usually the custodial parent, however, most of the responsibility for living up to these precepts falls to them and along with it the sense of responsibility and guilt for their children's suffering. Most divorcing couples experience considerable conflict and emotional upheaval, and women are rarely able to protect their children from it.

Also, it appears the second most crucial factor in children's recovery is the level of functioning of the custodial parent (usually the mother). Considering the unfair share mothers take on, their ability to cope is severely constrained. The divorced mother's own distress makes it more difficult to handle her children's distress, which can lead to a disorganized household, lax supervision, and inconsistent discipline. As illustrated by Helen's situation, perhaps the most central factor in the child's emotional well-being—their mother—is given the least social and economic support.

Once again, much research on divorce lends credence to the idea that ours would be a happy land again if only mothers would stay married because, it seems, mothers just can't do it all. However, the Furstenberg studies do lead the way toward rethinking the labeling of "divorced" families. Rather than talking about divorced mothers and their children versus married-parent families, the distinction between fragile families and healthy ones may turn out to be far more useful. It might even help reduce the growing anger at mothers who are so selfish as to divorce and leave their children without a father.

## SINGLE MOTHERS

If we can't blame mothers for working and divorcing—what about being single? Between 1982 and 1992, while the divorce rate leveled off at about 50 percent, the number of women who became mothers without marrying increased by 60 percent. The increase was especially steep among educated and professional women. At the same time, record numbers of single women now rely on welfare, even though the value of cash benefits has fallen sharply in the past two decades.* Close to one in three mothers is single, and yet her family is generally regarded as a mutant form of the "normal" two-parent mar-

---

*The number of single mothers on welfare has jumped by one third since 1984, even though benefits are at least 10 percent lower than in 1980 and 45 percent lower than in 1970. Jason DeParle. "Rise in Births Outside Wedlock," The New York Times. July 14, 1993, p. 1+.

ried family. In fact, there is a growing chorus in the land that seems to believe single motherhood is a sign of bad "family values" and a threat to the sanctity of marriage. Being a single mom is basically immoral and selfish, the reasoning goes, since it deprives children of an important paternal role model and source of support. Single mothers are also seen as engenderers of the underclass—the juvenile delinquents, drug addicts, and violent criminals who indeed plague the country. And of course, the real crime is that single mothers are generally impoverished (almost half are below the poverty line) and therefore need help.* Of course, since this help must be provided by the full community of adults, single mothers' plight is simply another reason to resent them. They are seen as a drain on our scarce resources rather than people who are doing the work of two adults with the pay of less than one.

The popular image of single mothers is that they are either Murphy Browns or black teen-age high school drop-outs—and that these are people who reject marriage. The truth is, however, that the vast majority of women having children outside of marriage are poor or working-class—in fact 40 percent have an income below $10,000. A big factor in their lack of a marriage partner is declining wages and jobs for lower-income men. Moreover, nearly 40 percent are non-Hispanic whites; teens are less than a third of unmarried mothers and black teens are 12 percent. Fifty-four percent are in their twenties. A woman's level of education is highly correlated with her single mother status: Almost 50 percent of births to high-school drop-outs occur out of wedlock; among college graduates, the proportion is just 6 percent.

Unwed motherhood is often a transitory state. One quarter of out-of-wedlock births involve women who had been previously married but were divorced, separated, or widowed before they became preg-

*The Census Bureau reports that 47 percent of the families headed by single mothers live in poverty, compared to 8.3 percent of families headed by two parents. (Jason DeParle, "Rise in Births Outside Wedlock," New York Times, July 14, 1993, pp. 1+.) Sixty-two percent of single-mother families with children under three live in poverty; in white single-mother families 50 percent of the children are poor; in black single-parent families, the figure is 70 percent; 73 percent for Hispanic. (S. D. Einbinder, "A Statistical Profile of Children Living in Poverty . . . 1990" [unpublished document from the National Center for Children in Poverty; New York: Columbia University School of Public Health, 1992].) Sixty-five percent of households headed by women have incomes of less than $20,000. (Lee Smith, "The New Wave of Illegitimacy," Fortune, April 18, 1994, pp. 81+.)

nant. Forty percent of mothers whose first birth occurs outside marriage marry within five years. And one in four married mothers has a live-in relationship with a man.[35]

The argument about single motherhood is complicated by race. Currently, three in five black families are headed by single mothers, compared to one in five white families.[36] Among white mothers, the major reasons for singlehood are divorce and separation. Among black mothers, divorce and separation also used to be the major causes of single parenthood, but no more. In 1991, 54 percent of one-parent black families were headed by women who had never married; two thirds of black children are born out of wedlock.[37] Therefore, one could say single motherhood is the norm for black families. And therefore, according to popular logic, black mothers are a prime source of social blight.

Single mothers have two main things in common: They are poor and they are lone parents. Beyond that, there is considerable variation. Single mothers may be adoptive parents,[38] lesbian and gay parents[39] or teens. They come in every racial-ethnic group, age, and financial station—characteristics that contribute to their uniqueness as subgroups. There are powerful demographic and economic reasons for black women not to marry, which are different from the reasons of teens, for example, or lesbians and gays, or the growing number of older, middle-class, financially secure single women. Single mothers may also be cohabiting, living with their own parents, or living with other unrelated adults, factors that significantly alter the environment in which their children are cared for.[40]

## SINGLE MOTHERS IN POVERTY

For obvious reasons, single mothers are far more likely than married-couple families or single fathers to live in poverty. In fact, 47 percent of all single-mother families live in poverty, compared with 20 percent of their male counterparts and 8 percent of married-couple families.[41] These are the same women who typically pay more than 25 percent of their income for child care![42] Among these single mothers, less than 75 percent who were awarded child support, actually receive it.[43] In 1989 the average annual award was $2,995 per year.[44] But even if women received all the child support they were due, only a quarter of the gap between their income and the poverty threshhold would be closed.[45]

In addition to delinquent fathers, the state has been a major contributor to the impoverishment of single mothers and their children. Between 1970 and 1991, the purchasing power of the average AFDC check fell by 42 percent.[46] Rent burdens among single-parent households skyrocketed between 1974 and 1987, from 38 to 58 percent of their incomes. The supply of low-income housing is so low that only one third of those who qualify for Housing and Urban Development (HUD) subsidies, receive them. Moreover, women with children face housing discrimination. A HUD survey found that 25 percent of all landlords barred tenants with children; another 50 percent had partial restrictions on the age or number of children.[47] Not surprisingly, many poor, female-headed families are rapidly falling through the publicly funded "safety net" and into homelessness. In fact, many mothers are receiving AFDC when they become homeless.[48] Poverty is likely to mean poor medical care, poor nutrition, poor housing, and poor schooling—for starters.

Surely the growing outrage about single mothers is based on knowledge that they are "bad for children." The thoughtful reader might wonder which aspects of their parenthood are most harmful. Is it their poverty? Their poor parenting skills? Their inability to enlist the support of the father? Or is it something else? Do fathers make a difference beyond their financial support? Are grandmothers just as psychologically good for children as fathers? Is the emotional weight of single motherhood, rather than poverty, the key burden in their children's lives? After all, single mothers have to contend with constant time and energy pressures. Does the social isolation experienced by many single mothers exacerbate the problems caused by lack of money? Is dependency on welfare, which is supposed to lower self-esteem and stigmatize the family, damaging to children? Does single motherhood cause juvenile delinquency?

## THE RESEARCH ON "SINGLE MOTHERS"

Answering these questions is complicated because there are so many different kinds of single mothers—from Murphy Browns to fifteen-year-olds. Even how long a mother is single varies widely. A "single mother" could be unmarried for just a year or two, or she might be someone who never married. She might have lived with the father of her child without marrying him; she might have lived with several men who each fathered a different one of her children; she might have lived with men who did not biologically father her children but helped nurture them; she might have lived in a household with other adults who contributed to the nurture of her children. The variations are significant.

Once again, however, social scientists have constructed the category of single motherhood out of certain unquestioned assumptions—in this case the paramount importance of marriage. And so, in studying these mothers, there are actually few consistent findings about the effects of single motherhood, per se, on the lives of children. Some studies show children from single-mother families are more likely to do poorly in school, to drop out of high school, to have emotional problems, and to become single mothers themselves than children from two-parent married families. Other studies fail to corroborate these findings, with one exception. One finding that is fairly consistent, is that children of "single mothers," on the average, perform less well in school than children from two-parent families.

Many social scientists believe that a significant portion of the single-mother "effect" on children's educational performance is due to the economic conditions of single motherhood.[49] However, the factors causing this poverty are related to children's academic performance in a variety of ways that have yet to be examined. As a group, single mothers are less educated and more likely to be of minority status than married parents (or single custodial fathers). These factors may compound the effects of poverty in unique ways.[50] Related to the problems of poverty is the question of the importance of a father. Much research seems to indicate that the primary deficit represented by the absence of a father is his financial contribution. When divorced or absent fathers visit frequently, this does not appear to enhance their children's school performance.[51] There is one correlation, though: The more financial support the father contributes, the less "problem behavior" his children exhibit.[52]

Other social scientists trace the poorer academic performance of the children of single mothers to the absence of fathers. This theory contends the parental authority structure is weaker in single-mother families because they lack a male role model and disciplinarian. But in the few studies that examine this matter, it appears that single mothers take on the aspects of the traditional father role, acting as both disciplinarians and role models for autonomy.

Still other social scientists link children's problems to the extreme demands of time and energy experienced by single mothers, which presumably leave less parental energy for child rearing and supervision. However, many studies indicate that single mothers give the time to their children that they would have had for themselves, so that the kids don't appear to be shortchanged.

Parents use both material and nonmaterial resources to create an atmosphere at home that fosters academic skills and motivation. Material resources may include the purchase of extracurricular lessons, books, computers, and so forth. Nonmaterial resources are interpersonal—being involved in the child's day-to-day activities, talking about school, planning course selection, helping with homework. Few studies have compared single mothers to single fathers in the relative use of these resources. However, in one such study some possible differences were noted that deserve further exploration. Researchers found that despite the material advantages that single fathers enjoy, children from single-father families perform no better in school than those from single-mother families. In fact, it appears that in single-mother families, where there is usually an economic deficit, women make up for their relative poverty with their interpersonal efforts—being more involved with their children's daily lives. Single fathers provide less in interpersonal resources and more in economic resources thus to some extent evening out the differences between mothers and fathers.[53]

One recent and unusually broad study by Sarah McLanahan and Gary Sandefur[54] no doubt will be added to the motherblame arsenal because it finds, consistently, that children of single mothers fair less well than children from two-parent families. (That the authors refer to single mothers as "disrupted families" makes clear from the outset that their study will be a search for deficits in comparison to the two-parent family, which they view as the only truly legitimate form.) McLanahan and Sandefur compared teenagers of similar racial and educational background who grew up with both biological parents at home to adolescents who lived apart from one of their parents during

some period of childhood. They found that the children who lived
with only one biological parent, regardless of whether the parent remarried, were twice as likely to drop out of high school, twice as likely
to have a child before age twenty, and one and a half times as likely to
be "idle"—out of school, out of work—in their late teens and early
twenties as children who grew up with both biological parents.[55]

But before we get in line to congratulate Dan Quayle and company,
let's examine some problems with this study that may limit its usefulness. First, all the single mothers in this study became single mothers
in the 1960s. Therefore, the diversity that now comprises single motherhood must certainly be absent in their sample. Mothers who became single in the 1960s were much more unusual and may turn out
to be more different from two-parent families than are contemporary
single mothers. Even today, however, single mothers are likely to be a
different group of people to begin with, than mothers who married
and stayed married. They are much more likely to be poor, black, and
Hispanic, less educated, and may even be more likely to have different kinds of relationships with men than married mothers. Families
with an alcoholic or abusive parent, for example, are more likely to
break up than other families. This means that if all single mothers suddenly wedded tomorrow (or stayed wedded), the differences between
the children of the formerly single mothers and those of married
mothers would still be quite evident.

The other point to keep in mind as the Republican Contracters
begin to wave the family values banner (with its new McLanahan-
Sandefur imprimatur) is that the differences that have been identified
constitute small percentages—the vast majority of children in single-
mother families in their study do just as well as those in two-parent
families. Single motherhood and the absence of fathers are not the
causes of school failure, early childbearing, and juvenile delinquency—these problems exist in significant numbers for all types of
families. For example, during the 1980s, the high school dropout rate
was about 19 percent overall, and about 13 percent for children who
lived with both parents. Clearly, most school failure is caused by
something other than single motherhood. On the other hand, children living with only one biological parent are at a greater risk than
their peers who have two parents at home. McLanahan and Sandefur
find that at least half of the six percentage points of difference be-

tween these groups is due to low income and the sudden drop in income associated with divorce. With sufficient economic support, then, instead of six more children in one hundred dropping out of school, only three more would drop out because of economic conditions associated with being in a single-parent family. They found most of the other half of the disadvantage was due to inadequate parental guidance and attention and the lack of ties to community resources.

Income is also highly related to other important factors that McLanahan and Sandefur call "social capital." Children from single-mother families are more likely to attend inferior schools with higher dropout rates. (Moreover, on the average, schools with more minority students spend less money per child and have higher teacher-student ratios than schools with fewer minorities, and minorities are more prevalent among single mothers, so the effects of racism are confounded with social capital and income.) Another aspect of social capital is how often children switch homes. This study finds that children in single-parent families experience the most stressful moves, whereas children in stepparent families experience the greatest number of moves as compared to those who stay in married families. Both kinds of residential mobility seem to undermine the children's social capital in the form of community ties. In fact, the authors claim that school quality and residential mobility account for a considerable portion of the educational deficit and early childbearing associated with living in single-parent and stepfamilies. Idleness among young men seems less related to these factors than some other factor, probably the availability of work in certain communities.

The third factor, in addition to income and social capital that McLanahan and Sandefur examined, was the role of parenting. They predicted that supervision and involvement are weaker in single-parent families because one parent has less time and less authority than two. Also, single-parent families and stepfamilies have less stability in terms of support "personnel" (grandmothers, mothers' boyfriends, and stepfathers are more likely to move in and out), which creates uncertainty about household rules and parental responsibility. They found, however, that single mothers tended to compensate for the time lost with their children in routines like sharing meals together and reading to their children, among other activities. Remarried mothers, on the other hand, were a bit less involved with their kids, although the differences were small. In this study, single mothers tended to indicate they exercise less control over their children than married mothers, leaving them on their own more often and enforcing fewer rules. The researchers also found that having a grandmother in the house does increase the amount of supervision, whereas having a male partner does not.

Even in this study, most children in single-parent families do as well as those in two-parent families, suggesting once again that against considerable odds the deviant mothers are doing a good job.

## HELEN HOLMESWORTH'S FRIEND

To have a better sense of what some typical single mothers and their children are like, let us imagine for a moment that Helen Holmesworth, the divorced mother mentioned earlier in this chapter, has a friend Jane, whose situation exactly mirrors Helen's. Now imagine that Jane has broken her engagement to her fiancé, Harold, and experienced another half decade of single motherhood. Jane's daughter Jennifer was especially upset by the break, as she had been flourishing with the attention she received from Harold's parents. In the meantime, Jane's ex-husband and his new wife moved to another state, and Jane no longer hears from him; she does not even know where he is. Most important, she no longer receives any child support. To make matters worse, the company where Jane worked for ten years decided to downsize and eliminate her job. She received two weeks' severance pay. She had not thought this possible, since she had been an excellent employee according to her various supervisors' ratings over the years and she worked for a large and, she thought, prosperous corporation. She was barely paying her bills as it was, and she needed another job immediately. After a week of tracking every lead for full-time work, she went to an agency that placed temporary workers. She got a job that paid $6.50 an hour and lasted for three days. Because this job was over an hour away and she did not want to risk being late, she had to make special child care arrangements for those days to cover the extra time away from her apartment. Then for a week, there were no temp assignments, and not even an interview for another full-time job. She was going to have trouble meeting her $400-a-month rent.

## THE WELFARE MOTHER

Jane realized her only recourse was to apply for public assistance. She felt very ashamed and told no one of her decision. Jane waited five hours at the welfare office the first day, and filled out a thirty-five-page form, only to be told that she had not brought sufficient documentation of her plight. In addition to the tax returns and pay stubs and personal ID she had brought, she was told she needed bank statements, rent and utility statements, and her children's birth certificates. She returned the next day, spending another five hours waiting to see someone. Fortunately, she had less than $1,000 in the bank and no car, so it appeared she would qualify. She would have to return in two to three weeks to see if this were so and to receive the initial benefit. In the meantime, she continued to look for work and borrowed money from her parents to pay the rent and buy food. Eventually (as she resided in the state with the second-highest benefits) she received a $663 monthly welfare check plus $168 worth of food stamps and a Medicaid card, which entitled her and her children to health benefits, or $9,972 per year with health benefits.[56] Her rent and utilities came to $476 per month, or $5,712 per year, leaving $4,260 to pay for a year's worth of food, transportation, and clothing. She had to cancel the tutoring that had been helping her son Alex, making up for what she felt were deficits in the public school he now attended. While Jennifer had been doing all right in school, Jane felt school was not really challenging her. In fact, Jane felt that Jennifer's teachers really did not expect very much from her. So Jane had enrolled her in a weekly dance class in which Jennifer had begun to excel. This, too, had to be canceled.

For a while Jane accepted temp work when it was available, but this required that she arrange for child care, which was unreliable since she could not afford to pay for it but had to swap favors with neighbors. She was too busy to have good friends at this point, and since her parents lived an hour away and also worked, there was really no help in sight. She actually netted less money in the months where she had some work, so she focused on just looking for full-time employment. After nine months she was so poor that when she spent $20 for cake mix and party favors to celebrate Alex's birthday, it meant she could not afford to do eight loads of wash. And things were getting worse. City budget cuts forced up the price of a monthly transit pass to $40 from $35. The children needed new clothes.[57]

Jane was on and off welfare for the next five years. When she did have periods of work, it was in the new "contingent" sector, so named because of the tenuous, on-again, off-again relationship to employers. Temps, together with part-time workers, independent contractors, consultants, and freelancers, now constitute 25 to 30 percent of the civilian workforce. The majority of them, especially at the lower levels, are women. These workers go without health insurance, sick pay, other benefits, and the kind of safety regulations that protect full-time workers. In Europe temp agencies must provide full benefits, including sick pay. The income from temporary work more than tripled between 1981 and 1991, from $3.5 to $11.4 billion. In fact, over a quarter of the new jobs in our current "economic recovery" are of this nature.[58] In the past year, Jane has worked for a bank, a pharmaceutical company, an advertising agency, and an insurance company. At the insurance company, she had a supervisor who constantly yelled at her as she had not mastered the hundreds of complicated forms peculiar to their business. She found herself crying quietly in the bathroom every day but afraid to quit for fear there would be no more work. This same supervisor insisted she lift heavy boxes full of files, causing her to injure her back. She was afraid to report this accident for fear of losing the work and was even afraid to report in sick in order to see a doctor.[59] Alex has now been diagnosed as learning disabled.

## ARE WELFARE MOTHERS TO BLAME?

Some people have argued that the expansion of welfare benefits is responsible for the growth of single motherhood in the United States. They claim that welfare reduces the cost of single motherhood and discourages young parents from marrying. While it is true that in some parts of the country, welfare offers poor women more economic security than marriage, this argument is flawed in several respects. First, the trend in welfare benefits between 1960 and 1990 does not match the trend in single motherhood very well. Both welfare benefits and single motherhood increased dramatically during the 1960s and early 1970s. After 1974, however, welfare benefits declined while single motherhood continued to rise.[60] Also, increases in welfare cannot explain why single motherhood grew among women from higher socioeconomic backgrounds who were not likely to be motivated by the promise of a welfare benefit. Moreover, welfare cannot explain why single motherhood is more common in this country than in other industrialized countries. Nearly all Western European countries have much more generous benefits for single mothers than the United States. In America, the poverty rate for nonemployed single mothers is 69 percent, whereas it is around 28 percent in countries such as Sweden, France, and the United Kingdom.[61] If we cannot blame single motherhood on welfare, can we blame welfare mothers for other social problems?

## JUVENILE DELINQUENCY

Of course, children of welfare mothers are more likely to experience special problems. But does it follow that we can blame welfare mothers (or single mothers) for juvenile delinquency? Most of the research on families as a cause of juvenile delinquency tends to be rather limited. For instance, researchers examine family structure—i.e., whether there is one parent, two parents, stepparents, and so forth—without examining the quality of relationships within those families. Most important, variations in socioeconomic status are not explored as an influence, with the exception of extreme urban poverty where the delinquency rates are much higher.[62] Few studies of the origins of juvenile delinquency look at the same children over a long period of their lives. Thus, the findings from this body of research are unreliable and full of contradictions. It is impossible to draw conclusions about marital status, per se, as a factor in juvenile delinquency.

However, there are several family factors that appear to be associated with juvenile delinquency regardless of social and economic context. They include parents' criminal record; poor parental supervision; cruel, passive, or neglecting parental attitudes; erratic or harsh discipline; marital conflict; and large family size. The parents' own criminality has the most striking and consistent association with their children's delinquency. Criminal parents provide a model of aggression and antisocial attitudes, if not of criminal activities as such. Also, a parent's criminality is associated with poor supervision, family discord, unemployment, reliance on welfare, and a host of other family factors.[63] As about 95 percent of convicted criminals are males, one might safely conclude that mothers of any sort are not a prime cause of juvenile delinquency.[64]

In fact, the only fairly clear correlation between family structure and juvenile delinquency is that children from divorced and separated families appear to be somewhat more likely to commit minor offenses, especially those involving drug and alcohol abuse. Adolescents who come from dysfunctional broken homes are significantly more likely to be involved in drug offenses than adolescents from functional broken homes, functional intact homes, or dysfunctional intact homes.[65]

Clearly, the quality of relationships within the family is more important than whether children are in a single- or two-parent family. There is some indication that a stepparent in the family increases the likelihood of delinquency because stepfamily relationships can be extremely difficult. Where there is conflict and a high degree of dysfunctional behavior, adolescents are more likely to misbehave.[66] It must be remembered that children are born with their own temperaments and, in the case of juvenile delinquency, it appears that those who become delinquents are more likely to have evidenced antisocial behavior since childhood, suggesting that certain innate personality characteristics are also associated with delinquency.[67]

But beyond the family, the school and peer environment are such powerful influences that regardless of family environment, they can create juvenile delinquents, although, most often, all these influences interact. The degree to which an adolescent is motivated to do well in school and the degree to which he or she is involved with delinquent peers, are, by adolescence, as influential as any family factors.[68] At a broader level, delinquency is also more common in urban environments, especially within the disenfranchised ghetto, where stable families and institutions have fled and the prospects for stable employment are low. The socioeconomic diversity that characterized the inner city even a decade ago, is no longer there. Minority professionals and even the working class who once attended school and shared the same commercial and recreational facilities with the poorest sectors of the city, have left and taken with them standards of mainstream behavior as well as a social network that was able to link those on the bottom with jobs and support. As prospects for employment diminish, alternatives to salaried work such as welfare and the underground economy have become a way of life. Related to this social isolation is the problem of juvenile delinquency, learned in the streets by boys who have no visible prospects of legitimate employment.[69] Another group of juveniles who tend to see less prospect for a bright future are girls, who find a role with some importance as young mothers.

## TEEN MOTHERS

Lorraine Lessope was unmarried and a school dropout when she became pregnant at the age of sixteen by her twenty-two-year-old uncle.* She went on welfare immediately and continued to receive public assistance for the next seventeen years, even while she was married (to someone other than the father of her child). The marriage lasted only three years. Lorraine eventually had three children by three different men, none of whom was her husband. She has been employed periodically but never for more than a few years at a time and never yielding enough income to lift her off the welfare rolls. Lorraine is now living alone with her three children and her two-year-old grandchild, the son of her now sixteen-year-old daughter. Lorraine's oldest son, Randy, lived with a varying combination of adults over his life. During his preschool years, he resided first with his mother and grandmother, then with his grandmother alone, before moving back with his mother after she married Randy's stepfather. The boyfriend Lorraine lived with during Randy's adolescence is "like a father" (his words) to him, and they keep in touch about every other month. Randy does not see his stepfather. As a preschooler, Randy had difficulty concentrating, was frustrated when asked to delay gratification, exhibited low self-esteem, and tested low in cognitive ability. At age seventeen, he drinks alcohol regularly but has not committed a crime. He is behind one year in school but plans to finish high school.

Harriet Hopewell became pregnant with Claudia at sixteen. At her parent's insistence, she delayed her marriage to Ned, the seventeen-year-old father of her child, until she had completed her schooling

---

*Once again, I am indebted to Frank Furstenberg for these prototypes, which I have altered slightly by adding the typical sexual seduction by an older male. (See: Frank Furstenberg, Jean Brooks-Gunn, and S. Philip Morgan, Adolescent Mothers in Later Life [New York: Cambridge University Press, 1987].)

and had a job. She lived with her parents until she was twenty, when she married Ned. She and Ned have been married for fourteen years and have a second child. Both have been steadily employed and now live in a suburban garden apartment. Harriet's mother was the primary caregiver during Claudia's first four years while Harriet went to school. Throughout Claudia's preschool years the grandmother was her regular baby-sitter and the two are very close. Claudia is a B student and plans to go to college.

The truth about teen motherhood is not as predictable as many believe. Social concern about teen mothers probably has more to do with the fact that they are not married than that they are teens. After all, at the height of the baby boom, close to half of all women wed in their teens and well over a quarter of all women had their first birth before the age of twenty.[70] The percentage of births to teens out of wedlock jumped from 14 percent in 1955 to 56 percent in 1984.[71] For the first time in American history, the link between marriage and sexual activity was severed. Attention to this problem was initially focused on black families, in part because they experienced the most dramatic changes in the last quarter century. Marriage among teenage blacks virtually disappeared over the past two decades. By the mid-1980s, 90 percent of children of black teenage mothers were born out of wedlock.[72] Indeed, in the Furstenberg study, one of the consistent problems for mothers and their children was the fleeting involvement of fathers and father figures.

Lorraine Lessope is no more typical of teenage mothers than is Harriet Hopewell. Both represent prototypes found in the largest (close to four hundred subjects), longest (seventeen years) study of teen mothers to date.[73] By now the reader should not be surprised that even the teen mother has been taking a bum rap. Most researchers agree that children of teen mothers are more likely to be disadvantaged compared to the offspring of women who delay childbearing because they are more likely to grow up in a single-parent household and are more likely to be poor. But while early childbearing increases the risk of social and economic disadvantage, the risk is not sufficiently great to justify the stereotype of the teen mother living on welfare with a flock of ill-cared-for children. Virtually all existing studies show tremendous variation in outcomes of early parenthood. A substantial proportion of adolescent parents manage to recover from the handicaps imposed by early parenthood. Moreover, some portion of the adverse consequences presumed to be the fault of early child-bearing is actually due to prior differences in the family backgrounds of teen mothers and later childbearers. Also, most studies of early childbearing focus on the years immediately following the birth of the first child, when the greatest difficulties are occurring. In the Fursten-berg study the researchers found that none of the initial attitudes expressed by the adolescent and her family—whether they were pleased or distressed, had considered an abortion or not—predicted how well the mother actually managed her child's life in the future. (So much for the predictive power of bonding theory!)

The women in the Furstenberg study, for the most part, displayed a remarkable commitment to their children by juggling school, work, and child care responsibilities. And indeed, the majority succeeded in their efforts, as evidenced by the small number of chronic welfare de-pendents, the larger number of high school graduates, and their rela-tively small families. A third of the adolescents in this study were in the college prep track in school. And two thirds plan to continue their education beyond high school. However, their demanding life cir-cumstances did affect the environment in which their children were reared, and the costs of teenage parenthood sometimes was borne by their offspring.

Most studies show few or no differences in the parenting skills of teens with young children compared to older mothers.[74] However, teen mothers typically share parenting. During their children's early years, 40 percent of mothers in the Furstenberg study were not the primary caregivers. One in four of the girls lived with her parents and often a grandmother or other relative took primary responsibility for the child while the teen finished school and went to work. Even when they were aided by relatives, though, the girls took an active part in caring for their children.

Most young mothers put a great deal of energy into caring for their children and take great pride in their accomplishments and show strong feelings of love for them. However, while children in the Furstenberg study fared quite well as preschoolers, as youth, they ex-hibited higher rates of such misbehavior as running away from home, seriously hurting someone, or stealing. In fact, adolescents of teen mothers are much more likely to exhibit delinquency and antisocial behavior. They are also much more likely to be sexually active earlier and are more likely to become pregnant than children of older mothers. The reasons for these differences include not only the family environment, but the wider socioeconomic environment that involves an especially strong peer and school influence in adolescence. Once again, the consistent not-looked-for finding of this research is that children are most influenced by their mothers' well-being. Young women who have a stable job and/or a stable marriage, better education, and fewer children have children who are better off. A number of recent studies now find that the negative effects of teenage childbearing have been overstated: Because these girls are disproportionately from disadvantaged backgrounds, their children would have suffered from the effects of poverty whether they had them early or later in life, although to a slightly lesser degree if they were born later in their mother's life.[75]

Families run by unmarried single parents are here to stay, and a number of factors explain their growth. The first factor is women's growing economic independence from men and their ability to support themselves outside marriage. Also, the decline in men's earning power relative to women's is a factor. While women were becoming more self-sufficient in the 1950s and 1960s, men's wages and employment opportunities increased as well. Consequently, marriage continued to be economically rewarding even though more women could afford to live on their own. After the 1970s, however, the picture changed.[76] In just two decades, 1970 to 1990, the economic gains associated with marriage had declined by fifteen percentage points. Between 1970 and 1990, women's earnings stagnated while men's earnings declined; those with less education suffered most. Women with a high school degree experienced a 2 percent decline in earnings while men with a similar education experienced a 13 percent decline. Low-skilled men were having a hard time finding work and a hard time fulfilling the breadwinner role. And of course, changes in sexual mores and the feminist movement also contributed to the increasing independence of women and their intolerance of abusive husbands.

## CONCLUSION

When will social scientists stop casting the majority of contemporary mothers as deviates? American mothers come in several varieties, and there is no clear evidence to suggest that any one type should be illegitimate or even that Harriet should be the central ideal.

What's really extraordinary in all this industrious investigation of changing families is the accidental finding that again and again, mothers bear the lion's share of responsibility for their children and shoulder it so very well—sacrificing their own needs in order to provide for their children. And it is extraordinary, too, that instead of focusing on the detrimental effects of poverty on mothers and children, researchers continue to search for damage inflicted by bad mothers.

And while they earnestly engage in scrutinizing the bad mother, the bad father is nowhere to be found. Isn't Dad, after all, an unmarried father, a single father, a divorced father, a teenage pregnant father, a lazy welfare father? One thing that is clear from this study of the family, is that his help and involvement could be very valuable (and I don't mean to the taxpayer).

# Fatherguilt?

## WHERE ARE THE GUILTY FATHERS?

Where are the reams of research zealously investigating the social problems caused by fathers? Why is there no handwringing about the failure of fathers to marry, their culture of poverty that makes them bad examples to their children, their irresponsibility in absenting themselves from their children? Where is the guilt literature for men who apparently have so much trouble balancing work and family that they are unable to do their share of housework and caregiving?

Only 60 percent of American fathers live with their own children. (In black families the figure is closer to 40 percent.)[1] Yet our leaders do not seem to lament the emotional deprivation their children have experienced from not having a dad at home to care for them. Men often abandon their families completely when they divorce. Half of all noncustodial fathers gradually lose all contact with their children.[2] Public discourse about the absent father (when it's not about delinquent dollars) however, revolves around the restoration of the Ozzie and Harriet fantasy—the psychological needs of children are really less important than a return to the old order à la "family values" or the needs of men to refashion their sex role.

Even the fathers' rights movement seems to be about the wronged rights of divorced fathers regarding equal access to their children and a desire to hold down support payments.[3] Yes, to be fair, fathers often care by providing financially, and, yes, many divorced fathers continue to care deeply about their children and struggle to be involved with them. But guilt about the effects on children of losing their fathers is not the prime force behind the fathers' rights movement.

Fathers who live with their families continue to resist doing their fair share of domestic work, even though their wives often divorce them for that very reason. In fact, in only 20 percent of families where both partners work full-time do men share the domestic work equally with women.[4] While the figure is up from two decades ago, the prime reason for men's increased participation is not so much a change of heart, as economic necessity occasioned by the fact that more wives are working and child care is very costly.[5] In at least 13 percent of these families, the fathers who fail to share the domestic work are not even the primary breadwinners! No headlines regarding the apparently incapacitating work/family conflict experienced by fathers are to be found, however.

According to the social scientists, one of the most powerful factors in predicting whether a child will grow up to become a criminal is whether a parent is a criminal, in which case 95 percent of the time, we are talking about Dad.[6] Yet no social reformers have taken up this research finding to blame fathers for high court and prison costs (that are certainly greater than welfare) or failing to preserve the morals of their children. Why all the outrage over the Murphy Browns of the land—most single fathers are certified criminals because they fail to pay court-mandated child support! Most single fathers, unlike most single mothers, have violated the law. Only one in three single mothers receives court-mandated child support from her children's father, in spite of recent legislation making it a federal crime to fail to pay up.[7] Of course, these "deadbeat dads" have recently acquired notoriety. But it is not because anyone suddenly realized the psychological damage they caused their children. Rather, these fathers are seen as draining tax dollars. Men owe $34 billion a year in child support, much of which is compensated for by welfare.[8] And by the way, $34 billion is *twice* what the federal government parcels out to those destitute women and children whose dependence is considered a sign of welfare *mothers'* moral decay.

Let me add one other commonly ignored fact: One of the prime factors preventing welfare mothers from working when they do find jobs is fathers who become threatened by the prospect of these women's independence. The men harass and even assault these women in order to make them quit their jobs.[9] And speaking of abusive men, one half of all parental abusers are fathers, yet they spend a fraction of the time with their children that mothers spend. Moreover, wife abuse is an epidemic in this country and is truly a cause of psychological damage to children (and in thousands of instances a year it actually causes death to mothers).[10]

Fathers are not even such great breadwinners. One in three men between twenty-five and thirty-four doesn't earn enough to lift a family of four above the poverty level.[11] In one out of three families in which the mother works full-time, she is the main breadwinner.[12] Among minority fathers, the picture is even bleaker. A significant portion of black fathers, for instance, are virtually not available as "desirable" marriage partners.[13] A significant number of the missing men are either in prison or prematurely dead; an even larger number simply cannot find work.[14]

Where is the guilt culture for men? While the "deadbeat dad" epithet is increasingly hurled at them, nowhere are they repenting, confessing their guilt, or fearing the possible damage they've done to their kids' psyches. They mostly seem worried about their rights in custody battles and whether it is really masculine to diaper a baby. The "million man march" of black men on Washington in October 1995 was supposed to involve "atonement." While it was never made clear exactly what the men were sorry for, one would hope the abandonment of their children might have been high on the list. In any case that idea got lost in all the boasting about the vast numbers of men who (having left the women and children behind) gathered peacefully and felt good about it. Granted, there are the New Fathers, middle-class young men who are interested in nurturing their infants and children, who publicly lament their "work/family conflict." But their involvement with their children is generally viewed as a nice bonus if not a fashionable accessory. The failure to be a New Father is hardly the occasion for paternal apology, nor is their "conflict" the product of having to do the lion's share of domestic work as well as salaried work, leaving behind little energy for their children.

Rather than take off on a father-blaming extravaganza like the one being leveled at mothers, we would certainly do better to help fathers become more supportive of their children and their children's mothers through concrete action. Fathers are, of course, suffering from the hazards of the job market and the effects of failed or hostile relation-ships with the mothers of their children. They are also suffering from lack of education about parenting. And, yes, fathers also need the benefits of a national family support policy and a reformed workplace to facilitate their greater caregiving involvement with their children. But at the moment it seems their accountability for their children's well-being is not genuinely recognized.

## THE BABY GURUS AGAIN

The lack of fatherblame, it must be pointed out, is once again facili-tated by our favorite voices of authority—child psychologists and pe-diatricians, who have failed to view fathers' personal involvement as central to their children's development. The fact is, in the psychope-diatric community, fathers are still an afterthought, a possible mother substitute. They are seldom viewed as important parents in their own right.

Dr. Spock has been the most progressive among the baby gurus, encouraging fathers since the mid-1970s to get involved with their children and share equally with their wives in the parenting tasks and domestic work.[15] By 1992 Spock even discusses some of the difficul-ties for parents related to their changing sex roles, including discrim-ination and lack of flexibility in the workplace.

Penelope Leach, on the other hand, continues to dwell in the Freudian '50s, where having a baby is a woman's "sexual fulfillment." She claims that "no man can take full care of a child and every woman can and we would do well to fully recognize the differences and stop trying to make men into mothers." Leach decries attempts at equal parenting as a violation of nature. Women, by virtue of their preg-nancy and then breast-feeding and "hormone-driven vigilance" were meant to be the involved parent. The father's role is to make it safe for the mother to mother. She needs to be loved so that she can pour out her love to the baby. Then, as the first year draws on, fathers lure their offspring from that enclosing, rightly dependent relationship with the female parent and out toward autonomy with glimpses of the big world.[16]

T. Berry Brazelton tries to be more modern. He extols the virtues of "parents' " bonding/attachment which is "instinctive" but "not instant and automatic." Brazelton does not discuss the specifics of fathers' "instinctive" attachment except to say that fathers interact with their babies in a "different rhythm" from mothers. But as the story of becoming attached unfolds, it is clear that only mothers' attachment has any consequences for the baby. "It may be that there are a critical number of months that a baby and mother must go through together before they can be separated without irreparable losses to both of them," Brazelton opines.[17]

None of these parenting experts sees fathers as essential to their children's psychological well-being. While a new industry in paternal advice-giving has sprung up in the past decade, there is no sense that fathers are responsible for how their children turn out. The new paternal parenting precepts reflect the underlying research literature in that father involvement is considered a nice bonus for men who can still be masculine if they participate according to XYZ guidelines for masculine fathering.

## RESEARCH ON FATHERING

While great volumes of psychological research are produced that search for deficits caused by faulty mothering, the research on fathers is comparatively small and generally fails to find fathers responsible for their children's problems. Moreover, minority fathers are almost entirely missing from the literature. Fathers' employment is certainly not considered a threat to their children's well-being, whereas studies of maternal employment, of course, constitute a mini-industry. There are almost no studies of fathers as progenitors of child psychopathology, whereas pathogenic "toxic" mothers abound in the clinical literature. In fact, in the 1980s, 48 percent of the studies of causes of child and adolescent psychopathology exclusively involved mothers whereas only 1 percent exclusively involved fathers.[18] And while about half of parental child abuse is committed by fathers, the vast majority of studies focus on mothers as perpetrators.[19] No matter what fathering factors psychologists study—fathers never seem to be considered essential to children's well-being.

The study of fathering instead revolves around the importance of masculinity. In fact, in the research literature it appears that either fathers produce only sons, or that their daughters are so contented by the mere knowledge of their fathers' existence that they require no particular type of paternal attention. Psychologists' main questions are: How do fathers affect (boy) children? And how do fathers differ from mothers? In the earliest studies of fathers that began in the 1950s and 1960s, fathers were studied to see if their own masculinity made for masculinity in their sons. (It didn't.) Then families where fathers were absent were studied to see if the sons suffered for lack of a resident male role model. (They didn't.) In the 1970s, psychologists began to observe what fathers actually did with their children when they lived with them. The main question was not "What is it that makes men good parents?" but rather "What does masculinity bring to the situation?" (Nothing, per se.) Can fathers do it as well as mothers? (They can.) Do fathers do it as much as mothers? (They don't.) And finally, in the 1980s, child psychologists began to study the effects of divorced fathers on their children. Does the fact that most divorced fathers are non-resident parents, adversely affect their children—especially the masculinity of boys? In a word: No.

In the 1950s researchers attempted to correlate the characteristics of fathers and sons especially regarding the effects of sex role. Researchers thought that masculine fathers would make for masculine sons. However, they found there was no real correlation. What they eventually discovered, is that boys wanted to be like fathers that they liked and respected. So fathers, regardless of their "masculinity," had masculine sons when they had a warm and involved relationship with their sons. Interestingly, the actual characteristics of the "masculine" sons in these good relationships changed as ideas about what is proper masculine behavior changed with the times, and in response to the women's movement. As masculinity came to include more of such "feminine" characteristics as warmth and nurturance, boys who had warm relationships with their fathers showed those qualities instead of the more macho qualities of the 1950s.[20] Researchers had also thought that fathers who were highly achieving themselves would, by virtue of being good sex role models, have sons who were also highly achieving. Once again, however, the important factor proved to be the warmth and closeness of the relationship, not the father's achievement. And similar findings occurred for emotional adjustment in children. In other words, it was the quality of the father's relationship that seems to have mattered, not the fact of his sex.

Research on "father absence" also began in the 1950s. The assumption was that by comparing the behavior and personalities of children raised with and without fathers one could essentially—by a process of subtraction—estimate what sort of influence fathers typically had. This literature is voluminous and controversial. It generally indicated that somewhat more boys growing up without fathers tended to have problems of gender identity, school performance, and psychosocial adjustment—especially in the area of aggressiveness. Researchers first tried to explain these differences in terms of the absence of a male sex role model with whom the boys could identify. The problem here, though, was that most boys without fathers seem to develop quite normally so far as sex roles and achievement are concerned. Several other factors seemed to be more important in accounting for the differences. First, there is the absence of a coparent, someone to help out with the child care and provide emotional support and supplemental resources. Second, there is the economic stress that goes along with single mothering. And related to the economic stress of the single mother is the accompanying emotional stress and social isolation. And finally, of course, in many cases there is also the postmarital or extramarital hostility and conflict with the absent parent. In other words, fathers' absence may be harmful not necessarily because a sex role model is absent, but because many aspects of the fathers' role—economic, social, emotional—go unfulfilled.[21]

In the early 1980s, child psychologists also began to explore the ways in which divorce and the trasition to fatherlessness might influence children's development. Children of divorce are affected primarily by the conflict that often precedes the marital separation; they are also affected by the declining economic circumstances that often follow the divorce; and by the social and emotional isolation and distress of their single mothers (see chapter 4). Most of the research conducted to date, however, would suggest that while children are affected by the perceived and often actual abandonment by their parent (usually their father), the absence of a male gender role model is much less important in explaining the effects of divorce than are these other broader effects of divorce.

When the absence of fathers is studied, of course, the reference is to fathers who do not live with their children. "Maternal absence," by contrast, has been described as "maternal employment."[22] To date, there are no studies in which fathers' employment is referred to as "paternal absence" or where their working or overworking is seen as a deterrent to their children's well-being. Despite the volumes of research mandating that mothers shoulder the work of attachment to children—there is absolutely no imperative for father attachment even though fathers attach. (It's not hard to see where judges making child custody decisions in the divorce courts get their ideas.)

## PATERNAL ATTACHMENT?

Prior to the late 1970s, psychologists saw the role of the father primarily as the breadwinner. But as the women's movement grew and the natural childbirth movement took off, a "New Fatherhood" became part of the male liberation movement in which fatherhood functioned as a kind of self-enhancing therapy. The new liberated father would now be a less macho, more nurturing man who attended expectant father classes, discussed his feelings with other men, and learned "infant message" to enhance attachment and experience the pleasures of nurturing. This new fatherhood would heighten men's self-awareness and revise their masculinity.[23] As men's personal involvement with their young children became somewhat more common, psychologists began to study this New Fathering—not as a biological imperative, but mostly to see how it compared with mothering.

Because the natural childbirth movement in the mid 1970s employed fathers as birth coaches for their mates, fathers became part of the bonding craze and for a while their behavior toward their newborns, termed "engrossment," was identified and celebrated in the research literature.[24] Soon fathers were observed attaching to their infants, but they were simply compared to mothers—there is no real theoretical base for paternal attachment.[25] These studies of bonding and attachment generally find that infants form attachments to mothers and fathers at around the same age and that they may have a secure attachment to one parent while having a different type of attachment to the other. In comparison to the research findings about mothers, very little is known about the range of either father-infant interaction or the quality of father-infant relationships. I find one of the great curiosities of this research to be that an infant often may have a strong attachment to her father even though he does not spend a lot of time with her. Some researchers believe this disparity can be explained by the fact that fathers' "strong emotional investment" "suffuses" their interactions and communicates a special caring to the infant. No such suffusion of care, however, has been identified in mothers (whose guilt about working might be eased by the discovery of their own Suffusion Factor?). Moreover, researchers do not seem to take father attachment seriously as an influence on their children's lives. Where minute variations in maternal attachment are said to account for a variety of aspects of child development, there are virtually no studies connecting father attachment to any later child behaviors or personality factors.[26]

## ARE FATHERS DIFFERENT FROM MOTHERS?

Most contemporary studies that include fathers compare their behavior to that of mothers and they find that fathers influence their children in ways that are very similar to mothers. For example, in one recent study, psychologists measured men's and women's responses to a crying infant. Volunteers were shown a videotape of a crying, obviously distressed infant, followed by another tape of a comfortable, cooing baby. Men's physiological response—i.e., quickened pulse rate, increased rate of respiration, overall alertness of the senses—and the subsequent relaxation response to the comforted infant, was indistinguishable from that of women.[27] In another study, psychologists carefully observed and videotaped fathers and mothers while they bottle-fed their newborns. Deciding when and how much to feed, when to burp, when to arouse a sleepy baby who has not fed adequately, and when to soothe and settle the overstimulated infant, takes skill that is often linked to maternal hormones. These researchers were therefore surprised to find that fathers solved feeding problems, burped and stroked, awakened and soothed appropriately, and most important, got as much milk into their babies in the allotted time as did their spouses.[28]

Contemporary research psychologists have also studied the "behavioral styles" of fathers compared to mothers. They find that mothers' interactions are dominated by caretaking, whereas fathers are defined more as playmates. Mothers actually spend more time playing with their children than fathers do, but play is the main thing fathers do. Parenting skills are usually acquired "on the job" by both mothers and fathers—and both do equally well when given the same experience. Given the disparity in their experience, however, mothers become more sensitive to their children, more in tune with them, and more aware of each child's characteristics and needs. By virtue of their lack of experience, fathers become correspondingly less sensitive and come to feel less confidence in their parenting abilities.

## HOW INVOLVED ARE FATHERS?

Another aspect of fathering that psychologists began to study in the mid-1970s was simply the extent of fathers' involvement with their children—a topic defined in quite a variety of ways. Fathers in a two-parent family where the mother is unemployed spend less than a quarter of the time the mother spends in direct interaction with their children. However, those fathers assume almost no responsibility for their children's care or rearing. In two-parent families in which the mother is employed, the father spends about a third as much time as the mother but still does not take responsibility for the children's care and rearing. (Note that when mothers are employed, the actual amount of time fathers spend does not increase, but rather the proportion of time, compared to mothers, increases.) Both parents spend more time in child care when the children are younger—a trend that contradicts the assumption that fathers become more involved as the children get older.[29] Not only do fathers spend less time in child care or household work tasks associated with children, they are also less involved than mothers in parent-child leisure or teaching activities. Some of the difference is, of course, due to the emphasis on fathers' main role as breadwinner and the fact that fathers spend more hours in paid work than mothers. But the net differences in fathers' and mothers' employment does not account for the lower involvement of fathers in children's lives.

There have also been a few studies of fathers who either share in or take primary responsibility for child care. These studies all agree that children with highly involved fathers have increased cognitive competence, increased empathy, fewer sex-stereotyped beliefs, and a greater sense of autonomy. Psychologists speculate that the effects re-

sult from the benefit of having two highly involved parents who provide a diversity of stimulation rather than just one. But fathers' involvement also seems to change the family context by making it more
possible for both parents to do more of what is uniquely satisfying to
each of them. In these studies, the fathers felt good about their involvement because they chose it. If they should become involved because of a layoff from work, however, there is likely to be resentment
from both parents and the effects of father involvement on children
could be adverse. What matters, then, is not so much who is at home
but how that person feels about being there.

Psychologists have recently investigated some of the factors that
tend to motivate men to become involved in caretaking. Their first
concern has been with masculinity, and they find that the women's
movement and the media hype about the New Father have been helpful in overcoming macho stereotypes that denigrate the masculinity of
men who like to care for young children. Another factor affecting men's motivation to care for young children is skills and self-
confidence. Even motivated men often complain that a lack of skills,
exemplified by ignorance or clumsiness, prevents their increased involvement. Many fathers do not realize that first-time mothers are just
as incompetent and terrified as they are. The third factor influencing
paternal involvement is support—especially from the family, more especially from the mother.[30]

Researchers seem to believe that there is no single "father's role" to
which all fathers should aspire. They find that high father involvement may have positive effects in some circumstances and negative effects in others, especially where there is high conflict or abuse. But
they do not seem concerned about how little time men are actually
spending with their children. They just breathe a sigh of relief that the
father doesn't have to be particularly masculine or highly successful
to have a good relationship with his children and that absent fathers
are less important than absent coparenting support.

How can we account for the persistent bias in parenting research
that fails to see the personal involvement of fathers as important to
their children's lives? Is there some scientific basis for the double
standard? Or is it simply the result of prejudice born of custom? Perhaps psychologists failed to examine fathering because they lacked
the inspirational animal research to guide them. Indeed, there were

no studies of rats, goats, or geese to illustrate the perilous course of paternal instincts in the battle for survival. Even the primate research failed to yield up the necessary parables—that is, until more women became involved in the research and until primates were studied over longer periods.[31]

## BIOLOGICAL BASES OF FATHERHOOD

As it turns out, among non-human primates, the animals closest to us genetically, males have the same potential for parental involvement as females. Moreover, males are far more involved with infants than is popularly believed. For example, in nocturnal species of monkeys, males perform all of the caretaking tasks and mothers are relatively uninvolved in infant care. Within these species, mothers must spend all of their time away from the nest feeding themselves to produce enough milk to nurse their infants. Pygmy marmosets typically give birth to twins. It is physically impossible for the mothers to feed the infants by themselves, so adult males assume most of the child care responsibilities, carrying and caring for the young at all times other than when the young are nursing.[32]

Among species such as savannah baboons, gorillas, and black howler monkeys, mothers normally spend most of their time nurturing their offspring. However, infants also develop close, enduring relationships with one or two adult males. These male "friends" maintain spatial proximity to individual infants, and they hold, groom, cuddle, and comfort them when they show signs of distress. Within these species there is much variation among individual males in terms of their involvement with infants.

Another kind of paternal infant involvement is mainly one of tolerance and benign neglect. In other species, such as rhesus monkeys, hamadryas baboons, chimpanzees, and lar gibbons, the primary bond is between mother and infant, with males typically involved mainly with other males. Even in these species, however, males also develop occasional affiliative relationships with infants. If the infant's mother is hurt or killed, an intense bond usually develops between the infant and an individual male who adopts the infant and exhibits all the nurturing behaviors that are typically observed in mothers—holding, grooming, comforting, and protecting.

Primate males, therefore, have the same potential for parental involvement as primate females—it is simply a variety of social factors and other features of the environment that influence this natural capacity. However, it is misguided, if not foolish, to describe the behavior of nonhuman animals in evolutionary terms and then suggest that any human behavior which fails to correspond is unnatural. Moreover, humans are not just biologically programmed creatures. They presumably distinguish themselves from nonhuman animals by possessing a conscience—humans see a right or wrong, where animals see survival—eat or be eaten.* So human fathers probably do know what is "right" regarding the care of their children. The question is, why aren't they doing it?

## THE PROBLEM OF MASCULINITY

To understand why fathers aren't more personally involved in the daily lives of their children, we need to revisit the changes in sex role and related economic functions established back in the nineteenth century. When the breadwinner/hearth angel dichotomy was invented in the 1830s, fathers were propelled on a long trajectory away from their families and toward full commitment to the workplace (see chapter 2). For both economic and social reasons, those bipolar roles are no longer very functional. Women, of course, have now established themselves in the public workplace and have successfully rebelled against the restrictions of their hearth angel identity. Men, however, have not undergone a corresponding gender renovation although there is currently much talk about their doing so. The discussion of men's need to change began in earnest in the 1970s with a fledgling men's movement that was largely pro-feminist. Men then focused on getting in touch with their gentler feelings and viewing women in a more egalitarian light. A change in the fathering role, however, was not a central feature in this rather introspective era. In the 1980s, the men's movement grew in a variety of directions that were often reactionary. One former pro-feminist "liberated" man,

---

*Actually, of course, animals display a remarkable altruism and caring, which scientists are just beginning to fit into their evolutionary model. However, nonhuman animals' ability to reason about this is considerably less than the human capacity for thought.

Warren Farrell,[33] complained that independent women were venting too much anger at men who were reduced to "success objects" by achievement-obsessed women. In Farrell's most recent book, *The Myth of Male Power,* he claims victimhood for men at least on a par with that for women, since men's lives have presumably been shortened by the burdens of being breadwinners. This reactive trend has taken some odd turns. In *Naked Nomads: Unmarried Men in America,* George Gilder, for example, echoing some of the assertions of sociobiologists, claimed men are an unsavory breed, "a baboon troop" of "naked nomads" who are far more likely when they are unmarried to become drug addicts, alcoholics, compulsive gamblers, criminals and murderers. Women must therefore prepare to wed or die because men will buy knives and guns and thus achieve a brief and predatory dominance, raping and pillaging, debauching and despoiling. (Gilder does not explain why marrying one of these predators is better than fending them off.) According to Gilder, by championing programs that allow wives to survive without their husbands (such as AFDC), feminists and liberals have seen to it that men were "cuckolded by the compassionate state." That explains the criminality of the underclass male who has gone astray without the civilizing effects of a wife. Marriage is the ultimate solution to reforming males.[34]

Of course, in the contemporary debate about masculinity, there have also been more works of feminist men who champion women's rights. For example, *Myths of Masculinity* and *The End of Manhood: A Book for Men of Conscience,* are by pro-feminist men dreaming of a kinder, gentler male gender. Another frequent theme in this movement is men's sorrow over the lack of closeness they had with their own fathers who were often either emotionally unavailable or absent. Samuel Osherson's *Finding Our Fathers: The Unfinished Business of Manhood*[35] and Robert Bly's *Iron John*[36] are of this genre. In fact, in the early 1990s, hundreds of thousands of mostly white, middle-aged, middle class men gathered in woodsy workshops in search of their lost manhood, longing for their lost (emotionally distant) fathers, letting loose the screaming "wild man" inside them which had presumably been held in check by women. (See chapter 2 for a description of a previous incarnation of this movement at the turn of the century.) *Iron John* topped the best-seller lists for more than thirty-five weeks in 1991.[37] Not surprisingly, rather than blaming their fathers for abandoning them, the men have managed to blame their mothers. According to Bly, women have invaded men's areas and treated them like boys. The Great Mother's (women's) authority has become too powerful. The single mother's son has become a nice boy who is too eager to please his mother. To restore the nice boy's male identity, Bly offers the story of Iron John, borrowed from a Grimm Brothers fairy tale in which a young man has to take back the power he has given to his mother and get away from pleasing mommy. (The alert reader might just be catapulted from her chair as she imagines Gilder and Bly debating how women manage to make men both too wild and not wild enough!)

On the scholarly front, the exploration of masculinity is now booming. A recent issue of *The Chronicle of Higher Education* listed close to thirty new books on men and masculinity whose common theme was expressed in the headline "Scholars debunk the Marlboro Man: Examining Stereotypes of Masculinity."[38] These books include histories of American manhood, a history of male heterosexuality, and several studies on how the presence of women in the workplace has affected men. There is also an analysis of Clint Eastwood and a look at how men's bodies are treated as "spectacle" in Hollywood films.[39] In suggesting guidelines for the New Man, however, few of these books express a concern for men as fathers (notwithstanding the fair number of victims of distant or absent fathers). Their main interest is in men as pro-feminists, men as homosexuals, male friendships, men who are able to be emotionally vulnerable, and the ways in which masculinity is depicted in art and popular culture. While men's exploration of the confines of masculinity shows little interest in the role of fathering, discussions of fathering positively turn on questions of masculinity.

## THE NEW FATHER

The New Fathers who love to nurture their children—especially infants—have been at it almost two decades now and it is doubtful their ranks are greatly expanding. In fact they now have competition from the "New Traditionalist" father (who may or may not have ties to *Good Housekeeping*) who is being promoted by conservatives who see the restoration of fathering as a means to reconstruct family relations in which men are "masculine" authorities over "feminine" women and their children. But even amongst the old New Fathers, there appears to be more concern about what is masculine—how fathering differs from mothering—than what children actually need in order to thrive.

The New Father, the one who focuses on nurturing babies, emerged as a prototype in the late 1970s. He was highly publicized in the media, where he was pictured as educated, middle-class, and zealous about his role reversal. He began to write and buy books about himself that started to map a new social territory. Indeed, fathers in droves began writing about their fathering experiences. Typical of the genre, in 1982, a newspaper reporter for the *Miami Herald,* Mike Clary, published *Daddy's Home,*[40] an account of his first two years at home as a full-time father of Annie and his daily "experiences in the realm of motherhood." According to Clary, other men persistently ask him when he's going to get a real job and he keeps coming down with "housewives' blues." However, Mike "confesses" to feeling enormously comfortable in the role of full-time parent and asserts he keeps getting better at it. (A Doonesbury cartoon on the subject spoofs the considerable self-celebration of these new father chronicles, showing new father Rick glued to his word processor chronicling his adventures in parenting while his neglected child tries in vain to gain his attention.) Comedian Bill Cosby's *Fatherhood,*[41] a humorous take on family life, was one of the bestselling books in publishing history. His is a world, though, in which the fathers are still breadwinners and disciplinarians and their children are just little people who don't have "enough energy" to do their chores but love to spend Dad's money. Men's interest in fatherhood sold a great deal of copy. It also sent men to infant care and parenting education classes sponsored by hospitals and businesses. In response, there was a burst of how-to books and even a magazine, nonthreateningly titled *Parents Sports.* The how-to books: *How to Father, The Expectant Father, Father's Almanac, Father Power, Father Love, How to Father a Successful Daughter,* and so forth, were also complemented by a couple more theoretical and research-based books such as *Fatherhood in America: A Historical Study* and *Fathers Care for the Next Generation.* There were even special-interest texts for part-time fathers, single fathers, stepfathers, and homosexual fathers.[42] In spite of all the armchair interest, though, fathers have actually increased their involvement very little.

## THE NEW STEREOTYPES

By the 1990s, the New Father trend was being assessed. The primary concern of those who describe him, however, is not how wonderful it is for his wife and children to have his involvement; not how it is changing his view of himself and what's important in life; but rather, that fathers are, in some fundamental, biologically based, stereotypical way, different from mothers. The difference theme is displayed in a recent *Time* cover story on fatherhood.[43] The article points out that while some commend the nurturing nature of the idealized New Father, many others cringe at the idea of genderless parenting and defend the importance of men being "more than pale imitations of mothers." (No doubt mothers who bring home a salary are simply pale imitations of fathers.)

According to the difference theorists, there is some uniquely male contribution that is essential for raising healthy kids. A mother's love is unconditional, a father's love is more qualified, more tied to performance. Mothers worry about an infant's survival, fathers about future success. Kids learn from their moms how to be aware of their emotional side; from dad they "learn how to live in society." Parenting of young infants is just not a natural activity for males. Women are made for it: Their voices are more soothing; they are better able to read the signals a child sends before he or she can talk, and so forth. Go to the park and watch father and mother next to a child on a jungle gym. The father encourages the kid to challenge himself by climbing to the top; the mother tells him to be careful.[44] What interests *Psychology Today* about the New Father is sons in search of their lost masculinity. Fathering is the most masculine thing a father can do. A father who gets to hang out with his children is reliving the joys of his own childhood.[45]

Yes, "Dads Do It Differently," *American Baby* pronounces. Fathers, they claim, tend to be more playful and may prefer taking the kids out someplace for fun. Some parents [sic] hate diapers and burping but really enjoy going to the zoo, the park, or a museum with them.[46] *Parents* is even more adamant about the difference. According to Jerrold Lee Shapiro, author of *The Measure of a Man: Becoming the Father You Wish Your Father Had Been,* "Fathers aren't assistant mothers." It is a "big mistake" to encourage men to be more like women in bringing up their children. Men are different. They hold children differently, for instance. When a mother picks up her infant, she tends to wrap the baby up toward her breasts, providing comfort, warmth, and security. By contrast, a father may well hold the child at arm's length and make eye contact, toss her in the air, turn her around so that her back is against his chest, or prop her up to look back over his shoulder. Each of these "daddy holds" underscores a sense of freedom. Fathers and mothers even play differently. Mothers almost automatically join at the child's level of play. By contrast, play with Dad resembles an apprenticeship. Instead of pitching himself at the child's level, a father posits himself as teacher of his activity. Play is "hand me the socket wrench." Mothers and fathers also discipline differently. When a mother disciplines a child, she uses "an invisible emotional umbilical cord" to adjust the discipline from moment to moment, to the child's current state of mind. A father, "lacking any such apparatus," disciplines by rules.[47]

While on the face of it, the assertion of such gender differences might sound reasonable (the emotional umbilical cord notwithstanding) and certainly describes many commonly observed patterns, it must be remembered such differences may be largely the product of custom. It would be a shame if observations of these differences led to new gender restrictions that prohibit men and women from expressing the full range of their humanity and developing their special talents in the parenting role.

## THE NEW TRADITIONALIST FATHER

The widespread concern with maternal/paternal difference is not merely an embroidering on the flimsy cloth of some loose-knit lifestyle trend; it is also embedded in a political struggle to reshape the family along more traditional lines. In the beginning of the decade, the argument was cast as a matter of "family values." But the family values crowd failed to capture widespread support, in part because

many women were not eager to return to the halcyon days of Harriet.
More recently, the campaign has been recast in the form of concern
for the "absent father." A growing group of conservative organizations have begun to decry our "fatherless America." They believe that
society should discourage unwed fatherhood and divorce. They are
pushing the idea that the old breadwinning, authoritarian father, with
some updating in the nurturing department, can repair the damage to
the family that they believe was caused by feminism.

William Kristol, director of the Project for the Republican Future
and a favorite GOP adviser, explains: "Ultimately, the revival of fatherhood implies challenging some of the premises of the sexual revolution and of radical feminism." Wade Horn, director of the
National Fatherhood Initiative, one of several groups trying to persuade fathers to take their responsibilities to heart, explains, "What
we are trying to counter is this sense in our culture that the mother
and father do the same thing." The literature of the National Fatherhood Initiative asserts: "At times of crisis or stress, the traditionally
male values—especially the ability to contain emotions and be deci-
sive—are invaluable."* Mr. Horn and his colleagues believe that fathers bring something irreplaceable and inherently masculine to a
family: qualities like discipline, risk taking, and decisiveness that are
the hallmarks of the traditional father. They fear that some of the emphasis on blurring the roles of mother and father has "conned" people into believing that families will do fine without fathers.[48]

David Blankenhorn, president of the Institute for American Values, chairman of the National Fatherhood Initiative, and author of *Fatherless America,* is one of the most tireless promoters of bringing
back a more traditional view of fatherhood. "My criticism of the New
Father paradigm is that it acts as if the only act worth crediting is nurture. But the deep meaning of masculinity for most men is the idea of
providing for, and teaching children, and that should be celebrated."
Mr. Horn and Mr. Blankenhorn say they are trying to curb the "excesses of feminism" and to reward fathers for their contributions.

---

*I always groan at this stereotype because it is so seldom questioned. While men contain the emotions
that make them vulnerable—they seldom let themselves cry—they seem to do fine expressing anger and
aggression. Note, for example, the differences in rates of child abuse, the prevalence of battered
women's shelters, and the convictions for violent crime. Yet, on the other hand, stereotype declares that
women become depressed and passive and tear-stained when they should get going.

They find it "oppressive to say that men will not become New Fathers unless they do half the diaper changes or bottle feedings."[49]

A colleague of Blankenhorn at the Institute for American Values, David Popenoe, laments the implicit goal of "androgyny" in discussions of the New Fatherhood. He claims that while social androgyny may be an appropriate goal in the working world, in family life it is not appropriate because unlike the workplace, family organization is based on biological differences between men and women.[50] The biological phenomenon of attachment, for instance, according to Popenoe, indicates that an infant must have just one caretaker with whom to form a relationship during the first two or three years of life. (See chapter 3 for a discussion of this assertion.) Females experience hormonal changes during and after childbirth that strongly motivate them to care for their newborns. These hormonal changes are linked, in part, to the woman's capacity to breast-feed. The father's mode of parenting is clearly not interchangeable with the mother's.

Many men, Popenoe claims, being of a "more independent spirit," will simply avoid marrying and having children if they face having to give up their independence and engage in "unnatural" nurturing and caretaking roles. This is why marriages that follow the New Father alternative, according to Popenoe, have a high likelihood of breakup. Marriages with New Fathers experience a "festering tension" because a couple must be different enough so that sexual attraction is maintained.[51] Males are more sexually driven and promiscuous while females are more relationship oriented, thus setting up a continuous tension between the sexes. According to Popenoe, among mammals, the primary function of males is to inseminate females and spread their genes widely; for females, to harbor the growing fetus and bind males to themselves for the long-term care of their offspring.[52] (Hohum. Will they ever stop trying to keep people in "their place" with this biology-is-destiny stuff?) In spite of the neoconservative agenda, however, a significant number of fathers are enjoying the role of primary caregiver of young children.

## FATHERS AS PRIMARY CAREGIVERS

According to the U.S. Census Bureau, men are now the primary caregiver in one out of every five dual-earner households[53] and children seem to benefit from the attention. In an intriguing study of such fathers, Yale psychiatrist Kyle Pruett was surprised to find that the children of fathers who had stayed home with them when they were infants scored higher than average (i.e., where mom, alone, stayed home) on most developmental tests.[54] In his five-year long study of seventeen New Fathers, he found there was nothing in their background or personality to distinguish them from men who do not choose to be a primary parent. There was one fundamental commonality, however—all the families had seen the father's becoming the primary caregiver of their child as a temporary situation. About a third of the fathers decided they would become primary caregivers prior to the pregnancy. They tended to be professionals, graduate students, and members of higher socioeconomic groups. The father typically wanted to take some time off from his career or education while the wife pursued hers and would care for the baby because it seemed the fair or interesting thing to do. These men also tended to describe their own fathers as uninvolved, and they seemed to identify more strongly with their nurturant mothers than their remote fathers. The middle third had generally stepped in when it had become increasingly clear that the mother's work would be jeopardized by maternity leave and the father's work could more easily withstand a leave of absence. The final third had the decision forced upon them at the last moment, usually for economic reasons—especially the father losing his job. These fathers were initially the most reluctant and uncertain. Most of the men had very little prior experience with young children. In spite of these differences, there were no corresponding differences in how well their children ultimately fared.

## BEN, ANNE, AND BABY HELEN

The role of one fairly typical New Father in the study, Ben Mellow, began when his wife, Anne, said soon after her delivery of baby Helen that she was beginning to wonder whether she really wanted to leave her career to stay home and raise Helen, although she had always planned to have children and fully intended to raise them herself. She was at a vulnerable stage in her career, having just been promoted when she got pregnant with Helen. Ben Mellow was surprised to find himself rather casually offering to "look after the baby for a while."

He reasoned that he could do his data analysis for the utility company that employed him from his home, and the company agreed to give him a kind of half-time paternity leave at one-third pay. His boss called it "inactive duty." Ben was contemplating a job change anyway amid rumors that his office was soon to be "absorbed." Ben and Anne's parents could not accept the arrangement at first. Anne's father worried about what was wrong with Ben that he "wanted to be a mother." At one point they consulted their priest, who told them the proper job for a young mother was to "follow in the image of the Virgin Mary and stay home and raise babies to the glory of God." Eventually, both families came around, but Ben and Anne started off by not feeling very supported.

In describing his early days with Helen after Anne returned to work, Ben said, "Suddenly, I began to figure her out. I was reluctant to admit that I had figured her out at first. I kept it to myself. But Helen became crystal clear to me. You know, like whether she was either tired or wanted to eat or play—that stuff. She responded instantly when I guessed right. That made me feel confident about what I was doing. Really, it was kind of like all of a sudden the feelings of being an outsider left, and I began to feel overwhelmed with the wish to raise her, to develop her the way I wanted her developed."[55] Ben initially experienced some guilt about his successful parenting of his daughter and would often attempt to "back off" when his wife returned from work in the evening. Helen, however, usually reacted instantaneously to such withdrawals and would fret or whine plaintively while he was trying to prepare dinner.

One of the things that most bothered him in his role as "housefather" was his being the only father he knew who was raising an infant. Early in his days as the primary caregiver, he was invited by several women in the neighborhood to join them on their morning "baby stroll" around their pleasant suburban neighborhood. He resisted initially, reporting a vivid memory of the times his sisters had tried to urge him in taunting, belittling fashion to "play dolls" and push their "babies" around in carriages with them.

"I hated this 'mothers brigade' at first. But then I noticed it provided relief from the loneliness and tedium of the soap operas, diapers and laundry. I began to feel some admiration from them for what I was doing. Now we're all fast friends."[56] When Helen was eighteen months old, the Mellows arranged for some in-home baby-sitting twelve hours a week, and a few months later put her in day care three afternoons a week. Meanwhile, Ben had returned to his office, putting in about twenty hours a week there. When Helen was three years old, a baby brother, Bruce, was born. Ben had planned to renew his half-time paternity leave, but his request was denied. His boss informed him that his company only allowed one paternity leave per family. As a result, Anne became the stay-at-home parent, having acquired an extended leave of absence (without pay) from her own firm. Helen, then three and a half, was at nursery school four mornings a week. Ben had a great deal of trouble feeling involved with his new son. He was depressed that he would not be able to have the same intensity of involvement he had experienced with Helen. Anne, on the other hand, felt more involved and happy as a mother than she had ever expected. She found herself sometimes calling her husband at the office for advice on how to handle infant problems. Ben, for his part, began to make his way out of his depression only by filing a lawsuit against his company regarding its paternity policy. Ben asserted that raising a child had changed his worldview, and he became an activist for passage of the ERA, which he felt would give both sexes more options.

## PETER, SUSAN, AND BABY HENRY

Peter and Susan Blue are another couple in the study. Mr. Blue carried Baby Henry in his left hand in the "football position" while he used his free right hand to answer the phone, make dinner, water plants, and warm up a bottle of breast milk for Henry. Mr. Blue explained himself: "I love looking after my son. But I would never have guessed it. In fact, if my old high school jock buddies ever knew I was doing it, they'd fall over dead from laughing. It wasn't easy at first, but it sure seems natural now. That bothers my wife a little . . . that it feels natural. She gets a little jealous sometimes."[57]

Peter Blue is a commercial artist with a studio in the apartment he shares with his wife, Susan, and son, Henry. When Susan found she could take only six weeks of unpaid maternity leave from her job as a court recorder, they decided that Peter would quit his part-time job as a salesman for a hardware company (which he did not like anyway) and stay home with the baby while she returned to her work. Both their families were aghast at their decision and predicted dire consequences for the child and the marriage.

Peter belonged to a group of young men who rode their dirt bikes on the weekend and had a "few beers together on Fridays." After Henry was born, Peter gave up his motorcycle, feeling suddenly that now that he was responsible for a child, he no longer wished to flirt with danger. Shortly after his wife had returned to work, Peter began, over Susan's objections, to take Henry with him to meet this group on Fridays at the local pub. At first, he said, Henry had a very sobering effect on the gatherings. But to his amazement, some of the other men became quite interested in what Peter did with Henry and in how he played with his son. Soon, one or two asked to hold him. After a couple of weeks, Henry had become a fixture at the Friday men's group. By the time Henry was two and a half, Peter was still spending an occasional Friday night "tossing down a few beers with the buddies" while Henry looked on.[58]

Peter found that since Henry's birth he felt more creative energy than he ever had before. "It's like I need to paint. I just think about him and it flows out of the brush and onto the canvas." Peter and Susan shared the child care arrangements. Peter was in charge of Henry Monday through Friday; Susan took Saturday, leaving Peter to work and run errands. Evenings and Sundays were "50-50 time." The Blues were feeling quite isolated during Henry's infancy, and some of the strain showed up in the way they competed over the role of "best baby-understander."

Henry seemed to go through a period of being more compliant with his mother than with his father, making her authority seem more effective than his. As Peter described it: "It was like I meant entertainment and she meant business—but we're over that now." Henry seemed to be making quite different use of his parents. As a young toddler, he brought dolls, stuffed animals, and clothes to his mother, who then became actively engaged in helping him clothe his "babies." He carried the baby bottle to his father after the babies were clothed. He always walked to his mother but ran excitedly to his father, initiating a tickling game while crawling up on his lap.

At two years Henry attended family day care at a neighbor's home three doors down the street. He was there a half day three mornings a week. By this time Susan was working as a paralegal and loved it and Peter had his own thriving sign-painting business. Henry had protested initially when he began attending family day care. Peter said, "He kicked up just enough of a fuss to let us know he loved us. Now they are all in love with one another down there. He can't wait to go."

All the children in Pruett's study scored far above average on a variety of developmental tests, although the rate of precocious performance slowed down as they got older. While the children were very clear about conventional gender stereotypes and expectations, their own views of men included the notion that men are important procreators and nurturers. Pruett initially speculated that the children's advanced development might be the result of a particularly stimulating, vigorous, and unpredictable handling style by fathers. This quality was observed throughout the study and neither waned nor diminished over time, adding support for the idea that it may be a characteristic of the American father-infant pair.* While the vigorous style may have contributed to higher scores, Pruett believes it was combined with several other enhancing factors. For example, the children were all firstborns, who generally get a lot more intense attention from everybody. Also there may have been an extra enthusiasm these fathers experienced because staying home with their infants was something they chose to do, not something that was expected of them. But, Pruett concludes, probably even more important, these babies may have been thriving because of the abiding commitment and involvement of two parents. Half of the fathers in the study retained the role of primary caregiver after two years, although some of them were now supplementing the care of their children with various combinations of day care, babysitting, or family day care. The most likely answer to the precocity phenomenon is that when children have several interested and involved adults in their lives, they will thrive be-

---

*Swedish fathers, for instance, do not show this style with infants when they are primary caregivers. They do not play with their babies as often as American fathers and have a more phlegmatic style of interaction. (Michael Lamb, "Why Swedish Fathers Aren't Liberated," Psychology Today, October 1982, pp. 74–77.)

cause they are getting the stimulation they need. It is also important to remember, however, that precocity is a short-lived phenomenon. Given half a chance, nature is the hidden tutor that will propel children along the developmental path, ultimately arriving at the same developmental milestones at the same general time.

## REVERSE SEXISM

While women who want to be very involved in their work face prejudice from every quarter, including the divorce court, men who want to take care of infants and be very involved with the daily tasks of nurturing their children also face prejudice. In a recent court case in Pennsylvania, a man who had legally adopted a nine-month-old Korean infant, was told by the adoption agency that the adoption was revoked because the man's wife had suddenly died of cancer.[59] Another adoption agency revoked its promise to place a child with a young couple because the couple had decided the father would be the primary parent while the mother worked full-time.[60] Paid male caregivers (a rare species) complain they are "second-class citizens," especially regarding infant care.[61]

The problem of males caring for infants can become even more complicated in the home. The new fifty-fifty coparenting imperative may be even more difficult than when the father becomes primary caregiver while the mother works. While most women need their husbands to be involved in child care, they are seldom prepared for the threats this care can pose to their deep-seated sense of identity. Women have been taught since birth that their self-realization as a woman is not complete until they become mothers. Being a doctor or an environmentalist is to be a secondary accomplishment. A female Nobel Prize winner who has no children is seen as somehow lacking. Add to this equation the thick poison of motherblame that permeates the media, polite conversation, and family relations, and you can well understand women's tendency to be defensive about this psychological territory: They will no doubt be blamed for anything that goes wrong.

From the magazines to the how-to books, there is a rising cry that men who want to share the care get to feeling very quickly that they can't do anything right. Their wife wants them to do 50 percent of the care, but she wants 100 percent of the decision-making power.[62] Part of the problem is that after birth the mother usually becomes the "expert" parent because she feeds the infant and spends more time with it. She, of course, is learning what to do as she goes along, but her husband, who has less hands-on learning experience, begins quickly to feel and to be less competent.

But there are reports of women who even feel guilty about letting their husband take the child to the pediatrician. They ask themselves if a really good mother would let "somebody else" take a sick child to the doctor. One woman gets annoyed over the way her husband dresses their child in clothes that are often mismatched, fearing that it will reflect badly on her. Another admits she sometimes feels a secret thrill when her husband acts ineptly, because it confirms her need to believe that mothers are naturally superior. Many women, it appears, monitor their husband's caregiving at every turn—thinking ahead for them and ultimately preventing them from learning by doing. It's easy to see how men might circumscribe their interactions with their young ones to the play-buddy role and special excursions where they are alone with their children.*

The workplace also penalizes men for getting involved with their children. First of all, of course, men make more money than women and therefore there is great pressure on them to place work before family time. One recent study by the Families and Work Institute indicates that fathers *are* increasing their involvement with their families and arranging more flexible schedules. But the increase is small. Men say that while they would like to take more time and take advantage of such new benefits as paternity leave when it is available, they are afraid to do so for fear it will be held against them. Managers still take men aside and warn them not to take paternity leave if they want to be taken seriously. In fact, men even fear losing their jobs if they reveal their fathering priorities.[63]

---

*To be fair, though, many men resist domestic and caregiving work tooth and nail. Hochschild's 1989 study showed this reluctance to be a major cause of divorce; the women's magazines are full of as many articles about husbands' civil disobedience tactics on the domestic front as complaints by the disenfranchised male caregiver. (Arlie Hochschild, The Second Shift [New York: Avon, 1989].)

According to some studies, however, there is now an invisible "daddy track." Many men are quietly shaping their career plans around family concerns, turning down promotions that would take more of their time, and selecting jobs with flexible schedules. Men lie about time off with their families, saying they are going to a meeting when they are meeting their child for a Little League game, or saying they are taking a sick day when they are staying home with a sick child.[64] Evidence presented to Congress in 1991 documented considerable willingness on the part of fathers to get out of the rat race and onto the daddy track.[65] In spite of the 1993 Family and Medical Leave Act, which requires companies with more than fifty employees to offer most workers, men and women alike, up to twelve weeks of unpaid leave after childbirth or adoption, most men are told it would be better for their status at work if they took a few vacation days instead.[66]

## HOPE

There are, of course, some sterling exceptions. The president of an urban design firm in Denver, for example, put a great deal of energy into building the firm in the 1980s. At the end of the decade, his son was born. He assembled his partners and his small, hardworking staff and told them he was "divorcing" them because the most important thing in his life was now his family. "I am not going to work Saturdays and Sundays and evenings anymore, and I am not going to value employees who work evenings and weekends. I will value people who work less and work smarter . . . and spend time with their families or their lovers or their boats . . ." His staff feared the company might start to fall apart, thought he might be having some irrational personal crisis. Nonparents in the company felt resentment, fearing they would have to take up the slack for the married workers. The transition took two years. Ultimately, most employees began to feel their lives had been out of balance whether they had children or not. They began to relish spending more time with family and friends and not feeling guilty about it.[67]

Men are going to have to fight to become nurturers of their families—but it is not mothers they need to fight, and it is not some new (or old) notion of masculinity they need to fight for. Like mothers, they need to hold social scientists and baby gurus accountable for their lack of interest in fathers' caregiving. Men also need to fight alongside mothers against business and government to break through the current public indifference to children's welfare. And one of the first goals they need to secure is quality child care for all children.

# The Real Culprit:
# American Child Care

Behind all the mother blaming, there is a rather nasty reality. No one wants to pay for the care of our young children. Rather than putting forth the effort and providing the funds for a first-rate day care system for these young children, for whom all the blamers profess such concern, mother castigation provides the useful smokescreen.

## THE NATIONAL SHAME

American child care is definitely something to feel guilty about, and it is not mothers who should feel the guilt. They, in fact, are responsible for cobbling together—with more opposition than assistance from business, government, or a well-wishing public—a supplementary system of care for our children.[1] At the beginning of the decade, two women nominated for the position of U.S. Attorney General were not confirmed by Congress because of a flood of disapprobation from the public. They, unlike any male counterpart, were questioned as to how they cared for their children. The first candidate, Zoe Baird, had failed to pay Social Security tax for her illegal alien nanny.* The second, Kimba Wood, had paid Social Security but was denied the appointment because the nanny was not legal, although she had applied for legal status which would eventually be granted. The message is clear to all mothers: Child care is solely their responsibility; any problems associated with it will be used against them in the workplace.

*Admittedly, this is not good for nannies or mothers.

It should not be surprising, then, that the mere handful of recent studies, which have finally begun to evaluate American child care in all its variety, indicate that our "system" is the worst in the Western world (see chapter 7). Day care centers, now used by 28 percent of parents with children under five, are a national shame. A 1995 study of four hundred centers concludes that the care provided by most American child care centers is so poor it threatens children's intellectual and emotional development! In fact, this study, conducted by child psychologists and economists, shows that only one in seven American child care centers provides a level of quality that promotes child development and learning. Infants and toddlers are worst off, with 40 percent of their care rated as "poor."[2]

Recent studies of family day care and care by relatives (used by a third of parents with children under five) provide an even more disturbing picture of quality. A study by the Families and Work Institute found that only 9 percent of providers could be rated as "good," while 56 percent provided only "adequate" or "custodial" care. Another 35 percent was so poor it could harm the children's development. An unexpected finding was that the children were more likely to feel secure with unrelated caregivers rather than with relatives, apparently because the relatives would rather not care for the children, but do so only as a favor.[3]

Don't assume that hiring your own private nanny is the answer. A 1992 Department of Consumer Affairs report calls the nanny placement industry a "free-for-all." It is a measure of how very haphazard child care is in America that nobody can say how many such workers there are. Estimates range from 75,000 to 353,000.[4] But with the vast majority of even legal nannies paid off the books, it's not surprising many are not eager to be counted. The demand for child care at home has been met by an unregulated patchwork of agencies, a few experienced nannies, and tens of thousands of immigrant and nonimmigrant women looking for jobs that require no training, no degrees, and often no papers. Usually, foreign nannies arrive with visas that are valid for a few months. Agencies sometimes lie about the legal status of the nannies they place and finding a good legal nanny is so difficult that many families are forced to break the law. The effects of this "system" on children, families, and the workers themselves has yet to be studied.

The poor quality of American child care is a direct consequence of the lack of funding and regulation. States with stricter child care regulations have more centers of higher quality. Almost everyone in this society who offers a service—from restaurateurs to plumbers to teachers—must be licensed and regulated. Very seldom are we poisoned, flooded, or incompetently taught (admittedly, the latter is debatable). Yet we seem to care so little about our young children that we do not enforce the most minimal standards for their guardianship. Perhaps we recognize that quality costs money. In the 1995 *Cost and Quality* study, researchers found the highest quality centers are those with access to extra money from federal or state governments, universities, or employers providing care at a work site.[5] High-quality child care is more likely to occur when centers have more adults taking care of children, pay better wages, and hire employees with training in how to care for children. Intense economic competition among centers, however, means that most charge similar fees regardless of quality, and in those that are subsidized, of course, parents naturally get more for their money. Therefore, quality tends to be highest among nonprofit centers and lowest among for-profits.

The biggest detriment to quality is the high turnover rate, which is due primarily to the low wages. We currently pay workers on average $5 per hour to mind our children—less than we pay people to serve a hamburger, park our car, care for animals at the zoo, or collect our garbage. The nation's child care providers, 98 percent of whom are women, experience a 42 percent turnover rate, compared to 18 percent for all other occupations, primarily because of the low wages and low status of the work.[6] And of course, in centers with higher turnover rates, children suffer emotionally, socially, and intellectually. Moreover, high turnover is a problem for working parents, who have the added burden of seeking new child care arrangements; and for child care workers who are demoralized by the instability and expanded workload caused by having to do extra work while new staff is being found and trained.

In addition to the generally poor quality of care, there is the problem of who has access to the better care. Child care consumes the largest portion of family budgets after food, housing, and taxes. In 1990 the average fee paid by parents was about $3,173 per year for full-time, center-based care and $2,565 in family day care for each child. Among low-income parents who pay for child care, the expenditure consumes an average of 24 percent of family income. Single parents spend 21 percent of their income, on average, whereas two-parent families spend 9 percent.[7] But the ability to pay does not correspond directly to the quality of services paid for. While children from low-income and minority families tend to be in the lowest-quality family day care, the quality of the situation varies wildly from provider to provider.[8] For example, in 1990, in Washington, D.C., a woman was ordered to stop running her unlicensed family day care business after police found fifty-four children in her home, among them nine babies strapped in car seats. State legislators seeking to crack down on the problem noted that many responsible parents defended the woman's operation because they are so desperate for affordable care. In contrast, a Washington area working couple are so pleased with their neighborhood family day care provider that they have written her into their wills as their children's guardian.[9]

In general, though, there are some consistent patterns in the quality of care. Poor people are more likely to have access to subsidized center care than working-class and middle-class people. But even in subsidized care, there are serious problems that impede quality for poor children and these are largely the product of prejudice and racism. In one analysis of care for the poor, researchers concluded that while center care for poor children was likely to pay better salaries and have a better ratio of the number of teachers to children, the teachers tended to be less sensitive and more harsh. Only a minority of care for the poor, however, qualifies as "good." On the other hand, the most uniformly poor quality of care is to be found in the predominantly middle-class centers, which are seldom subsidized and often run for profit.[10] The affluent, of course, have more choices, and access to better-quality centers, although evaluating those choices is not easy for parents.[11] Even very wealthy children sometimes receive inferior care from nannies and au pairs who are neither regulated nor trained.

In addition to socioeconomic class discrepancies in the quality of care, there is the general problem of availability. Though the nation's day care capacity has increased by 80 percent since 1970, the crazy quilt of commercial, nonprofit, and home-based facilities forces the average parent to spend five full weeks searching for a slot.[12] While there is now generally enough care for three- to five-year-olds, there is still too little care available for infants and toddlers, sick children, special-needs children, and for care during nontraditional hours.[13] Unfortunately, families who are under some of the greatest social and psychological stress are more likely to lack good care. Parents who live apart or who work split shifts, weekends, or long hours, have difficulty finding decent care because their work often falls outside the standard weekday hours for center and family day care.[14] The current picture of availability will be obliterated, of course, if the drastic welfare-to-work proposals currently afloat are actually effected, as none of our august reformers has thought to plan day care for the estimated 10 million children who will be disenfranchised from maternal care.[15]

One of the most shocking findings of the 1995 *Cost and Quality* day care center study is that while the researchers found the vast majority of day care centers to be "poor" or "mediocre," 90 percent of the parents in the study rated their children's care as "good." The researchers conclude that "inadequate consumer knowledge" reduces incentives for some centers to provide good quality care.[16] But the fact is, parents can only do so much. Assessing the quality of care requires both sophistication and access to information not always readily available. Factors such as teacher-child ratios and group size can be confusing, since a variety of aides and volunteers may alter the equation. The salaries and benefits of teachers and the staff turnover rates may also be difficult to obtain. The "process variables"—the kinds of things that should happen in teacher-child interactions—may be difficult for the untrained parent to evaluate.

It is not surprising, then, that parents have difficulty selecting care for their children. It is difficult and expensive even to get time off from work in order to visit a sufficient number of child care facilities to have an adequate perspective. Once parents choose a child care setting, they must often rely on reports from their children. A recent survey of parental attitudes toward child care revealed that many found looking for care so stressful that they usually settled on the first situation that seemed halfway acceptable, which often meant they had to find an alternative arrangement a short time thereafter.[17] Parents need official accrediting authorities to set standards and actively and regularly assess and monitor care. In the meantime, however, I want to give parents a vivid picture of some of the psychological factors they might consider in thinking about their children's care.

## DAY CARE CENTERS

A descriptive glimpse into the personal dynamics of day care for the poor illustrates some of the factors enumerated in the recent evaluations cited above. Care for the poor, unless subsidized, often tends to be detrimental to children's well-being. For example, outside one not-atypical inner city child care center housed in a crumbling building with a churchfront facade, a neon sign flickers weakly, CHRIST DIED FOR OUR SINS.* Inside, forty-five preschool children are watching afternoon cartoons in a cavernous basement room. As the preschoolers chatter and giggle, an exhausted-looking teacher stands up and threatens to turn off the television. "Anyone who talks will have to sit at a table with their head down, where everyone can see," she warns. Seven toddlers are cordoned off in a small corner of the room, wandering in circles as another staff person watches from behind a desk. On the floor, an infant in a bassinet cries incessantly but is only picked up—carelessly—a couple times over the course of two hours.

"We usually have five teachers, but two were out sick yesterday," says Dorothy Beasley, the head teacher. "So three of us had to take care of fifty-eight kids." She points to empty shelves lining the cracked walls. "We don't have enough toys or books, and we don't have money to keep up the facility. Right now, the kids are sleeping on mats that are more than fifty years old."

While there are many such impoverished centers, in poor communities, subsidized programs—whether they are public school-sponsored, community-based, or Head Start—have more resources. The Head Start program provides a comprehensive approach that includes health care for the children, nutritious food, social services, and parent education. However, as with many programs that serve "at risk" children, the widespread view that the poor are responsible for their own degraded fate often trickles down to teachers' views that

---

*Based on a description of an inner-city center by Linda Baker, "Day-Care," The Progressive, June 1994, pp. 26–27.

poor children are inferior because of their poverty. The pervasive deficit model indicates that the "culture of poverty" in which these children reside retards their development and requires them to experience a far more "structured" experience than middle-class children. But "structure," as seen through the lens of prejudice against the poor, and executed by women in low-status, low-paying jobs, can be a disastrous formula for children.

## MAPLE SHADE HEAD START

The Maple Shade Head Start program is housed in a pleasant, well-equipped, one-story building in the center of an urban metropolitan area. The program offers half-day classes for four-year-olds Monday through Thursday and parent education and Home Start visits on Fridays. Home Start visits are for three-year-olds who also may attend a morning class twice a week. The children served in the three classrooms are about 50 percent black, 25 percent white, and 15 percent Hispanic and a few recent immigrants who speak little English. The Head Start teachers who have child development credentials earn an average salary of $13,000.* Mrs. Bias's classroom is divided into several carefully made play areas—there is a beauty shop, a fire station, a block building, a quiet corner, an arts and crafts center, and a popular loftspace. Child-made art is confined to a small pinup board. Necklaces hang above each area and children are required to wear one around their neck when entering each picture-labeled area. When all the necklaces are taken, no more children may visit the area at that time. Of course, many children actually play in the areas without necklaces and leave the area, forgetting to place their necklaces back on the hook. They are, after all, four years old.

Three boys are at the easels during "choice time": Chris, Jeremiah, and Yasser. Yasser and Chris have pocketed small wooden cars from the block area and secretly sneaked them over to the easel area. Jeremiah has painted "a curvy road" with a series of arrows pointing in one direction and a stop sign in red. Chris and Yasser are trying to

---

*This composite portrait is drawn from the study of several Head Start and public school centers described in Valerie Polakow's Lives on the Edge: Single Mothers and Their Children in the Other America (Chicago: University of Chicago Press, 1993).

drive their cars on the road made by Jeremiah without touching the wet paint, saying, "we going to Chicago—vroom." Mrs. Bias strides over and snatches the cars from the boys, saying, "We do not drive cars over the easel, this is for painting only—you boys never pay attention; go over to the table and sit with your arms folded." Chris and Yasser run away and collide with each other, and Chris shouts, "You dummy, you asshole" at Yasser as Mrs. Bias physically separates them and places them at opposite sides of the table, telling them they will miss outside time today. She tells the researcher, "These two boys are real problems. Chris has no father and his mother is always running around, and Yasser doesn't understand anything you tell him."

Jeremiah, Chris, and Yasser are Mrs. Bias's "problem" children. Chris, who is the white child of a single teenage mother, is seen as the repository of his mother's "immoral" ways, and Yasser, an Arab child, is seen to be intellectually deficient because of his language difficulties. Jeremiah is black and he and his younger sister and mother were homeless for a year. At the end of the day, Mrs. Bias tells Jeremiah's mother "You people better do something about your kids." She also tells her teacher aide, Dee, whom the researcher observed frequently hugging the children, "You're too soft on these kids."

Children receive breakfast, snack, and lunch in the program and a number of them have insatiable appetites and constantly ask for seconds and thirds. Snack is served at midmorning—crackers with peanut butter. Mrs. Bias twice reprimands Jeremiah for comments that the snack "looks real yummy." As Jeremiah has talked out of turn, he is passed over and has to wait for his snack until the children at the table behind him receive theirs. Jeremiah begins to protest, "Gimme mine—no fair—gimme," and he grabs at the tray. Mrs. Bias grabs him and wipes his runny nose with a look of distaste and takes him to the time-out chair. At this point he is sobbing and yelling, "no fair" and is forced to sit on the chair for fifteen minutes as he looks hungrily at the others eating. Mrs. Bias says this is part of her "classroom management plan" with Jeremiah, as "food is what he really cares about." She has been taught that these "at risk" children need behaviorist condi-

---

*Of course there are excellent Head Start and public preschool programs for poor children, but the quality varies widely and the prejudice that blames poor women for their poverty often affects their children. In fact, Head Start is considered justified only when it proves to have increased three- and four-year-old

tioning techniques as part of a more structured environment because their lives outside the classroom are so disordered.*

## TINY TOTS FOR PROFIT

Lower-middle-class people are more likely to have some choices, for which they pay a considerable portion of their income. But this care isn't necessarily based on the notion that child care is an important task to be shared by the community. The for-profit centers, which are most likely to be used by middle-income people, tend to put profit before quality in a business where there is little margin for profit in the first place. Children end up paying the price.

Tiny Tots is a large, owner-operated, profit-making, licensed child care center serving a largely working-class population of low to moderate means. Parents pay an average of $3,800 per year. When four-year-old Jerry Spinoza arrives at Tiny Tots each morning at 7:30, he likes to hang on to his mom's skirt for a while as he becomes attuned to the bustle of activity surrounding him.† They stand in the entry to what doubles as a church, with a high, pitched roof, stained glass windows and partitions that stand about five feet high and are removable. Finally his mother nudges him and he runs to store his coat and day pack in one of the open wooden cubbies. As usual, he has trouble finding an empty coathook because his cubbie is already crowded with the belongings of three other children who share it with him. Even though the licensed capacity of Jerry's classroom is 36 children, more than sixty children, some part-time, some full-time, are enrolled in this room alone. Because of the children's irregular schedules, Jerry is never quite sure which friends he will have to play with or for how long on any given day. Jerry heads toward the tables in the "morning art area" in the center of the room, covered with coloring books, used computer paper, and broken crayons. Jerry avidly searches the crowd for friendly, familiar faces. Today he sees Gilda, the head teacher,

---

*children's test scores, never for simply providing pleasant, safe care for little children who happen to be poor.*

*†I am indebted to Lynda Beardsley,* Good Day—Bad Day: The Child's Experience of Child Care *(New York: Teachers College, Columbia University, Teachers College Press, 1990). The following center portraits are drawn largely from the prototypes presented in that study, which is the product of extensive on-site child care research.*

chatting by the book corner with another grown-up. He has never been sure what her name is, so, like most of the other kids, he just calls her "teacher." Happily, he spots his pal Jamila, busily coloring at the art table, so he runs to join her. "No running, Jerry!" Gilda calls out.

"Hi, Jamila! Watcha doin'?" asks Jerry.

"Coloring," Jamila replies and looks up with a smile. "You wanna, too?"

As Jerry eagerly pulls a chair up next to Jamila, Gilda yells out once again from across the room, "No, no, Jerry, there are already too many kids at the art table! You will have to find something else to do." Just then, a new girl, Alicia Woodbury, appears with her mother, clutching a stuffed lion. Mrs. Woodbury introduces Alicia to Gilda, and Alicia gives Gilda a big grin and pipes right up, "I three years old and I got a new puppy. Him name Tugger!" She is about to continue when Gilda looks at her watch, gives her a wan smile and a pat on the head and refers the newcomers to an assistant teacher, as it is time for her break now. They are shown to a cubby and Mrs. Woodbury says, "Now you hold on to Leo, honey. I have to leave for work." Gilda's instructions to her were that she should leave right away. "I'll be thinking about you all day and missing you." She gives Alicia a big hug and Alicia bursts into tears. Mrs. Woodbury looks around desperately for some assistance, big tears filling her eyes, too. No one intervenes but Ruth, an assistant, who tells her to leave and that everything will be fine. "They soon get over it." Mrs. Woodbury leaves, and Alicia flings herself onto the floor and cries. Ruth comes over and pulls her up. "Come on, now. Only babies cry." Alicia pulls away from her and flings herself back down on the floor. Ruth then notices Alicia's lion and picks it up.

"Is this yours?" Ruth asks, dangling the lion in front of Alicia's now terrified gaze.

"Leo! Leo!" Alicia screams as she grabs the lion out of Ruth's hands and clutches him to her chest.

"Alicia, you're gonna need to put that lion in your cubby, 'cause if you don't, some other kid might try to snatch it. That's why we have a rule that no one is supposed to bring toys to school." Alicia continues to hang on to the lion and sob.

In order to maintain control over the large and ever-changing group of children in their care, the Tiny Tots staff stick to a rigid, assembly-line schedule. Children eat at the same time, participate in assigned activities at the same time, nap at the same time (whether they need to or not). They participate in activities whether or not they find them interesting and must curtail things they do find interesting according to the schedule. The caregivers expect all the children to remember a large number of rules that exclude many opportunities for children to make the kinds of decisions that contribute to intellectual and social skills. As more prestige is associated with what were commonly called nursery schools, many day care centers advertise that they are academically oriented preschools. They often hire teachers who are trained to teach elementary school and fail to realize that preschoolers need a far different approach, one that builds on their interests and teaches through activities rather than drills and lectures. In these centers, there is not time for teachers to develop a relationship with parents.

Children may attend the program for two to eleven hours per day, from 7:00 A.M. to 6:00 P.M. To control costs, the center operates at the state licensing minimum of one teacher for every twelve children. Staffing costs at Tiny Tots comprise less than 50 percent of the program budget. Only the head teacher in each classroom is assigned a regular, full-time position. The majority of the remaining staff earn $5 per hour or less. The program employs twenty-nine teaching staff plus twenty high school student aides. Most staff work fewer than twenty hours per week. The annual staff turnover rate exceeds 50 percent. All teachers have had at least twelve college-level semester units in early childhood education but have not necessarily been supervised through a student-teaching experience.

## SPROUTS FOR CHILDREN

Sprouts Children's Center is a small private nonprofit early childhood program serving children from one to five years of age. When four-year-old Jerry Spinoza arrives each morning around 8:00, his teacher, Louise, always jumps up to greet him with a hearty "good morning!" and a big hug. He also gets a happy greeting from Juanita, the morning teaching assistant, and "Hi" and "Jerry's here!" from the other children already busily at play. The center is in a remodeled home with large sunny rooms and a spacious play yard. As he hangs up his coat in the cozy cubby corner near the door, he scans the other fifteen cubbies to see whose coats have arrived ahead of his. "Great, Jamila's here today," he thinks to himself.

As Jerry eases himself into another full day with his preschool class-mates, his mom, Annie Spinoza, hangs her coat on the parent coatrack and then signs in. There is a place on the daily sign-in sheet for par-ents to alert staff to any special needs their child might have that day and also for the staff to leave messages for the parents at the end of the day. As Annie writes, Louise, the head teacher joins her and reads her comments. Annie expresses concern about her son's recent irri-tability and mischievous behavior. Louise responds, "You know, we've been seeing a lot more agitation among the four- and five-year-olds like Jerry who are getting ready to enter kindergarten in a few months." Together, they discuss the problem and decide to contact the local kindergarten teachers and arrange a preview visit for the children who will soon be entering kindergarten.

Teacher Juanita looks up from the couch where she is snuggled be-tween Latosha and Katie, reading from a pile of books the girls have selected. "Bye now, Annie, have a great day at work! Let me know when you put those red shoes on sale. I want 'em!"

Annie smiles and gives Jerry one last kiss and heads off for a long day as manager of a local shoe store.

Louise turns on the lights in the other rooms of the house, since the rest of the children will soon be arriving. The early birds pursue what-ever activities they choose. Louise helps Latosha put on a smock so she can paint at the easel. She looks up to see that Alicia Woodbury, the newest child in the program, and her mother have arrived. Even though Alicia has been spending some time at Sprouts for the past two weeks, this is her first full day of regular child care. Louise knows that they will both be feeling a bit apprehensive and hurries over to make them feel welcome. She notices Alicia clutching her stuffed lion. "I see you brought your lion friend again today. Is his name Leo?" Alicia nods and Louise continues. "You know, he doesn't have to stay in your cubby. It's okay for him to stay with you today if you like." Ali-cia looks relieved.

Sprouts consists of a preschool area that serves sixteen three- to five-year-olds per day with a staff of two (1:8 adult-child ratio) and an infant toddler area that serves six one- and two-year-olds per day with a staff of two (1:3 ratio). In addition, there are two part-time teachers who work in the busy morning and afternoon hours. Most children attend the program five days per week from 9:00 A.M. to 4:00 P.M. but there is also extended care allowing them to arrive at 8:00 and leave as late as 5:30. Parents volunteer their own labor two hours a month, whether it's for a yard cleanup or extra help in the classroom or serving on the parent advisory committee or the fund-raising committee. There are four full-time certified teaching staff who are trained to support children's development in all areas, not just intellectual. Even though Sprouts teachers are paid at the highest levels for their profession, they are still not paid as much as public school teachers. Staff compensation at Sprouts is by far the most expensive component of the program.

## FAMILY DAY CARE

Family day care is distinguished by small group size (typically six or fewer children) and generally mixed-age groups and is run in women's own homes. Providers fall into one of three broad categories: young mothers in their late twenties and thirties who have their own young children at home and want to supplement their family income while keeping their children at home with them; women in their forties and fifties who care for at least one related child, often a grandchild; women in their thirties to fifties who care only for unrelated children, although they may have begun providing care with their own children at home. The turnover among family day care providers is over 40 percent per year. In one study, 63 percent of the providers saw their work as temporary, partly because they were providing care as a means of subsidizing the care of their own children at home; partly because of struggling to find a balance between loving the children in their care and becoming too attached to them; and partly because of their isolation from other adults. Family day care workers are paid the lowest wages, in part because of their reluctance to put a price tag on caring. They do not get sick days, their negotiations with parents are often difficult and their weekly income fluctuates in part because neither parents nor providers are comfortable with translating intimacy into a cash relationship. The struggle to make caring into a business has both financial and emotional costs.

Since even providers define their wages as being paid out of what the child's mother earns, this puts a very low ceiling on what "affordable" means in practice. And while these women gain autonomy and power by working in their own home, they lose privacy and reliable time boundaries because parents don't always pick up their children on time.[18]

## ANGELA DOUBTHART'S FAMILY DAY CARE

At one family day care home, Angela Doubthart stands in the hallway of her old Victorian house with its long shuttered French windows that go all the way to the floor.* Morning light floods the front room where Angela's four-year-old daughter Rita plays with a Barbie doll. Jimmy Wurkert has just arrived with his mother and rushes over to join Rita in selecting an outfit for Barbie. Angela's one-year-old infant wiggles around in a crib under the window. Two more children, a five-year-old boy and a two-year-old girl, will soon arrive. Angela is twenty-eight years old, married, and has been providing family care for four years in order to stay home with her own children. She earns about $8,000 a year, with no benefits, not even a sick day. Angela is like a second mother to these children, who generally play freely in unstructured activities. While Angela occasionally has activities planned for them, they mostly play together, paint at the easel, build with blocks, or listen to stories read by Angela. Sometimes they become bored and frustrated with the lack of adult management and fewer age-appropriate toys and projects. The toddler is often quite a problem as she is constantly invading areas of the house and yard that are not toddler-proofed. Angela prides herself on the emotional quality of the care she provides, however. "There's no two that need the same amount of loving and the same amount of reprimanding," she explains to Janie Wurkert. "Each one needs a little extra something of

*This portrait is based on my own observations of family day care and the studies of Margaret Nelson, Carollee Howes, and Laura Saki. (Margaret Nelson, "Mothering Others' Children: The Experiences of Family Day-Care Providers," Signs: Journal of Women in Culture and Society 15, no. 3 [1990]: pp. 586–605; Margaret Nelson, Negotiated Care: The Experience of Family Day Care Providers, [Philadelphia: Temple University Press, 1990]; Carollee Howes and Laura Saki, "Family Day Care for Infants and Toddlers," in Family Day Care: Current Research for Informed Public Policy, Donald Peters and Alan Pence, eds. [New York: Teachers College Press, 1992], pp. 115–128.)

some sort." Angela feels that unlike a day care center, where there is more emphasis on routines and learning activities, what she provides in this more intimate setting, is love. It is, in fact, the difficulty of this love that is causing Angela to "burn out." "You see," she says, "it's like they're my own children. I love them like a mother. It's my real reward when they tell me they love me. But that's also a problem. I love these children and I feel terrible when I lose one. But I'm not their mother. I don't have that kind of control over them. Eventually, they must leave. It's a delicate balance you have to keep so you don't get too attached. I know I reserve something knowing they're not mine. I don't want to get too attached. I did that in the beginning. I had one little boy from six months till he was almost four. His mother put him in a preschool and I haven't seen him since. It broke my heart. Especially since I think he needed me more than ever when he left. His parents were divorcing and it was awful hard on him. I kept him here when she couldn't pay, 'cause I knew one more loss would break his heart. I was the one stable and available person who was there for him. For the last six months I had him, she never paid. It was my fault. I let her do it. But I couldn't just abandon him. Then she moved to another part of town and put him in preschool. I never heard from them again. So now I reserve something. I hold back a little. I have to be real careful. I had one little girl here, she was really neglected. One day I bathed her and fixed her hair. The next day she said, 'Oh please bathe me.' I was afraid the mother might see it as a criticism and take her away. So I had to be careful."

Janie is surprised. Her own concern was that Angela should have a child-rearing philosophy similar to her own—especially regarding discipline. And of course, in the back of her mind, she worried about the possibility of abuse. For her part, Angela had been concerned about Janie picking up Jimmy on time and also paying on time. In a few weeks, however, they began to see one another as compatible and reliable, and Janie discovered that not only did Jimmy develop a love of Angela, he also became better behaved. Janie realized she may just have been spoiling him a bit out of her own guilt about working. Happily for Jimmy, his mother and caregiver came to like and respect each other. Angela and her children were invited to Jimmy's birthday celebrations, and they kept in touch with occasional phone calls and greeting cards throughout Jimmy's childhood.

## NANNIES

Carol Lansbury, an attorney married to a stockbroker, has two children, now two and five years old.* She has employed three nannies and a dozen or more baby-sitters. Through an agency, Carol found twenty-seven-year-old Wanda Jefferson to become Jason's nanny when he was four months old. (Carol had employed a baby nurse prior to Wanda.) Wanda was paid $450 a week, had her own room and bath, sick leave, health insurance and time to take piano lessons. Wanda had two years' training at a prestigious British nanny school, where she studied both child psychology and infant health. "Wanda was like a daughter to me. We used to talk about her future, her boyfriends, clothes, and, of course, Jason. She knew more about how to care for him than I did. This sometimes made it a little difficult for me. I don't mean I was jealous. But it wasn't always easy to assert my authority. Like when to call the doctor or what to feed him. But we usually worked it out. I was really devastated, though, when she left. She had everything with us. But she left after only a year. I guess what she didn't have was her own life. She moved in with her boyfriend and took a job in a day care center. For a while she still baby-sat for Jason (at $10 an hour). But now she's moved away. Next was thirty-four-year-old Marie from the West Indies. We were told she was legal. In a way she was—she had two sets of documents with two different names on them."

According to Marie from the West Indies, "Carol was my fifth family in five years. When they know you need the job, they can make any conditions they want. They tried to make me cook and clean, they even lent me out to their friends. 'Oh, I'll send Marie over, she'll help you with your party tonight.' I hate that. Like I'm a piece of property they can just use. I can't make a better life for my daughter if I stay back home. I don't want her to have to work for $135 a week like I had to. She's going to college and she knows it. She lives with my sister and she's a good student. I'm putting money away for her college.

---

*This portrait is a composite based on interviews I conducted with parents and nannies and accounts in the following articles: Melinda Beck et al., "Mary Poppins Speaks Out," Newsweek, February 22, 1993, pp. 66+; Carin Rubenstein, "No Good Nannies: Find a Good Family," New York Times, September 16, 1993, p. C2; Susan Cheever, "The Nanny Track," The New Yorker, March 6, 1995, pp. 84 +.

But here, they can fire you and not give you a good reference if you don't do what they say. You don't have any rights. Carol is nice. But I have to be careful. Women get jealous if their kids love you too much. But if you're always there for them, of course they're gonna love you. So I keep it a little cool when she's around. But Jason is just a little kid. I think about him on my day off. Did she get his lunch yet? He's probably hungry. Do they know it's library day at Kidspace? It's hard to separate yourself. And the families, they can't get along without you. They're always asking you to work extra. The mothers, they sometimes want to be friends with you. But they talk to you different from the way they talk to their friends."

## CHILD CARE "CHOICES"

Barbara Johnson has a Ph.D. in physiology and is a science writer who works at home; her husband Richard is a journalist and is out of the house twelve hours a day.* Their daughter, Virginia, is now four years old. Barbara gave herself two months with Virginia before she returned to her work; Richard, however, benefited from a recent paternity leave lawsuit at his newspaper, which allowed him to take off four months full-time and two more half-time (without pay, of course). For two months, Richard and Barbara interviewed fifteen nannies and finally hired Alice, who became Virginia's auxiliary caregiver. Alice, a recently divorced grandmother in her fifties, cared for Virginia in Richard and Barbara's home at first, but soon she took Virginia with her wherever she went during the day—to visit friends, in their homes or even in bars. Virginia loved Alice and vice versa. But at about eighteen months, Richard and Barbara felt Virginia should have a stable group of children to play with in an environment geared to children's learning. They lived in the city and sent her to the nearby, rather posh, Old Spruce Center, which was a steep $135 per week. The preschool

---

*This portrait is based on my own interviews with some two dozen parents, which I conducted simply as a reality check to compare with the published research on the experience of parents, I assumed I would be reading. Alas, there is very little research on their experience—whether we are looking at their own caregiving, or their attempts to secure auxiliary care. The interviews were primarily with middle- and upper-middle-class parents, were informal, although I did use a seven-question protocol to assure that consistent categories of information had been addressed. I was not interested in establishing any group characteristics, but simply gathering parent's stories.

was beautiful and even had color-monitor computers for the children. The Spruce Center was very much a school, however, with many teachers and children on different shifts. Virginia cried every day for the first several weeks. Barbara found herself "sneaking" over to the school and "spying" on her. Virginia, she found, was a bit withdrawn, aloof, bewildered, so after a few months, Barbara withdrew her. Alice still cared for Virginia in a pinch, and she took over for a few weeks while Barbara found another center. After a month, Barbara and Richard found Just for Kids, which was a smaller, less education-oriented center that involved parents. Virginia soon adjusted to this, and Barbara started to make friends with the other parents. When Virginia was thirty months old, however, Barbara and Richard moved to the suburbs. Virginia attended the local Quaker preschool which she loved, but at $185 a week they simply could not afford to keep her there. Another interim period of nanny Alice and baby-sitters followed until Barbara, in the middle of a difficult aspect of a book she was writing, could locate a more affordable and appropriate place. After a month of searching, she found Jennifer Hart's family care. Jennifer cared for her own infant and three-year-old daughter, along with a full-time four-year-old boy and a part-time brother and sister, two and four, respectively. In this more intimate group, Virginia was most happy, and Jennifer and Barbara have become friends. Alice is considered a family member and is invited to family celebrations and still occasionally cares for Virginia in a pinch. Virginia appears to be a normal, well-adjusted little girl.

Yolanda, a Head Start aide whose husband is also employed, continued to work through the birth of her first child, Roberto.* Subsequently Yolanda paid, on the average, $35 a week for caregivers. First, she used a neighbor across the hall in her housing project to care for Roberto when he was an infant, but there were problems. "She took care of him until he was about a year old. One day—it was two weeks before summer vacation, I remember—I got there to pick him up and his face was marked. I asked her what had happened, and

*This woman is interviewed in an ethnographic study of child care in a working-class community. (Caroline Zinsser, Raised in East Urban: Child Care Changes in a Working Class Community [New York: Teacher's College Press, 1991], pp. 138–143.)

she was in a very bad mood, and she tells me, 'I fell down, and he hit himself on the cabinet.' I just looked at her. The redness was all over his face. It was like somebody had just slapped him from side to side. The child was so depressed. I had noticed the change in him. I get the chills just talking about it and remembering. I went home and looked him over, and I cried. I never took him back."

During the two weeks remaining until Yolanda's summer vacation from Head Start, her husband's stepmother stayed with the family to baby-sit for Roberto. She turned out to be "another problem." She would take the child along when she visited her friends, which Yolanda did not object to, but would forget to feed him. Although Yolanda provided jars of food for the baby, he was often fed only crackers because the stepmother did not take the time or trouble to heat up the baby food.

When Yolanda went back to work in the fall, she found another baby-sitter. "She was a good person as far as feeding him. She had him really nice and clean when I picked him up. But she took care of four or five other children, and one day I noticed on Roberto's leg there were scars, like a bite. I showed her. She said, 'I'm not aware of anything that happened. But I do take care of a little boy that used to have the habit of biting, but I took that habit away from him by smacking him in the mouth. But if that's so, I'll have to watch him.' A couple of days later Roberto came home with a bite on his back. A deep bite. I was really upset. She kept taking care of the boy [who was biting] and I tried looking for another baby-sitter. I didn't find anybody else. I had to leave him there. He went through a lot of things like that. One time he had his fingers smashed in the door because there were so many kids she took care of."

The next baby-sitter, she discovered, did not feed Roberto properly. Yolanda would give the baby-sitter food for Roberto, but she used the food for her own child instead. Yolanda once found the baby-sitter's child eating a can of spaghetti and meatballs that she had brought, while Roberto had been given only a small bit of spaghetti mixed with chopped boiled potato. Roberto subsequently had a difficult start in school and has received various diagnostic labels from psychologists and educators.

## IS MOTHER BEST?

Our glimpse into the world of nonmaternal care is incomplete without the counterbalancing inside look at care by a variety of mothers who stay home with their children. But unfortunately, there is no parallel range of descriptive studies of mothers at home with children. We know in general, of course, that mothers who devote themselves exclusively to their children range from the saintly to the abusive. Hopefully there is more love, commitment, and attention for children in situations where mothers do not work outside the home, but observations would no doubt also reveal considerable flaws in the stay-at-home mother setting. Isolation and boredom for mothers and children must be common features. Frustration, lost tempers, tears, and tantrums (from adult and child alike) no doubt complement the rosy, soft-focus moments of tranquility and love pictured by the experts. Some mothers are even overinvolved and overcontrolling. Parental psychopathology, especially substance abuse and depression, can also disturb children's development. Persistent parental conflict and conflict-filled divorces can have devastating effects on children's emotional well-being, yet such features of home care do not figure into the mothercare/othercare equation. As we develop an appropriate sense of outrage at the quality of our othercare patchwork, it is important to keep in mind that care experienced in the isolation of the private home may benefit from the counterbalancing of more public care.

## THE RESEARCH ON CHILD CARE

We've paid a price for being so tied to the maternal gold standard. As a result, child psychologists are out of touch with the reality of most children's lives, which would benefit greatly from the educational and social advantages that high quality day care can provide. Of course, day care has long been recommended for children of poor families—since the days of the infant schools in the early part of the nineteenth century which were designed to reform and socialize the poor (see chapter 2). A contemporary version of this social welfare type of care is the Head Start program, launched in 1965 as part of President Lyndon Johnson's War on Poverty. Researchers at that time claimed that the problem with poor children was poor "stimulation." To compensate, the children would attend preschool to stimulate and enrich their minds while their mothers (fathers weren't in the equation) were instructed in how best to mind them. But Head Start's high political profile soon led to its depiction as a program designed to improve school performance, which then led to the measurement of IQ as a means of assessing the success of the programs. Indeed it appeared that children's IQ did increase while they attended Head Start. However, it soon faded when the children left the program. A poorly funded Follow Through program was then established but the federal effort was constantly dogged by wavering commitment and funding. While Head Start is widely praised, there is actually so much diversity among Head Start programs that few consistent findings about its effects on poor children are available except it appears that the programs need improvement if they are to accomplish the kind of goals claimed for them.[19]

There is good evidence, however, that extended preschool programs of high quality can be very effective. The Perry Preschool Program in Ypsilanti, Michigan, which began in 1962, enrolled 128 African-American children from low-income families and randomly assigned them to control and intervention (an enriched preschool experience) groups. Beginning when they were three to four years old, children received two and a half hours of class instruction several days a week, thirty weeks per year. In addition, mothers (nope, no fathers) and children were visited at home weekly for about ninety minutes. The children continued to be followed after the initial program; they are now in their late thirties. Children in the enrichment program continued to have higher achievement scores in adolescence, were more likely to graduate from high school, were more likely to be employed and not to have been arrested at age nineteen, earned more, and were less likely to have had a history of frequent arrests by age twenty-eight, and were less likely to go on welfare. It is estimated that an average investment of $12,356 per child resulted in benefits through age twenty-eight of $70,876, reflecting the additional costs of completed education and higher wages and the lower costs of incarceration and welfare.[20]

While these efforts were under way to help poor children in the late 1960s, middle-class mothers were entering the workforce in ever greater numbers and securing others to care for their children. This "problem" threatening attachment became so great that in the 1970s researchers conducted several studies to find out to what degree day care was damaging to these three- and four-year-old children. By the early 1980s, the results of several studies, mostly conducted in high-quality day care centers, had fostered a widespread consensus that, contrary to the dire predictions of psychologists, nonmaternal care begun in the third year of life or later does not have adverse effects on development.[21] In fact, investigators found that children between two and four years, who attend day care, experience cognitive development that is advanced while they are in day care. (By the time children have gone through the first grade, however, those who did not attend preschool have caught up with them.) Good day care centers also appear to enhance children's social development: Children are likely to be more self-confident, outgoing, assertive, and self-sufficient, more comfortable in new situations, less timid, more cooperative, and more verbally expressive. They are also more independent and determined to get their own way, and they do not always have the social skills to achieve this smoothly.[22]

Such conclusions must be qualified, however, because most of the studies involved atypically good programs and ignored family day care and in-home care by relatives and paid caregivers. Researchers also paid no attention to the characteristics that distinguished parents who tended to use the different kinds of care, nor did they pay much attention to the differing personalities of the children. Mostly, they continued to study high-quality center care, continuing to suspect deficits and failing to find them. Research on preschoolers trickled along, exploring whether day care makes these children less compliant than children reared at home (quality care may actually make them more independent).[23] High quality center care also has positive effects on children's self concept and intellectual development regardless of their family background.

While some psychologists continued to explore the experiences of a small minority of middle-class three- and four-year-olds, the real arena of controversy shifted to infants and toddlers. Jay Belsky, of course, led the assault with his 1986 study[24] (see chapter 3). Currently, Belsky has produced a new study claiming again that infants who experienced more than twenty hours per week of nonmaternal care are headed for trouble. However, in this study, Belsky analyzes a variety of factors in the family environment and the day care situation and notes their interaction. Again, he finds trouble in more of the families that use infant day care, in part because infant care in this country is generally poor, in part because much of the time families spend together is stressful due to work and other pressures, and, related to this, families are less familiar with how to manage their infant's behavior so that when they become toddlers (hitting the "terrible twos") the parents find them more difficult.[25]

In addition to looking for what's wrong with day care, some researchers have begun to examine the "attachment-like" relationships that infants form with their caregivers. They find that the sensitivity and involvement of the caregiver tends to predict which of the relationships will be "secure," "avoidant," or "difficult."[26] Moreover, it appears that children in day care don't shift their allegiance from mothers to care providers as the primary objects of attachment; infants can love several people at once. While some studies show associations between infant day care and later aggressiveness, this seems more likely to be the product of poor relationships with the care providers rather than the result of separation from the mother, as attachment theorists would predict.[27]

Perhaps most telling of all, studies of Swedish infants who entered day care in the second half of the first year of life show that these infants actually score better on tests of cognitive ability and achievement. Since Swedish centers are generally of very high quality and since infants from a wide variety of backgrounds have this experience, it is likely that far from being harmful, quality infant day care is even good for infants. It also helps babies whose mothers are depressed.[28]

Overall, however, few differences between infants raised at home and infants experiencing quality day care have been documented. It is unlikely that clear answers regarding infant day care will soon appear because of all the methodological problems with such studies— for example, the continued use of ambiguous tests and the lack of evidence that infants who "flunk" attachment tests behave any differently in future years than those who ace them. While psychologists have been so busy scrutinizing gradations of attachment they have failed to turn their attention to the inadequate care available for special-needs children, even though they constitute a surprisingly large portion of our population—around 10 percent of all children under six years old.[29]

There is at least one study underway that promises to be a more comprehensive examination of child care. A five-year, $5-million study, begun in 1991 by the National Institute of Child Health and Human Development, employs some of the country's most experienced researchers. They are cooperating in the venture in which children have been periodically observed in any child care arrangement in which they spend at least ten hours a week. The researchers identified over 1,300 infants at birth from a wide range of family backgrounds. The study proposed to examine how social relationships in the family "moderate" child care; assess the influences of children's individual differences; determine the effects of "maternal employment"; document the typical matrix of care used by families; identify the elements of quality child care; and identify what influences parents' choice of child care. On the face of it, this all sounds progressive and helpful, but unfortunately, this study is still burdened by assumptions about the maternal gold standard so that fathers continue to be an afterthought and "nonmaternal" care is still viewed as suspect along with "maternal employment." The study still categorizes children raised by mothers at home as one kind of care to which "nonmaternal" care is then compared using measures of maternal attachment as a prime assessment tool. And of course, the focus is still on identifying the effects of child care on children rather than seeing care, families, and work as part of an interacting system.[30]

## AMERICA'S CONTEMPT FOR CHILDREN

America's contempt for children has reached new lows with the GOP assault against the poor that suggests that children be put in orphanages if their mothers cannot find sufficient work to support them. Such irresponsible nastiness springs from a widespread undercurrent of disregard for children. American families are saddled with a crazy quilt of unregulated, underfinanced child care that is detrimental to children's development because most adults simply do not care.*

---

*There is a significant demographic factor in this lack of concern. Families with children have become an increasingly small proportion of families: In 1991, only 26 percent of all households contained a mar-

Family policy in every other modern country is substantial (see chapter 7). In the United States it is niggardly and piecemeal.* American families with children receive a very modest Earned Income Tax Credit available to working families making under about $27,000.[31] In 1994 the federally funded Head Start program enrolled 750,000 children at a cost of about $4,434 per child. In 1991 Congress passed the Act for Better Child Care ("ABC"), which distributed $732 million to the states for child care for children under thirteen whose family income is no greater than 75 percent of the state's median income. These funds are sometimes used for mothers who are getting off welfare through employment, but assistance is limited in most cases to a year. These programs do not begin to address the needs of our millions of families with young children.

While the child care needs of its infants are especially critical, America has yet to take any serious initiatives to help them. Many dual-wage earner families now work alternate hours so they can care for their infant, but this places a tremendous strain on the marriage and may therefore result in inferior care for their child. Single parents are in the worst bind. They cannot stay home and cannot find affordable quality care.[32] Of course, one of the reasons for poorer quality care for infants is that such care is highly labor-intensive and therefore expensive. Full-time infant care costs about one third more than care for older preschoolers. One possible solution to the problem is to improve the availability of affordable, quality, out-of-home infant care by subsidizing it; the other is to provide more extended *paid* parental leave from work during their child's infancy.

In February 1993 the federal government enacted the Family and Medical Leave Act. This act requires companies with more than fifty employees to allow up to twelve weeks of unpaid leave for the birth or adoption of a child or to care for a child, parent, spouse, or oneself

---

*ried couple with children compared to 40 percent in 1970. (Robert Suro, "For Women, Varied Reasons for Single Motherhood,* New York Times, *May 26, 1991, pp. A 12+.)*

*\*In a comparison of countries that shows how taxes and benefits lower the percentage of children who are poor (1987), the United States is outstanding: In the United States the percent of poor based on income was 23 percent, after taxes and benefits, 21 percent; in France, the poor were 25 percent, but after taxes and benefits, 6 percent; the United Kingdom: 30 percent, reduced to 7 percent; and so forth. (The poverty line used is 50 percent of the median family income.) (Organization for Economic Co-operation and Development,* Measurement of Low Incomes and Poverty in a Perspective of International Comparisons, Labor Market and Social Policy Occasional Papers, *no. 14 [Paris, 1994], Table a. 6, p. 43.)*

during a serious illness. It requires companies to maintain health benefits during the leave and to reinstate the employee to his or her previous job or an equivalent position upon return. Employees whose earnings are in the top 10 percent and whose leave would cause serious hardship for the employer are exempted. However, because of the exemption of small business, the law covers, at most, only 39 percent of the total workforce. Moreover, employers are flouting even this meager break for parents. In a major study of compliance during the first year of the law, a survey of three hundred employers found that four in ten were failing to allow twelve weeks' leave, to guarantee jobs, or to continue benefits during leave. Two thirds of women who did take leave say they had considerable trouble with their employers. Only a very small minority of companies are really trying to implement the law.[33]

Typical of employer resistance is the case of a woman who was looking forward to taking twelve weeks off with her new baby until her employer turned her down flat. "The law is only for sick newborns," a benefits manager told her. The soon-to-be mother protested it was for all newborns and was told, "Honey, every woman would like to be able to stay home and play with her new baby . . ." In another case, a maintenance worker needed family leave to help care for his infant twins, who were born two months prematurely. But when he approached his boss a month before he wanted to begin his leave, the boss, he said, "was on me as soon as I hit the door. When I told him family leave was a federal law now, he said, 'I don't have to abide by federal law!' Then he called me some names and told me I had an attitude problem." After the worker gathered information about the law, a foreman forced the manager to approve the request. Some employees say they experienced retaliation when they returned to work after leaves. Shortly after a senior purchasing assistant with nearly thirteen years at a major oil company started a two-and-a-half-month leave with his new baby, he says friends at work called and told him his bosses had ransacked his office in clear view of coworkers. When he returned to work, he found someone else in the space. He had been given a much smaller office, his high-tech phone had been replaced with a cheaper model, and his computer passwords and e-mail had been erased. Then, he says, his boss gave him a warning letter citing the loose ends left when he rushed off to attend his wife's premature labor and stripped him of most job duties. He finally sued the oil company in federal court, alleging violation of the family-leave law.[34]

Critics maintain that such leaves impose significant costs on employers, resulting in reduced employment, higher costs to consumers, lower wages, and discrimination against women of childbearing age. On the other hand, proponents argue that by increasing the attachment (if I may use the term loosely) of workers to their employers, such leaves induce efficiency and thereby improve productivity. The one matter seldom discussed, however, is the cost to women who temporarily or permanently leave jobs for childbearing. One recent study estimated that the total earnings loss for women who bear children and return to work within two years is $12.9 billion annually. Those with access to leave sacrifice 51 percent of their prebirth annual earnings, and those without leave lose 86 percent. Furthermore, taxpayers must pay an additional $108 million in public assistance for many of these women.[35] (Why does no one accuse business and industry of that morally corrupting welfare dependence?)

On the other hand, child care–related absenteeism costs businesses $3 billion a year. A few American corporations have crafted generous family leave policies to head off such losses and to compete for the best employees, who are often young people with children. At IBM, for example, new parents may take up to one year of paid leave and up to two additional years of unpaid leave during which they must be available for part-time work. Health benefits are maintained during the entire leave period. Although large and medium-size firms tend to make leave available either through disability insurance or through paid sick leave, a substantial majority of employees in small, medium-size and large firms have no leave time available for infant care.[36] Of course there are less tangible, longer-term benefits of family leave, such as stronger families and better lives for children, but these consequences are not figured into cost-benefit analyses.

Even the most limited cost-benefit analysis, however, would indicate that pro-family policies are good for business. For example, in one company of 1,600 employees, until recently, at least two employees per day woke up and felt forced to tell a lie—they would call in sick to stay home and care for a sick child. That amounted to about 2,200 days a year. Like a growing number of businesses, the company decided to open an on-site child care center for infants to five-year-olds, with a "Sniffles and Snuggles" room for mildly ill youngsters up to age twelve. Figures from the first six months of operation showed that Sniffles and Snuggles saved the company more than it costs to administer the program.[37]

## IT *DOES* TAKE A WHOLE VILLAGE

The psychological research on child care has been so obsessively focused on the bogus mothercare/othercare dichotomy, that it has woefully failed parents and children. The fact is, exclusive mothercare is a social anomaly in human history and might better be viewed as of questionable importance. In fact, in most traditional societies, mothers have not been the primary caretakers of infants, let alone of young children.[38] Multiple caretaking, it turns out, is most common in societies that show a great deal of concern for children; where caretaking by the mother, alone, prevails, surveys show there tends to be more neglect of children.[39] In traditional societies, while young children may be reared cooperatively, the cast of caregivers remains fairly constant.

There is no precedent for the variety of unstable early relationships that so many infants and toddlers now experience in our own society. We *need* good, unbiased research to help us chart these untested waters, although we already know a great deal about what is best for these children—i.e., the kinds of social supports for families that are so badly missing in our society.

Multiple caretaking is here to stay—yet there are few adequate guidelines for its organization in contemporary America. However, most modern societies have at least made a good start toward providing high-quality multiple caretaking for all families at affordable rates. There are certainly quite a few good models from which to draw our own plan, and I'll take them up in the next chapter.

7

# Reformed:
# Child Care in
# Other Countries

## AMERICA IS THE WORST

We're so used to our culture of motherguilt and motherblame that it's hard to imagine any other paradigm. But in fact, most other modern countries have reformed the exclusive mothering ideal to fit the needs of the modern family. In other words, they *value* women's work outside the home. They pay to support it. They *value* their children. They pay to support them. America apparently still just doesn't get it. Therefore, on any number of indexes the U.S. has the worst record regarding the care of its young children.[1]

In Western Europe, Eastern Europe, Scandinavia, Canada, Israel, and Japan, as well as many industrializing nations, the care of young children isn't laid solely at mothers' feet; it is viewed as a collective responsibility, and public funds are allotted to subsidize both individual families and collective child care. Universal subsidized preschool for children from the age of two and a half to six has clearly emerged as the policy choice of the advanced industrial nations. Any differences in policy have to do largely with care of one- and two-year-olds. For toddlers, some countries stress child care services more, while others stress cash benefits to permit at-home parental care, and some offer a menu of options.

In more than one hundred countries around the world, employees get at least three months of paid maternal/paternal leave, and often as much as six to twelve months in the European and Scandinavian countries. One result of these leave policies, of course, is that out-of-home infant care is not an issue in many countries. Even where there are very high labor force participation rates for women with children under three—rates that are far higher than in the United States—very few children under age one are in care. In most countries, the benefit that is provided to protect the family against loss of income following childbirth is equal to either 100 percent of the mother's or father's insured wage or a major portion of the insured wage. And in most countries the benefit is tax-free. This support of families and children is based on needs to increase birthrates, regulate women's labor, and educate and socialize a future labor force, as well as an altruistic concern for children.[2]

It is probably no accident that attachment theory, which continues to insist on the superiority of stay-at-home mothering, has its origins in the United States and Great Britain, which are both near the bottom on measures of child-friendliness. And while we have exported attachment research to a host of other countries, those nations seem to have little use for it as a cautionary tale for working mothers since they have fully embraced their responsibility to subsidize families and child care. Clearly the precepts of attachment, far from being universal, scientifically established verities, are more than anything a rationalization that manipulates mothers into feeling solely responsible for the early care of their children. Attachment is a notion based on constructs regarding women's proper role, the structure of the labor market, the population needs of the nation, cultural values related to the egalitarian or hierarchical ideals of a society, values of cooperation and competition, and a variety of complex factors that have little to do with any universal psychological needs of children. Other societies have quite different and even opposite notions about early mother-child relations. Yet they produce perfectly psychologically healthy children and adults. On the Israeli kibbutz, for instance, the ideal has been to separate infants from their mothers at birth and raise them in "children's houses." In Sweden, nine out ten mothers of young children are in the labor force. All are paid to stay home for the first twelve months with their infants, who receive excellent subsidized care thereafter. There is no notion that attachment needs should keep mothers of infants and young children from working.

America is distinguished from the other nations by a combination of cultural values and labor market realities. Certainly, we tend to view workers as dispensable—a view made possible by a continual influx of immigrant laborers, abundantly available since the mid-nineteenth century. Therefore, neither women's labor nor a high native birthrate have been seen as crucial to the economy. Slavery and its legacy of racism has kept us divided against ourselves, disposing us to see the largely minority poor as inherently different and inferior. The rich, on the other hand, are every American's dream. And indeed, at the turn of the century, street corner boys did indeed go from rags to riches with real frequency. The ideal of every man for himself, based on that now-elusive dream of success through hard work, perpetuates the notion that individual families should also be able to fend for themselves. The collectivity of other countries may thus seem alien to Americans.

But in the interests of inspiring us to develop a more appropriate plan, let me briefly survey how a few other countries have put children first without holding mothers' feet to the fire.

## SWEDEN

Parents and children in Sweden are beneficiaries of the most advanced family policy of any country. Child care is considered a basic human need to which everyone has a right, along with food, shelter, work, and education. Sweden has a remarkably comprehensive, well-integrated, and carefully planned national family policy. The Swedish program developed in response to three major concerns: (1) worry about a low birthrate; (2) a desire to encourage women's employment; (3) a desire to liberate men and women from gender stereotypes and promote equality between the sexes.

Swedish parenting policies have three major components: direct economic family subsidies; significant paid family leave; and an extensive network of high quality subsidized and regulated child care facilities. The cornerstone of economic subsidy is the child allowance of about $1,500 a year, paid to families for each child under sixteen. In addition, single parents (about 15 percent of families with children) receive special protection: a child support advance (in 1990 about $645 per month tax-free) if the noncustodial parent fails to pay child support. If he or she is unable to pay the mandated amount, the state will make up the difference. Moreover, the custodial parent continues to receive payment (from whichever source) even if she (about 85 percent of single parents are women) or he remarries. Families also get a housing allowance. Low- to moderate-income families with children can obtain a nontaxable monthly housing allowance indexed to family income, number of children, and housing costs. In 1980, 80 percent of single parents received a housing allowance, compared to about 30 percent of married or cohabitating parents. The allowance covered 40 percent of the rent for the recipients who were single parents and about 13 percent for married couples.[3]

Sweden has developed the most extensive parental leave system to date. As a result, practically all Swedish children are at home with one of their parents until they are at least twelve months old. The higher the parent's educational status, the *earlier* they tend to place their children in outside care. About 35 percent are home when their children are between one and two, and 25 percent when their children are between two and three years old. Just under half of all children younger than three are cared for only by their parents, 34 percent receive publicly funded or "municipal" day care, leaving 13 percent cared for by relatives or in paid private day care.[4] Pregnant women whose health is in jeopardy have the right to stop work during the last sixty days of their pregnancy and receive 90 percent pay. In 1986, about 21 percent of pregnant women used an average of thirty-eight of these days. Fathers are allowed to take a ten-day leave of absence within sixty days of childbirth, also at 90 percent of pay.[5] Currently, once the child is born, fathers and mothers are given eighteen months parental leave. Twelve months are compensated at 80 percent of earnings; a further three months is paid at a low flat rate (about $10 a day); and the final three-month period is not paid. Parental leave can be taken in one block of time, or several shorter blocks, and at any time until a child is eight. Both parents cannot claim paid leave at the same time. Parents may also reduce their work week to thirty hours with a right to return to full-time work after two months' notice to the employer. This reduction in work time was motivated by concern with the length of time many children spend in day care. In the 1970s, half of all children younger than three spent more than nine hours per day in day care. Now, fewer than 40 percent of children average more than seven hours per day.[6] Benefits can be used as full, half, or quarter days.

Parents are also entitled to 90 percent of their salary for care of a sick child for up to one hundred twenty days per year if the child under twelve is unable to stay in the place where care is normally provided. (The high number of allotted days is out of concern for handicapped and severely ill children.) A certificate from a medical doctor is needed if a child is sick for more than a week at a time. In 1986, this benefit was used for 48 percent of all children under twelve, for an average of seven days. Benefits were used to a larger extent by parents with children ages one to four; 41 percent of those who used benefits were men. Parents also receive two "contact days" where they can simply visit with their child in the care facility. Sweden's parental insurance specifies that the parent's working conditions should not be impaired because he or she used parental rights (for example, by a transfer to an inferior position). In a 1986 study, 97 percent of parents who had returned to full-time work reported no adverse impact on their subsequent earnings as compared to 90 percent who had reduced their hours. In 1989–90 the government's costs for the parental insurance benefits amounted to 3.9 percent of government expenditures and 1 percent of GNP.[7]

To promote parental leave and especially leave-taking by fathers, nationwide advertising campaigns were launched in the 1970s, picturing wrestlers, soccer players, and other "masculine" men holding, feeding, and walking babies. Despite these efforts to promote fathers' taking parental leave, the numbers are still rather low. Ten percent take advantage of parental leave during the first six months after birth; generally, mothers breast-feed babies for the greater part of this period, so it is possible fathers do not wish to interrupt that process. During the next three-month period, about 28 percent of men take paternity leave for some part of this time. Utilization of other types of leave by fathers is higher. Eighty-three percent take paternity leave at the time of birth of a child, averaging nine of the ten days available. Among parents taking time off to care for sick children, 41 percent were fathers, while 34 percent of parents taking advantage of "contact days" were men.[8] As a consequence of these disappointing fathering figures (Sweden is dedicated to full equality between men and women), the Rikstag passed a new law in 1995—"the father's month"—mandating that at least one month of the first subsidized twelve months of parental leave be taken by the child's father.[9]

Sweden has a comprehensive system of heavily subsidized public child care, including day care centers, family day care, and after-school facilities. Parents have a variety of child care options available to them. Day care centers are open all day and provide high-quality care and education for children between nine months and six years of age whose parents are employed or in school, and for children in need of developmental support. The centers have a cognitive and a developmental program and a trained staff of preschool teachers and nurses. The average ratio of children to annual employees was 4.3 to 1 in 1985. There are also some night care centers for parents with inconvenient working hours. Part-time preschools—"play schools"—provide educational activities for three hours per day free of charge for children aged four to six years who are not in day care centers. Open preschools provide activities in which children who are cared for by parents or family day care providers can participate periodically with their caregiver.[10]

In addition to day care centers, there are parents' clubs where the municipality provides premises and a preschool teacher to assist parents who are at home with their children, regardless of their age. There are also kindergartens, for four-, five- and six-year-olds. Most municipalities also support family day care. "Day mothers" are paid a salary by the municipality to care for unrelated children in their own homes. And there are private alternatives. The most common is the unregulated day mother who is paid directly by the parents. There are also parent cooperatives and day care centers run by various religious or secular associations. In the case of parent cooperatives, a number of parents get together, rent premises, and employ one or more preschool teachers. Very few day care centers are run on a private enterprise basis. Some children are also cared for by nursemaids in the child's own home. Most nursemaids come only during the day; few live in. Finally, some children are cared for by relatives, either in the child's or the relative's home.[11]

The cost for places in municipal day care centers and family care is shared such that the state and municipality each contribute just under half, while parents pay an average of 10 to 15 percent of the real cost of child care. The state's share of the cost is covered by a general social insurance contribution that all employers have to pay to the state.

The municipalities' child care costs are covered by the municipal tax levied on both companies and individuals.

Of course, Sweden has national regulations and norms for staff size and training, group size, daily routines, and the design of the child care environment. Considerable research has been conducted regarding the well-being of children in day care, and while the studies suffer from limitations of scope, sample size, and so forth, they indicate either no effects or positive effects for day care.[12]

Sweden has done the most to acknowledge that both mothers and fathers have legitimate economic and caregiving roles. In fact, women's wages currently equal about 90 percent of men's for equal work, although women are less likely to be found in the higher managerial levels of work and upper echelons of the professions. Fathers as well as mothers work fewer hours in the labor market when they have young children. Nearly half the female work force works part time; 86 percent of women with young children are in the workforce.[13] In one study of gender and the effects of Swedish family policy, it was found that fathers still played a considerably less involved caregiving role than mothers. Those fathers who had taken more leave tended to be more involved in child care in the future, in large part because they felt more capable as a result of their caregiving experience. Two thirds of women in the study preferred part-time work while their children were small, compared to a quarter of fathers. The study suggested that parental leave policy may even reinforce women's unequal position in the labor market as they are expected to and enabled to devote more energy to child care than are men. The study also found that when women take leave, they tend to return to less satisfying jobs and promotion chances as their longer leave is more disruptive to their workplace.[14]

Swedish family policy officially began in the 1930s in response to the Depression and out of concern with declining birthrates related to a serious labor shortage. As part of this pro-natalist policy, maternity aftercare and preventive child health centers were established, and there was no charge for obstetrical services. In 1947 national family allowances were established for children up to the age of sixteen. In 1964, a special allowance for child care was recommended, to make it possible for women to work and have as many children as they wanted. This contribution would enable mothers to stay home during their child's infancy, but also to choose gainful employment. Sweden had actually introduced subsidies into day care centers and playschools (the latter were what we would call kindergartens) as early as 1943, but these subsidies were inspired by an acute labor shortage, and public attitudes did not substantially support day care centers until the mid-1960s.[15]

Because Sweden was one of the few European countries to stay out of World War II, it entered the postwar era ready to produce and export goods to a variety of nations in need of reconstruction. As a result, the country went through an unprecedented economic boom that lasted several decades during which lack of labor was almost the only threat to further economic growth. During the 1950s Sweden solved its lack of manual workers by a massive importation of people from Finland and southern Europe. During the 1960s, when importation of workers was not enough, there was an increasing proportion of women in the workforce. It took the concurrent forces of a strong national economy, the continuing shortage of labor, the women's liberation movement, and the generally leftish political climate of the 1960s to tear down the resistance toward public day care that existed in the Swedish Parliament. The Labour Organisation, the Social Democratic, the Liberal, and the Communist parties all viewed the expansion of public child care as a major condition for equality between men and women.[16]

In 1991, however, Sweden elected a conservative government, toppling the left wing Social Democrats for only the second time since World War II. As a result, the budgets of public child care centers, among many other benefits, were cut. Teachers were laid off, and more children were herded into fewer classes. This caused the typical class size for a three-year-old to rise from eight to twenty-four, with only two adults per group. However, the conservatives were ousted in the fall of 1994, as most Swedes saw, in three years, the benefits of their social democracy dismantled to the point where many felt they were losing their very identity as an egalitarian society. As one citizen put it, "This was always a country that took care of its people. Are we still Swedish?" A 1994 poll found that 78 percent of Swedes did not want their taxes reduced if such a move would lead to further cuts in benefits. Social welfare spending in Sweden was 40 percent of the gross national product, compared to 26 percent in the European Union, and 15 percent in the United States. However, Sweden's unemployment rate is 13 percent, compared to 11 percent in Europe and 6 percent in the United States. Productivity is down, and the budget deficit is high. It remains to be seen how social welfare and economic prosperity can be balanced in the changing global economy. One factor that is bound to be a significant influence: Forty-one percent of the Swedish parliament is female, the highest in the world.[17] In my own conversations with members of the parliament, child care researchers and workers, the press, and assorted Swedish citizens in March 1995, it was clear that the Swedes are still very committed to the democratic (90 percent of Swedes vote, compared to 55 percent in the United States[18]) Social Welfare State. The commitment to family subsidies and quality child care remains strong, and many officials believe reductions in funding for the family are temporary.

## FRANCE

In Europe, preschool programs are viewed as very advantageous for all children for purposes of child development as well as preparing them for primary school—regardless of the parents' labor force status, family income, cultural background, or capacities as parents. Almost all children between two and a half and six years of age attend these programs on a voluntary basis. The programs are all heavily subsidized, operate largely within the public sector, are free or charge modest, income-related fees, and cover, at least, the normal school day.

In France, as in Sweden, parenting support involves direct family subsidies, significant paid family leave, and an extensive network of subsidized and regulated child care facilities. The French terms for out-of-home-care of young children are "programs of welcoming" (*programmes d'accueil*) and "programs of awakening" (*programmes d'éveil*). The French believe that every child benefits from working and playing cooperatively with other children. They point to national census data showing that preschool attendance improves children's chances of passing first grade, which is a critical indicator of later school success across all social and economic classes. Despite the fact that only about 60 percent of the mothers of children aged three to five are in the labor force, more than 95 percent of children that age participate in these programs. During the 1970s, most middle-class and wealthy French parents preferred to use nannies. But attitudes changed radically after research demonstrated that socialization is important and that children who had been in *crèches* and *écoles maternelles* did better in the first years of elementary school.[19]

Currently, public child care programs for young French children are remarkably comprehensive. For France's children under six, the constellation of child care offerings is vast, and all are linked to health care. There are day care centers, or *crèches,* and day care homes for children three months to three years of age, which charge fees on a sliding scale. They serve about 27 percent of all infants and toddlers; another 3 percent are cared for by unlicensed home-based caregivers. Virtually all French children between three and six attend nursery school: the *écoles maternelles,* for children two and a half to five years old, which are free; or parochial nursery schools, which are heavily subsidized.[20] The *écoles maternelles* are generally located in new, bright, spacious, well-maintained, specially designed buildings. They emphasize developmentally appropriate activities and are supervised by pediatric nurses who have special training in public health, child development, and program administration. Infant-toddler centers are housed at a single location. National standards for infant-toddler centers specify ratios of one adult staff person for every five children who do not walk and one for every eight children who do. Centers are usually open from 7:00 A.M. to 7:00 P.M. All municipal *crèche* directors have apartments in the same building, enabling them to keep a child past 7:00 P.M. Parents pay on a sliding scale that is based primarily on income.[21]

By contrast, family day care networks consist of a number of licensed home-based caregivers who are recruited, trained, and supervised from a central hub, which also sponsors regular activities for them and the children they care for. Family day care providers must pass medical and psychological exams and their homes are inspected for safety. Each network of family *crèches* has a hub linked to as few as six or as many as thirty-five family day care homes. The hub pools administration, training, activities, and equipment and is directed by a specially trained pediatric nurse. To offer an antidote to the isolation of home-based care, the hub staff organizes small-group sessions for caregivers and children, typically once a week for half a day at a special facility.

There are also independent licensed family day care providers who provide care for no more than three children other than their own. Each one is advised and monitored by a specially trained pediatric nurse who visits her home at least once every three months and sometimes as often as once every three weeks.[22] The French government reimburses parents for the payment of the providers' social security taxes and gives them a special tax deduction for using licensed rather than unlicensed caregivers.

Government-run free preschools are open from 8:30 A.M. to 4:30 P.M. To accommodate the schedules of working parents, most preschools are linked with "wraparound" programs offered before and after school.[23] The core program of these nearly full-day, noncompulsory schools consists of three morning and three afternoon hours of language arts and developmentally appropriate exercises, crafts, games, dance, singing, rest, and play. All preschool teachers have training equivalent to a master's degree. Each one is responsible for a class averaging twenty-eight students, of whom twenty-two normally attend. A teacher is assisted by an aide and by lunch and naptime staff, and has two hours at midday for lunch and class preparations. (In the United States the optimal adult/child ratio for preschools is considered 1:9.) However, despite the large number of French children per adult, studies by American experts show the quality of *écoles maternelles* to be as high or higher than the best American day care centers. Apparently the excellent teacher training and the French style of teaching, which involves careful planning of daily activities and constant monitoring of the children, allow them to deliver good results to larger groups of children.[24] In 1991 the starting annual salary for teachers was $11,347 a year plus free housing, plus the regular fringe benefits of government employees. Their salary rises to a maximum of $23,300 per year. French day care teachers are well educated and have a relatively low turnover rate.[25]

Several small-scale infant-toddler programs meet special needs and preferences that are not limited to those of working parents. For example, *garderies* offer drop-in, part-time care for mothers who care most of the time for their own children. France also offers parent-run day care cooperatives and short-term drop-in programs. Municipalities put up money to build the cooperatives and provide a child development specialist to work with parents. Government-run *garderies,* which are akin to indoor playgrounds, offer a few hours' respite for parents. For immigrant mothers who may be acculturated to keeping the child at home, the occasional short-term use of the drop-in center at the suggestion of a social worker or public health nurse may serve to ease the mother's way to sending her child to a nursery school where he may begin to learn French and have a better start in public school. Paris is experimenting with a center for children in difficult family situations; it provides special care night and day, supervised by a psychologist and social worker. It works with the court system and social service agencies.

Various incentives promote quality in child care. Family day care providers are entitled to employee benefits and social security once they become licensed. Students training to be preschool teachers receive cash stipends in addition to a free education; they agree, on entering a training program, to spend five years in the field after graduation. All preschool teachers and directors have training equivalent to a master's degree in early childhood and elementary education, and they earn salaries equivalent to those of elementary school teachers. Directors of infant-toddler programs are pediatric nurses who have professional training in public health, child development, and administration. Infant-toddler educators have a degree that is equivalent to two years of college in the United States and an additional two-year professional course in early childhood education and child development.

An extensive national service of preventive health care for mothers and their infants has reduced France's infant mortality rate to the fourth-lowest in the world. The Maternal and Infant Protection Service is a comprehensive health service for all children from before birth to age six. As of 1989, it cost about $55 per child per year. A number of mechanisms link the service with all forms of out-of-home infant and toddler care and preschools. Proof of regular medical exams is required at the time of a child's admission to, and at intervals during, every public child care program. The service readily gives these exams at no charge to parents. By law, a child must have a medical exam once a month until nine months of age and then at six-month intervals until six years.

Family benefits in France are predominantly financed by employers through a universal payroll tax of 9 percent. (Employees do not contribute.) This levy supports the national system of family allowances that provides significant income supplements to families. For example, a family with two young children presently receives $1,117 annually, regardless of its income. Needier families receive higher supplements, and there are numerous formulas to cover specific conditions and needs such as the care of a handicapped child. France's maternal leave law gives all working mothers paid leave (in 1993 mothers received 84 percent of their base salary) with job security during the last 6 weeks of pregnancy and for ten weeks after childbirth. Ten weeks of paid leave are given for adoptions. At the end of her leave a woman returns to her former job in its identical form and including all former benefits. Either parent has the right to request an unpaid leave of absence for up to two years after a child's birth or adoption. Alternatively, or consecutively, a parent can ask for part-time employment during this period. (Employers having fewer than one hundred employees can request, and often receive, an exemption.) This "parent education" leave is viewed as time off from one set of responsibilities that are important to society to learn another set that are critical to society. However, in reality, this extended leave is used infrequently, primarily by women in lower-paying jobs and by mothers of children having health or other problems.

Parents may also receive a nonemployed parent's allowance (about $468 per month) if the family has at least three children, at least one child under three, and the parent staying home with the children has a history of at least two years of paid work in the ten years preceding the birth. In the baby's third year, the parent who has gone back to work half time is entitled to a monthly stipend of $234.[26]

American and French taxpayers' attitudes toward spending on social services are very different. Americans spend on their child care and development programs about half of what the equivalent French programs would have to spend if their country was as big as the United States. However, American programs do far less than half as much as the French programs do to provide child care that will allow parents to hold jobs. Almost half of France's gross domestic product goes to taxes, compared with less than a third in the United States.[27] But even with France's growing concern about its budget deficit and high payroll taxes, the French are clamoring for more, not less, spending on child care. The solution has been to continue building day care centers and charge wealthy families more. France spends over $7 billion annually on infant and child health and education. If the United States were to commit equivalent public resources to child care and linked health services, this would approximate $23 billion a year— triple our present public expenditures.[28]

One of the central forces behind France's family-friendly policy has been the wish to increase the birthrate by reducing the difficulties mothers have in rearing children. Economically, France was always capable of supporting a larger population than it possessed as there was considerable spare agricultural land. Until the 1970s, there was never a national unemployment problem. Military reasons have also been strong since the time of Napoleon, who offered to fully support every seventh son of a couple if he joined the army; and related to this there was frequently a need to replace a population devastated by war. Catholic enthusiasm for large families has also been a factor, as has been French feminism, which linked women's rights to their freedom to both raise children and work in the public sector.[29] The fact that French benefit programs do not narrowly focus on the poor, in which immigrant and minority populations figure disproportionately, has preserved support for them. (About 10 percent of the French population consists of recent immigrants.) Moreover, the French recognize the importance of socializing minority populations in order to maintain the superior status of the French nation.

## ISRAEL

When Americans think of nonmaternal care, one of the common examples that comes to mind is the Israeli kibbutz. The kibbutz is, in many ways, a very radical arrangement that has now been scrutinized by social scientists. Psychologists have been especially interested to see how it affects the personality of the child. Kibbutz infants are taken from their mothers immediately after birth to live in communal infant houses where they share a caregiver with other infants and are visited a few times a day by their mothers. Psychodynamic and attachment theory would certainly predict a different and probably dysfunctional personality for the kibbutz-raised person. The kibbutz was, indeed, designed to create a different personality, though certainly not a dysfunctional one.

In the early twentieth century the Jewish population of Israel was largely built through waves of immigration from Europe, Eastern Europe, and northern Africa. The immigrants attempted to transform this conglomeration of peoples into a modern and different generation of Jews, speaking one language and adhering to the ideology of equality and fraternity. The first priority was to guarantee their survival. Throughout the land, the community's responsibility for the health of its young was expressed through the establishment of a network of mother and child centers that attended to the needs of pregnant women and their infants. The "new Israeli" children were to be the foundation on which the new culture and society would be built. They had to be "cleansed" of any traces of the "mentality" of the stereotypical diaspora Jew. In many cases these pioneers disqualified themselves as parents competent to rear their own children. After all, they did not know the language that was supposed to be their children's mother tongue, and they could not rid themselves of some of their old customs and habits. So they turned to the professional educator, who was supposed to provide answers and models for the socialization of their children.

The most extreme but representative example of this trend was that of the children's homes in the kibbutzim. Ideology, the practical necessities of life, and later on, reasoning based on psychodynamic theory, led to a social system where children from the first days of life were reared in communal homes, spending only a few hours a day with their parents. This system enabled both parents to work, which was not only an economic necessity but also an ideological norm. It further enabled the community to provide the housing, hygiene, medical care, and safety facilities needed to ensure the survival of its young. Thus, while their parents lived in tents and were plagued by illness, undernourishment, and fever, the young generation lived in houses, received the best food available, and were raised by carefully chosen caregivers trained in both the latest ideas of public health, modern education and the most revered principles of social revolution. The provision of a professional educator was expected to help both child and parent overcome the bourgeois past, as well as to avoid the intergenerational psychological strain of nuclear family existence. Today, the kibbutz movement encompasses only 4 percent of the population. However, in the 1930s and 1940s, close to 8 percent of the Jewish population lived in kibbutzim.[30]

The history of the kibbutz intentional community extends over seventy years. The first kibbutz communities started in the second decade of the century, were independent Zionist agricultural enterprises struggling for survival. The kibbutz was an ideal solution to the problem of colonizing Palestine in the years before the founding of the State of Israel. Settling the land with groups of young people having attachments to the collective, rather than individual homesteading families, was more militarily defensible. The kibbutz was also idealistic, believing in the virtue of a return to nature through agriculture, and aiming for a true egalitarianism where people would be less selfish and more generous. The change in social structure was expected to lead to a psychological change in every individual.

Two basic principles were the underpinnings of child-rearing philosophy in the kibbutz. The first was that communal child rearing would work against individualism and identification with the family unit. The second was that experts in child rearing could inculcate the ideology of the kibbutz with greater ability and objectivity than could parents. The primary socializing agents would become the nurses, teachers, and peer groups. The founders of the kibbutz were also in open rebellion against their own parents and the institution of the family, which was seen as promoting selfishness, individualism, and inequality between the sexes.

The kibbutz child-rearing system, of course, has undergone many changes over the decades, but until the 1970s, it can generally be described as follows: Several days after the birth of a baby, which takes place in the maternity ward of a regional hospital, mother and infant return home to the kibbutz. The mother returns to her own quarters, which she shares with her husband, while the infant is placed in the "infant house." Henceforward, the child is, with rare and exceptional interruptions, primarily in the company of his peers until he graduates from high school at the age of eighteen and becomes eligible for adult membership in the kibbutz. The infant house accommodates about twenty children from the first week of life to about fifteen months, with one section for the very young and another for those who have been weaned.

Demand feeding is the rule in the kibbutz, so the mother is available, usually for breast-feeding, whenever she is needed. The feeding lasts about twenty minutes but the time of contact is extended to about forty-five minutes. The mother also changes diapers, carries the infant, plays with him, and finally puts him to sleep. In some instances she may sleep in the infant house for several weeks, especially if late-night feeding is necessary. Once the infant is six weeks old, the mother resumes working on a half-time basis until he reaches about four months of age, and the child is gradually weaned. The mother continues to play the major part in the care of her infant until he is about nine months old. The evening feeding and putting the child to bed is still her prerogative until he is about a year old.

A *metapelet* is responsible for the house; she monitors the health of the child, comforts and plays with him, washes him regularly, and keeps close watch over the infant when the mother is not around. The literal meaning of the word *metapelet* (plural: *metaplot*) is "the one who takes care" of the child—the nurse. When the infant is nine months old, his group of six infants gets their own *metapelet,* who stays with the group for the next five years. Parents and siblings may visit during prescribed hours.

In the 1970s, the kibbutz parents began to keep their infants with them in their own quarters. This trend was partly due to the improvement in the living standards of the parents' homes, as well as the lack of privacy and therefore difficult conditions involved in feeding and settling the infants for the night in the infants' house. Also, medical practice regarding infectious childhood diseases helped ease parents' fears of exposing infants to the outside world. And finally, there was a general trend in the kibbutz movement to strengthen the family. By then, it was generally agreed that children brought up in the earlier kibbutz were well-adjusted, developed close ties with their parents, and grew up without any special intellectual or psychological deficits—so the shift to more emphasis on parents was not born of a need to reform a deficient institution. Rather, the main reason for the change seemed to be the desire of parents, especially mothers, to be more directly involved in the raising of their children. In the 1980s, mothers tended to delay moving infants to the children's houses for six and even twelve months, simply because they wanted the personal involvement with their child.[31]

Studies of the outcomes of the kibbutz communal child-rearing philosophy are frought with bias, both in favor and against such an arrangement. One of the most widely read and influential studies, written by Bruno Bettelheim and published as *The Children of the Dream*,[32] describes the children of this collective education as introverted, hostile, and insecure. The book is based on clinical observations by a psychoanalyst who did not speak the language of the people he was studying, was in their company for a few weeks, and pursued an impressionistic rather than systematic course.

Bettelheim proposed that kibbutz children would experience a diffusion of identity because of the "diffusion" of early relationships and this would lead to a reduced capacity or need for intimacy. He alleged the kibbutz-reared children displayed "flatness of affect," were incapable of intimacy, had low initiative, and had acquired a "collective superego." Bettelheim did not attempt to compare them to a control group of children raised in nuclear families. Bettelheim was widely criticized, especially by Israelis, for having had excessive expectations for the kibbutz children, and, upon failing to find his "angels," painting a rather vindictive portrait. He was also criticized for his ethnocentrism, his "unexamined and unwarranted assumption that child-rearing methods that are standard in middle-class Western culture are best for all cultures."[33]

A more systematic study in the same era did compare kibbutz children with rural children reared in more conventional nuclear families. Researchers found few differences between the children. There was some variation in the rates of development and differences in values based on what they had been taught. But they found no characterological differences.[34] More recent studies have more systematically compared adult groups of kibbutz-reared children to family or *moshav*-reared groups. One study of adults reared in kibbutz and *moshav* in the 1950s found that there were no significant differences between the two groups in fulfilling their adult roles in their respective communities. In both groups, the rates of marriage and parenthood were nearly identical; educational levels were quite similar; kibbutz members were more likely to be officers in the army; *moshav*-reared adults tended to evaluate their childhood in more positive terms than their kibbutz counterparts, even though kibbutz children experienced greater permissiveness; kibbutz members tended to be more critical of marriage and their marriage partners. Kibbutz members were a bit less likely to have a single "best friend" with whom they had a close relationship. This difference is thought to be due to the experience of having been able to find several "best friends" in the peer group in which kibbutz children were reared and their subsequent capacity to find a number of "best" friends in adulthood.[35] Kibbutz members also described themselves as more anxious and critical than *moshav* respondents. This is thought to be due to their ability to be more open and self-analytical. The two groups have similar self-esteem and seem to be similarly psychologically healthy.

This study tried to evaluate the quality of interpersonal attachments and found differences that suggest a different interpersonal style of intimacy and friendship. While *moshav* adults have very strong emotions in relationships, both positive and negative, the kibbutz adults experience less of either extreme. Since the kibbutz caretaking situation was perceived as lying somewhere between maternal deprivation on the one side and normal maternal contacts in the traditional family on the other, it has often been assumed that the relative "deprivation" would have its effects in the form of a greater prevalence of psychopathology. Such an effect was never found. In sum, the personality of the kibbutz-born adult appears to be nonpathological, effective, and shows moderated but positive attachment to others.[36]

## MODERN ISRAEL

In Israel today the Jewish population, about 80 percent of its people, take it for granted that educating and rearing young children is the responsibility of the whole community. The Arab population, while changing, retains the more traditional view that early child rearing is the responsibility of women in the extended family. In the Jewish population most parents believe that it is important for two- to three-year-old children to be in some type of group setting, and feel they do not meet their children's developmental needs adequately if they are kept at home. Family benefits and child care subsidies do not match those in Europe and Scandinavia, but are far more generous than the United States. Family benefits include maternal leave, which enables working mothers to receive 70 percent of their salary while staying home for twelve weeks following delivery and an additional nine-month unpaid leave while their job is held secure; each family also receives a special grant upon the birth of a child. A network of mother and child centers ("a drop of milk") provides free pre- and postnatal care, immunization, nutrition, and screening of all infants for mothers and children up to the age of three.

In the typical subsidized preschool for three- to six-year-old children, the curriculum is predominantly oriented to socializing immigrants into a homogenized Hebrew culture. In addition to free public nursery schools there is a network of privately owned nursery schools serving two- to five-year-olds, which is paid for by the parents. A large number of preschool programs are located within day care and community centers serving three- to five-year-olds where costs are covered by the parents, the women's organizations, and the Ministry of Labor and Social Welfare. The preschool system was conceived of primarily as an educational program designed to prepare children for life in a Western society and not as a service for working mothers. As such, it has always operated as a half-day program. In recent years, however, families with working mothers have pressured the local authorities to open afternoon programs for children three to six, which they have done. Salaries of day care workers remain among the lowest in the country, and the women's organizations find it difficult to staff the centers.

Sponsored family day care, where a woman takes a group of children into her own home, is sponsored by either the local community center or by the local welfare department, but regulation of standards and supervision are nationally controlled. The rapid growth of this program can be explained by the fact that it does not require investment in building and it is perceived by both parents and professionals as the best alternative care for infants and toddlers. The caregiver is required to participate in a two-month, preservice training course and to receive individual supervision in her home on a weekly basis. For every eighteen homes there is a coordinator with academic training either in social work or early childhood education.[37]

What characterizes family policy in Israel, and links it to Europe and Scandinavia, is a tradition of seeing child rearing as an essential means of guiding the future of the nation. But Israel is also unique in the degree to which this child socialization was also a necessary means of homogenizing a diverse immigrant population.

## JAPAN

The chief natural resource of Japan, a small island nation of 121 million, is its well-educated and motivated citizenry. Researchers have studied the Japanese family, the system of compulsory schooling, and its business organizations in an attempt to understand the Japanese "economic miracle." As some Westerners marvel at the high achievement levels of the Japanese, a recent trend has been to investigate the roots of this success in children's early experiences before compulsory schooling takes over.[38] While day care and kindergarten have become much more widespread in the past three decades, Japan's strong family system makes a unique contribution as well. Until very recently, a wife's involvement in the Japanese marriage has been primarily with her children, and secondarily with her husband. Typically his primary relationship is with his business.[39]

In Japan, the nuclear family became the predominant form in the 1960s, and now about 70 percent of families describe themselves as nuclear. The general decline of the traditional extended family has given greater responsibility for child care to mothers and child care facilities such as day nurseries. At the same time, there has been a slow increase in the number of three-generation families since the 1960s—in fact, at least one grandparent (80 percent of whom are paternal grandparents) lives in the home of 28 percent of Japanese families (compared with 3 percent in the United States). As a result of the declining birthrate (Japan now averages 1.7 children per woman), the number of families with three or more children is 18 percent, which means that the segment of their lifespan Japanese women devote to the maternal role is far less than ever.[40] Also, Japanese children have fewer playmates at home today than ever before, and combined with the decline of the neighborhood as the center of social life, child care facilities have gained importance as the locale of peer and parent interaction.

Japan has become a very affluent society, which has supported the growing number of private child care facilities that have appeared in Japan since the 1960s. Day care and preschool programs have nearly doubled each decade since 1960.[41] Middle-class consciousness has fed into the heightened educational aspirations and commitment of many families. Competition for social and occupational status is based in Japan on the prestige of one's academic degrees, so much so that the term "schoolism" (gakureki-shugi) has been coined to describe this emphasis on educational attainment. The emphasis on competitive education has trickled down to early childhood education, as some parents push their children to enter prestigious kindergartens and thereby enhance their potential for later academic success. In fact, in one recent survey, half the parents said they had their preschoolers tutored to gain a competitive edge. At the age of three, children are sent to "cram schools" where they are tutored in everything from memorizing stories to taking achievement tests.[42] Mothers are generally held responsible for children's school attainment and the term "education mom" (kyoiku mama) is a popular depiction of her assigned role. Because many day nurseries have openings only for employed mothers, a growing number of mothers take jobs just so their children can be enrolled in nursery school.

The Japanese government is both encouraging women to participate more fully in the workplace, as well as calling for an increase in the birthrate. Child care therefore has become a focus of national concern. Demand has increased because more women now continue to work outside the home after having children. Japanese women are critical of their working conditions, especially the absence of adequate child care, as well as the expected complaints about lack of job opportunities and traditional attitudes that women belong in the home. However, looking at the types of child care used by employed women, Japan's use of group facilities outside the home (mainly kindergartens and day nurseries) was, until recently, significantly higher than in the United States and Western Europe. By 1982, 65 percent of Japanese parents used day nurseries or kindergartens for children under five, compared to 31 percent in the United States and 40 percent in France. Millions of women entered the labor force during the economic growth years of the 1960s to fill a labor shortage of unskilled workers. Many women also went into the labor force in the 1970s because two incomes were necessary to support a family in that decade of growing expectations, rising educational costs, and slowing economic growth. Yet in the 1990s, Japanese mothers must contend with the general attitude that no other job is better or more suitable for women than mothering. Parents who work longer hours simply because longer child care hours are available, are seen as selfish.[43]

In Japan the day nursery and kindergarten are the predominant facilities for nonmaternal child care. Half of employed mothers use day nurseries for the care of their children. Close to a third report using grandparents as baby-sitters. Japanese society has developed very little in the way of family day care, and parents generally do not feel secure leaving their children in private homes. Most parents are uneasy entrusting their children to a nonprofessional "outsider." However, family day care for children under three did emerge in the 1960s. These women are called "childcare moms" (*hoiku mama*) and most often serve infants. They receive no government financing, but local governments set basic standards for care and licensing and arrange individual contracts between families and caregivers. A final alternative to maternal care is paternal care, which until recently was uncommon. There has been some shifting of societal values in support of greater paternal involvement, especially as there is a growing number of single-parent fathers.

The day nursery (*Hoikusho*) is the most utilized alternative to maternal child care for employed mothers. The curriculum for older day nursery children was made similar to the kindergarten educational curriculum in 1965, such that the final year of the day nursery experience is more comparable to a U.S. kindergarten. Although the large majority of day nursery children are over the age of three, there has been a small trend in recent years for day nurseries to serve younger babies. Day nursery and kindergarten teachers are usually young female junior college graduates and the child/teacher ratios are high: 6

to 1 for six months to two years; 30 to 1 for ages four and over. More than 90 percent of day nurseries operate between eight and eleven hours daily. Parents pay on a sliding scale according to their income.

The day nurseries were originally designed to serve the working class, whereas the kindergarten was for the middle class, but the differences have pretty much faded. Kindergartens are considered educational facilities rather than child care facilities, although they emphasize motivation and socialization rather than cognitive matters, and serve three-, four-, and five-year-olds. The Japanese are now clamoring for better infant care, and day nurseries now accept children from six months.

In general, day nurseries and kindergartens are licensed and regulated by the government, but some large-scale group facilities are not licensed. In fact, some private kindergartens and other facilities, which are more profit, rather than child centered in their philosophy, tend to hire young inexperienced workers and even to encourage staff turnover in order to minimize salary expenses. The baby hotel, originally located in hotels as short-term baby-sitting for children of hotel guests, is one form of unlicensed child care that has gained an inordinate amount of public attention because of deaths and accidents that occurred in these facilities in the 1970s. They are still popular, however, as they are open twenty-four hours a day and charge fees on an hourly basis and are easily accessible. Child care workers generally lack prestige and are poorly paid.

Paternal leave is extremely rare. The number of companies providing paid maternal leave has increased in recent years but remains under 20 percent, even though the 1991 child care law allows mothers or fathers up to twelve months of leave, which may be unpaid or partially paid depending on the employer or type of parental insurance.[44] Japan spends even less of its GNP for social welfare (12 percent) than the United States (15 percent).

Clearly, regardless of how very different are the values and governments of the modern nations, all consider young children to be a collective responsibility and have been willing to pay for their care. All recognize the need to support families now that children are no longer primarily a direct economic asset to the family, but rather will provide their future labor to business and the state. America needs to learn from these models and draw up a plan that catapults us from the bottom of the heap to the top. We *could* just provide the best care for children in the world if we would give up the outmoded hearth-angel icon and remember that our children are our future. Taking collective responsibility for child rearing would indeed do a lot to improve our family values.

# The Way
# It Ought to Be

The key to ending the litany of motherblame from parenting experts, public officials, and even mothers themselves is to first recognize that mothers are not causing the problems afflicting American children. Mothers have once again become scapegoats to exonerate the rest of us from fundamental social and economic conflicts we do not wish to face.* Restoring the 1950s middle-class family ideal will not stop the violence, end the mistrust, or avert economic decline, nor will it restore children's lives. In fact, the prime factor preventing people from marrying and staying married and at least forming the touted two-parent biological family is economic. The majority of single mothers are in their twenties and are poor and working-class women whose male counterparts face high unemployment and low wages unless they have a college degree. Young adults increasingly view marriage as an ideal that is beyond their grasp because they do not believe they can expect a strong economic future.

But the popular mend-all of "family values" can transform our lives only if they reside in business and government, in the aging population and the young, in school and in art, as well as inside the happy

---

*Typical of this wrong-headed set of priorities, for instance, is the proposal before Congress to require federal health and safety regulators to prove a regulation is "cost effective" by providing a cost-benefit analysis of potential hazards for any regulations they wish to administer. Thus, they would have to decide how much is lost in dollars when a child dies because her pajamas were not flame retardant; or when a baby is strangled because the slots on her crib were far enough apart to let her squeeze her head through—and whether these costs ultimately outweigh the wages and profits gained by the production of such materials. (Bob Herbert, "Safety? Too Costly," New York Times, April 19, 1995, p. A23.)

home. The nuclear family cannot save a society that puts individual rights before collective responsibilities or profits before people.

American children are suffering from the stupidity of a nation of adults who fail to see themselves as responsible stewards of the new generation. It is a squabbling nation that lacks the unity of purpose to recognize that our children are ourselves. It is our children who will write our laws and enforce them, who will mind our environment, provide for us in our old age, create our entertainment, tend our produce, forge new inventions, and manage our complex institutions; they will also be our prisoners, illiterates, unemployed, slackers, drug dealers, gangsters, addicts, abusers, muggers, rapists, bombers, mentally ill, and entirely alienated. They are the civilizing or uncivilizing force that will be guiding us in the very near future.

As reformed motherblamers, there are several practical, concrete changes that we must effect if our children are to become a future we can look forward to. First, it is time for mothers to downsize their operations. American motherhood simply cannot thrive in its current form. Mothers can no longer afford to prop up the economy with their domestic and reproductive subsidy. They need to balance their own mental and physical budget if they are going to be able to continue to provide the human capital that is the basis for the nation's very survival. Mothers must effect more profitable mergers with fathers. They must also outsource some of their operations to employers who also have vested interests in the new generation. And they must require the provision of infrastructure from their government on a par with the roads, bridges, subsidies, and tax breaks that facilitate the male-dominated business enterprise. One of the first things mothers must do, however, to enhance their enterprise is see that their domestic advisers undergo retraining. Social scientists and parenting experts must become more aware of their own biases. The history and sociology of social science and medicine must become required coursework in the college curriculum.

## A MORE OBJECTIVE FAMILY PSYCHOLOGY

Parents who seek guidance from experts have a right to expect a more sensible and complex family psychology in which researchers actually listen to mothers and fathers as well as children instead of fabricating endless variations of the "exclusive-mothering" mythology. At a time when mothers are being threatened with losing their children to institutions if they can't find work, or losing them to ex-husbands if they work too hard or well, at a time when fathers' interest in their infants is being considered fashionable, at a time when child care is used by the vast majority of parents, it is important to get the "attachment" story right. Unfortunately, the psychopediatric priesthood has gotten the story wrong because of its love affair with the housewife. The attachment theory of John Bowlby and Mary Ainsworth is certainly the greatest cultural invention since the "hearth angel" was discovered beating her wings against the heartlessness of the Industrial Revolution back in the early nineteenth century. But it has not served families well. It has isolated mothers and children in the private home, denying them the social and intellectual stimulation that constitutes a rich life.

Yes, all children need and should have secure relationships to loving, responsible, consistent caregivers. Their livelihood depends on it. But let's not put the awesome responsibility for nurturing children solely on mothers' shoulders—and let's not claim that scientific research "proves" that mothers put their infants at risk if they return to work. The exploitation of attachment theory has inspired a research industry on mothers' work outside the home that is truly a morass of paltry and conflicting results. Any study that presumes the mother as the sole architect of "her" children's character must be seen as suspect. The question of whether mothers should work is irrelevant to modern family life. In fact, it is really reprehensible that a whole body of research persists in this superstitious obsession with the mother-child dyad and fails to even acknowledge that most women must work and want to work. Psychologists need to recognize and study how mothers' employment *contributes* to their children's lives and stop the endless search for deficits. As close to a third of American children live in poverty, it is reprehensible that psychologists waste so much effort on creating endless gradations of attachment violations when they could be documenting the truly damaging effects of poverty.

Because both parents now work, child care is as essential to family life as the telephone and the pizza. Social scientists need to discard their false mothercare/othercare distinction and explore what constitutes an appropriate amount of *parental* devotion to employment and what makes for good child care. More than anything, psychologists should be engaged in documenting the deficits in children's lives caused by poor-quality, underfinanced, unregulated, or unavailable professional child care. The truly damaging inferiority of American child care has eluded most psychologists because they have been so busy arguing over whether middle-class stay-at-home mothers (clearly a minority group) are better than quality day care centers (an even greater minority). Paradoxically, of course, their racial and class prejudice prevents them from concerning themselves with the real-life problems of poor and minority parents and their children except as examples of deficit parenting.

If we are to have a sufficiently complex family psychology, researchers will have to pay much more attention to individual differences in children. Do shy children do better in family day care? Does aggression in boys need to be handled differently from that in girls? How should special-needs children be cared for? We must take into account how families differ too in their ability to pay, their working needs, the harmony of their relationships—since all are part of the interacting dynamic of early care.

The varying quality of caregiving situations, the continuity of care, the combinations of care, and the way child care functions for the entire family are essential matters researchers have failed to explore in depth. Most children in real life experience caregiving from mothers, fathers, relatives, paid baby-sitters, and some kind of group care—in different combinations, at different phases of their lives. Increasingly, contemporary parents are forced to slap together a patchwork of caregivers who come and go, frequently with little warning. The detrimental effects of these tenuous relations on parents, children, and caregivers need to be explored. The whole question of payment also needs to be addressed. The complicated dynamics involved in paying someone or being paid for caregiving profoundly affect the child care experience for all parties.

So far, psychologists have adopted a child-centered assumption about the principal purpose of child care. Therefore, they have not explored how child care affects how a family functions. Does it make couples less depressed, improve marital relations, or make for better parenting? What effects can improving the quality and availability of child care have on parents' employment, career advancement, income '

capacity, and job satisfaction? To understand the stresses of balancing work and family life in the United States, psychologists need to
look at the psychic costs of our *lack* of family supports.

It is true, of course, that there are some progressive studies that
have begun to pay attention to these matters and move toward a more
complex family psychology. Let's hope they quickly light the way.

Social scientists, in their research on family structure, have been
equally prejudiced against mothers in their assumption that the two-
parent family is best and that all other family forms constitute "disrupted" families. Researchers might do better to distinguish between
"solid" families and "fragile" families as conflict and instability are
clearly detrimental to children. Not all two-parent families are harmo-
nious. Statistically speaking, after all, the two-parent family is the most
dangerous place for a woman to be, and many single mothers may
have especially good reasons for being single.* Moreover, millions of
survivors of the nuclear family flock to therapy groups that offer to
heal the "inner child" from damage inflicted by that hallowed two-
parent family life. At best, the family can teach us the finest things,
such as generosity and love; it is also, all too often, where we learn
about hate and rage and shame. Yet the social science study of the
family headed by a single mother is simply a search for deficits—never
for advantages, even though there are clearly deficits to be found in the
Nelsonian family. With so many variations of family a reality, it makes
no sense to single out one permutation as a gold standard.

Divorce and bad marriages are an unfortunate commonplace in our
society. We need more clear information about which aspects of bad
marriages and divorce are most detrimental to children's well-being.
Social scientists must move past the notion that divorce, per se, damages children. We need to map the whole range of changing family relations in an attempt to help guide all members of the family through
them, not just children. More than anything, we need to know more
about what factors are likely to lead to divorce in order to help save

---

*About 4 million women a year experience severe or life-threatening assaults from a male partner in an
average twelve-month period in the United States. (Toni DeAngelis, "Women's Safety Illusory When
Males Turn Violent," The APA Monitor, 25, no. 9 [September 1994]: 1.) In 1993, according to FBI
figures, 1,530 women were killed by their husbands or companions. In about 3.4 percent of 60 million
American couples, the man will inflict severe violence, such as punching, kicking, choking, or threatening with a gun or knife in any year. (Daniel Goleman, "An Elusive Picture of Violent Men Who Kill
Mates," New York Times, January 15, 1995, p. A22.)

more people from having to go through such a difficult transition. It would also be useful to know more about what keeps women from marrying in the first place; why couples prefer to cohabit; and what facilitates multigenerational parenting.

## REINVENTING FATHERHOOD

After setting her guardians straight, the New Mother must call on men to be New Fathers—not as a chic trend among a small segment of the male population, but as a wholehearted commitment from all fathers. More than ever, children and mothers need the warm, loving, committed involvement of fathers. The argument over fathering, of course, is largely about power. Mothering, in spite of all the ideology surrounding it, is low-status work. It receives no pay in a society that measures most things monetarily. It is easily taken for granted and easily maligned. Should men expand the parameters of masculinity to include mothering, they will not gain the high status and financial rewards that women accrued when they proved themselves in the traditionally male world of work, and this is surely an impediment to progress. The fears men seem to have about losing their masculinity and becoming like women when they take on the role of nurturers need to be recognized as having a great deal to do with losing power and dominance. I don't in any way dismiss issues of sex and gender. It is important for us to know a great deal more about the ways our biology influences our behavior. If we can examine such factors with a clear eye, we may be far better able to socialize our children along paths that produce the best human qualities in all people. At the moment, however, there is considerable irrationality and sheer silliness in much thinking about gender, especially as it relates to fathering.

Men and women are going to experience the best relationships when they exhibit the positive qualities traditionally attributed to both sexes. Those who are both nurturant and independent, for instance, may never need the divorce court, while those who are aggressive and dependent will experience discord. Studies are beginning to show quite clearly that the happiest and healthiest marriages are those termed "peer" marriages—where husbands and wives view each other as equals and distribute the breadwinning and domestic work according to each of their unique talents and desires rather than the roles once automatically ascribed to gender.[1] We need to worry far less about whether a behavior is masculine or feminine, and far more about whether it is humane. Then we will have children whose needs for loving adult involvement and diverse role models will be met. And perhaps then men will become full partners in the child-rearing equation and families will begin to receive the support they deserve. First, however, they will have to overcome some prejudice.

Reconciling the ideals of fatherhood with the realities of men's employment and the needs of families is essential to providing children with a loving, stable environment. When men stop being penalized by the workplace for giving time to their families, they will be far more likely to seek responsibility for the day-to-day care of their children. Should men's parenting skills become more highly valued, men who are underemployed and unemployed may still feel important to their children and contribute what they can rather than argue about what they are unable or unwilling to provide financially. They may also take less desirable jobs (as mothers do) because they feel more involved with their children.

## EDUCATING FATHERS

While the workplace still may not be friendly to fathers (or mothers), there is increasing recognition that education can help fathers to get involved with children. There are a growing number of programs for fathers that range from company-based workshops on childbirth and infant care, to programs for young unwed fathers. One widely publicized unwed father program that has had some dramatic results should provide considerable hope to those who lament we are in a fatherless America.

A program implemented by Charles Ballard eleven years ago under the auspices of the National Institute for Responsible Fatherhood and Family Development has helped unwed fathers between ages eighteen and thirty. The first thing that Ballard teaches these young fathers is that they can be vital to their children's future, even if they are at present unable to make any financial contribution. As frequently happens, the *ability* to provide financial support is driven by the *desire* to provide financial support. Ballard also works to establish an atmosphere in which women are honored and respected. Spirituality

(Christian teaching) is also an important ingredient for transforming these men's lives. A recent evaluation of the program shows that 90 percent of the young men formerly enrolled in the program are providing financial support for their children. Seventy percent have not had additional out-of-wedlock children. A mere 8 percent had jobs when they entered the program; now 60 percent have full-time jobs and another 11 percent are working part-time. Most of the men were high school dropouts who are now finishing or have finished high school. Even more heartening, since it was not a goal of the program, 11 percent are enrolled in college.[2]

Probably one of the best programs to promote fathers' involvement, however, is the one that begins at home. How to raise little boys to be good men is a question of growing concern. There is currently a mini-boom in books about raising boys to become psychologically healthy men. Some New Parents are trying to raise boys differently, trying to show them to care more about how other people feel and to be unafraid to cry. While they worry about their son's level of aggressiveness, they often find themselves using biological explanations to excuse it. Probably the greatest influence on boys' sex role, however, will be the examples of their own fathers' nurturance and sensitivity. The men's movement and the feminist movement, because they both aim to expand the range of acceptable behaviors that are characterized as masculine or feminine, have much to contribute to our knowledge of how to socialize our children and how to recast family relations.

## EDUCATION FOR FAMILY LIFE

But fathers are not the only ones who need education. The time to start formally educating people about family life is in public school. There are many good curriculum models for teaching children to prevent early reproduction and to educate them about married life, including the costs and responsibilities of having children. Young people should also learn about child development and parenting skills before they graduate from high school. Moreover, given the level of contentiousness and even violence in every institution of the society, courses in emotional intelligence that teach awareness of emotions and conflict resolution should also be requirements for high school graduation, if not for all pay raises of people employed in the

public and private sector. But education cannot go very far in preventing bad marriages, early reproduction, or family violence unless
family members can expect to make a decent living. In the interests of
guiding us toward a more truly valued family, mothers can help to ini-
tiate come critical new fiscal directions.

## OUTSOURCING SOME OF THE MATERNAL ENTERPRISE

The reason mothers are having difficulty "balancing work and children" is that they are being asked to choose between two full-time
jobs. The impossibility of this choice must be addressed. Children
benefit from the involvement of several adults throughout their childhood. Businesses must be required to provide such easily arranged
reforms as flextime, more part-time work, job sharing, and telecom-
muting. They must stop penalizing parents for caring for their children. Businesses need to recognize that retaining mothers (and
fathers) on reduced work schedules is less costly than losing them
completely for years at a time and then having to retrain them or their
replacements. Both the child care situation and the workplace must
be reformed so that women do not have to choose and children can
receive the care of the "whole village" as they deserve.

Although most mothers do not expect to divorce, almost half of
them will have that experience. They would be wise, then, for the sake
of their children and for their own benefit, to continue developing
their work skills through education or part-time employment in a
workplace designed to accommodate parents. A divorced mother is
otherwise far more likely to become a poor mother with poor children. But while the workplace must change, the single most direct
way to help families is through a first-rate national family policy.

## DEMANDING THE PROVISION OF INFRASTRUCTURE FOR THE FAMILY

Because of the high cost of infant care and the importance of allowing parents to get to know their own infants, America would do well
to provide substantial parental leave. Parents should be guaranteed
leave of six months at 80 percent of pay, the cost of which would be

borne by an insurance fund to which business, workers, and government contribute. The proportion of payments could be on a sliding scale for businesses as well as families. An additional six to twelve months of partial leave at partial pay would allow parents to maintain some of their work responsibilities while continuing their involvement with their infants. Certainly the Swedish model of the "father's month(s)" would be essential to making it permissible and possible for men to be involved in the daily care of their children. Parents of infants who are unemployed or underemployed must be subsidized by the national child care fund.

A genuinely adequate family infrastructure would require us to replace welfare with a package for families that will break down the distinction between "welfare" and programs for paid workers. Using a variety of incentives, we must help poor, single mothers to compete for low-wage jobs and provide assistance to poor working parents to give American children the life they deserve. One plan, designed by economists Heidi Hartman and Barbara Bergman is a sensible model that requires spending more for family support in the short term, that will result in spending less money on social problems associated with poverty, from remedial education to prisons, in the long run.[3] They estimate that if medical coverage and child care for preschool children and after-school care for older children, as well as the earned income tax benefit, were provided for the working poor, 60 percent of women now on welfare would voluntarily switch to employment. The remaining unemployed single parents, who may be virtually unemployable because of health or psychological problems, would receive about $100 a month in cash plus vouchers for rent, utilities, public transportation, and a food stamp credit card. Overall, the short-term increase in spending would be about $86 billion. *Sacré bleu!* You can already hear the cry on Capitol Hill, where the whir of the budget axe has so far only grazed the billions in welfare for business and defense while virtually releasing the guillotine on the necks of the nation's poor mothers and children.[4]

## TOWARD A NEW IDEAL OF SHARED CARE

American child care is characterized by hostility to women and contempt for children. It is a sickly creature, suffering not only from financial starvation, but also from a climate of stinginess shored up by modern psychology. The use of child care is fraught with suspicion, nursed by the ideology of exclusive mothering and fed by the low value placed on women's work. Because of the long-standing ideology of exclusive maternal care in our society, the psychology of the young child is often distorted so that shared caregiving is seen as a mother's failure rather than the most natural and advantageous opportunity for both children and families. Such an atmosphere promotes the neglect of children by thwarting the establishment of a first-rate child care system. Class differences that distinguish poorly paid caregivers from their better paid maternal employers also militate against a more collective endeavor, as does the pervasive racism that promises inferior care for children of minority parents. But parents and children are already members of a new culture of caregiving, one in which there is actually far greater potential for meeting the needs of families than ever before. New caregiving roles appropriate to this culture, however, cannot be forged while the old ideals of exclusive mothering are still embedded in the minds of parents, the studies of academics, and the laws of Congress.

Asking parents to find and pay for child care on their own is like asking individuals in the late nineteenth century to organize and fund their own schools. We need a national system that is well funded and well regulated. Our children are really everyone's responsibility and everyone's opportunity. They are little people who deserve adult protection, and we are certainly failing them. They are the future adults who will, however well or ill, be supporting and leading the rest of us in our old age. Without a well-educated, well cared-for, respectful youth, we are all doomed to be the victims of young people who are not skilled readers or thinkers, whose abundant energies are used for random destruction, and who are likely to make a poor generation of leaders. To insist that mothers of children are alone responsible for their early upbringing, that their care is a burden, that this women's job is unimportant, is to sentence not only our children to neglect and abuse, but ourselves as well. Child rearing must become a cooperative, collective, prideful endeavor, instead of the niggardly, scapegoating, uncaring project its official overseers currently promote.

## ENDING CHILD POVERTY THROUGH SUBSIDIZED CHILD CARE

The most critical problem facing mothers and children in America is poverty. A first-rate national child care system could help to eliminate child poverty. One out of four American children officially lives in poverty. Three out of five single mothers live in poverty. Women who work earn two thirds of what men earn. With one careful act, however, we can help eliminate welfare, put single mothers above the poverty line, go a long way toward easing women's unequal work burden, further the goal of equal pay between men and women, and facilitate a rapprochment between mothers and absent fathers.* With a universal child care system, we can even create much-needed jobs. Finally, we can socialize children whose physical and mental health, whose languages and customs, whose neglect and even abuse, may inhibit their partaking of the best educational opportunities and congenial social environments. A first-rate national subsidized child care system would accomplish all these goals with the benefits going directly to children.

The math is very simple: Providing child care could boost the incomes of impoverished parents by about 20 to 25 percent—right over the poverty line—with the children as the direct and undisputed beneficiaries. Employed single mothers with children under five who depend on purchased child care spend a quarter of their income for that purpose. Mothers who attempt to leave welfare cannot transcend their level of welfare income because a quarter of their earned income would be required to pay for child care. With a national child care system, most mothers who work full-time even at minimum-wage jobs would be lifted above the poverty line (assuming they were provided with health insurance coverage).[5]

As unemployment is built into the system, we might also need to expand the AmeriCorps national service program that has helped build houses, provide remedial education, clean up pollution, replenish wildlife populations, help walk children to school through dangerous areas, clean up vacant lots and other drug-user hangouts and

---

*Many fathers resist involvement with their children because the financial obligation is overwhelming.*

turn them into gardens or other community resources, deliver hot meals to the elderly, and aid in the immunization of infants. Ameri-Corps members receive a $600 a month allowance and health benefits worth $1,200 a year. After one year with the program, they are entitled to a voucher worth $4,725 that can be used only for education expenses. AmeriCorps mothers could tend their own children part of the time and provide Corps services part of the time in a graduated, parent-friendly approach. This plan has the added benefit that expensive job training programs that now cost the taxpayer billions of dollars and have a low placement rate would not be as necessary as most mothers could manage minimum-wage jobs without prior training; some might even find their way into the work of trained and well paid caregivers.[6] In addition to the considerable turnover in low wage jobs that would make work available to them, the provision of quality child care would create hundreds of thousands of new jobs, since there are nineteen million children under five years old in the United States, most of whom suffer from inadequate child care. The monetary costs for AFDC and food stamps, which currently run about $32 billion, could be radically reduced. The even more important costs of the demoralizing welfare trap could also be virtually eliminated.

Providing the lowest-income fifth of the population with free, high-quality child care and the next two fifths with partially subsidized care on a sliding scale would cost about $36 billion annually.[7] High-quality child care that is free to low- and middle-income parents, whether they are married or single, could provide a safe, nurturing environment for children that could insulate them from some of the stresses of a struggling community, providing them with preventive health care and nutritional meals.

In order for a national child care program to succeed, it would have to be organized differently from the current public education system, which is clearly failing children, especially poor children. To avoid these pitfalls, the program should be based on a voucher system, which parents can use for private or public providers and be far more locally controlled. The standards of these providers must be far more rigorous than they are currently, however. Both proper training and adequate supervision are needed to ensure quality care. While general national standards must be set, including decent salaries for caregivers, local authorities, either public or privately contracted,

The Way It Ought to Be

could actually regulate the system. Child care workers subsidized by the government and business would command pay and benefits that would attract more trained and talented people and lower the now high turnover rates endemic to the profession. Underwriting child care fees (restricted to licensed facilities) would increase parents' demand for higher-quality care. Some of the programs we now have, such as Head Start and half-day kindergarten, could be restructured as full-time programs.

## PARENTAL ACTIVISM

Parents of young children are going to have to become a political force and fight for their kids. Demographically, they are a smaller group than ever before in our society because of the low birthrate and our longer lifespan, which increases the size of the aging population. Much can be accomplished at the local level by forming groups that gather critical information, work with community leaders, and know how to use the media. For example, in Boston, one woman started a citywide parents' organization in 1987 that has succeeded in making some important changes. She began by taking her idea for a group that would be "the voice of parents" to leaders of child advocacy organizations and got them to agree to be sponsors. She then had membership cards printed that said "Parents United for Child Care" and began speaking to organizations—churches, day care center boards, and community housing projects—about the need to create a citywide organization for parents.[8] And everywhere she went, she handed out membership cards. People joined "Parents United" on the spot. At their first meeting, in 1988, the new members discovered they agreed that quality child care is a community issue, not just a personal family issue. So if things were going to get better, it was essential that parents end their isolation.

Their first task was to define the problem: How much child care was available in Boston? Who provided it? Who used it? How much did it cost? It didn't take the group long to discover that there was very little information available to answer these basic questions. Parents United soon became "experts" with more knowledge about this problem than anyone else. And still they had to push for change. School officials claimed they didn't know the locations of after-school

programs that parents used, so Parents United developed a guide list-
ing every after-school program in Boston along with where the kids in
each program attended school. Thus the school system was persuaded
to incorporate the after-school programs into its bus routes.

To effect a widespread change in public policy, however, mothers
and fathers also need to go to Washington as lobbyists and legislators
with a clear agenda they are ready to do battle for. The National Commission on Children was authorized by federal legislation passed in
1987 with a mandate to propose new directions for public policy affecting children. The Children's Defense Fund, headed by Marian
Wright Edelman, has been a leader in lobbying the federal executive
branch and the Congress on behalf of poor children. Parent Action,
which Dr. T. Berry Brazelton helped to start, is a national lobbying
organization that has pushed for parental leave, flexible work arrangements, and quality day care. Much of the machinery is in place but it
needs to be powered by all of us who care about our children.

## WE CAN'T AFFORD NOT TO CHANGE

Many Americans seem to be dubious that governmental agencies can
deliver high-quality services to children or manage the purchase of
such services from private providers. Indeed, curing the problems of
mothers and children in the United States requires more than having
government agencies write checks. It requires cooperation, involvement, and commitment from all facets of the society—from local
communities, to national coalitions of parents and children's rights
advocates, to businesses and even vaunted experts. But more than
anything, it requires a new commitment to solving the problems of
children and a greater trust that we can work together to reform our
really criminal treatment of children.

Instead of rooting out discrimination, encouraging adequate wages,
promoting full and flexible employment, and implementing the kind
of child care and other family supports common in most industrialized countries, policy makers in the United States have simply turned
to racist and sexist scapegoating. Subsidies to women and children
are thus provided with contempt. The term "welfare mother" (have
we ever lamented the "unemployment compensation fathers"?) is
an epithet equivalent to all the other "scoundrel" terms and is in-

creasingly used interchangeably with "single mother," expanding the calumny.

The contempt for non-Nelsonian mothers is facilitated by the fact that women's domestic work is not counted officially as work. The housewife who spends her days preparing food, setting the table, serving meals, clearing food and dishes from the table, washing dishes, dressing and diapering her children, disciplining the children, taking them to day care or to school, disposing of garbage, dusting, doing the laundry, going to the supermarket, paying bills, putting away toys, books, and clothes, doing the family shopping, and so forth, is performing totally unproductive labor, according to the current international economic accounting system. On the other hand, a pimp and heroin addict in a big city regularly pays graft. While his services and his consumption and production are illegal, they are, nonetheless, marketed. Money changes hands. His activities are part of America's hidden economy and will be recorded as part of the fruits of America's productive labor. He works, she does not.[9] It is not surprising, then, that a 1995 United Nations study of thirteen industrial countries shows that 66 percent of women's economically valuable work is unpaid, compared to 34 percent for men.[10]

Yet, as I hope to have established, children can be viewed as vital human capital who, to date, cannot be manufactured by anyone but women.[11] The maternal enterprise, however, is subjected to a double standard that becomes apparent when we look at male-run institutions and our government's support of them. The federal government finances more than 125 programs that subsidize businesses (run primarily by white males) at a net cost of $85 billion a year.* Add the corporate tax breaks, and the figure becomes $100 billion a year: half the annual federal deficit. Many defend these programs, arguing that they strengthen strategic industries and thus protect high-paying jobs. But what could be more strategic than the socialization of the fu-

---

*In addition to price supports for agriculture and subsidies to large and profitable utility companies, it also spends $110 million a year advertising American products abroad. In 1991 taxpayers spent $10 million promoting Sunkist oranges, $2.9 million selling Pillsbury muffins and pies, and $1.2 million boosting the sales of American Legend mink coats, and $465,000 advertising McDonald's Chicken McNuggets. (Stephen Moore, "How to Slash Corporate Welfare," New York Times, April 5, 1995, p. A25.) As of September 1995, this program has won a 29 percent increase. (Michael Wines, "Where the Budget Ax Turns Dull: Government Benefits for Business Are Mostly Spared," New York Times, August 30, 1995, p. D1.)

ture labor force?[12] And even the most deluxe family support won't cost $100 billion.

Only a few select companies receive these benefits (some say those most influential with Congress), and the jobs are disappearing anyway. America continues to provide $6 billion a year in research and development subsidies alone to some of America's richest corporations, including Amoco, AT&T, Citicorp, Du Pont, GE, General Motors, IBM, and Motorola, hoping to create an array of new technologies generating hundreds of thousands of high-wage, high-skill jobs. Between 1990 and 1994, however, those companies cut their U.S. workforce by 329,000.* The combined profits of those eight companies for 1994 was $26 billion. The return to the taxpayer from their licensing and royalty fees amounted to one fifth of a penny on the dollar.[13]

The federal government, led of course by the U.S. Congress (90 percent male), makes decisions about taxation that transfer even more income to those who need it least. As part of their "Contract with America" (which I don't remember signing), it is proposed that $99 billion a year in taxes be cut from the incomes of the wealthiest 10 percent of households. To help pay for the measure, more than $60 billion will be cut out of social service programs (food stamps, school lunches, housing assistance, day care allowances, Medicaid, and Medicare) by the year 2000. Low-income families would absorb two thirds of the spending cuts, but reap only 5 percent of the tax cuts.[14]

Moreover, the United States has a child poverty rate that is four times the rate of Western European countries. In fact, America has the most unequal distribution of wealth in any of the wealthiest nations. The richest 1 percent of households control 40 percent of the nation's wealth—twice as much as the figure in Britain, which has the greatest inequality in Western Europe. American chief manufacturing executives are paid twenty-five times the pay of their workers (compared to ten times in Japan).[15] The average CEO "earned" as much as 157 factory workers in 1992.[16] While some income disparity motivates

---

*Some of these millions of R&D tax dollars helped to provide: fancier fireworks at Disneyland; a better way to peel chili peppers; a coloring book titled Technology Transfer with Space Pup; a study of the benefits of planting shade trees in big cities; an Outward Bound–type program to turn government rocket scientists into business tycoons; and so forth. Gilbert Gaul and Susan Stranahan, "How Billions in Taxes Failed to Create Jobs," Philadelphia Inquirer, June 4, 1995, pp. 1+.

work and creativity, the widening chasm in our country is positively debilitating for those who are increasingly disenfranchised.

Adding to the burden on women and children is the fact that the United States is the world's top military spender. In 1993 the U.S. military budget was $277 billion. The combined military budgets of our eight most likely enemies is $66 billion.* The next biggest spender is Japan, at $40 billion, then France at $36, Britain, $35, and Germany $31 billion each. The other nine nations in the top ten military spenders in 1993 spent a total of only $238 billion combined.[17] Transferring spending from the military to child care could end our child care crisis overnight.

## A SEA CHANGE IN ATTITUDE

Whether a change in policy comes from altruistic feelings about the well-being of other people or from the pragmatic recognition that it is in our economic and social interests to see that the least fortunate members of our society are not too unfortunate, we need to develop a new attitude toward mothers. Women's domestic work must be counted as essential to the economy. It must migrate from the separate sphere of women and become a cooperative endeavor in which men and women share equally. Only then will the "family values" so many long for become a widespread humanity.

All the concern about our loss of family values is not only the lament of adults regarding the poverty, violence, and corruption of a civilization in trouble, it is also a male cry of recognition that men are increasingly disconnected from women and children. The host of assertions that the two-parent family is best for children are really a plea to return to marriage as the predominant family form—one that in its former incarnation restricted women's lives to the role of mother and domestic dependent. The redress increasingly suggested is to punish women for divorcing or having children out of wedlock, by taking away public assistance; even controlling women's freedom to have children outside of wedlock; and forcing men to pay for their estranged families. But if we want more people to marry and stay mar-

---

*In 1993, Russia spent $29, China, $22, Iraq $9, North Korea $2, and Iran, Syria and Cuba, $1.2 billion each. (Frank Holzman, "Pentagon Overkill," New York Times, February 1, 1995, p. A20.)

ried in order to create more rich and secure financial and emotional environments for children, men will have to undergo a masculinity makeover to the same degree that women were liberated from their "femininity" twenty-five years ago. Men are going to need to get down off their pedestals, roll up their sleeves, take low-paying work or get education for better-paying work just like mothers have done, and pitch in as equal partners with women to make their families work.

However, a household with a quarrelsome but paying spouse or ex-spouse, is not going to engender moral values. A household with an abusive husband is not going to promote a better world; one with two full-time wage earners but only one who doubles as a domestic servant is bound to bust. A family where both partners are out of work and trying to rear children on $13,000 a year is in distress. A family in which the woman works, acts as a housewife, and attempts to shore up an unemployed or underemployed husband is under strain. A family in which the woman is educated and the only prospective husbands are uneducated, unemployed, and alienated, is a family divided. A family that fails to conform to the mom-and-pop stereotypes of the 1950s, whether the parents are gay, or single, or related women, is disenfranchised by the family values agenda. It is a mistake to think that only married couples make good parents. Single mothers, single fathers, divorced and stepparents, gays and lesbians, grandparents acting as parents, adoptive and foster parents—all are capable of successfully nurturing children. Such non-Nelsonian families are here to stay, and they deserve our genuine support.[18]

Marriage, of course, and the love and commitment that often attend it, is still seen by most people as the ideal for raising a family. But the reasons for marrying are changing. For a woman, marriage is no longer her main option in life for obtaining status, security, income, and access to motherhood. For a man, becoming a bridegroom no longer secures his position as a head of household, offers him a housekeeper for life, or guarantees his children are his property. The touted morality of the "family values" marriage was shored up by shotgun marriages and it concealed the nastiness of mental, physical, and sexual abuse. New marriage faces the toughest test. They are increasingly based on what one person can offer another in terms of commitment, respect, sex, love, friendship, and understanding. Given the extraordinary changes that have taken place in the past few decades—reproductive technology, the sexual revolution, improved education for women, and no-fault divorce—it is almost amazing that people marry as much as they do. In fact, they marry not once, but even twice, and three times, apparently trying to get it right.

We increase our chances for healthy, long-lived relationships when both adults can negotiate from a position of economic and emotional strength. Restricting mothers' economic independence will do nothing to enhance the well-being of the family. Viewing tax breaks, child care, and income subsidies to mothers as a burden rather than ethical and pragmatic will contribute nothing to the ideal of a good family life. Only with a marriage model of independence and equality in mind can we begin to reconstruct a more cooperative set of rules that define where self-fulfillment ends and selfishness begins, where the needs of children outweigh the needs or whims of their parents, and decide what constitute the rules of healthy parenting.

Mothers who work, divorce, never marry, or parent their grandchildren, are doing a superb job and deserve to be congratulated for doing it with so little support. Blaming mothers for the ills of a changing society is like blaming the village goat for the adultery, thieving, and lying of the villagers—it is scapegoating of the most superstitious kind. If we, as a society, are to live well—as our tremendous wealth promises—we must all become like mothers. Only then can we truly understand motherguilt.

# *Notes*

## INTRODUCTION

1. Natural childbirth reformers in the 1970s had been pushing for obstetric wards to allow fathers to participate in the birth. Bonding was taken up by this movement because it advocated a birth in which the entire family was present to help solidify the new relationships. The research on bonding, however, was frankly nonsense. No maternal hormones were ever monitored to indicate some universal or instinctual phenomenon in women, nor was there evidence of mothers rejecting their children because of separation after birth. Postpartum bonding, however, became a rigid doctrine so that by the early 1980s, psychologists who had withheld their criticism because they wanted the reforms began to open fire with critical reviews of the studies that discredited the claims. About the same time, bonding research virtually ceased, not so much because of the devastating criticism, but because its mission to reform hospital birth had already been accomplished. In fact, in spite of the criticism, postpartum bonding remained part of standard obstetric practice, as there was little political incentive to remove it from official hospital policy.

## CHAPTER 1. MOTHERBLAME

1. Gwen Kinkead, "Spock, Brazelton and Now . . . Penelope Leach," *The New York Times Magazine,* April 10, 1994, pp. 32+.
2. Penelope Leach, *Children First: What Our Society Must Do—and Is Not Doing—for Our Children Today* (New York: Alfred Knopf, 1994), p. 45.
3. Penelope Leach, *Your Baby and Child: From Birth to Five* (New York: Knopf, 1989), as cited in Susan Chira, "Still Guilty After All These Years: A Bouquet of Advice Books for the Working Mom." *The New York Times Book Review,* May 8, 1994, p. 11.
4. T. Berry Brazelton, *Infants and Mothers* (New York: Delacorte, 1981), pp. 163–164. In the 1983 edition, he reiterates, "My bias is that a woman's most important role is being at home to mother her small children" but then concedes to the realities of moms' lives; pp. 172–175.
5. T. Berry Brazelton, *Working and Caring* (New York: Addison Wesley, 1983).

6. T. Berry Brazelton, "Working Parents," *Newsweek,* February 13, 1989; also see T. Berry Brazelton, *On Becoming a Family* (New York: Dell, 1992), pp. 187–191.

7. Interview with T. Berry Brazelton by Bill Moyers, *The World of Ideas* (New York: Doubleday, 1989), p. 149.

8. Benjamin Spock and Michael Rothenberg, *Dr. Spock's Baby and Child Care* (New York: Pocket Books, 1985), pp. 41–42; Spock and Rothenberg, *Dr. Spock's Baby and Child Care,* 6th ed. (New York: Pocket Books, 1992), p. 35.

9. Dr. Benjamin Spock, *A Better World for Our Children: Rebuilding American Family Values* (Bethesda, MD: National Press Books, 1994), pp. 142–143.

10. Between 1975 and 1993, the number of dual-earner families rose from 42 percent to 64 percent. Betty Holcomb, "How Families Are Changing for the Better, *Working Mother,* July 1994, pp. 30+.

11. A 1995 Federal Department of Labor study. Constance Hays, "Increasing Shift Work Challenges Child Care," *The New York Times,* June 8, 1995, p. C4. Statistical Abstracts, *Facts About Women,* 1991, p. 41, cited in Congressional Economic Leadership Institute, *A Briefing for the Congressional Competitiveness Caucus* (Washington, D.C.: September 1992); Barbara Willer, *The Demand and Supply of Child Care in 1990* (Washington, D.C.: National Association for the Education of Young Children, 1991), p. 8.

12. Peggy Kline, "Time, Guilt, Insecurity and Fatigue," *Parents,* February 1991, pp. 100–103.

13. Karen Levine, "Top-Ten Guilt Trips," *Parents,* April 1992, pp. 58+.

14. Nancy Samalin, "Guilt Busters, *Parents,* September 1994, pp. 133+. Also see: Josie Oppenheim, "Stay-at-Home Moms," *Good Housekeeping* 211, September 1990, pp. 114+; "Good Housekeeping and Child Care," *Good Housekeeping* 211, September 1990, pp. 95+.

    Stay-at-home moms experience less guilt than working moms: Carin Rubenstein, "Guilty or Not Guilty?" *Working Mother* 14, May 1991, pp. 53–57. Results of a survey of 3,000 readers show only 16 percent of their readers, median income $60,000, feel guilty about working: Leslie Bennetts, "Guilty?" *Parents,* July 1991, pp. 91+; Benjamin Spock, "Who's the Boss?" *Redbook,* April 1991, p. 30; Janna Malamud Smith, "Mothers: Tired of Taking the Rap," *The New York Times Magazine,* June 10, 1990, pp. 32–38; Ron Taffel, "The Real Trouble with Working Mothers," *McCalls,* June 1992, pp. 52+; Dianne Hales, "Letting Go of Guilt," *Working Mother* 15, September 1992, pp. 47+.

15. Researchers who have studied sexual abuse in day care estimate the risk is about 6 children per 10,000 enrolled, compared to about 9 per 10,000 who are likely to be sexually abused in their own household. More than half the

abusers are not professional day care workers, but janitors, bus drivers, and so forth. Unfortunately, this research must be viewed with caution as these investigators often do not question the methods by which children's "memories" are recovered. Robert J. Kelly, "Sexual Abuse in Day Care," in *Psychosocial Issues in Day Care,* ed. Shahla Cherazi (Washington, D.C.: American Psychiatric Press, 1990), pp. 205–217.

16. Paul and Shirley Eberle, *The Abuse of Innocence: The McMartin Preschool Trial* (Buffalo, NY: Prometheus Books, 1993); Alexander Cockburn, "McMartin: Anatomy of a Witch Hunt," *Playboy* 37, June 1990, pp. 45+; Ginia Bellafante, "Chronicle of a Witch Hunt," *Time,* May 22, 1995, pp. 69+; Abby and Myra Mann (producers, scriptwriters), *Indictment: The McMartin Trial* (HBO movie, aired May 20, 1995); Evelyn Nieves, "After 10 Years, Prosecutors Drop Charges of Sex Abuse, *New York Times,* December 3, 1994, p. 25; Neil Mac Farquhar, "Ex-Nursery Worker to Sue over Ordeal of Sex Charges," *New York Times,* May 11, 1995, p. B4; AP, "Court Rejects 2 Convictions for Sex Abuse, *New York Times,* May 3, 1995, p. A21.

17. The McMartin case began when one parent reported to police that her son had been sexually abused at the preschool. Within twenty-four hours parents were sent a letter informing them that Raymond Buckey had been arrested on suspicion of child molestation and asking them to question their own children to discover if they had been either witnesses or victims. A quick check of school records would easily have revealed that the boy in question was at the school for a total of fourteen days and had never been in the accused Ray Buckey's class, but regular police protocol seems not to have occurred in that zealous atmosphere. Moreover, a medical report indicated that the boy himself had told a doctor examining him for signs of abuse that the boy's own father "poked him" in his anus. Eberle, *The Abuse of Innocence: The McMartin Preschool Trial,* p. 93. All the children initially denied any abuse. But as rumors swept the community, parents became concerned, even though they did not believe their children had been molested. They were encouraged by public officials to have their children interviewed at an agency that cares for abused children to see if their traumatic experiences could be unearthed. There, an unlicensed therapist interviewed most of the children and pushed them to "reveal" their abuse. The resulting accusations led to more than two hundred charges in which child witnesses testified that they were raped by their teachers not only in the school but on an airplane and in a tunnel under the school, subjected to satanic rituals, and forced to watch animals being killed, including the bludgeoning of a horse with a baseball bat (whether in the tunnel, on the plane, or in the classroom was never clear). The children also identified community leaders, gas station attendants, and store clerks as molesters. In addition to the lack of sound corroborating physical evidence in these cases,

another reason for their being overturned is new research illustrating children's suggestibility. For instance, researchers at McGill and Cornell universities tested four- to six-year-olds to see how easily they might be influenced to make things up. For each child, they made up a list of events, two that actually occurred and eight that had not. Then they repeatedly reviewed the list with the children, each time asking, "Did this ever happen to you?" In one case, a four-year-old boy was asked eleven times about one of the phony items on his list, whether he had been taken to the hospital because his finger had been caught in a mousetrap. The first time he answered, truthfully, that he hadn't. The second time he answered "yes," that he had been to the hospital and he had cried. Each time thereafter the story grew until, by the eleventh interview, he had concocted an elaborate and wholly fictitious tale: "The mousetrap is down in the basement next to the firewood . . . I was playing a game called 'Operation' and then I went downstairs and said to Dad: 'I want to eat lunch,' and then it got stuck in the mousetrap . . ." Malcolm Gladwell, "Children's Testimony No Longer Gospel in Day-Care Abuse Cases," *Washington Post,* September 3, 1994, p. A3.

In the McMartin case, in every taped interview of therapists and children offered in court the child was told that large numbers of children and parents had already told the "secrets." In one typical interaction, a child who was being prodded said, "Ray never touched me." He was told once again that all of the other children and parents knew: "Johnny told us. You're just as smart as he is, aren't you?" Finally, after a lengthy interrogation, he reluctantly pointed to the therapy doll's genitals. The interviewer loudly exclaimed, "What a great kid! You're so smart! Your mom and dad will be so happy!" The boy later testified that he had been abused. Eberle, *The Abuse of Innocence: The McMartin Preschool Trial,* p. 201; Gladwell, "Children's Testimony No Longer Gospel in Day-Care Abuse Cases," p. A3. It must be emphasized that there is sometimes a fine line between helping children to reveal a shameful experience and pushing them to make one up. Moreover, fantastic details do not necessarily discredit a child's story. In these cases, however, it seems the fine line was crossed.

18. The New Traditionalist ads presented grainy photos of former careerists cuddled in their renovated Cape Codder homes, surrounded by adoring and well-adorned children. "America is coming home to *Good Housekeeping*" was a typical ad's final sentence and was the clue to what these ads were really about. Journalist Susan Faludi asserts that the "trend" was actually manufactured by the magazine to recapture a declining readership. In the 1980s the circulation of traditional women's magazines had fallen by about 2 million readers, and *Good Housekeeping* was the worst off. "Well-established brands will be big sellers in the future once the retrotrend takes

hold," the publisher of *Good Housekeeping* promised his advertisers, according to Faludi. Susan Faludi, *Backlash* (New York: Crown, 1991), pp. 92–95. For further examples of this pseudo-trend see: Josie Oppenheim, "Stay-at-Home Moms," *Good Housekeeping,* September, 1990, pp. 114+; Linda Stern, "Can You Afford to Quit?" *Parents,* August 1990, pp. 74+; Claudia Morrell, "One View: Staying Home," *American Baby,* July 1990, pp. 30+; Anita Jones-Lee, "Afford to Quit?" *Parents,* September 1992, pp. 121+; Margery Rosen, "Working Mom's Makeover," *Ladies' Home Journal,* February 1993, pp. 98+; Karen S. Peterson, "Many Women Say Their Place Is in the Home," *USA Today,* September 20, 1993, Life section, p. D1; Christine Davidson, *Staying Home Instead: Alternatives to the Two-Paycheck Family* (New York: Lexington Books, 1992); Darcie Sanders and Martha M. Bullen, *Staying Home: From Full Professional to Full-Time Parent* (Boston: Little, Brown, 1992); *Good Housekeeping* officially dropped the New Traditionalist campaign in 1995 in favor of a new one that asserts GH is "the magazine America trusts" by promoting the testing center that gives out its seals of approval. Stuart Elliott, *"Good Housekeeping* Drops a Celebration of New Traditions and Goes Back . . ." *New York Times,* April 10, 1995, p. C1.

19. It is true that in the spring of 1994 *Barron's* (the cover is a picture of June Cleaver in full apron holding out a pie) proudly claimed to see a trend of middle-class mothers staying home. But, alas, the data suggest a small blip affecting a select few, at best. The percentage of working women age twenty to twenty-four fell from a high of about 73 percent in 1986 to a low of about 70 percent by December 1993. Among women twenty-five to thirty-four the percentage flattened at about 74 percent during the same period. Some of the change, however, is related to a baby boomlet resulting from the 1967 tightening of draft deferments, which inspired many would-be soldiers to become fathers. Their daughters reached prime childbearing age during this period. Maggie Mahar, "Working Women: Goin' Home," *Barron's,* March 21, 1994, pp. 33+; Letters: mailbag, *Barron's,* April 4, 1994, p. 58. Other trend watchers, although they have no statistics, claim their research indicates a significant portion of women—primarily from upper-income brackets—are temporarily staying home to rear children but will return to the workforce when their children are older, a trend that began in the late 1980s. *Advertising Age* sees it as a rare upper-class status symbol—"stopping out" they call it. "Mom Stops Out," *Advertising Age,* September 18, 1994, p. 16.

20. See: Neala Schwartzberg, "Stuck on You, How Attachment Grows," *Parents,* October 1987, pp. 100+; Robert Karen, "Becoming Attached," *Atlantic,* February 1990, pp. 35+; Marcelle Clements, interview, "The Ties

That Bind: Can a Mother's Style of Attachment Determine Her Child's Romantic Life?" *Elle,* 1994, pp. 88+; Robert Karen, interview with Ray Suarez, *Talk of the Nation,* National Public Radio, September 21, 1994.

21. Advertisement for a book by Robert Karen, *Becoming Attached* (New York: Warner, 1994) in *The New York Times Book Review,* March 6, 1994, p. 18.

22. Paul Klein, "The Needs of Children," *Mothering,* Spring 1995, pp. 39+.

23. A 1993 national survey of working women by the Labor Department's Women's Bureau shows that while 80 percent either like or love their jobs, their number-one problem is the difficulty of balancing work and family. Tamar Lewin, "Working Women Say Bias Persists," *New York Times,* October 15, 1994, p. 9.

24. Tamar Lewin, "Demands of Simpson Case Land Prosecutor in Custody Fight," *New York Times,* March 3, 1995, p. 38.

25. "Day Careless?" *Time,* August 8, 1994, p. 28. At this writing, the Prost case is still on appeal. The status of Marcia and Gordon Clark's battle remains private. "People," *US News & World Report,* November 20, 1995, p. 40.

26. Lini Kadaba, "Custody: Now Issue Is Time," *Philadelphia Inquirer,* March 19, 1995, p. A1. In other, less-publicized cases the double standard is also applied. For instance, in South Carolina, real estate agent Ruth Parris lost custody of her son because a judge decided that, as an "aggressive, competitive individual" who was "not particularly family oriented," Parris could not care for her son as well as the boy's father, a developer. While Parris had taken a year off after her son's birth and had been closely involved in his daily care, religious and secular education, and activities, the judge gave more weight to the father's domestic virtues: making the morning coffee, often cooking weekend meals, attending the boy's swim meets, and sometimes taking him to the doctor. Elinor Brecher, "For Divorced Women of the '90s, the Decision to Work Can Mean Losing Their Kids," *Miami Herald,* March 11, 1995. In Phoenix, Arizona, Stephanie Orr, executive director of Phoenix's Center Against Sexual Abuse was ordered by a divorce mediator to leave her job in the middle of the afternoon to pick up her eight-year old daughter from school. Orr agreed to be at home after 3:30 P.M., as she risked having a judge order her daughter to take a school bus to the home of her father, who now has a second child and a stay-at-home wife. (Mr. Orr would not be at home at that time, but the new wife would.) Ms. Orr would also have to fire a nanny who had cared for her daughter since the child's birth. Orr was fortunate in being able to arrange to make up the work time on the nights and weekends when her daughter visits her father. Cathryn Creno, "The Custody Crunch Demands of Courts: Workplace Play Havoc with Moms' Lives," *Arizona Republic,* June 17, 1995. One legal expert at the National Center on Women and Family Law in New York, Joan

Zorza, believes the double standard is applied far more frequently to women on the upper rungs of the career ladder. "We aren't seeing judges do this to women working at McDonald's or at part-time jobs," she says. Personal interview, October 1995.

27. Christine Berardo, *Because Mommy Works* (original screenplay), first draft, August 15, 1994 (unpublished, furnished upon request by Warner Bros. Television).

28. Susan Smith, it must be noted, had her children while she was married and was not on welfare. Her own parents appeared to have been exemplars of churchgoing, community-leading, tax-paying middle-class Republican virtue, although when Susan attempted to commit suicide, at age thirteen, her mother and stepfather denied her treatment. When she was fifteen, her stepfather began to sexually molest her. Barbara Ehrenreich, *Time,* August 7, 1995, p. 78. Two men and a woman have been charged with murdering Ms. Evans because they wanted a baby. The father of Ms. Evans, Sam Evans, decried Gingrich's remarks, declaring: "It's terrible to use this for politics, it's an outrage!" The murdered woman's mother, Jacalyn Arnold, was prompted to defend her daughter, saying, "Debra was on welfare, but she was one of the most caring people in the world. Even though she was on welfare, she opened her house to people. She gave other people food when she didn't have much." Alison Mitchell, "Gingrich's Views on Slayings Draw Fire," *New York Times,* November 23, 1995, p. B18.

29. Twelve percent require AFDC because they were working and their earnings fell. Statistics are for 1993 from the 1994 Green Book, House Ways and Means Committee. "Welfare: Who Gets It? How Much Does It Cost?" *New York Times,* March 23, 1995, p. A23. Curiously, Gingrich's righteous wrath is only for poor mothers who receive public assistance apparently because it requires collective tax dollars which, for the average family (the median income in 1993 was $52,200 [Edward Wolf, "How the Pie Is Sliced," *The American Prospect* (summer 1995), p. 59]) is about $157 per family. Dan Meyers and Jeffrey Fleishman, "Reform Poses Consequences for Poor," *Philadelphia Inquirer,* January 22, 1995, pp. 1+.

30. Verne Barry, David Cooney, *et al.,* "What Will Happen to the Children?" *Policy Review* (winter 1995), p. 7.

31. Charles Murray, "What to Do About Welfare," *Commentary,* December 1994, p. 27.

32. Sarah Ferguson, "The Home Front," *Village Voice,* February 1, 1994, p. 20.

33. The average annual fee for child care is $3,173 for full-time center-based care for each child. Research and Policy Committee for Economic Development, *Why Child Care Matters* (Washington, D.C.: Committee for Economic Development, 1993), pp. 21–22; Demie Kurz, *For Richer, For*

*Poorer: Mothers Confront Divorce* (New York: Routledge, 1995), pp. 24, 119.

34. Kristin Luker, "Dubious Conceptions: The Controversy Over Teen Pregnancy," *The American Prospect,* no. 5 (spring 1991), pp. 73–83.

35. Results of a 1991 study of more than 300,000 teenage mothers around the country by the National Center for Health Statistics. Mike Males, editorial, "Unwed Mothers: The Wrong Target," *New York Times,* July 29, 1994, p. A27. Mike Males, "In Defense of Teenage Mothers," *The Progressive,* August 1994, pp. 22–23.

36. Katha Pollitt, "Subject to Debate," *The Nation,* January 30, 1995, p. 120.

37. Steven Holmes, "Birthrate for Unwed Women up 70% Since '83 Study Says," *New York Times,* July 20, 1994, p. A1. Never mind that in one recent survey it was found that three quarters of "illegitimate" births were registered by both parents, a rising proportion of whom already live together at the time of registration. Moreover, there is growing evidence that the increasing custom of cohabiting is not less stable than marriage. In one study of illegitimate births, five years after the birth, 77 percent of the couples were still cohabiting and nearly half had married. Moreover, single-parent families are overwhelmingly the product of marital breakdown—the proportion of single-parent families headed by a mother who has never been married is less than one third. Anthony Gottlieb, "Why Can't We Behave?," review of *The De-Moralization of Society,* by Gertrude Himmelfarb, *The New York Times Book Review,* February 19, 1995, p. 12. The studies were by the Office of Population Censuses and Surveys in Britain and Susan McRae of the Policy Studies Institute, 1992. Most officials tend to confound illegitimacy with single motherhood and to assume that lack of a marriage license means lack of a coparent. We do know that in America, single mothers (including never-married mothers, divorced, widowed, and separated mothers) head over 25 percent of all families with children. Just under 10 percent of all mothers are never-married—the fastest growing category of all family groupings. Among white women and women who attended college, the percentage who became mothers without marrying doubled between 1982 and 1992. It is not known how many of these women may be living with partners, male or female, without benefit of wedlock. For women who had attended at least a year of college, the rate rose from 5.5 percent in 1982 to 11.3 percent in 1992. For white women, the rate rose from 7 percent to 15 percent. For black women, from 49 percent to 56 percent. For Hispanic women, the figure rose from 23 percent to 33 percent. (Figures are for women between eighteen and forty-four who never married.) The study, by Amara Bachu, a census analyst, is called "Fertility of American Women, June 1992," reported by Jason DeParle, "Big Rise in Births Outside Wedlock," *New York Times,* July 14, 1993, pp. A14 L+. In

1991, women headed 58 percent of all black families with children, as against 19 percent among whites. In 54 percent of those black families, the mothers were never married—up from 15 percent in 1970. Single fathers head fewer than 4 percent of all families. Robert Suro, "For Women, Varied Reasons for Single Motherhood," *New York Times,* May 26, 1992, pp. A12+.

38. Drummond Ayers, "Quayle Defending '92 Speech, Returns to Family Values Theme," *New York Times,* September 9, 1994, p. A16.

39. Barbara Dafoe Whitehead, "Dan Quayle Was Right," *Atlantic Monthly,* April 1993, pp. 47+.

40. Even the growing number of single mothers who are financially secure and are choosing to have babies without a father because a congenial mate cannot be found are considered unacceptable by these arbiters of family values. For women with professional or managerial jobs, the rate of single motherhood rose from 3.1 percent to 8.3 percent between 1982 and 1992. (Figures are for women between eighteen and forty-four who never married.) Jason DeParle, "Big Rise in Births Outside Wedlock," pp. A14+.

41. David Blankenhorn, *Fatherless America: Confronting Our Most Urgent Social Problem* (New York: Basic Books, 1995).

42. Popenoe actually uses the term "single-parent" families. However, 93 percent of single (in-charge) parents are women. David Popenoe, "The Controversial Truth: Two-Parent Families Are Better," *New York Times,* Op-Ed, December 26, 1992, p. 21.

43. Michiko Kakutani, "If Gingrich Only Knew About Victoria's Secret," *New York Times,* May 19, 1995, p. E5. The GOP plan would freeze federal spending on AFDC and transfer responsibility but not adequate dollars to the states. It would also eliminate Medicaid coverage for as many as 4.4 million children by the year 2002, cut nutrition assistance to 14 million children, reduce child abuse protection by nearly 20 percent, and deny assistance to nearly 16,000 homeless children. The Food Research and Action Committee, a nonprofit group in Washington, estimates that one in twelve American children suffers from hunger and predicts these numbers will sharply worsen if Congress enacts planned cuts in social services. Richard Russo, "Feeding Body and Soul," *New York Times,* November 1, 1995, p. A23. Bob Herbert, "Kiss and Cut," *New York Times,* October 23, 1995, p. A15. It would even reduce, if not eliminate, the Earned Income Tax Credit, which aids almost 14 million families who are poor but make too much to qualify for welfare.

44. Just consider that the average welfare payment is $373 a month! Figure is for 1993 from the House Ways and Means Committee, the 1994 Green Book; "Welfare: Who Gets It?" p. A23.

45. But the disproportion of black mothers needing public assistance is facili-

tated by the fact that black males between twenty-five and forty-four have dwindled as potential husbands as a result of high unemployment and an increasing cycle of alienation and crime. In 1995, one in three black men in their twenties were in prison, on probation or parole, not because crime by blacks is getting worse, but because the percentage of arrests of black drug users is so high, much higher than the rates for white. While African Americans make up 12 percent of the nation's population and consititute 13 percent of all drug users, they represent 35 percent of arrests for drug possession, 55 percent of all convictions for drug possession, and a stunning 74 percent of all prison sentences for drug possession. Fox Butterfield, "More Blacks in Their 20's Have Trouble with the Law," *New York Times,* p. A18. Black men, more than any other segment of the population, lost their jobs in the 1970s and 1980s as the blue-collar jobs that had sustained them were lost to improved technology and cheap labor outside the country. Black women found work in the service sector, and more tend to be more educated than black men. Farai Chideya, *et al.,* "A World Without Fathers," *Newsweek,* August 30, 1993, pp. 16+.

46. Kevin Sack, "In Mississippi, Will Poor Grow Poorer with State Welfare Plan?" *New York Times,* October 23, 1995, p. 1.

47. In New Jersey, then-governor Jim Florio made headlines in 1993 when he announced New Jersey's "family cap" rule had reduced births to women receiving AFDC by 16 percent. Legislators across the country—including the House and Senate Republican majorities and President Clinton—rushed to introduce similar laws. While there has been a decline in the AFDC birth rate, it mirrors a more general decline and has yet to be proven the result of Florio's policy.

48. Several states, including Colorado, Connecticut, and Florida, have proposed bills to provide subsidies to welfare recipients who accept Norplants. Fertility rates of AFDC recipients, while they are receiving assistance, are lower than among the general population. Alexander Cockburn, "Beat the Devil: Welfare, Norplant and the Nazis," *The Nation,* July 18, 1994, pp. 79+. Moreover, fully 56 percent of all pregnancies in the United States are unintended—one of the highest rates in the industrialized world, but hardly a problem specific to poor women. L. B. Williams and W. F. Pratt, "Wanted and Unwanted Childbearing in the United States: 1973–1988," data from the National Survey of Family Growth, *Advance Data from Vital and Health Statistics,* no. 189 (Hyattaville, MD: National Center for Health Statistics, 1990).

49. Norman Atkins, "Governor Get-a-Job, Tommy Thompson," *The New York Times Magazine,* January 15, 1995, pp. 22+.

50. It's true that a disproportion of welfare mothers are black. In 1995, 12 percent of the population was black and 39 percent of all welfare parents were

black, while 38 percent were white and 17 percent were Hispanic. Dan Meyers and Jeffrey Fleishman, "Reform Poses Consequences for Poor," *Philadelphia Inquirer,* January 22, 1995, pp. 1+. Of those who received AFDC assistance for two years or less: 65 percent were white and "other," 23 percent were black, 13 percent were Hispanic; for more than five years; 43 percent were white and "other," 34 percent were black, 23 percent were Hispanic. Source: study by La Donna Pavitti, The Urban Institute. Celia Dugger, "Iowa Plan Tries to Cut Off the Cash," *New York Times,* April 7, 1995, p. 1. But the disproportion of black mothers needing public assistance is facilitated by the fact that black males between twenty-five and forty-four have dwindled as potential husbands as a result of high unemployment and an increasing cycle of alienation and crime. Butterfield, "More Blacks in Their 20's Have Trouble with the Law," p. A18; Chideya, *et al.,* "A World Without Fathers," pp. 16+.

51. Atkins, "Governor Get-a-Job," pp. 22+.
52. Thompson's welfare rules now penalize mothers for not working, and where he has tried the program, more mothers are at work. However, their increased employment seems to be due to a regional employment boom. Atkins, "Governor Get-a-Job," pp. 22+. Keep in mind that the average AFDC benefit is $3,274 per year. The average food stamp benefit is $816 per year; only 9 percent of AFDC families are in public housing, 12 percent receive federal rent subsidies. "Welfare: Who Gets It? How Much Does It Cost?" p. A23.
53. AFDC payments are $13.1 billion per year, out of $644.2 billion in federal entitlement spending for Social Security ($281.9 billion), Medicare ($147.9 billion), Medicaid ($69.6 billion), unemployment ($36.4 billion), retirement and disability ($57.4 billion), food stamps ($20 billion), and Supplemental Social Security ($17.9 billion). U.S. Bureau of Census, *Consolidated Federal Funds Reports,* 1992. The cost to federal and state budgets combined, is $25 billion. Erik Eckholm, "Solutions of Welfare: They All Cost Money," *New York Times,* July 26, 1992, pp. 181+.
54. Mickey Kaus, *The End of Equality* (New York: Basic Books, 1992).
55. Sack, "In Mississippi, Will Poor Grow Poorer . . . ?," p. 1.
56. Kaus, *The End of Equality.*
57. See George Gilder, *Wealth and Poverty* (New York: Basic Books, 1980); Charles Murray, *Losing Ground: American Social Policy 1950–1980* (New York: Basic Books, 1984); Michael Novak, *The New Consensus on Family and Welfare: A Community of Self-Reliance* (Washington, D.C.: American Enterprise Institute for Public Policy Research, 1987), p. 5; Susan L. Thomas, "From the Culture of Poverty to the Culture of Single Motherhood: The New Poverty Paradigm," *Women and Politics* 14, no. 2 (1994): p. 82.

58. Charles Murray, "What To Do About Welfare," *Commentary,* December 1994, pp. 26–34.

59. See June Axinn and Amy Hirsch, "Welfare and the Reform of Women," *Families in Society,* November 1993, p. 569. The study on hunger was conducted by the Food Research and Action Center, a nonprofit group in Washington, D.C. Richard Russo, "Feeding Body and Soul," *New York Times,* November 1, 1995, p. A23.

60. As of 1990, 20 percent of married-couple families had a strictly breadwinner/homemaker division of labor, compared with nearly 70 percent in 1940. *Population Today,* September 1992, p. 2. U.S. Department of Labor, Bureau of Labor Statistics, *Employment and Earnings,* January 1994, p. 76. Between 1976 and 1991, the percentage of married couples with children under six in which the father worked and the mother stayed home, dropped from 55 percent to 34 percent. As a percentage of all families with children under six, such "traditional" families are now just 27 percent, down from 47 percent in 1976. Unpublished tabulations from March 1991 and March 1976, *Current Population Survey,* U. S. Department of Labor, Bureau of Labor Statistics as cited in the Research and Policy Committee of the Committee for Economic Development, *Why Child Care Matters* (Washington, D.C.: Committee for Economic Development, 1993), p. 5.

61. An article with stunning photographs of handsome colorful buildings, reports that 70 percent of all the prison space in use today has been built since 1985 at a cost of $32.9 billion. Only 11 percent of the nation's classrooms were constructed during the 1980s. David Anderson, "America's Best Buildings," *The New York Times Magazine,* February 20, 1994, pp. 38–41.

62. Income from the paychecks of wives allows 8 million American families to stay above the poverty line, and without these earnings, the poverty rate of those families would double. From a study by Martha N. Ozawa, a social work professor at Washington University. Reported in "Newsview," *USA Today.*

63. The Legal and General Insurance Company study shows housewives spend an average seventy-one hours a week on domestic chores and a woman with a part-time job still works an average fifty-nine hours at home. Even those with a full-time job have an average domestic working week of forty-nine hours. Lindsay Cook, "Wives Are Valued at 349 Pounds a Week" or $572. (The dollar figure is for a fall, 1995 exchange rate.) London *Times,* February 3, 1993, p. 36. The total current value of all unpaid household work is estimated to be about one third of the conventionally measured Gross Domestic Product. That which is devoted specifically to the care of children might be put at roughly 2 to 4 percent of the Gross Domestic Product, on the order of $120 to $240 billion annually. This estimate is made by the Committee on Economic Development, Research and Policy Committee of

the Committee for Economic Development, *Why Child Care Matters,* p. 7.

64. In the last two decades, women have increased their unpaid domestic labor. Women with full-time paid jobs increased their total annual hours of work by 160 hours between 1969 and 1987, an average of an extra month each year. Juliet Schor, *The Overworked American* (New York: Basic Books, 1992), p. 37. According to a recent UNICEF study, poor women represent the principal variable for the policies of adjustment to the current global economic crisis. Through women it is possible to ensure the survival of at least that third of the population with the lowest incomes by extracting huge amounts of labor that are not socially recognized. *Alternative Women in Development, Reagonomics and Women: Structural Adjustment U.S. Style— 1990–1992* (Washington, D.C.: Alternative Women in Development, 1992).

65. Peter Kilborn, "More Women Take Low-Wage Jobs Just So Their Families Can Get By," *New York Times,* March 13, 1994, p. 24.

66. Arlie Hochschild, *The Second Shift* (New York: Avon Books, 1989), pp. 3, 9.

67. Ibid., p. 212.

68. U.S. Department of Labor Women's Bureau, "Facts on Working Women," no 93-3, June 1993, p. 1. Some of the inequity in pay is caused by the custom of paying more for work that is traditionally male. For example, a sales worker in hardware and building supplies, which requires basic reading and math skills, makes $333 per week; a sales worker in apparel, also requiring basic reading and math, makes $238. Naomi Barko, "Equal Pay in Your Pocketbook," *Working Mother,* November 1993, pp. 41+. The ghettoization of women's salaried work is well known. In 1990, 71 percent of women were employed in just six job categories: nurses and health technicians; elementary and secondary schoolteachers; sales clerks in retail trade; clerical workers; apparel and textile workers; and service workers. Black women are confined to even fewer occupations than white women and predominate in such jobs as chambermaids, welfare service aides, nurses' aides, and child care workers. While the earnings of black women are similar to those of white women, black women are 2.5 times as likely to be unemployed as white women. U.S. Department of Labor, Bureau of Labor Statistics, 1989. pp. 514–537. Kurz, *For Richer, For Poorer: Mothers Confront Divorce,* p. 29.

69. "Facts on Working Women," p. 1.

70. The number of Americans who fell below the poverty line in 1993 was 15.1 percent, compared to 13.1 percent in 1989. Jason DeParle, "Census Sees Falling Income and More Poor," *New York Times,* October 7, 1994, p. A16. Forty-seven percent of families headed by single mothers lived in poverty in 1989, as against 8.3 percent of families headed by two parents. DeParle, "Big Rise in Births Outside Wedlock," pp. A14. The median income for a

female head of household is $16,692 compared to $28,351 for a male head of household. This figure is for 1991. "Facts on Working Women," p. 1. This means that the median income of single mothers in America is very near the official poverty line! Adding to their burden, decent child care for one child costs a quarter of the median income of a single mother with one preschool child.

71. U.S. Bureau of Census, *Poverty in the United States: 1990,* Current Population Reports, series P-60, no. 16 (Washington, D.C.: GPO, 1991). In the 1980s, nearly two thirds of those who earned minimum wage or less were women. In 1990, a single mother working full-time earning the minimum wage would earn more than 20 percent below the official poverty level. But because minimum wage work is unlikely to provide health insurance or other benefits, and because child care is unaffordable, mothers are forced to turn to AFDC to receive Medicaid and insure their children are looked after. In 1990, though, the maximum AFDC benefit for a family of three averaged 55 percent below the poverty level. *The State of America's Children, 1991* (Washington, D.C.: The Children's Defense Fund, 1991), pp. 21–35, 26–27.

72. Some mothers must work to anchor their families to the middle and upper classes (about 15 million), far more (37 million) must work to keep their families out of poverty. Kilborn, "More Women Take Low-Wage Jobs Just So Their Families Can Get By," p. 24. Economist Hilda Scott estimates that two thirds to three fourths of working-age women who are not poor would be poor if they had to support themselves and just one dependent. Hilda Scott, *Working Your Way to the Bottom: The Feminization of Poverty* (London: Pandora Press, 1984). In a 1995 Lou Harris survey, half of working women say they bring home half the household income. In a Bureau of Labor Statistics survey married women who worked full-time throughout 1993 contributed 41 percent of the family's income. Tamar Lewin, "Women Are Becoming Equal Providers," *New York Times,* May 11, 1995, p. A27.

73. S. D. Einbinder, "A Statistical Profile of Children Living in Poverty: Children Under 3 and Children Under 6, 1990" (unpublished document from the National Center for Children in Poverty, New York: Columbia University, School of Public Health, 1992); "Single Women and Poverty Strongly Linked," *New York Times,* February 20, 1994, sec. I, p. 35.

74. In fact, only 14 percent of able-bodied women on welfare are not in school, working, or looking for work. Study by Institute for Women's Policy Research, cited in Heidi Hartman, "Exploding the Welfare Myth," *Working Woman,* December 1994, p. 16; also see Joel F. Handler, *The Poverty of Welfare Reform.* (New Haven: Yale University Press, 1995). A substantial share of women on AFDC have substantial impediments to full-time work

including: 60 percent who have experienced abuse or neglect as adults, 35 percent who have partial disabilities; 25 to 40 percent who have learning disabilities, and 16 percent who have substance-abuse problems. Findings based on survey in Washington State. USN&WR-Basic data: U.S. Dept. of Health and Human Services, Urban Institute. "Welfare, the Myth of Reform," *U.S. News & World Report,* January 16, 1995, pp. 30+.

75. Kathleen Harris, "Work and Welfare Among Single Mothers in Poverty," *American Journal of Sociology* 99, no. 2 (September 1993): pp. 317–352.

76. This country has not seen full employment since the industrial system took hold in the 1840s. In our system about 6 percent of the population who want to work will not be able to do so because there simply are not enough jobs. So far, at any rate, unemployment seems built into the system. Moreover, even those lucky enough to be employed full-time, can still be counted among the homeless (three fourths of whom are woman-headed families) and hyperpoor because even the minimum wage, which again, businesses require in order to remain competitive, puts even workers earning the minimum wage well below the poverty level. U.S. Department of Labor Women's Bureau, "Facts on Working Women," p. 1; Valerie Polakow, *Lives on the Edge: Single Mothers and Their Children in the Other America* (Chicago: University of Chicago Press, 1993), pp. 44–45. It is clearly mothers who are keeping American business afloat by living in poverty while raising the future labor force. Yet the poor (primarily mothers and children) are blamed for poverty as if they themselves had invented it.

77. Deborah Swiss and Judith Walker, *Women and the Work/Family Dilemma* (New York: John Wiley and Sons, 1993), p. 194.

78. Barko, "Equal Pay in Your Pocketbook," pp. 41+.

79. Sue Shellenberger, "Many Employers Flout Family and Medical Leave Law," *Wall Street Journal,* July 26, 1994, p. B1. Yet 75 percent of women with children between the ages of six and thirteen were in the workforce in 1991 compared with 56.6 percent in 1980. Karen Levine, "Is Today's Workplace Really Family-Friendly?" *Parents,* August 1993, pp. 30+. Moreover, the number of women with infants under one year, rose from 31 percent (of all women with infants) in 1975, to 53 percent in 1987 where it remained in 1990; and 75 percent of those mothers worked full-time. Rosalind C. Barnett, "Research on the Effect of Women's Outside Employment," Center for Research on Women, Working Paper Series (Wellesley, MA: Wellesley College, 1991), p. 14.

80. Michele Cohen Marill, "Will Motherhood Cost You Your Job?" *Redbook,* May 1993, pp. 84+; Barbara Noble, "An Increase in Bias Is Seen Against Pregnant Workers: New Mothers May Be Targets in Staff Cuts," *New York Times,* January 2, 1993, pp. 1+. One psychologist recently conducted an interesting experiment. She filmed a woman performing certain job functions

in an office when she was nine months' pregnant, then doing them exactly
the same way five months after the childbirth. Both male and female viewers rated the woman's performance much lower when she was pregnant,
saying she was too emotional, distracted, or just didn't belong in an office.
Jane Halpert, director of industrial psychology, DePaul University in
Chicago. See: "Pregnancy As a Source of Bias in Performance Appraisals,"
*Journal of Organizational Behaviors* 14, no. 7, December 1993, pp. 649–663.

81. Mary Lord, "Pregnant and Now Without a Job," *U.S. News & World Report,* January 23, 1995, p. 66.
82. Priscilla Painton, "The Maternal Wall," *Time,* May 10, 1993, pp. 44+.
83. Betty Holcomb, "How Families Are Changing for the Better," *Working
Mother,* July 1994, p. 29.
84. In fact, women, especially women with children, end up paying propor-
tionately more taxes than any other group. Teresa Amott, *Caught in the Crisis: Women and the U.S. Economy Today* (New York: Monthly Review
Press, 1993).
85. The divorce rate then leveled off to a point where 50 percent of first marriages end in divorce; 60 percent of second marriages do. Stephanie Coontz,
*The Way We Never Were: American Families and the Nostalgia Trap* (New
York: Basic Books, 1992), pp. 82–83; David Eggebeen and Peter Uhlenberg, "Changes in the Organization of Men's Lives: 1960–1980," *Family
Relations* 34 (April 1985), pp. 251–257.
86. T. Espenshade and T. Goodis, *America in Transition: Benefits for the Future*
(Washington, D.C.: Employee Benefit Research Institute, 1987), p. 11.
87. Between 1969 and 1993, the percentage of men twenty-five to thirty-four
years old earning less than the amount needed to lift a family of four above
the poverty line had more than doubled from 13.6 in 1969 to 32.3 in 1993;
likewise the percent of children living in households headed by women increased from 11 percent to 23.3 percent in the same period. In 1990, 43 percent of men in their thirties who earned less than $10,000 were married
compared to 83 percent of men of similar age who earned more than
$50,000. Steven Holmes, "Low-Wage Fathers and the Welfare Debate,"
*New York Times,* April 25, 1995, p. A2.
88. Robert Griswold, *Fatherhood in America* (New York: Basic Books, 1993),
pp. 222–223.
89. Jason DeParle, "Census Sees Falling Income and More Poor," *New York
Times,* October 7, 1994, p. A16.
90. Keith Bradsher, "Gap in Wealth in U. S. Called Widest in West," *New York
Times,* April 17, 1995, p. A1.
91. Coontz, *The Way We Never Were,* p. 272. Over the last twenty years, the
compensation for CEOs rose from an average of forty times the pay of all
workers to nearly two hundred times that. Over the same period, moreover,

the economy slowed and pay stagnated for most workers. Michael Weinstein, "The Rich: Why They Deserve It," *The New York Times Magazine,* November 19, 1995, p. 103. In Japan, CEOs are paid two times more than their workers. Bradsher, "Gap in Wealth in U. S. Called Widest in West," p. A1.

92. Barbara Ehrenreich, *Fear of Falling: The Inner Life of the Middle Class* (New York: Harper Perennial, 1989), pp. 200–210.


CHAPTER 2. FRAMING MOTHERHOOD

1. Stephanie Coontz, *The Way We Never Were: American Families and the Nostalgia Trap* (New York: Basic Books, 1992); Mary Frances Berry, *The Politics of Parenthood: Child Care, Women's Rights, and the Myth of the Good Mother* (New York: Viking, 1993).

2. In their writings, Puritans and planters referred primarily to their fathers' child-rearing involvement. Cotton Mather, the New England Puritan, did not even discuss his mother in his memoirs. Thomas Jefferson's earliest recollections included being physically cared for by slaves and nurtured by his father. Catherine Beecher, born in 1800, remembers her preacher father as the primary nurturer in her family. Berry, *The Politics of Parenthood,* pp. 46–47, 50. In fact, family law until the early nineteenth century provided that "in consequence of the obligations of the father to provide for the maintenance . . . education of his infant children, he is entitled to the custody of their person and to the value of their labor and services . . . while the child is under fourteen years of age." Brenner *et al., Children and Youth in America,* vol. 2, 1600–1885, cited in Berry, *The Politics of Parenthood,* p. 364; "Legal Rights of Children, 1880," U.S. Bureau of Education Circular of Information, no. 3.

3. Berry, *The Politics of Parenthood,* p. 51.

4. J. Matthaei, *An Economic History of Women in America* (New York: Schocken Books, 1980), pp. 38–39.

5. Berry, *The Politics of Parenthood,* p. 48.

6. Theresa LaFromboise and Anneliese Heyle, "Changing and Diverse Roles of Women in American Indian Culture," *Sex Roles* 2, pp. 455–476.

7. E. Fox-Genovese, *Within the Plantation Household: Black and White Women of the Old South* (Chapel Hill: University of North Carolina Press, 1988); Deborah White, *Ar'n't I a Woman?: Female Slaves in the Plantation South* (New York: W. W. Norton, 1985); Alan Kulikoff, "The Beginnings of the Afro-American Family in Maryland," and Herbert Gutman, "Persistent Myths about the Afro-American Family" in *The American Family in Social-Historical Perspective,* 2d ed., ed. Michael Gordon (New York: St Martin's Press, 1978). The ex-slave and abolitionist Frederick Douglass

could not even remember seeing his mother until he was seven. See Frederick Douglass, *My Bondage and My Freedom* (1885; reprint, New York: Dover, 1968), p. 48.

8. White, *Ar'n't I a Woman?*, p. 169.

9. Gutman, *The Black Family in Slavery and Freedom: 1750–1925*, p. 191.

10. G. F. Moran and M. A. Vinovskis, "The Great Care of Godly Parents: Early Childhood in Puritan New England" in *History and Research in Child Development: In Celebration of the Fiftieth Anniversary of the Society for Research in Development*, eds. J. Haben and Alice Smuts (Chicago: University of Chicago Press, 1986), pp. 24–37.

11. Throughout the country until 1950, personal service was the largest census category of women employees and they mostly "lived in" until after World War II. Phyllis Palmer, *Domesticity and Dirt: Housewives and Domestic Servants in the United States, 1920–1945* (Philadelphia: Temple University Press, 1989), p. xiii.

12. Ann Dally, *Inventing Motherhood: The Consequences of an Ideal* (New York: Schocken Books, 1983), p. 92; Barbara Ehrenreich and Deirdre English, *For Her Own Good: 150 Years of the Experts' Advice to Women* (New York: Doubleday, 1978); Bernard Wishy, *The Child and the Republic: The Dawn of Modern American Child Nurture* (Philadelphia: University of Pennsylvania Press, 1972).

13. Steven Mintz and Susan Kellogg, *Domestic Revolutions: A Social History of American Family Life* (New York: The Free Press, 1988), pp. 46–49; Mary P. Ryan, *Cradle of the Middle Class: The Family in Oneida County, New York, 1790–1865* (Cambridge: Harvard University Press, 1981), pp. 71–72, 85–86.

14. Jean-Jacques Rousseau, *Emile* (1762; reprint ed. Michael Launey, New York: French and European Publishers, 1966). Interestingly, Rousseau's philosophy didn't reverse the practice of fathers abandoning their children. He put his own five infants into a foundling hospital. See John Boswell, *The Kindness of Strangers* (New York: Pantheon, 1988). Pestalozzi, in his novel *Leonard and Gertrude*, presents Gertrude as the ideal mother-teacher who sets up a village school where she is a self-sacrificing exemplar of gentleness and piety. J. H. Pestalozzi, *Leonard and Gertrude* tr. and abridged by Eva Channing (Boston: D. C. Heath, 1969).

15. In 1833 Amariah Brigham began his campaign. These schools, which taught two- to four-year-olds, flourished in New England through the 1830s. D. May, and M. A. Vinovskis, "A Ray of Millennial Light: Early Education and Social Reform in the Infant School Movement in Massachusetts 1826–1840" in *Family and Kin in American Urban Communities, 1840–1940*, ed. T. K. Hareven (New York: Watts, 1977), pp. 62–99.

16. Before the Civil War almost 90 percent of Americans were farmers or self-

employed businessmen; by 1910 the figure was less than one third. Robert L. Griswold, *Fatherhood in America: A History* (New York: Basic Books, 1993), p. 207.

17. Berry, *The Politics of Parenthood;* Ehrenreich and English, *For Her Own Good,* p. 23; J. Matthaei, *An Economic History of Women in America.*

18. Carl Degler, *At Odds: Women and the Family in America from the Revolution to the Present* (London: Oxford University Press, 1980), pp. 27–65; Ehrenreich and English, *For Her Own Good,* pp. 22–26; Christopher Lasch, *Haven in a Heartless World: The Family Besieged* (New York: Basic Books, 1977), p. 10; Barbara Welter, "The Cult of True Womanhood: 1820–1860," in *American Vistas (1607–1877),* 3d ed, eds. L. Dinnerstein and K. Jackson (New York: Oxford University Press, 1995); Wishy, *The Child and the Republic.*

19. Welter, "The Cult of True Womanhood," p. 187.

20. Wishy, *The Child and the Republic,* p. 32.

21. Ibid., p. 29. Yet for every middle-class Victorian family with a domestic angel in charge at home, there was an Irish or German girl scrubbing floors, a black girl doing the family laundry, a black mother and child picking cotton, and a host of very poor children and women sent to textile mills, where they slaved twelve hours a day to make cloth that was then sewn in a sweatshop by a Jewish or Italian woman. Berry, *The Politics of Parenthood.*

22. While most Native American and African-American women were poor, those who were not emulated the white middle-class cult of true womanhood. See Berry, *The Politics of Parenthood,* pp. 62–63.

23. Sam Warner, *Streetcar Suburbs: The Process of Growth in Boston, 1870–1900* (Cambridge, MA: Harvard University Press, 1962).

24. Wishy, *The Child and the Republic,* pp. 115–135.

25. Glenn Davis, *Childhood and History in America* (New York: The Psychohistory Press, 1976), p. 45.

26. Ehrenreich and English, *For Her Own Good,* pp. 182–210; Wishy, *The Child and the Republic,* pp. 81–113.

27. Ellen Key, *The Century of the Child* (New York: G. P. Putnam, 1909), p. 2.

28. At the turn of the century, two and a half million children were full-time laborers in coal mines, glass factories, in the cigar industry, and in the homes of the wealthy. Four-year-olds worked sixteen-hour days sorting beads or rolling cigars in New York City; five-year-old girls worked the night shift in southern cotton mills. Ehrenreich and English, *For Her Own Good,* p. 186. Coontz, *The Way We Never Were,* p. 213.

29. Charles E. Rosenberg and Carol S. Rosenberg, "The Female Animal: Medical and Biological Views of Woman and Her Role in Nineteenth-Century America," in *Women and Health in America,* ed. J. W. Leavitt (Madison: University of Wisconsin, 1984), pp. 12–27.

30. Ehrenreich and English, *For Her Own Good,* p. 127.

31. Jane Addams, *Twenty Years at Hull House* (New York: Macmillan, 1911).

32. Just before the turn of the century, many of these centers appeared in Boston, New York, and Chicago, providing care from 6:30 A.M. to 9 P.M. They took infants as young as a few days old. See Sheila Rothman, "Other People's Children," *Public Interest* 30 (1973), pp. 11–27; Margaret Steinfels, *Who's Minding the Children? The History and Politics of Day Care in America* (New York: Simon & Schuster, 1973).

33. The number of licensed day care centers increased from 206 in 1905 to a high of 695 in 1916, certainly a tiny drop in an ocean of need. See Rothman, "Other People's Children."

34. Social commentator Thaddeus Wakeman writing in 1890 as quoted in Paul F. Boller, Jr., *American Thought in Transition: The Impact of Evolutionary Naturalism 1865–1900* (Chicago: Rand-McNally, 1969), p. 120.

35. Ehrenreich and English, *For Her Own Good,* p. 185.

36. Editorial, *Ladies' Home Journal,* October 1911, p. 6.

37. Caroline Hunt, *The Life of Ellen Richards* (Washington, D.C.: The American Home Economics Association, 1958).

38. Ehrenreich and English, *For Her Own Good,* pp. 161–167.

39. Christine Frederick, "The New Housekeeping" (serialized), *Ladies' Home Journal,* September–December 1912.

40. Ehrenreich and English, *For Her Own Good,* p. 191.

41. Wishy, *The Child and the Republic,* p. 117.

42. Hall himself did no experimental work of any note. By the late 1880s he had already abandoned the tedious empiricism of the lab (measuring reflex times, spatial perception, etc.) to found the new field of child study. His experimental efforts in child study were, by ordinary scientific standards, little short of absurd as there were not even any consistent categories of information to make comparisons with. In one study he mailed out 102 questionnaires to parents, asking about their children's moods, fears, dolls, imagination, speech, religious sentiments, affection, games, and sense of self. There was no way to draw conclusions from the resulting "data" and no "results" were ever published. Ehrenreich and English, *For Her Own Good,* p. 198.

43. G. Stanley Hall, "Some Practical Results of Child Study," in *The Work and Words of the National Congress of Mothers* (New York: Appleton, 1897), p. 165.

44. E. Lomax, Jerome Kagan, and B. Rosenkrantz, *Science and Patterns of Child Care* (San Francisco: W. H. Freeman, 1978).

45. John B. Watson, *Psychological Care of Infant and Child* (New York: W. W. Norton and Co., 1928), pp. 9–10.

46. Watson, *Psychological Care of Infant and Child,* p. 17.

47. The experts paid little attention to fathers who were occasionally called in as playmates or could stand aloof as role models. Robert Griswold, *Fatherhood in America: A History* (New York: Basic Books, 1993), p. 116.

48. Ehrenreich and English, *For Her Own Good,* p. 217.

49. W. Grubb and Marvin Lazerson, *Broken Promises: How Americans Fail Their Children* (New York: Basic Books, 1982).

50. Celia Stendler, "Psychological Aspects of Pediatrics: Sixty Years of Child Training Practices, Revolution in the Nursery," *Journal of Pediatrics* 36 (1950), pp. 122–134.

51. Griswold, *Fatherhood in America.*

52. Michael Kimmel and Michael Kaufman, "The New Men's Movement: Retreat and Regression with America's Weekend Warriors," *Feminist Issues* (fall 1993), p. 13.

53. Women were then relegated to what became the pink-collar ghetto of clerical and service workers. Coontz, *The Way We Never Were,* pp. 158–159.

54. Berry, *The Politics of Parenthood,* p. 105. Some mothers who managed to work during the Depression experienced a brief period of assistance from a nursery school project sponsored by the Works Progress Administration (WPA). Once again its purpose was not so much to assist working mothers as to supply jobs for the unemployed. By 1937 there were 1,900 nursery schools serving 40,000 children, which were run by the WPA, but by 1940 they were disbanded because of the booming war industry. See Steinfels, *Who's Minding the Children?*

55. Griswold, *Fatherhood in America,* pp. 157–158.

56. Victoria Gettis and Maris Vinovskis, "Child Care in the United States to 1950," in *Child Care in Context,* eds. Michael Lamb, Kathleen Sternberg, Carl-Philip Hwang, Anders Broberg (New Jersey: Lawrence Erlbaum, 1992).

57. V. Kerr, "One Step Forward, Two Steps Backward: Child Care's Long American History," in *Child Care, Who Cares? Foreign and Domestic Infant and Early Childhood Development Policies,* ed. P. Roby (New York: Basic Books, 1973), pp. 20, 157–171.

58. Many of the leftover WPA centers were used. They were terminated in 1946, and scholars estimate they served between 60,000 and 100,000 children. See Gettis and Vinovskis, "Child Care in the United States to 1950." (Estimates vary on this figure.)

59. After the war, the term "day care" disappeared from public discussion and did not reappear until the 1960s. The term "baby-sitting" was used to refer to nonmother care. See Berry, *The Politics of Parenthood,* pp. 20, 110.

60. Betty Friedan, *The Feminine Mystique* (1963; New York: Dell, 1983).

61. Sigmund Freud, "Some Psychical Consequences of the Anatomical Distinction Between the Sexes," *Standard Edition of the Complete Psychological Works,* vol. 19 (1925; reprinted London: Hogarth Press and Institute of Psychoanalysis, 1962), p. 192.

62. Nancy Chodorow, *The Reproduction of Mothering: Psychoanalysis and the Sociology of Gender* (Berkeley: University of California Press, 1978); Freud, "Some Psychical Consequences of the Anatomical Distinction Between the Sexes."

63. The prevailing prescription for motherhood was stretched to the limit as part of an official propaganda campaign directed by the U.S. Office of War Information, which engaged in a massive effort to persuade Americans that married women should be hired in fields drained by the enlistment of men. Maureen Honey, *Creating Rosie the Riveter: Class, Gender and Propaganda During World War II* (Amherst: University of Massachusetts Press, 1984), p. 28. This propaganda was essential. A preliminary government survey had discovered that only 19 percent of wives with children were ready to work. No more than 30 percent of husbands thought it acceptable for their wives to work, regardless of whether they had children. Degler, *At Odds,* p. 420.

64. Honey, *Creating Rosie the Riveter,* pp. 118–120, 133.

65. E. Boll, "The Child," *The Annals of the American Academy of Political and Social Science* 229 (September 1943): p. 75.

66. Father Flanagan of Boys Town, a refuge for wayward boys. See Griswold, *Fatherhood in America,* p. 167.

67. *The Saturday Evening Post,* 1945, as cited in Honey, p. 133.

68. L. Banner, *Women in Modern America: A Brief History* (New York: Harcourt Brace Jovanovich, 1974), p. 223.

69. In 1900, 18 percent of the American labor force was female; in 1920 it was 20 percent; in 1930, 22 percent. The proportion jumped dramatically, however, from 25 percent to 36 percent between 1940 and 1945. Women returned to the home after the war, and the percentage dropped to 28 in 1947. But by 1951, 31 percent of the labor force was female and by 1973, the figure was 42 percent. Banner, *Women in Modern America,* pp. 205, 219, 279. In 1940 less than 10 percent of mothers with children under six held jobs; in 1950, the proportion was almost 12 percent; by 1970 it was over 30 percent and still rising. Degler, *At Odds,* p. 418. But the major increase came in spheres of work that were stereotypically women's, particularly office work. Sheila Rothman, *Woman's Proper Place* (New York: Basic Books, 1978), p. 224.

70. Degler, *At Odds.*

71. Marriage rates were high, and the age of first marriage dropped while the size of families increased, creating the "baby boom." Banner, *Women in Modern America,* pp. 236–237. Between 1945 and 1960, the gross national

product grew by almost 250 percent. During the war years millions of Americans were sharing housing—typically adults with children lived with their own parents. By 1960, 62 percent of American nuclear families owned their own homes compared to 43 percent in 1940. Eighty-five percent of the new homes were built in the suburbs, where the nuclear family found privacy and togetherness. These trends were facilitated by the role of government, which provided generous education benefits for men with the GI Bill and housing assistance. Coontz, *The Way We Never Were,* pp. 24–29. Before World War II banks often required a 50 percent down payment on homes and issued mortgages for only five to ten years. The postwar Federal Housing Authority required down payments of only 5 to 10 percent and guaranteed mortgages of up to thirty years with interest rates of 2 to 3 percent. Almost half the housing in suburbia depended on such federal financing. Coontz, *The Way We Never Were,* pp. 76–77.

72. Margaret Ribble, *The Rights of Infants* (New York: Columbia University Press, 1943), p. 107.

73. Millett, *Sexual Politics,* p. 206.

74. Farnham based the book on her clinical work in psychiatry. With her collaborator, Ferdinand Lundberg, a sociologist (both were Freudians), they proclaimed that contemporary women "in very large numbers" are psychologically disordered. They based their case on studies that seemed to show high rates of neurosis among army draftees and career women and increasing alcoholism and impotence among American men.

75. Ethel Kawin, *Parenthood in a Free Nation,* vol. 1, *Basic Concepts for Parents* (1954; New York: Macmillan, 1967), p. v.

76. John Bowlby, *Maternal Care and Mental Health,* 2d ed. (Geneva: World Health Organization, Monograph Series no. 2, 1951); Ehrenreich and English, *For Her Own Good,* p. 231. Bowlby's 1951 report advised that subsidies be provided to mothers to keep them from economic pressure to work and that family systems be evaluated and treated because they were engenderers of mental illness. But these remedies cost money and even involved the possibility of changing the family system. They were ignored.

77. David Levy, *Maternal Overprotection* (New York: W. W. Norton, 1944).

78. David Riesman, *The Lonely Crowd* (New Haven: Yale University Press, 1950); William Whyte, *The Organization Man* (New York: Simon & Schuster, 1956).

79. Caroline Zinsser, "Dr. Spock's Book," (unpublished paper: 1986).

80. Benjamin Spock, *Common Sense Book of Baby and Child Care* (1945; New York: Pocket Books, 1976), p. 40.

81. Ehrenreich and English, *For Her Own Good,* p. 280.

82. Friedan, *The Feminine Mystique,* p. 22.

83. Ehrenreich and English, *For Her Own Good,* pp. 280–283.

84. Mary Anderson, *Thinking About Women: Sociological Perspectives on Sex and Gender,* 2d ed. (New York: Macmillan, 1988), p. 115; Degler, *At Odds,* p. 418.
85. Friedan, *The Feminine Mystique,* p. 84.
86. Millett, *Sexual Politics.*
87. In 1985, 34 percent of all female-headed households (13 percent of male-headed); 27 percent of white female-headed households (11 percent white male); 51 percent of black female-headed households (23 percent of black male); 53 percent of Hispanic families headed by women (18 percent of Hispanic male), lived below the poverty line. See Anderson, *Thinking About Women,* p. 130. In 1975, 80 percent of maids were black women.
88. La Fromboise and Heyle, "Changing and Diverse Roles of Women in American Indian Culture," pp. 455–476. More recent immigrants from Asia, Mexico, Puerto Rico, and so forth, were less interested in sex-role reform than being freed of racism and economic discrimination.
89. Judith Hole and Ellen Levine, *Rebirth of Feminism* (New York: Quadrangle Books, 1971), p. 85; Rochelle Gatlin, *American Women Since 1945* (Jackson: University Press of Mississippi, 1987), pp. 77–96. In 1967 Congress enacted the Work Incentive Program (WIN) which required AFDC mothers to obtain jobs or lose benefits. President Richard Nixon's Family Assistance Plan expanded WIN's punitive approach, broadening the work requirement and providing meager custodial care. See Berry, *The Politics of Parenthood,* p. 135. Also see Jack Rosenthal, "President Vetoes Child Care Plan as Irresponsible," *New York Times,* December 10, 1971, pp. 1, 20; Berry, *The Politics of Parenthood,* pp. 132–37. In 1976 President Ford's National Commission on Observance of International Woman's Year reported that the shortage of day care left 6 million in need and again advocated nationally financed day care. Ford vetoed the bill, claiming it was an interference with states' rights. See Berry, *The Politics of Parenthood,* p. 141.
90. Birth managed by midwives, on the other hand, is supportive of birthing women's vastly different needs and allows nature to take its course. The doctor is called in to use his specialized skills in only a small percentage of births. Diane Eyer, *Mother-Infant Bonding: A Scientific Fiction* (New Haven and London: Yale University Press, 1992), chaps. 6 and 7. As part of a rebellion against this regime, and in keeping with a romantic view of nature (anything "natural" was inherently good), women and their husbands, part of a widespread natural childbirth movement, began to have their babies at home and in the alternative birth centers managed by midwives, which burgeoned in the 1970s.
91. One psychologist, for example, studied the visual perception of infants and found they preferred looking at patterns rather than colors—they especially

liked the pattern of the human face. Robert Fantz, "The Origin of Form Perception," *Scientific Perception* 204: pp. 66–72.

92. Dozens of studies by Mark Rosenzweig and his colleagues explored this phenomenon. See for instance: M. Rosenzweig and E. Bennett, "Effects of a Few Hours a Day of Enriched Experience on Brain Chemistry and Brain Weights," *Physiology and Behavior* 3, no. 6 (1968): pp. 819–825; M. Rosenzweig and E. Bennett, "Cerebral Changes in Rats Exposed Individually to an Enriched Environment," *Journal of Comparative and Physiological Psychology* 80, no. 2 (August 1972): pp. 304–313; P. Ferchmin, E. Bennett, and M. Rosenzweig, "Direct Contact with Enriched Environment Is Required to Alter Cerebral Weights in Rats," *Journal of Comparative and Physiological Psychology* 88, no. 1 (January 1975): pp. 360–367.

93. Alvin Toffler, *Future Shock* (New York: Random House, 1970).

94. Mothers are given elaborate instructions on how to enhance their infant's development at every minute step of the way. For instance: "the Phase II baby who is eight to ten weeks old, should have objects placed six to eight inches away from his eyes to facilitate the development of hand-eye coordination" p. 21, Burton White, *The First Three Years of Life* (New Jersey: Prentice Hall, 1975), pp. xiii, 1, 54, 95. As of 1993, White was still adamant that mothers (he's pretty mum on fathers) should stay home with their children for the first three years.

95. Anderson, *Thinking About Women,* p. 115.

96. The divorce rate then leveled off to a point where 50 percent of first marriages end in divorce; 60 percent of second marriages do. See Coontz, *The Way We Never Were,* pp. 82–83; David Eggebeen and Peter Uhlenberg, "Changes in the Organization of Men's Lives: 1960–1980," *Family Relations* 34 (April 1985): 251–257.

97. A 77 percent increase; see Anderson, *Thinking About Women,* p. 116.

98. Just over half the mothers awarded child support received the full amount, a quarter received partial payment, and over a fifth received nothing at all. Edward Walsh, "Going After Fathers Who Turn Their Backs," *Washington Post Weekly* 10, January 11–17, 1993, p. 32; U.S. Bureau of the Census, "Child Support and Alimony, 1987," Current Population Reports, series P-23, no. 167, June 1990, 3, table B. One study found that men's monthly car payments typically exceeded the amount requested for child support. Lucy Marsh Yee, "What Really Happens in Child Support Cases: An Empirical Study of the Establishment and Enforcement of Child Support Orders in the Denver District Court," *Law Journal of Denver* 57 (1980): pp. 21–36.

99. In 1959 the figure had been 23 percent. Valerie Polakow, *Lives on the Edge: Single Mothers and Their Children in the Other America* (Chicago: University of Chicago Press, 1993) p. 59. Children who live with their mothers are

far more likely to live in poverty: 51 percent of such children were poor in 1989 compared to 22 percent in single-father-headed families and 10 percent in two-parent families. Polakow, *Lives on the Edge,* p. 59. More than 20 percent of American children were living in poverty—one in eight children under age twelve actually went hungry; almost 100,000 were homeless. Coontz, *The Way We Never Were,* p. 2.

100. Typical of the experts' remedies is an article in which "work/family expert" Ellen Galinsky shows a newspaper editor mom how to add regular exercise and better nutrition to her already tight schedule. Her college professor husband appears to feel no conflict regarding his work, and it is not suggested he accommodate in any way for the care of their ten- and fourteen-year-old boys. Nor is it suggested the editor-mom attempt to change her workplace. A postscript to the article informs the reader that this advisee resigned from her career, apparently despairing that the only solution to her problems was her time management "makeover." Marjorie Rosen, "Working Mom's Makeover: How to Stop Driving Yourself Crazy," *Ladies' Home Journal,* February 1993, pp. 98+.

101. Lynn Langway *et al.,* "Bringing Up Superbaby," *Newsweek,* March 28, 1983.

102. Coontz, *The Way We Never Were,* p. 18.

103. About putting her child in day care, Brazelton warned: If she is left out [by competing day care workers], she is likely to grieve about losing him [her child] and may begin to detach at an unconscious level in order to defend herself from feelings about having to share him. T. Berry Brazelton, *On Becoming a Family* (New York: Dell, 1992), p. 190. By 1984, almost half of women with children under three were in the labor force, and Brazelton (one might say, to keep his job) modified his stance on attachment, claiming it was now really only the first year that mattered. Ruth Sidel, *Women and Children Last: The Plight of Poor Women in Affluent America* (New York: Penguin, 1986), p. 127.


CHAPTER 3. CRIMES OF ATTACHMENT

1. (The alert reader might note that separation must first occur before this pleasurable biochemical response can occur.) Richard Saltus, *Boston Globe,* "Research Shows Mother and Child Can Get Hooked on One Another," *Philadelphia Inquirer,* January 12, 1994. This article reports on research conducted at the University of Wisconsin School of Medicine by Steven Shelton and Ned Kalin, both in the department of psychiatry. The authors study the neuropsychopharmacological underpinnings of fear-related experiences of infant rhesus monkeys. See: R. Davidson, N. Kalin, and S. Shelton, "Lateralized Response to Diazepam Predicts Tempera-

mental Styles in Rhesus Monkeys," *Behavioral-Neuroscience* 107, no. 6 (December 1993), pp. 1106–1110.

2. *Oprah, Donahue, Geraldo,* 1989.

3. Ken Magid and Carole McKelvey, *High Risk* (New York: Bantam, 1988); *Oprah, Donahue, Geraldo,* 1989.

4. Schroeder begins: "We live in a time of transition . . . sixty-five percent of all mothers with children under eighteen years of age work outside the home. There are more single-parent families, and because of our mobility, there is less extended-family support to help us meet the demands of balancing work and family. An attitude held by many employers is that if a woman chooses to become a mother, she should stay home. The days when that may have been a choice for most of us are long gone. Surveys continue to verify that the majority of women in the workforce are there because of financial necessity. If you are a working mother reading this book, I am sure you will experience, as I did, moments of grief and guilt as you reflect on the difficult choices you have had to make . . ." Ken Magid and Carole McKelvey, *High Risk* (New York: Bantam, 1988), foreword.

5. Linda Blum, "Mother, Babies, and Breastfeeding in Late Capitalist America: The Shifting Contexts of Feminist Theory," *Feminist Studies* 10, no. 2 (summer 1993): pp. 291–311.

6. See Renee Bacher, "Confessions of a Breast-feeding Dropout: My Baby and I Were Both in Tears—If Nursing Was Supposed to Help Us Bond, Why Was I Starting to Think of My Newborn as Jaws?" *Redbook,* November 1994, pp. 71+; "Surgeon General Elders Urges Doctors, Hospitals to Push Breast-feeding, *Jet* 86, no. 17, May 9, 1995, p. 28.

7. Benjamin Spock and Michael Rothenberg, *Dr. Spock's Baby and Child Care* (New York: Pocket Books, 1992).

8. Lauren Lipton, "TV Programs on Parenting," *Philadelphia Inquirer,* May 26, 1991, p. 5-L.

9. Sam Griffiths, "Put Apprentice People First Again," London *Times Educational Supplement,* April 15, 1994, p. 8.

10. Janny Scott, "The Baby Makers," *New York Times,* January 5, 1995, p. C1.

11. T. Berry Brazelton, *On Becoming a Family: The Growth of Attachment Before and After Birth* (New York: Dell, 1991), p. 11.

12. Penelope Leach, *Children First: What Our Society Must Do—And Is Not Doing—For Our Children Today* (New York: Knopf, 1994), p. 97.

13. Spock and Rothenberg, *Dr. Spock's Baby and Child Care,* p. 15.

14. "The crucial importance to women of the effects of pregnancy, birth and breast-feeding is generally acknowledged, but the equal importance to men of being unaffected is not. It is not only that men have to accept their partners' primacy in the production of their joint children, it is also that no physical experience will ever tell them whether they have fathered a child or

not . . . The baby who belongs to both parents needs to wake up to independent life through his mother and to get a firm hold on that life through her nursing, her hormone-driven vigilance and the next stage of an attachment . . . The mother is the person who is uniquely equipped to meet these first infant needs but that does not mean that the father has no role; he is crucially important in making it emotionally safe—as well as practically possible—for her to do so . . . What both she and his baby need him to do is to acknowledge, accept and approve of her feelings and behavior, privately and publicly, welcoming the efforts she makes for the baby . . . the male needs to be there to facilitate the female's mothering." Leach, *Children First,* pp. 37–45.

15. Diane Eyer, *Mother-Infant Bonding: A Scientific Fiction* (New Haven: Yale University Press, 1992), pp. 48–49.

16. Rene Spitz and Katherine Wolf, "Anaclytic Depression," *Psychoanalytic Study of the Child* 2 (1946): pp. 313–342.

17. For a critical review of this research, see: Michael Rutter, *The Qualities of Mothering: Maternal Deprivation Reassessed* (New York: Jason Aronson, 1972).

18. John Bowlby, *Maternal Care and Mental Health,* 2d ed. (Geneva: World Health Organization: Monograph Series no. 2, 1951).

19. Ibid, p. 157.

20. Ibid, pp. 93–100.

21. See Harry Harlow, "The Nature of Love," *American Psychologist* 15 (1958): 673–685.

22. See, for example, Konrad Lorenz, *The Year of the Graylag Goose* (New York: Harcourt Brace Jovanovich, 1979).

23. John Bowlby, *Attachment* (New York: Basic Books, 1969).

24. Mary Ainsworth, *Infancy in Uganda: Infant Care and the Growth of Love* (Baltimore: The Johns Hopkins University Press, 1967); Mary Ainsworth and M. Blehar, E. Waters, and S. Wall, *Patterns of Attachment: A Psychological Study of the Strange Situation* (Hillsdale, NJ: Lawrence Erlbaum, 1978).

25. Ellen Carder, "When Mother Must Go Away: Her Small Son Called Her 'Bad Mommy' Because He Didn't Understand Why His Mother Had to Leave," *Parents,* November 1960, pp. 58+; Evelyn Mellon, "Who Takes Care of the Baby? How to Ease a Little Child's Loneliness and Fear When You Must Be Separated from Him," *Parents,* November 1960, pp. 59+; Selma Fraiberg, "How a Baby Learns to Love," *Redbook,* May 1971, pp. 76+.

26. By 1984, 51.8 percent of women with children under six were working. See Margaret Anderson, *Thinking About Women: Sociological Perspectives on Sex and Gender,* 2d ed. (New York: Macmillan, 1988), p. 115.

27. Jerome Kagan, R. Kearsley, and P. Zelazo, *Infancy: Its Place in Human Development* (Cambridge, MA: Harvard University Press, 1978).

28. In 1989 the average teacher's salary was $12,074; 47 percent were paid below $10,000. Valerie Polakow, *Lives on the Edge: Single Mothers and Their Children in the Other America* (Chicago: University of Chicago Press, 1993), p. 120. Teacher's aides, of course, were paid even less.

29. M. Klaus, J. Kennell, P. Jerauld, N. Kreger, W. McAlpine, and M. Steffa. "Maternal Attachment: Importance of the First Postpartum Days," *New England Journal of Medicine* 286, no. 9 (March 2, 1972): pp. 460–463; Also see: M. Klaus and J. Kennell, *Maternal-Infant Bonding: The Impact of Early Separation or Loss on Family Development* (St. Louis: C. V. Mosby Co., 1976).

30. For an analysis of the politics as well as the faulty "science" of the research, see Eyer, *Mother-Infant Bonding.*

31. M. Svejda, J. Campos, and R. Emde, "Mother-Infant "Bonding": Failure to Generalize," *Child Development* 51 (1980): pp. 775–779.

32. Eyer, *Mother-Infant Bonding,* chaps. 2 and 4.

33. See, for example, the forthcoming John Kennell and Marshall Klaus, *Bonding* (Reading, MA: Addison-Wesley).

34. Benjamin Spock, "How Mothers Learn to Love Their Newborn Babies," *Redbook,* May 1976, pp. 22+; also see: Spock, *Baby and Child Care.*

35. These studies have been thoroughly discredited, but Spock continues to peddle the idea. See: Eyer, *Mother-Infant Bonding.*

36. Diane E. Eyer, "Babies and the Bonding Myth," *USA Today Weekend,* May 7–9 1993; T. Berry Brazelton, "Working Parents: How to Give Your Kids What They Need," *Newsweek,* February 13, 1989, pp. 66+. See T. Berry Brazelton, "The Miracle of Birth: How Babies See Their World," *Redbook,* March, 1978, pp. 112+; T. Berry Brazelton, "Welcoming Your Baby," *Redbook,* September, 1979, pp. 35+.

37. *Thesaurus of Psychological Index Terms* 7th ed., Alvin Walker, Jr., ed. (Washington, D.C.: American Psychological Association, 1994).

38. Subject search on "Psych Lit" on-line index by Diane Eyer.

39. Neala Schwartzberg, "Stuck on You! How Attachment Grows," *Parents,* October 1987, pp. 100+.

40. Katherine Karlsrud, Column, "Birth to One Year," *Parents,* May 1987, p. 198.

41. Jay Belsky, "Infant Day Care: A Cause for Concern?" *Zero to Three* 6 (1986): pp. 1–7; also see: Jay Belsky, "The Effects of Day Care Reconsidered," *Early Childhood Research Quarterly* 3 (1988): pp. 235–272.

42. See C. Wallis, "Is Day Care Bad for Babies?" *Time,* June 22, 1987, p. 63; for a discussion of the ensuing controversy, see Ellen Ruppel Shell, "Babes in Day Care," *Atlantic Monthly,* August 1988, pp. 73–74.

43. The normal distribution of types of attachment is considered to be: 66 percent: "secure"; 22 percent: "insecure-avoidant"; 12 percent "insecure-resistant." In Belsky's study, 26 percent were rated "insecure-avoidant." The groups to whom he compared the day care infants had between 65 and 79 percent "secure" attachment. See an entire issue of *Early Childhood Research Quarterly* which is devoted to assessing the infant day care scare and concludes there are "too many methodological problems" in this research to provide a valid cause for alarm. See especially Ross Thompson, "Effects of Infant Day Care: Through the Prism of Attachment Theory: A Critical Appraisal," *Early Childhood Research Quarterly* 3, pp. 273–82. A number of studies of children from their first year through as many as thirteen years show that children who entered high-quality center-based care before the age of one, in fact, were rated better in social and cognitive skills than children who had entered center care later or those who remained home; they also tended to be less aggressive and exhibit greater emotional well-being. More important, there is no evidence to date that the age a child enters non-maternal care has any substantial effect on children's development. S. Scarr and M. Eisenberg, *Annual Review of Psychology.* 44 (1993): pp. 613–644.

44. See, for example, William Arney, *Power and the Profession of Obstetrics* (Chicago: University of Chicago Press, 1982).

45. While Bowlby and Ainsworth did not study fathers, a few of their followers did. There was a brief flurry of studies in the late 1970s and early 1980s comparing father attachment to mother attachment. In the late 1980s there were some that compared the attachment to husbands of employed versus unemployed mothers. But the vast majority of attachment research (about 95 percent) is on mothers; fathers, who are seldom studied, are simply viewed as a form of othercare compared to the gold standard of mothercare. Louise Silverstein, "Transforming the Debate About Child Care and Maternal Employment," *American Psychologist,* October 1991, p. 1030; author's Psych Lit Index survey. There were just a few studies of the effects of fathers' early ("bonding") contact with infants, sometimes called "engrossment," but there were no clear results of these studies. Susan Goldberg, "Parent-Infant Bonding: Another Look," *Child Development* 54 (1983): p. 1377. See chapter 5 for a discussion of the fathering research.

46. For a more in-depth discussion of the problems of research design as it pertains to the bonding research, see Eyer, *Mother-Infant Bonding,* chap. 2.

47. John Bowlby, *Forty-four Juvenile Thieves and Their Characters and Home Life* (London: Balliere, Tyndal and Cox, 1946).

48. See the work of Jerome Kagan for a more complete discussion of this issue; e.g., Kagan, Kearsley, and Zelazo, *Infancy: Its Place in Human Development.*

49. Michael Lamb, Ross Thompson, William Gardner, Eric Charnov, *Infant-*

*Mother Attachment: The Origins and Developmental Significance of Individual Differences in Strange Situation Behavior* (Hillsdale, NJ: Lawrence Erlbaum, 1985).

50. Lamb, Thompson, Gardner, Charnov, *Infant-Mother Attachment;* Marinus van IJzendoorn, "Developments in Cross-Cultural Research on Attachment," *Human Development* 33 (1990): pp. 3–9; Judy Dunn, *Young Children's Close Relationships: Beyond Attachment,* Individual Differences in Development Series, vol. 4 (London: Sage Publications, 1993).

51. M. Sigman and J. Ungerer, "Attachment Behaviors in Autistic Children," *Journal of Autism and Developmental Disorders* 14 (1984): pp. 231–244.

52. Attachment with a caregiver even helps children who would otherwise be troubled: C. Howes, C. Rodning, D. Galluzo, and L. Myers, "Attachment and Child Care: Relationships with Mother and Caregiver," *Early Childhood Research Quarterly* 3 (1988): pp. 403–416.

53. D. Rajecki and Michael Lamb, "Toward a General Theory of Infantile Attachment: A Comparative Review of Aspects of the Social Bond," *The Behavioral and Brain Sciences* 3 (1978): pp. 417–464.

54. Robert Hinde and Joan Stevenson-Hinde, "Attachment: Biological, Cultural and Individual Desiderata," *Human Development* 33 (1990): pp. 62–72.

55. John Condry and Sandra Condry, "Sex Differences: A Study of the Eye of the Beholder," *Annual Progress in Child Psychiatry and Child Development* (1977): pp. 289–301.

56. R. Ruth Bleier, *Science and Gender: A Critique of Biology and Its Theories on Women* (New York: Pergamon Press, 1984).

57. Richard Herrnstein and Charles Murray, *The Bell Curve: Intelligence and Class Structure in American Life* (New York: The Free Press, 1994).

58. For a fascinating description of this "science," see Stephen Jay Gould, *The Mismeasure of Man* (New York: W. W. Norton, 1981).

59. Sociobiologist David Barash claims that sociobiology relies heavily on the biology of male-female differences and that nature itself appears to be "sexist." Therefore, according to Barash, "it may be that human rapists in their own criminally misguided way are doing the best they can to maximize their fitness"—that is, to leave as many offspring as possible. David Barash, *The Whisperings Within* (New York: Harper and Row, 1979), p. 283.

60. Mario Mikulincer, Victor Florian, and Aron Weller, "Attachment Styles, Coping Strategies, and Post-traumatic Psychological Distress: The Impact of the Gulf War in Israel," *Journal of Personality and Social Psychology* 61, no. 5 (May 1993): pp. 817–826.

61. Kelly Brennan and Phillip Shaver, "Attachment Styles and the 'Big Five' Personality Traits: Their Connection with Each Other and with Romantic

Relationship Outcomes," *Personality and Social Psychology Bulletin* 18 (October 1992): pp. 536–545.

62. Seymour Feshbach, "Psychology, Human Violence, and the Search for Peace," *Journal of Social Issues* 48, no. 1 (spring 1990): pp. 183–198.

63. Linda Stevens, "Attachment to Pets Among Eighth Graders," *Anthrozoo* 3, no. 3 (winter 1990): pp. 177–183.

64. Patrick Pistroni, "Attachment-Detachment and Non-Attachment," *Journal of Analytical Psychology* 38, no. 1 (January 1993): pp. 15–55.

65. Alistair Lawrence, "Mother-Daughter Bonds in Sheep," *Animal Behaviour* 42, no. 4 (October 1991): pp. 683–685.

66. Antonio Madrid and Melissa Schwartz, "Maternal-Infant Bonding and Pediatric Asthma," *Pre- and Peri-Natal Psychology Journal* 5, no. 4 (summer 1991): pp. 347–358.

67. Mary Muller and Sandra Ferketich, "Factor Analysis of the Maternal-Infant Fetal Scale," *Nursing Research* 42, no. 3 (May–June 1993): pp. 144–147.

68. Sidney Blatt and Erika Homann, "Parent-Child Interaction in the Etiology of Dependent and Self-Critical Depression," *Clinical Psychology Review* 12, no. 1 (1992): pp. 47–91.

69. Kathleen Hart and Maureen Kenny, "The Relationship Between Parental Attachment and Eating Disorders," *Journal of Counseling Psychology* 39 (October 1992): pp. 521–526.

70. Malcolm West, *et al.,* "Borderline Disorder and Attachment Pathology," *Canadian Journal of Psychiatry* 38, supp. 1 (February 1993): pp. 16–22.

71. Pamela Alexander, "Application of Attachment Theory to the Study of Sexual Abuse," *Journal of Consulting and Clinical Psychology* 60 (April 1992): pp. 185–195.

72. William Rholes, Julia Nelligan, and Jeffrey Simpson, "Support Seeking and Support Giving Within Couples in an Anxiety-Provoking Situation: The Role of Attachment Styles," *Journal of Personality and Social Psychology* 62 (March 9, 1992): pp. 434–446.

73. Rogers Kobak and Mary Dozier, "Adult Attachment Interview," *Child Development* 63 (December 1992): pp. 1173–1180.

74. This case is fictional, a composite based on several actual cases; Rebecca Hegar, "Assessing Attachment, Permanence, and Kinship in Choosing Permanent Homes," *Child Welfare League of America* 72, no. 4 (July–August 1993): pp. 367–378.

CHAPTER 4. DEVIANT MOTHERS

1. Around the world, for instance, about one third of families are headed by a woman alone. Iris Young, "Making Single Motherhood Normal," *Dissent* (winter 1994): pp. 88–93. Divorce rates in Western countries more than

doubled between 1960 and 1990. (However, the United States has the highest prevalence of single-parent families.)

2. They are 27 percent of all married-couple families with children under six. In 1940, nearly 70 percent of married-couple families had a strictly bread-winner/homemaker division of labor. *Population Today,* September 1992, p. 2. U.S. Department of Labor, Bureau of Labor Statistics, *Employment and Earnings,* January 1994, p. 76.

3. Of these single-parent households, about 61 percent are maintained by di-vorced or separated women, 31 percent by never-married women, and 6 percent by widows. Twenty-seven percent of children are born to unmar-ried mothers, and it is estimated that one in four births to unmarried women are to a cohabiting couple, a majority of whom eventually marry; and nearly a third are born to divorced or separated mothers. Half of all children will reside in a single-parent family for about six years before they reach sixteen. Suzanne Bianchi, "The Changing Demographic and Socioeconomic Char-acteristics of Single-Parent Families," in "Single-Parent Families: Diversity, Myths and Realities," S. Hanson, S. Heims, D. Julian, M. Sussman, eds., *Marriage and Family Review* 20, nos. 1/2 (New York: The Haworth Press, 1995), pp. 71–97.

4. Andrew Cherlin and Frank Furstenberg, Jr., "Stepfamilies in the United States," *Annual Review of Sociology* 20 (1994): pp. 359–381.

5. Figure is for 1987. Patricia Evans, "Targeting Single Mothers for Employ-ment . . . " *Social Service Review* (Chicago: University of Chicago Press, Sep-tember 1992), pp. 378–398. "Welfare mothers" are 20 percent of divorced mothers and 55 percent of never-married mothers. Mark Lino, "Income and Spending Patterns of Single-Mother Families," *Monthly Labor Review,* May 1994, p. 29.

6. Ron Taffel, "The Confident Parent: The Real Trouble with Working Moth-ers," *McCalls',* June 1992, pp. 52+.

7. Paul Klein, "The Needs of Children," *Mothering,* spring 1995, pp. 39+.

8. Julia Kagan, "Mom-to-Mom Report '94," *Child,* May 1994, pp. 74+; Eliza-beth Fishel, "Through the Eyes of a Child," *Child,* May 1994, pp. 80+.

9. See: P. Barglow, B. Vaughn, and N. Molitor, "Effects of Maternal Absence Due to Employment on the Quality of Infant-Mother Attachment in a Low-Risk Sample," *Child Development* 58, pp. 945–954.

10. For reviews, see: J. Belsky, "The Effects of Infant Day Care Reconsidered," *Early Childhood Research Quarterly* 3 (1988): pp. 235–272; A. Clarke-Stewart, "Infant Day Care: Maligned or Malignant?" *American Psychologist* 44 (February 1989): pp. 266–273; Louise Silverstein, "Transforming the Debate About Child Care and Maternal Employment," *American Psycholo-gist,* 46 (October 1991): pp. 1025–1032; S. Scarr, D. Phillips, and K. Mc-Cartney, "Working Mothers and Their Families," *American Psychologist* 44

(June 1989): pp. 1402–1409; R. Thompson, "Infant Day Care: Concerns, Controversies, Choices," in *Employed Mothers and Their Children,* eds. J. Lerner and N. Galambos (New York: Garland, 1991), pp. 9–36.

11. For example, some studies have reported negative outcomes for boys, in that sons of middle-class working mothers report a lower grade-point average than do sons of middle-class nonworking mothers. A. Bronfenbrenner and A. Crouter, "Work and Family Through Time and Space," in *Families That Work: Children in a Changing World,* eds. S. Kamerman and C. Hayes (Washington, D.C.: National Academy Press, 1982). Although this finding has been widely reported, an analysis of the data reflects a tiny (five-point) difference in grade-point averages and only reaches significance with large sample sizes. See E. Greenberger, Bronfenbrenner, *et al.,* "Revisited: Maternal Employment and Perceptions of Young Children" (paper presented at the 97th Annual Convention of the American Psychological Association, New Orleans, LA, 1989).

12. S. Scarr, D. Phillips, and K. McCartney, "Facts, Fantasies and the Future of Child Care in the United States," *Psychological Science* 1, no. 1 (January 1990): pp. 26–35.

13. Also see: A. Clarke-Stewart, "Predicting Child Development from Day-Care Forms and Features: The Chicago Study," in *Quality in Child Care: What Does Research Tell Us? Research Monographs of the National Association for the Education of Young Children,* vol 1, ed. D. Phillips (Washington, D.C.: National Association for the Education of Young Children, 1987), pp. 21–42.

14. M. Weinraub, E. Jaeger, and L. Hoffman, "Predicting Infant Outcomes in Families of Employed and Non-employed Mothers," *Early Childhood Research Quarterly* 3 (1988): pp. 361–378.

15. S. Scarr, *Mother Care/Other Care* (New York: Basic Books, 1984).

16. C. Hill and F. Stafford, "Parental Care of Children . . ." *Journal of Human Resources* 15 (1980): pp. 219–239. Another recent study shows mothers spend as much time caring for their children as they did in 1965, primarily because families are now smaller and parents do not reduce the amount of caregiving time when they have fewer children. J. P. Robinson, "Caring for Kids," *American Demographics* 11, no 7 (1989): p. 52.

17. Although increased employment reduces the time spent caring for very young children (under three years old), employed mothers actually spend more time caring for their older children than do unemployed mothers (in two-parent homes). The study is by time-use expert Keith Bryant. Reported by Susan Lang, "Mother's Time," *Human Ecology Forum* 20, no 2 (spring 1992): pp. 27–29.

18. About half of parents' primary child care time is spent doing "custodial" activities—dressing, feeding, or otherwise tending to the physical needs of

children. Another 15 percent is spent chauffeuring children to school, to lessons, or to other places. The remaining one third is spent interacting with children—talking to them, helping them with homework, or playing with them. Secondary activity is when parents care for their child while they are doing other activities, such as housework or watching television. Parents spend four hours a week doing child care as a secondary activity. Children of single parents receive two to three fewer hours of care per week from the custodial parent than do children in two-parent households. Mothers with college degrees spend an average of more than ten hours a week in primary care compared to six hours for mothers who did not complete high school. Robinson, "Caring for Kids," p. 52.

19. They also ignore studies that show that higher levels of interaction between nonemployed mothers and their children may become strenuous for mothers and dangerous for children. Research in the area of family violence, for example, indicates that women employed full-time are less likely to be violent toward their children than mothers who are employed part-time or are not employed. David Demo, "Parent-Child Relations: Assessing Recent Changes," *Journal of Marriage and the Family* 54 (February 1992): pp. 104–117.

20. For some of the more complex approaches, see: Adele Gottfried and Allen Gottfried, *Maternal Employment and Children's Development* (New York: Plenum, 1988), p. 253; Weinraub, Jaeger, and Hoffman, "Predicting Infant Outcomes in Families of Employed and Non-employed Mothers," p. 376.

21. In Silverstein, "Transforming the Debate About Child Care and Maternal Employment," pp. 1025–1032, Silverstein asserts: "Psychologists have not yet begun to frame research questions that examine the devastating consequences of the lack of societal supports for balancing the demands of work and family life. The search for possible negative consequences of maternal employment and substitute care continues despite two decades of exhaustive research that has failed to document consistent (i.e., replicable across several studies) meaningful negative findings (p. 1025) . . . A new agenda is proposed that would document the negative consequences of *not* providing high-quality, affordable child care. This new agenda would also acknowledge that fathers and family process are as central to developmental outcomes in children as are mothers (p. 1026) . . . Psychologists must refuse to undertake any more research that looks for the negative consequences of other-than-mother care" (pp. 1029–1030).

22. For responses to Silverstein, in *Journal of Social Behavior and Personality* 8, no. 1 (1993), see: M. Hojat, "Abandoning Research on Consequences of Nonmaternal Care: A Disservice to the Science," pp. 5–8; Frances Haemmerlie, "Intolerance Within Psychology: A Disservice to the Profession,"

pp. 9–11; Anita Barbee, "Political Agendas Versus Research Agendas: The Day Care Dilemma," pp. 13–16; Nancy Struthers, "New Directions Are Needed for Research on Child Development," pp. 17–20; Virginia Colin, "Public Policy, Attachment and Science," pp. 21–23. Also see in *American Psychologist* 48, no. 6 (June 1993): pp. 689–694; J. Maddux, "Social Science, Social Policy, and Scientific Research"; K. McCartney, D. Phillips, and Sandra Scarr, "On Using Research as a Tool"; NICHD Early Child Care Network, "Child-Care Debate: Transformed or Distorted?"; N. Shpancer, "Transforming the Child-Care Debate."

23. Maddux, "Social Science, Social Policy, and Scientific Research," pp. 689–694.

24. Hojat, "Abandoning Research on Consequences of Nonmaternal Care: A Disservice to the Science," pp. 5–8.

25. See: K. MacEwen and J. Barling, "Effects of Maternal Employment Experiences on Children's Behavior," *Journal of Marriage and the Family* (1991): pp. 635–644; L. Otto and M. Atkinson, "Feedback: Maternal Employment . . . a Reanalysis and Comment," *Journal of Marriage and the Family* 56 (1994): pp. 501–510; Lois Hoffman, "Maternal Employment and the Child," in *Parent-Child Interaction,* ed. M. Perlmutter (Hillsdale, NJ: Lawrence Erlbaum, 1984); Aurora Jackson, "Black, Single, Working Mothers in Poverty," *Social Work* 38, no 1 (1993): pp. 26–38.

26. Barbara Dafoe Whitehead, "Dan Quayle Was Right," *Atlantic Monthly,* April 1993, pp. 47+.

27. Frank Furstenberg and Julien Teitler, "Reconsidering the Effects of Marital Disruption," *Journal of Family Issues* 15, no. 2 (June 1994): pp. 173–190.

28. For reviews of the research on the effects of divorce on children, see: Paul Amato, "Children's Adjustment to Divorce: Theories, Hypotheses and Empirical Support," *Journal of Marriage and the Family* 55 (February 1993): pp. 23–38 (commentary on the review: pp. 39–54); Demo, "Parent-Child Relations: Assessing Recent Changes," pp. 104–117; Frank Furstenberg and Andrew Cherlin, *Divided Families: What Happens to Children When Parents Part* (Cambridge, MA: Harvard University Press, 1991); Robert Emery, *Marriage, Divorce and Children's Adjustment,* Developmental and Clinical Psychology and Psychiatry 14 (Newbury Park, CA: Sage Publications, 1988).

29. Some of the best statistical data on the process of divorce comes from the National Survey of Children, a representative sample of children followed from the mid-1970s to the present. The period when marriages come apart is often a time of severe marital strife, about one third of the time culminating in some physical violence. Furstenberg and Cherlin, *Divided Families,* p. 13. For example, see: P. Lindsay Chase-Lansdale and E. Mavis Hether-

ington, "The Impact of Divorce on Life-span Development: Short and Long Term Effects, in *Life Span Development and Behavior,* Vol. 10, eds. David Featherman and Richard Lerner (Hillsdale, NJ: Lawrence Erlbaum, 1990), pp. 105–151.

30. It has commonly been thought that children of single parents do best when they live with the parent of the same sex. However, upon further examination, it appears that while there may be special instances where this is so, it does not generally hold true. Douglas Downey and Brian Powell, "Do Children in Single-Parent Households Fare Better Living with Same-Sex Parents?" *Journal of Marriage and the Family* 55 (February 1993): pp. 55–71.

31. See: Judith Wallerstein, "The Long-Term Effects of Divorce on Children: A Review," *Journal of the American Academy of Child and Adolescent Psychiatry* 30, no. 3 (May 1991): pp. 349–360.

32. Frank Furstenberg and Julien Teitler, "Reconsidering the Effects of Marital Disruption," pp. 173–190.

33. Amato, "Children's Adjustment to Divorce: Theories, Hypotheses and Empirical Support," pp. 23–38 (commentary on the review: pp. 39–54).

34. Furstenberg and Cherlin, *Divided Families.*

35. Margaret Usdansky, "Single Motherhood: Stereotypes vs. Statistics," *New York Times,* February 11, 1996, p. E4.

36. The number of white mothers who have never married has increased rapidly, from less than 3 percent of one-parent families in 1970 to 19 percent in 1991; for blacks, the increase was from 15 percent in 1970 to 54 percent in 1991; for Hispanics, the rate rose from 23 percent to 33 percent. Teen pregnancy among blacks has not increased much, but the rate of marriage among teenagers has dropped. Robert Suro, "For Women, Varied Reasons for Single Motherhood," *New York Times,* May 26, 1992, pp. A12+.

37. U.S. Bureau of the Census, *Poverty in the United States: 1991,* Current Population Reports, series P-60 (Washington, DC: U.S. Government Printing Office), p. 181.

38. Single-parent adoptions comprise 15 percent of all nonrelative adoptions. Shirley Hanson *et al.,* "Single-Parent Families: Present and Future Perspectives," *Marriage and Family Review* 20, nos. 1/2 (New York: The Haworth Press, 1995), pp. 1–26.

39. Considering the often virulent hostility directed at gays and lesbians in our society, it is rather surprising to find that their children do quite well. A review of the studies of the children of lesbian mothers reveals these children's development is perfectly normal. C. Patterson, "Children of Lesbian and Gay Parents," *Child Development,* October 1992, pp. 1025–1042.

40. Among single mothers, almost one third will live at some point in their par-

ents' home for an average of two years. Suzanne Bianchi, "The Changing Demographic and Socioeconomic Characteristics of Single-Parent Families," in "Single-Parent Families: Diversity, Myths and Realities," eds., S. Hanson, S. Heims, D. Julian, M. Sussman, *Marriage and Family Review* 20, nos. 1/2 (New York: The Haworth Press, 1995), pp. 71–97.

41. U.S. Bureau of the Census, *Who's Minding the Kids?*, Population Reports, Special Studies, series P-70, no. 20 (Washington, D.C.: GPO, 1990), table 7, part B.

42. Mark Lino, "The Economics of Single Parenthood: Past Research and Future Directions," in "Single-Parent Families: Diversity, Myths and Realities," pp. 99–114.

43. U.S. Bureau of the Census, "Child Support and Alimony: 1987," series P-23, no. 167, p. 34. Among mothers with an absent father, only 50 percent were even awarded child support in 1989. Of the women not awarded child support, 64 percent desired it, but the father was deemed unable to pay or could not be located. Of the women due child support, 51 percent reported receiving the full amount, 24 percent received less than the full amount, 25 percent did not receive any support at all. G. H. Lester, "Child Support and Alimony: 1980," Current Population Reports, series P-60, Bureau of the Census (Washington, D.C.: GPO), p. 173.

44. Teresa Amott, *Caught in the Crisis: Women and the U.S. Economy* (New York: Monthly Review Press, 1993), p. 108.

45. U.S. House of Representatives, Committee on Ways and Means, *Overview of Entitlement Programs: 1991 Green Book* (Washington, D.C.: WMCP: 102–9, 1991), appendix G.

46. National Low Income Housing Coalition, *Unlocking the Door: An Action Program for Meeting the Needs of Women* (Washington, D.C.: NLIHC, 1990), p. 2.

47. Marcia Steinbeck, "Homeless Female-Headed Families: Relationships at Risk," in "Single Parent Families: Diversity, Myths and Realities," pp. 143–160.

48. See, for example, S. McLanahan, "Family Structure and the Reproduction of Poverty," *American Journal of Sociology* 90 (1985): pp. 873–901; E. M. Hetherington, K. Camera, and D. Featherman, "Intellectual Functioning and Achievement of Children in One-Parent Households," in *Assessing Achievement,* ed. J. A. Spence (San Francisco: W. H. Freeman, 1983), pp. 205–284.

49. Douglas Downey, "The School Performance of Children from Single-Mother and Single-Father Families," *Journal of Family Issues* 15, no. 1 (March 1994): pp. 129–147.

50. Ibid.

51. See Andrew Cherlin, *Marriage, Divorce and Remarriage* (Cambridge, MA: Harvard University Press, 1981).

52. Frank Furstenberg, S. Morgan, and P. Allison, "Paternal Participation and Children's Well-being After Marital Dissolution," *American Sociological Review* 52 (1987): pp. 695–701.

53. Unfortunately, in this research comparing single-father and single-mother families, there was no attempt to account for differences in the amount of time a child was in a single-parent family, thus making the "findings" quite tenuous. Douglas Downey, "The School Performance of Children from Single-Mother and Single-Father Families," *Journal of Family Issues* 15, no. 1 (March 1994): pp. 129–147.

54. S. McLanahan and G. Sandefur, *Growing Up with a Single Parent: What Hurts What Helps* (Cambridge, MA: Harvard University Press, 1994).

55. The authors extract data from four national surveys of thousands of children, conducted for other purposes, that cover a number of years of the lives of those children. They believe that stepfamilies are disadvantaged compared to families with both biological parents present, and they attempt to define the factors causing disadvantage in stepfamilies as well as those for single mothers. Nine out of ten single parents are single mothers.

56. AFDC benefits for a three-person family in 1990 ranged from $120 a month in Mississippi to $891 in Alaska. Marcia Steinbock, "Homeless Female-Headed Families: Relationships at Risk," in "Single-Parent Families: Diversity, Myths and Realities," pp. 143–160.

57. Based on a real case described in: Laura McClure, "Working the Risk Shift," *The Progressive,* February 1994, pp. 23+.

58. McClure, "Working the Risk Shift," pp. 23+.

59. Ibid.

60. The real value of the welfare benefit package (AFDC plus food stamps) for a family of four fell from $10,133 in 1972 to $8,374 in 1980, and to $7,657 in 1992, a loss of 26 percent between 1972 and 1992. U.S. House of Representatives, Committee on Ways and Means, *Overview of Entitlement Programs* (Washington, D.C.: GPO, 1993).

61. The actual rates are difficult to discern, however, because some groups are more aggressively arrested, and reporting also differs among groups. See Michael Rutter and Henri Giller. *Juvenile Delinquency: Trends and Perspectives* (New York: The Guilford Press, 1983), pp. 132–145, 180–181.

62. Rutter and Giller, *Juvenile Delinquency,* pp. 180–181.

63. Van Voorhees, *et al.,* "The Impact of Family Structure and Quality on Delinquency: A Comparative Assessment of Structural and Functional Factors," *Criminology* 26 (1988): pp. 235–261.

64. Of the total state prison population in 1991, 728,246 were males; 39,917

were females. Clifford Krauss, "Women Doing Crime, Women Doing Time," *New York Times,* July 3, 1994, p. E3.

65. For a review of research on broken homes, see M. D. Free, "Clarifying the Relationships Between the Broken Home and Juvenile Delinquency: A Critique of the Current Literature," *Deviant Behavior* 12, no. 2, (1991): pp. 109–167.

66. Robert Sampson and John Laub, *Crime in the Making: Pathways and Turning Points Through Life* (Cambridge, MA: Harvard University Press, 1993), pp. 6–24.

67. Ibid., pp. 99–122.

68. Ibid.

69. See William Julius Wilson, *The Truly Disadvantaged: The Inner City, the Underclass, and Public Policy* (Chicago: University of Chicago Press, 1987).

70. Cherlin, *Marriage, Divorce, Remarriage.* It is true that between 1955 and 1970 the number of births to fifteen- to nineteen-year-olds rose by a third and lifted the relative share of all births to teenage mothers from 12 percent to 18 percent during the same fifteen-year-period. However, this growth was due to the large numbers of baby boom girls at that age level, and their relative high rate of birth compared to the declining rate among older women.

71. One million of America's 9 million girls between fifteen and nineteen get pregnant each year, and about half give birth. Lee Smith, "The New Wave of Illegitimacy," *Fortune,* April 18, 1994, pp. 81+.

72. Furstenberg, Brooks-Gunn, and Morgan, *Adolescent Mothers in Later Life,* p. 5.

73. Ibid.

74. Researchers compared the child development scores of children of sisters who experienced their first births at different ages and found no differences in the scores. Arline Geronimus and Sanders Korenman, "The Socioeconomic Costs of Teenage Childbearing: Evidence and Interpretation." *Demography,* Vol. 30, No. 2, May 1993, pp. 281–296.

75. See Saul Hoffman, Michael Foster, Frank Furstenberg, Jr. "Reevaluating the Costs of Teenage Childbearing." *Demography,* Vol. 30, No. 1, February 1993, pp. 1–31.

76. The gender gap in earnings (women's earnings divided by men's earnings), which had remained at about 60 percent, began to narrow after the 1970s. In the 1980s, women between twenty-five and thirty-four who worked full-time earned 65 percent as much as men, and in 1990 they earned 74 percent as much as men. Between 1980 and 1990, the earnings of college-educated women grew by 17 percent while the earnings of college-educated men grew by only 5 percent (for ages twenty-five to thirty-four working full-

time). McLanahan and Sandefur, *Growing Up with a Single Parent,* pp. 141–142.

CHAPTER 5. FATHERGUILT?

1. Aaron Sachs, "Male Responsibility in an Overpopulating World," *World Watch,* March/April, 1994, pp. 12–19; Farai Chideya *et al.,* "Endangered Black Family," *Newsweek,* August 1993, pp. 17+.
2. Edward Krek, "The Disengaged, Noncustodial Father," *Social Work,* 39, issue 1 (January 1994): pp. 15–25.
3. Several examinations of the fathers' custody movement describe the disparity between the rhetoric of equality and shared custody and the actual practice of the fathers who mostly seem angry that they have lost control of their children. Rather than seeking equal responsibility and care of their children after divorce, they seek equal access to their children, information about them, and decision-making rights. Moreover, in discussing the matters of equity, fathers do not recognize the nonmonetary contribution of the mothers' daily care of their children in their considerations of equality. Fathers do not seem to imagine the lifestyle consequences for their children in the absence of their support payments. Carl Bertoia and Janice Drakich, "The Fathers' Rights Movement," in *Fatherhood: Contemporary Theory, Research and Social Policy,* ed. William Marsiglio (London: Sage, 1995), pp. 230–254; see also Martha Fineman, *The Illusion of Equality: The Rhetoric and Reality of Divorce Reform* (Chicago: University of Chicago Press, 1991); Robert Griswold, *Fatherhood in America: A History* (New York: Basic Books, 1993), chap. 11.
4. Betty Holcomb, "How Families Are Changing for the Better," *Working Mother,* July 1994, pp. 30+.
5. Employed mothers spend twice as much time caring for their children as fathers (employed or unemployed), although fathers spend just as much time as mothers in the more enjoyable and influential aspects of child care—talking to them, playing with them, helping them with homework. Fathers spend less time tending to their physical needs, chauffeuring them, and so on. J. P. Robinson, "Caring for Kids," *American Demographics* 11, no. 7 (1989): p. 52. One survey found that the percentage of children whose fathers cared for them during their mothers' working hours rose to 20 percent in 1991, after holding stable at around 15 percent since 1977. The survey also found an increase in unmarried fathers caring for their children, to 7 percent in 1991, from 1.5 percent in 1988. The study's author, Martin O'Connell, attributed the increase to the high cost of child care, a growing number of parents who work night shifts or part-time, and changing social

attitudes. Susan Chira, "Census Data Show Rise in Child Care by Fathers," *New York Times,* September 22, 1993, p. A20.

6. Angela Phillips, "Like Father, Like Son," *New Statesman and Society,* November 1993, pp. 32+.

7. Karen Schneider, "All Agree That Welfare's Flawed," *Philadelphia Inquirer,* September 5, 1993, p. 1. Ninety-seven percent of noncompliant, noncustodial parents are fathers. In 1992 they owed $34 billion to their 23 million children. Ellen Goodman, "Hitting Them Where They Drive," *Washington Post,* July 30, 1994, p. A17.

8. Theda Skocpol and William Julius Wilson, "Mesh Welfare Reform with Family Realities," *New York Times,* 1994, in *Arizona Daily Star,* February 14, 1994.

9. Jason de Parle, "Welfare Mothers Find Jobs Easy to Get But Hard to Hold," *New York Times,* October 24, 1994, pp. 1+.

10. Every year between 10 and 20 percent of women are beaten by a male intimate. Demie Kurtz, *For Richer, For Poorer: Mothers Confront Divorce* (New York: Routledge, 1995), pp. 52–53. Estimates of abuse in families varies widely because of the range of definitions of abuse and the disinclination to report the abuse to authorities. However, 3 million American children per year are reported to be neglected or physically or sexually abused—triple the number in 1980. *The Progress of Nations,* UNICEF, 1994, p. 41.

11. In April 1992, an Annie Casey Foundation study using 1992 census data showed that the percentage of men twenty-five to thirty-four earning less than the poverty level for a family of four more than doubled to 32.2 percent in 1993 from 13.6 percent in 1969. Steven Holmes, "Low-Wage Fathers and the Welfare Debate," *New York Times,* April 25, 1995, p. A12.

12. Judsen Cabreth, editor in chief, *Working Mother* magazine, Letters to the Editor, *New York Times,* June 29, 1994. Fathers' incomes have declined 15 percent since 1980, and husbands now bring in only two thirds of the family income. The median family income of married-couple families in which the wife worked was $47,000 in 1990, compared with $30,000 where the wife did not work. *Population Today,* September 1992, p. 2.

13. In 1970, 9 percent of young black males twenty to twenty-four were neither employed nor in school; by 1980 the figure had risen to 27 percent, and by 1990 it was 28 percent. The trend for young white males was in the same direction, at 13 percent in 1990, up from 9 percent in 1970. F. Welch, "The Employment of Black Men," *Journal of Labor Economics* 8, no. 1 (1990): pp. S26–S74.

14. I put "desirable" in quotes, because in the best of all possible worlds, male marriage partners would not be judged solely on their employability but also on their human capacity to love and nurture. The decline of income of

men since 1969 has been paralleled by a decline in the marriage rate, suggesting that men's lowered income discourages marriage. Holmes, "Low-Wage Fathers and the Welfare Debate," p. A12. In 1980, there were only 56 employed black men for every 100 black women in the Northeast between the ages of twenty and forty-four. Ellis Cose, "Protecting the Children," *Newsweek,* August 30, 1993, pp. 28+.

15. Benjamin Spock, *Baby and Child Care* (New York: Dell, 1976, 1985, 1992).

16. Penelope Leach, *Children First: What Our Society Must Do—and Is Not Doing—For Our Children Today* (New York: Alfred Knopf, 1994), pp. 31–47.

17. T. Berry Brazelton, *On Becoming a Family: The Growth of Attachment Before and After Birth* (New York: Dell, 1992), pp. xvi, 190.

18. While the proportion of studies in early child development that focus on fathering has increased from about 1 in 20 in the 1950s to about 1 in 5 in the 1990s, the research maintains its maternal-sculptress bias. According to a search of the psychological research journals, between 1974 and 1986, out of 1,849 studies of parents and infants, only 195 involved fathers; between 1987 and 1994 out of 2,435 studies of parents and infants, only 284 involved fathers. D. Eyer, *Psych Lit Index,* April 1995. In a review of family studies in the research journal *Child Development,* in 1985, 22 percent included fathers; in 1990, 20 percent included fathers. The vast majority of these studies focused on mothers as the prime architects of their children's development. G. Russell and M. Radajevic, "The Changing Role of Fathers? Current Understandings and Future Directions for Research and Practice," *Infant Mental Health Journal* 13, no. 4 (winter 1992): pp. 296–311.

19. Vicky Phares, "Where's Poppa? The Relative Lack of Attention to the Role of Fathers in Child and Adolescent Psychopathology," *American Psychologist,* May 1992, pp. 656–664.

20. Michael Lamb, "Paternal Influences on Child Development" (presentation made to the Conference on Changing Fatherhood, Tilburg, The Netherlands, May 1994).

21. Ibid.

22. Phares, "Where's Poppa?"

23. Robert Griswold, *Fatherhood in America: A Historical Study* (New York: Basic Books, 1993), chap. 11.

24. According to a search of the psychological research journals, between 1974 and 1986, out of 79 infant bonding/attachment studies, 7 were primarily concerned with fathers; between 1987 and 1994, out of 103 infant bonding/attachment studies, 8 were primarily concerned with fathers. Diane Eyer, *Psych Lit Index,* April 1995.

25. Russell and Radajevic, "The Changing Role of Fathers?" pp. 296–311.

26. Ibid.

27. Michael Lamb, "Qualitative Aspects of Mother-and-Father-Infant Attach-
    ment," *Infant Behavior and Development* I (1978): pp. 265–275.

28. Ross Parke, *Fathers* (Cambridge, MA: Harvard University Press, 1981),
    p. 35.

29. Lamb, "Paternal Influences on Child Development."

30. Ibid.

31. Some of the persistent popular misconceptions about evolutionary influ-
    ences on paternity are based on earlier primate research that showed that
    primate males are more aggressive than females; males dominate females;
    males have short-term bonds with sexually receptive females; and males are
    uninvolved with infants. However, new research, involving more female re-
    searchers and spanning longer periods of time—ten to fifteen years—has
    now yielded quite different results. Newer research shows a very complex
    picture where males' need to get their genes into the gene pool are only one
    of several important variables in deciding how reproduction is organized. It
    appears that female influence is very important to the social group, and
    male aggressive dominance hierarchies are less important than was thought;
    there are long-term affiliative, as well as short-term sexual relationships, and
    varying amounts of male involvement with infants. Louise Silverstein, "Pri-
    mate Research, Family Politics, and Social Policy: Transforming 'cads' into
    'dads,'" *Journal of Family Psychology* 7, no. 3 (1993): pp. 267–282.

32. Michael E. Lamb, "Biological Determinism Redux: Comment on Silverstein
    (1993)," *Journal of Family Psychology* 7, no. 3 (1993): pp. 301–04.

33. In Warren Farrell's book, *The Liberated Man* (1974; New York: Berkley
    Publishing, 1993), he set out parameters for the feminist male who would
    be freed from the economic burden of supporting a family alone and from
    the physical and mental strain of proving masculinity and repressing "fem-
    inine" emotions. He also led men's consciousness-raising groups.

34. George Gilder, *Men and Marriage* (Gretna, LA.: Pelican, 1986); *Naked No-
    mads: Unmarried Men in America* (New York: Quadrangle, The New York
    Times Book Co., 1974); *Wealth and Poverty* (New York: Basic Books,
    1981).

35. Samuel Osherson, *Finding Our Fathers: The Unfinished Business of Man-
    hood* (New York: Free Press, 1986).

36. Robert Bly, *Iron John: A Book About Men* (Reading, MA: Addison-Wesley,
    1990).

37. Brian Johnson, "The Male Myth," *Maclean's,* January 31, 1994, pp. 38+.

38. Scott Heller, "Scholars Debunk the Marlboro Man: Examining Stereotypes
    of Masculinity," *The Chronicle of Higher Education,* February 3, 1993, pp.
    A6+.

39. Also see, for example: Martin Green, *The Adventurous Male: Chapters in the*

*History of the White Male Mind* (University Park, PA: Pennsylvania State University Press, 1993); Anthony Rotundo, *American Manhood: Transformation in Masculinity from the Revolution to the Modern Era* (New York: Basic Books, 1984); Paul Smith, *Clint Eastwood: A Cultural Production* (Minneapolis, MN: University of Minnesota Press, 1993); Griswold, *Fatherhood in America;* Peter Middleton, *The Inward Gaze: Masculinity and Subjectivity in Modern Subject* (New York: Routledge, 1992); Peter Nardi, *Men's Friendships* (Thousand Oaks, CA: Sage, 1992); Steven Cohan and Ina Rae Hark, *Screening the Male: Exploring Masculinities in Hollywood Cinema* (New York: Routledge, 1992).

40. Mike Clary, *Daddy's Home* (New York: Seaview Books, 1982).
41. Bill Cosby, *Fatherhood* (New York: Berkley, 1994).
42. Nancy Gibbs, "Fatherhood" (cover story), *Time,* June 28, 1993, pp. 53+.
43. Ibid.
44. Ibid.
45. Frank Pittman, "Fathers and Sons: What It Takes To Be a Man," *Psychology Today,* September/October 1993, pp. 52+.
46. Maureen Weldon Fegan, "Dads Do It Differently," *American Baby,* April 1991, pp. A17+.
47. Jerrold Lee Shapiro, "Daddy Love: Why It's Special," *Parents,* June 1994, pp. 165+.
48. Susan Chira, "War Over Role of American Fathers," *New York Times,* June 19, 1994, p. 22.
49. Ibid.
50. David Popenoe, "The Proper Study of Men: Parental Androgyny," *Society,* September/October 1993, pp. 5–11.
51. Ibid.
52. Sociobiologists commonly made the claim that natural selection favors males who mate with many females and invest little time and energy in the care and protection of their offspring. Males that use this reproductive strategy are referred to as "cads," in contrast to males who mate with only one female and invest a large amount of time and energy in their children, who are referred to as "dads." However, more recent research shows that paternity certainty, that is, the male's genetic relation to infant offspring, is only one of many circumstances that leads to high paternal investment in the nonhuman animal kingdom. Paternal investment also varies according to social, demographic, and ecological variables. Louise Silverstein, "Primate Research, Family Politics, and Social Policy," pp. 267–282.
53. Kyle Pruett, *The Nurturing Father* (New York: Warner Books, 1987).
54. Ibid.
55. Ibid., p. 86.
56. Ibid., p. 89.

57. Ibid., p. 122.

58. Ibid., p. 138.

59. L. McCrary and L. King, "A Widower Had Won the Right to a Korean Girl . . . ," *Philadelphia Inquirer,* September 27, 1994, p. B2.

60. Pruett, *The Nurturing Father,* p. 279.

61. One such educator, Michael Myerhoff, complained. "Whenever I attempted to [care for an infant], one of the senior staff members would snatch the baby away and say, 'Oh, let me do that.' On the other hand, I was routinely singled out for certain chores such as moving the sandbox, carrying in supplies, putting together cribs, etc. I felt like the proverbial female who finally gets a promotion to the managerial ranks of the company only to find that all she is asked to do is make coffee during the important meetings." Myerhoff's recent professional observations of hundreds of day care centers around the country convince him that things haven't changed much. However, the center Myerhoff first integrated two decades ago now recruits male high school students to join the girls as intern caregivers. Michael Myerhoff, "Of Baseball and Babies," *Young Children,* May 1994, pp. 17–19.

62. Sally Abrams, "Do You Really Want Him to Be a Great Dad?" *Redbook,* June 1994, pp. 152+; Gayle Kimball, *50/50 Parenting* (Lexington, MA: Lexington Books, 1988); Ron Taffel, *Why Parents Disagree* (New York: William Morrow, 1994).

63. Richard Louv, "How Fathers Feel (survey)," *Parents,* December 1993, pp. 226+.

64. In one study, 60 percent of the fathers under thirty-five said they were shaping their career to spend more time with their families. Study by Douglas T. Hall, Boston University School of Management, cited in Shirley Fader, "Are Men Changing?" *Working Mother,* February 1993, pp. 49+.

65. House of Representatives, 102d Congress, 1st session, June 11, 1992, "Babies and Briefcases: Creating a Family Friendly Workplace for Fathers." Hearing before the Select Committee on Children, Youth, and Families.

66. Susan Chira, "Fathers Who Want Time Off for Families Face Uphill Battle," *New York Times,* October 21, 1993, p. C6.

67. Richard Louv, *Father Love* (New York: Pocket Books, 1993), pp. 51–54.

CHAPTER 6. THE REAL CULPRIT: AMERICAN CHILD CARE

1. In 1991, about 23 percent of the preschoolers were cared for exclusively by their mothers at home. Among the three quarters of American preschoolers not cared for at home by their mothers, almost 10 percent of them were cared for by their mothers at their mother's place of work. Another 20 percent (of that three quarters) received primary supplemental care from their

fathers and 16 percent from their grandparents. Among nonrelatives, family day care constituted about 23 percent of the choices; day care/preschool centers represented about 24 percent. Charles S. Clark, "Child Care: The Issues," *CQ Researcher* 3, no. 47 (December 17, 1993): p. 1107.

2. In 76 percent of the centers, safety and health needs are being met, but the need to grow and develop are not. The researchers examined 400 child care centers in California, Colorado, Connecticut, and North Carolina in the spring of 1993 and tested 826 children from those centers. Susan Chira, "Care at Child Day Centers Is Rated as Poor," *New York Times,* February 7, 1995, p. A12; Suzanne Helburn, *et al., Cost, Quality and Child Outcomes in Child Care Centers,* executive summary (University of Colorado at Denver, University of California, Los Angeles, University of North Carolina, and Yale University, January 1995). Another comprehensive study of centers estimates 70 percent are substandard. Marcy Whitebrook, Carollee Howes, and Deborah Phillips, *The National Child Care Staffing Study* (Oakland, CA: Child Care Employee Project, 1990).

3. Ellen Galinsky, Carollee Howes, Susan Kontos, Marybeth Shinn, *The Study of Children in Family Child Care and Relative Care* (New York: Families and Work Institute, 1994).

4. As cited in Susan Cheever, "The Nanny Track," *The New Yorker,* March 6, 1995, p. 84. Melinda Beck *et al.,* "Mary Poppins Speaks Out," *Newsweek,* February 22, 1993, pp. 66+.

5. The study concluded that to provide higher quality care, centers had to spend about 10 percent more than those that provided mediocre care. The difference in nonprofit and for-profit centers is less in states where child care is well regulated. Helburn, *et al., Cost, Quality and Child Outcomes in Child Care Centers.*

6. Edward Zigler and Mary Lang, *Child Care Choices: Balancing the Needs of Children, Families, and Society* (New York: The Free Press, 1991); salaries range from about $5.35 an hour to $8.85 at the top end, or about $8,890 to $15,488 a year, which puts child care workers below the poverty line. Clark, "Child Care: The Issues," p. 1112. Few child care workers receive health insurance and almost none receive retirement benefits. Linda Baker, "Day-Care," *The Progressive,* June 1994, pp. 26–27.

7. Research and Policy Committee of the Committee for Economic Development, *Why Child Care Matters* (Washington, D.C.: Committee for Economic Development, 1993), pp. 21–22.

8. Sue Shellenberger, "Poor Quality Found in Family Day Care," *Wall Street Journal,* April 8, 1994; Galinsky, Howes, Kontos, and Shinn, *The Study of Children in Family Child Care and Relative Care* (New York: Families and Work Institute, 1994).

9. Clark, "Child Care: The Issues," pp. 1107–1115.

10. Deborah Philips, Miriam Voran, Ellen Kisken, Carollee Howes, Mary Whitebrook, "Child Care for Children in Poverty: Opportunity or Inequity?" *Child Development* 65, (1994): pp. 472–492.

11. Wealthy counties have access to 50 percent more of the nation's 80,000 day care centers than do low-income neighborhoods. Research and Policy Committee of the Committee for Economic Development, *Why Child Care Matters*, p. 1.

12. Between 1976 and 1990, the number of child care centers tripled and the number of children cared for in these programs quadrupled as day care and nursery schools became more alike to accommodate the dramatic migration of mothers into the labor force. Research and Policy Committee of the Committee for Economic Development, *Why Child Care Matters*, p. 20.

13. Research and Policy Committee of the Committee for Economic Development, *Why Child Care Matters*, p. 20.

14. Martha Zaslow, "Variation in Child Care Quality . . ." *Journal of Social Issues* 47, no. 2, (1991): p. 133.

15. Baker, "Day-Care," pp. 26–27.

16. Helburn, *et al.*, *Cost, Quality and Child Outcomes in Child Care Centers.*

17. EDK Associates, *Choosing Quality Child Care* (prepared by the Child Care Action Campaign, Sponsored by Dayton Hudson Foundation, January 1992).

18. Margaret Nelson, "Mothering Others' Children: The Experiences of Family Day-Care Providers," *Signs: Journal of Women in Culture and Society* 15, no. 3, (1990): pp. 586–605.

19. E. Zigler and S. Muenchow, *Head Start: The Inside Story of America's Most Successful Educational Experiment* (New York: Basic Books, 1992); E. Zigler and S. Styfco, "Head Start: Criticisms in a Constructive Context," *American Psychologist* 49 (1994): pp. 127–132.

20. W. Barnett, "Benefit-Cost Analysis of Preschool Education: Findings from a 25-Year Follow-up," *American Journal of Orthopsychiatry* 63, no. 4 (1993): pp. 500–508.

21. J. Belsky and L. Steinberg, "The Effects of Day Care: A Critical Review," *Child Development* 49 (1978): pp. 929–949; Jerome Kagan, R. Kearsley, and P. Zelazo, *Infancy: Its Place in Human Development* (Cambridge: Harvard University Press, 1978); A. Clarke-Stewart and G. Fein, "Early Childhood Programs," in *Handbook of Child Psychology*, eds. M. Maith and J. Campos, series ed. P. Mussen, vol. 2. *Infancy and Developmental Psychobiology* (New York: Wiley, 1983), pp. 917–999.

22. Clarke-Stewart, "Developmental Consequences of Child Care," pp. 63–82.

23. Alison Clarke-Stewart et al.; "Does Day Care Affect Development?" *Journal of Reproductive and Infant Psychology* 9, no. 23 (April–September 1991): pp. 67–78.

24. Jay Belsky, "Infant Day Care: A Cause for Concern?" *Zero to Three* 6 (1986): pp. 1–7; also see Jay Belsky, "The Effects of Day Care Reconsidered," *Early Childhood Research Quarterly* 3 (1988): pp. 235–272.

25. Belsky, Woodworth and Crnic, "Trouble in the Second Year: Three Questions About Family Interaction," in press, *Child Development.*

26. Carollee Howes and Ellen Smith, "Children and Their Child Care Caregivers: Profiles of Relationships," *Social Development* 4, no. 1 (March 1995): pp. 44–61.

27. C. Howes, M. Whitebrook, and D. Phillips, "Teacher Characteristics and Effective Teaching in Child Care: Findings from the National Child Care Staffing Study," *Child and Youth Care Forum* 21, no. 6 (1992): pp. 319–414.

28. Bengt-Erik Andersson, "Public Policies in Early Childhood Education," *European Early Childhood Education Research Journal* 2, no. 2 (1994).

29. In one survey, close to 42 percent of centers polled would not accept special-needs children. Yet their families may have more need for child care services because of the extra stress of parenting a handicapped child. Research and Policy Committee of the Committee for Economic Development, *Why Child Care Matters,* p. 20.

30. Sarah Friedman, *et al.,* "Child Care and Development: The NICHD Study of Early Child Care" (unpublished report, December 27, 1993).

31. As of 1991 the average credit was $808, suggesting a considerable proportion of beneficiaries worked part-time. For higher incomes, the benefits were lowered, ceasing altogether for a family with an income of $27,000 or more. Barbara Bergmann, "Child Care: The Key to Ending Child Poverty" (paper presented at the conference on Social Policies for Children, Woodrow Wilson School of Public and International Affairs, Princeton University, May 1994).

32. Research and Policy Committee of the Committee for Economic Development, *Why Child Care Matters,* p. 40.

33. Sue Shellenbarger, "Many Employers Flout Family and Medical Leave Law," *Wall Street Journal,* p. B1.

34. Ibid.

35. Roberta Spalter-Roth and Heidi Hartman, *Unnecessary Losses* (Washington, D.C.: Institute for Women's Policy Research, 1988).

36. Research and Policy Committee of the Committee for Economic Development, *Why Child Care Matters,* p. 41.

37. Dee Moran, "Saving Money by Caring for Children," *Wall Street Journal,* August 22, 1994, p. A10.

38. In surveys of traditional societies, only 46 percent of mothers are the primary caretakers of infants—40 percent of the time, there are multiple caretakers. Mothers are principal caretakers of the young 20 percent of the time; in fact, another 20 percent of young children spend most of their time away

from their mothers. H. Barry and L. Paxson, "Infancy and Early Childhood: Cross-cultural Codes 2," *Ethnology* 10 (1971): pp. 466–508.

39. Margaret Mead, "A Cultural Anthropologist's Approach," in *Deprivation of Maternal Care,* Mary Ainsworth, *et al.* (Geneva: World Health Organization. 1962), pp. 45–62.


CHAPTER 7. REFORMED: CHILD CARE IN OTHER COUNTRIES

1. Of the twenty-three industrialized nations, including Europe, Scandinavia, Canada, and Japan, the United States has the highest rate of child poverty— more than twice the rate of the country with the second highest rate; the United States has the second highest rate of deaths from infant abuse; and is the only country that does not provide paid maternity leave. UNICEF, *The Progress of Nations* (report) (1994). One hundred fifty nations provide paid maternity leave—the United States does not; the infant mortality rate in the United States is higher than in thirty other nations. *Starting Points: The Carnegie Corporation Report* (1994), p. 20.

2. Sheila Kamerman, "Child Care Policies and Programs: An International Overview, *Journal of Social Issues* 47, no. 2 (1991): pp. 179–196.

3. Marianne Sundstrom, "Sweden: Supporting Work, Family and Gender Equality," in *Child Care, Parental Leave, and the Under 3s: Policy Innovation in Europe,* eds. Sheila Kamerman and Alfred Kahn (New York: Auburn House, 1991), pp. 171–199.

4. Phillip Hwang, "Scandinavian Experience in Providing Alternative Care," *Pediatrics* 91, no. 1 (January 1993): pp. 264–270.

5. In Sweden employed women have had the right to maternity leave since 1931. At that time the leave was only one month and the pay was low. See Sundstrom, "Sweden: Supporting Work, Family and Gender Equality," pp. 171–199.

6. Sundstrom, "Sweden: Supporting Work, Family and Gender Equality," pp. 171–199.

7. Ibid.

8. Hwang, "Scandinavian Experience in Providing Alternative Care," pp. 264–270.

9. Author's personal interviews with Rikstag members, March 1995.

10. Sundstrom, "Sweden: Supporting Work, Family and Gender Equality," pp. 171–199.

11. Philip Hwang and Anders Broberg, "The Historical and Social Context of Child Care in Sweden," in *Child Care in Context: Cross-Cultural Perspectives,* eds. Michael Lamb and Kathleen Sternberg (Hillsdale, NJ: Lawrence Erlbaum, 1992), pp. 27–53.

12. Ibid.

13. Gertrude Goldberg and Eleanor Kremen, *The Feminization of Poverty: Only in America?* (New York: Praeger, 1990).

14. In this study of over three hundred parents, about 27 percent of fathers had taken leave; moreover, they took less than 20 percent of the parental leave available to them. Linda Haas, "Gender Equality and Social Policy: Implications of a Study of Parental Leave in Sweden," *Journal of Family Issues* 11, no. 4 (December 1990): pp. 401–423.

15. Sundstrom, "Sweden: Supporting Work, Family and Gender Equality," pp. 171–199.

16. Between 1960 and 1975 the percentage of women aged twenty-five to forty-four that were part of the labor force rose from 37 percent to 57 percent. In 1990 the birthrate was 2.07, high for the industrialized world. At the same time, infant mortality was 0.6 percent, among the lowest in the world. Hwang and Broberg, "The Historical and Social Context of Child Care in Sweden," pp. 27–53.

17. Editorial, "A Parliament That Looks Like Sweden," *New York Times,* September 27, 1994, p. A11; Dick Polman, "Swedes in an Identity Crisis as Welfare State Shrinks," *Philadelphia Inquirer,* June 26, 1994, p. C1.

18. This figure is for the 1992 presidential election. In the 1990 congressional elections, 37 percent of those eligible voted. Voter Registration Reform, *Congressional Digest,* March 1993, p. 67.

19. Kamerman, "Child Care Policies and Programs: An International Overview," pp. 179–196; Gail Richardson and Elisabeth Marx, "A Welcome for Every Child: How France Achieves Quality in Child Care: Practical Ideas for the United States," *The Report of the Child Care Study Panel of the French-American Foundation* (New York: French-American Foundation, 1989); Marie-Gabrielle David and Christophe Starzec, "France: A Diversity of Policy Options," in *Child Care, Parental Leave and the Under 3's: Policy Innovation in Europe,* pp. 81–113; Steven Greenhouse, "If the French Can Do It, Why Can't We?" *The New York Times Magazine,* November 14, 1993, pp. 50+.

20. The central government pays for the teachers and educational administration, while local governments pay for the auxiliary personnel and buildings. There are private nursery schools, mostly sponsored by religious organizations, which are partially subsidized by government funds and are attended by 12 percent of children in nursery school. *Ministère de l'Éducation Nationale de la Jeunesse et des Sports,* Repères et References Statistiques sur les Ensignements et la Formation (edition 1992), p. 13.

21. In Paris, where costs are generally higher than elsewhere in France, parents typically pay an annual fee for one child that is set at 14 percent of their yearly income and ranges from $1,750 to $4,000. The poorest families pay $195 and the richest pay $4,725 a year for one child (1989). The overall cost

of sending a child to a Parisian day care center was $10,000 a year in 1993. Poor families paid $390 per year, middle-class families paid about $3,200, and the rich paid $5,300. French-American Foundation, *Report of the Child Care Study Panel of the French-American Foundation.*

22. Parents pay $11 to $18 a day per child (in 1989). French-American Foundation, *Report of the Child Care Study Panel,* p. 15.

23. The yearly cost per pupil (in 1989) is $2,100. Of this amount, public funding pays $1,890 for the core costs of teachers' salaries and buildings. Parents pay the remaining $210 for the wraparound programs if they choose to use them. French-American Foundation, *Report of the Child Care Study Panel of the French-American Foundation,* p. 15.

24. A. Atkinson, "French Preprimary Education: A Tradition of Responding to Children," *Early Child Development and Care,* 46 (1989): 77–86; Carollee Howes and Elizabeth Marx, "Raising Questions About Improving the Quality of Child Care: Child Care in the United States and France," *Early Childhood Research Quarterly* 7 (1992): pp. 347–366.

25. Ministère de l'Éducation Nationale et de la Culture, 1992, "Le Coût de l'Éducation."

26. Caisse Nationale des Allocations Familiales, 1991; CAF Statistiques: Présentations Familiales, 1992.

27. French-American Foundation, *Report of the Child Care Study Panel of the French-American Foundation.*

28. These figures are for 1989. French-American Foundation, *Report of the Child Care Study Panel of the French-American Foundation,* p. 15.

29. Michael Hardey and Graham Crow, *Lone Parenthood* (Toronto: University of Toronto Press, 1991), pp. 123–125.

30. Miriam Rosenthal, "Nonparental Child Care in Israel: A Cultural and Historical Perspective," in *Child Care in Context: Cross-Cultural Perspectives,* pp. 305–330.

31. Mordecai Kauffman, Esther Eizur, and Margalit Rabinowitz, "Early Childhood in the Kibbutz: The 1980s," in *Kibbutz Members Study Kibbutz Children,* ed. Zvi Lavi, Kibbutz Studies Series, no. 1 (New York: Greenwood Press, 1990), pp. 17–33.

32. Bruno Bettelheim, *The Children of the Dream* (New York: Macmillan, 1969).

33. Introduction to ed. Zvi Lavi, *Kibbutz Members Study Kibbutz Children,* p. 6.

34. A. I. Rabin, *Growing Up in the Kibbutz* (New York: Springer, 1965).

35. Introduction to ed. Zvi Lavi, *Kibbutz Members Study Kibbutz Children,* p. 6.

36. A.I. Rabin and Benjamin Beit-Hallahmi, *Twenty Years Later: Kibbutz Children Grown Up* (New York: Springer, 1982).

37. Rosenthal, "Nonparental Child Care in Israel: A Cultural and Historical Perspective," pp. 305–330.

38. David Shwalb, Barbara Shwalb, Seisoh Sukemune, Shin Tatsumooto, "Japanese Nonmaternal Child Care: Past, Present and Future," in *Child Care in Context: Cross-Cultural Perspectives,* pp. 331–353.

39. Sumiko Iwao, *The Japanese Woman: Traditional Image and Changing Reality* (New York: The Free Press, 1993).

40. Moncrieff Cochran, ed., *International Handbook of Child Care Policies and Programs* (London: Greenwood Press, 1993), pp. 666–667.

41. Edith Lassegard, "Japan," in *International Handbook of Child Care Policies and Programs,* pp. 313–331.

42. Sheryl WuDunn, "In Japan, Even Toddlers Feel the Pressure to Excel," *New York Times,* January 23, 1996, p. C26.

43. Iwao, *The Japanese Woman,* pp. 142–143.

44. Ibid.

CHAPTER 8. THE WAY IT OUGHT TO BE

1. Pepper Schwartz, *Peer Marriage: How Love Between Equals Really Works* (New York: The Free Press, 1994).

2. Susan Chira, "Fathers Who Want Time Off for Families Face Uphill Battle," *New York Times,* October 21, 1993, p. C6.

3. Ann Crittenden, "A Humane Plan to Help Working—and Welfare—Parents," *Working Woman,* June 1995, p. 16.

4. See Michael Wines, "Where the Budget Ax Turns Dull: Government Benefits for Business Are Mostly Spared," *New York Times,* August 30, 1995, p. D1. The ten countries in the world with the highest military budgets spent a combined $238 billion in 1993—$38 billion less than the United States spent alone. Franklyn D. Holzman (economist), Letters to the Editor, "Pentagon Overkill," *New York Times,* February 1, 1995, p. A20.

5. A plan to eliminate child poverty through subsidized child care based on the French model is proposed by economist Barbara Bergman, at American University. Barbara Bergmann, "Child Care: The Key to Ending Child Poverty" (unpublished paper presented to the Conference on Social Policies for Children, Woodrow Wilson School of Public and International Affairs, Princeton University, May 25–27, 1994), p. 9.

6. There are some mothers receiving welfare who are taking drugs and have serious personal problems that prevent them from working and are also likely to prevent them from good parenting. These women need social services and should be required to obtain them with the goal of rehabilitating them to a point where they can manage employment.

7. A study relating current costs of private and public child care centers to measures of quality suggests costs on the order of $4,800 per child per year would be required if good quality care were to be procured (averaging the

costs of providing care for infants and for the older children). Suzanne Helburn, "Cost of Quality Child Care," Department of Economics, University of Colorado at Denver, 1994.

8. Salley Shannon, "From Fed Up to Fired Up," *Working Mother,* June 1994, pp. 39+.

9. Marilyn Waring, *If Women Counted* (New York: Harper Collins, 1988).

10. The study is by the United Nations Human Development Program. Barbara Crossette, "U.N. Documents Inequities for Women as World Forum Nears," *New York Times,* August 18, 1995, p. A3.

11. Frankly, I don't like this argument because children should be seen as our most natural and vital responsibility—one we take pleasure in fulfilling. But, alas, I must contend with a society that apparently desires to live by the almighty cost-benefit analysis.

12. Stephen Moore, "How to Slash Corporate Welfare," *New York Times,* April 5, 1995, p. A25.

13. Gilbert Gaul and Susan Stranahan, "How Billions in Taxes Failed to Create Jobs," *Philadelphia Inquirer,* June 4, 1995, pp. 1+.

14. Editorial. "Alms for the Affluent," *New York Times,* April 7, 1995, p. A34.

15. Keith Bradsher, "Gap in Wealth in U.S. Called Widest in West," *New York Times,* April 17, 1995, p. A14.

16. Holly Sklar, "The Snake Oil of Scapegoating," *Z Magazine,* May 1995, pp. 49–56.

17. Frank Holzman, "Pentagon Overkill," *New York Times,* February 1, 1995, p. A20.

18. See Yvonne Roberts, "We Are Becoming Divorced from Reality," *New Statesman and Society*, September 24, 1993, p.16+.

# Index

ABOUT THE AUTHOR

DIANE EYER is author of *Mother-Infant Bonding: A Scientific Fiction,* a highly praised analysis of how the bonding myth was created. Dr. Eyer is a psychologist who is in the vanguard of a new discipline: the history and sociology of psychology. She has taught courses in psychology including the History and Sociology of Childhood and the Science and Politics of Child-Rearing Advice at the University of Pennsylvania and Rutgers University. She is currently at work on a book about the shift from religion to psychology as a source of parenting advice and its effect on family values. Dr. Eyer has also been a producer and a writer on a series of documentary films on literacy in Morocco. She lives in Bucks County, Pennsylvania.